LAST SHOP STANDING

PROPER
MUSIC PUBLISHING

Library of Congress Control Number: 2010901530

ISBN: 978-0-9561212-3-3

Cover Designer: James Weston
Picture Research: Graham Jones

Every effort has been made to trace the copyright holders of the photographs in this book, but one or two were unreachable. We would be grateful if the photographers concerned would contact us.

Typeset by: Phoenix Photosetting, Chatham, Kent, United Kingdom
Printed by: Friesens Corporation, Altona, Manitoba, Canada

Published by Proper Music Publishing
P.O. Box 34114
Pensacola, FL 32507-4114
Proper Catalog No. PMOUS100

The views expressed in this book are of Graham Jones and not necessarily of Proper Music Publishing.

10 9 8 7 6 5 4 3 2 1

Printed in Canada

LAST
SHOP
STANDING

This book is dedicated to those shops that tried.

Contents

Foreword

by David Sinclair

There is a romantic image of the local record shop which Nick Hornby captures with exquisite detail in his novel *High Fidelity*. "The shop smells of stale smoke, damp and plastic dust-covers, and it's narrow and dingy and dirty and overcrowded.... this is what record shops should look like, and only Phil Collins' fans bother with those that look as clean and wholesome as a suburban Habitat."

The shop in Hornby's book is staffed by a bunch of oddballs, united by an obsessive love of recorded music and committed with an almost missionary zeal to the business of supplying it to the public. The owner measures out his life in an endless succession of music-related lists – everything from his Favourite Records (Singles) to his Top Five Dream Jobs.

Graham Jones, one of the founders of Proper Music Distribution has been doing his dream job – or variations on it – for most of his life, and the true story of his time spent working in and around the world of independent record retailing is every bit as colourful, funny, strange, and occasionally sad as any fictional yarn.

Graham has some lists of his own, and in *Last Shop Standing* he has amassed many extraordinary tales of the best shops he has done business with over the years and hilarious accounts of the worst. He reveals the truth about chart hyping and shines a light on some of the extraordinary shenanigans that have regularly gone on behind the scenes as record companies go about promoting some of their biggest hits (and misses).

But the most shocking list is the one that begins and defines *Last Shop Standing*: a roll call of some of the 540 record shops that have closed in the last four years alone. For record retailing is an industry in crisis. Beset by the onward march of the supermarkets, the growing popularity of music downloading and a host of other rapidly emerging market trends, the traditional record shop has become an endangered species.

While Graham recognises such problems, and explains them with an insider's knowledge and eye for detail, he remains committed to the future of the industry that he loves. As well as being a eulogy to an era that is fast fading into history, *Last Shop Standing* is also a celebration of the unique spirit of comradeship and entrepreneurial ingenuity that has enabled so many shops to keep operating successfully in such a harsh trading environment.

All of which makes this a most timely and important book.

Graham has amassed a fantastic collection of anecdotes on his travels around the record shops of Britain, and *Last Shop Standing* is a unique slice of social history and record industry folklore. It is also a damn good laugh.

David Sinclair
December 2008

Introduction

In 2009 I released the book Last Shop Standing (What ever Happened to Record Shops). I did so because I really love record shops but they were closing at such an alarming rate and nobody seemed to care. I felt that if I could highlight the situation then the public might support their local shop. When I set out to tour the UK and interview the 50 shops that I felt would be the Last Shops Standing, deep down I felt I was writing the obituary of the record shop. However, after interviewing the great characters that owned record shops I was convinced that they had a great future and I made it a personal mission to champion them. 2009 was the year that record shops fought back. One of the big factors in this comeback has been the impact Record Store Day has had on raising the profile of these great institutions. Record Store Day was the first time in years I saw queues outside record shops other than for a closing down sale. I decided to write a new edition of Last Shop Standing to let the world know that the record shop has a future and for any music fan to put the third Saturday in April in their diary. Make sure you attend an event at your local record shop. Check out the website at www.recordstoreday.com

I asked two people at the forefront of Record Store Day, Michael Kurtz, one of the founders in the USA and Spencer Hickman who is responsible for Record Store Day in the UK, if they would contribute to an updated version of Last Shop Standing to help promote Record Store Day. I asked Spencer if he would give the reader a background to Record Store Day. These are his words:

A man walks into a record shop…

No joke.

He really does.

If you pay attention to the music press and chatter of the online-communities you would be forgiven for thinking the humble record store had closed its doors a long time ago. A relic of the past viewed only with nostalgia; the footnote in a Nick Hornby novel.

Well I'm sorry I just don't buy it. While it's true that many stores have ceased to be over the last five years, there is a huge number that are not only still going but also thriving even in these uncertain economic times.

There are stores all over the world that still sell huge amounts of music on physical formats, help break new bands and engage with customers young and old.

The myth that record stores are finished is, well, frankly bullshit. On Rough Trade East's packed shop floor right now there are a few record nerds scouring the racks, a group of businessmen in the snug having a meeting, teenage girls causing havoc in the photo booth and one of our regulars buying a lot of 7" singles. He's 14 years old and he's BUYING RECORDS. It just goes to show how wrong the perception of music retail is. This kid and a lot of other kids and adults still come in and pay for a piece of plastic that they take home, listen to, learn the words and cherish forever.

Sure the industry as a whole seems to be careering into the toilet at an alarming rate after years of record company indifference about still trying to keep the product as a premium lifestyle accessory. Not having the inclination or infrastructure to address the emergence of the downloader was also a case of head-in-the-sand syndrome. By the time they'd realised it was too late.

Until recently the independent sector was crumbling due to people not wanting to lose their identity and share information. The 'I'm alright Jack' mentality, that perpetuated during the boom-time of the 80's is, in the noughties, retail suicide.

The stores that looked inwardly have closed – they just weren't good enough to survive. The ones that are still here are embracing the latest technologies; they're evolving and are here to stay. They are in touch with their customers like never before, they love what they do and most importantly the punters love them for it.

Don't tell me the record shop is dead because from where I'm standing it looks very much alive and thanks to events like Record Store Day the future looks even brighter.

Record Store Day has gone a long way to help kick independent stores back to life. For the first time in 25 years shops around the world are coming together to celebrate the record store and all that's great about it. They are communicating with each other. They're sharing ideas, information and tips. They're discussing the problems that were historically faced alone.

Record Store Day has captured the imagination of the public and the shop owners, proving that customers are still willing to spend money if they can get an 'experience' that's not available online.

You can't get free in-store gigs online. You can't get exclusive product, fanzine workshops, print clubs and an atmosphere that you want to be part of with genuine human interaction online. You can in a record shop.

Chatting to someone face to face who is as passionate as you are about music is something that never gets old. Discussing the merits of the week's new releases both good and bad is still as exciting to me as it was 20 years ago. The customer is now our friend and we like it like that.

Coordinating Record Store Day has been both hugely rewarding and maddeningly frustrating. In the beginning it saw me banging my head against the wall trying to make labels understand not only what the day was about but also what we were trying to achieve. The bruises were worth it and now labels jump on board offering exclusives without having to be badgered.

I'm hugely proud of what we've achieved with Record Store Day. Every single label and distributor is now committed to it and are all planning big things for the future. It's immensely gratifying to be involved and spread the word about how special and culturally important the record store is.

Why did I take it on? Because the record store is in my blood, it's what I do and I really love it. I couldn't see the shops disappear without having fought my very hardest.

Ever since I was a spotty 14-year-old Goth working on Saturdays in Birmingham's Vinyl Dreams my life has been soundtracked by the record stores I've worked in. I've made lifelong friends, met lovers and created enemies in them. I've been drunk, taken drugs, had sex, been sick, beaten up and slept in them. They've been the only constant things in my life.

Record stores are not only a huge part of my life they are also important to the millions of people who shop and work in them.

The level of support for Record Store Day from punters, labels and celebrities alike has been immense. Of course, one day a year will never be enough to sustain our businesses indefinitely, but the fact that it's helping to bring back lapsed customers and entice children as young as five to join in a global celebration of the record store is encouraging and exciting. Roll on next year.

Spencer Hickman
Rough Trade East
Dray Walk
91 Brick Lane
London E1 6QL

Do you remember any of these music retailers? These are my customers I have lost since I first decided to write this book:

101 Records – Croydon
A1 Records – London
Abbey Records – Ainsdale
Adagio Records – Harrogate
Ainley's Records – Leicester
Alan Fearnley Records – Middlesbrough
Andy Cash Records – Birmingham (3 shops)
Andy's Records – (37 shops)
Apex Home Entertainment – Manchester
APS Records – Crewe
Atom Records – Bridgend
Audiosonic – Gloucester
Backbeat – Aberdeen
Backbeat Records – Aberystwyth
Backtrack – Leicester
Badlands – Huddersfield
Bang Records – Brighton
Bassline 182 – Bexhill-on-Sea
Bernard Dean – Scarborough
Big Pink Music – Manchester
Birmingham CD & Tape Exchange – Birmingham
Blast From The Past – Eastbourne
Blaze Records – Cramlington
Blitz Retail – Ilkeston
Bradleys Records – Halifax
Bridge Records – Walsall
Brown Sugar Records – Manchester
Buzzard Records – Leyton Buzzard
Castle Records – Darwen
Castle Records – Loughborough
Cardiff Music Shop – Cardiff
Cavern Records – Aberdeen

CD Centre – Keighley
CD Centre – Leeds
CD City – Sutton-on-Trent
CD Heaven – Belfast
CD Heaven – Hitchin
CD Shop – Swindon
CD World – London
CD Zone – Halifax
Chalmers & Joy – Dundee
Changes 1 – Whitley Bay
Chart CDs – Loughton
Classical Rock – Harpenden
Classic Music – Bedford
Classic Tracks – Leicester
CMS – Milton Keynes
Compact – Falmouth
Con Brio – Sheffield
Concepts – Durham
Craigavon Music – Craigavon
Crossing Point – Bourne
Dawson's – Abingdon
Deck of Cards – Dartmouth
Disc N Tape – Bristol
Discmonger – Lincoln
Diskit – Sutton-in-Ashfield
Discus Music – Newmarket
Disque – Islington
Dominion Records – Chepstow
Dorset Music House – Sherborne
Dots & Squiggles – Halesowen
Double 4 Records – Stockport
Dragon Disc – London
D'vinyl – Watford
Dyscworld – Scarborough
EA Music (7 shops)
Ears Are Alight – West Kirby
East Coast Music – Bridlington

Easy Listening – Birmingham

Edinburgh Records – Edinburgh

Ellisons – Filey

Emporium – Diss

Epsom Record Centre – Epsom

Essential (4 shops based in the South)

Euphonics – Burnham-on-Sea

Fab Music – Crouch End

Fastlane – Sheerness

Fat Tracks – Weston-super-Mare

Fopp Ltd – (20, although 6 stores have re-opened under HMV ownership)

Fence – St Andrews

Filco – Edgely

Forever Changes – York

Forest Records – Lymington

Freedom Music – High Wycombe

Funhouse – Margate

Gallery Sounds – Bournemouth

Garon Records – Cambridge

Gemini Records – Liverpool

Global Beat – Bradford

Go Ahead – Little Missenden

Goldrush Music – Perth

Goodfellas – Birmingham

Good Music – Uckfield

Good Roots – Manningtree

Good Vibrations Record Shak – Thurso

Greensleeves – North Allerto

Happy Daze – Newport

Hedgehog – Ely

High St Records – Wisbech

Highway61 – Wolverhampton

Hillsborough Music – Sheffield

Hitman – Newport

Honkytown Jukebox – Wellingborough

Hot Wax – Edinburgh

House of Jazz – Brough

Hyde Music – Hyde

Imperial Music – Bristol

In Other Words – Plymouth

Inswing Music – Birmingham

Jazz House – Leicester

Jazz & Swing – Worcester

Jazzbox – Exeter

Jingles – East Grinstead

JJ Records – Birmingham

Just Classics – Maidstone

Just Shetland – Lerwick

Just Music – Newhaven

Kavern Records – Rhyl and Llandudno

Kays – (5 shops Bristol area)

Kemble's Records – Leicester

Ken Palk – Stockport

Kenny's Records – Sheffield

Knighton Music – Leicester

Laser Discount – Chelmsford

Leading Edge – Staines

Left Legged Pineapple – Loughborough

Lemon Tree – Poole

Let's Buy Some Music (2 shops in Kent)

Lizard – Norwich

Longplayer – Tunbridge Wells

Lounge Lizard – Keighley

Lucia Bop – Holt

Magic Music – Clacton

Magpie – West Bromwich

Malmesbury Music – Malmesbury

Mandala Music – Falmout

Martin's – Ashby de la Zouch

Mary's Music – Accrington

Max Millward – Wednesfield

MB – Scarborough

Melody's – Clacton

Mere Green Records – Sutton Coldfield

Meresborough – Sittingbourne

MG Music – Leicester

Midas Music – Derby

Mike's Country Room – Aberdeen

Millennium Music – Okehampton

Mischief – Croydon

Missing Records – Glasgow

Mister CD – London

Mix Music – Harrogate

Modern Music – Abingdon

Mole Jazz – London

Mongo Denoon – Bristol

Montpellier Records – Cheltenham

More Than Music (6 stores based in the Midlands)

Morlings – Beccles

Morph's Music – London

Mrs Yarrington's – Battle

Musicbank – Cheam

Musical Bond – Tewkesbury

Music Box – Grantham

Music Exchange – Alsager

Music Factory – Street

Musicfolk – Falmouth

Music Madness – Dartford

Music Mania – Glasgow

Music Meltdown – Brighton

Music Options – Pembroke

Music Room – Ashford

Music Room – Stornaway

Music Shop – Edinburgh

Music Stop – Bristol

Music Studio – Carrickfergus

Music to My Ears – Port Talbot

Music Zone (50 shops)

Music Word – Henley

Musiquarium – Swansea

MVC – (95 shops)

Newmarket Tapes – Aberdeen

No 9 Music – Ilkley

Noise Annoys – Sheffield

Nova Music – Littlehampton

Oakstone Classics – Worcester

Obsession – Fleetwood

Off Limit – Birmingham

Oldies Museum – Edinburgh

Omega – Northwich

Onyx – Bristol

Old Tyme Music – Eastbourne

Orbit – Longeaton

Orpheus – Southsea

Outlaw – Newcastle-under-Lyme

Out of Step – Leeds

Parliament Records – Hertford

Parrot Records – Cambridge

Past & Present Records – Watford

Paul for Music – London

Phase 1 – Wrexham

Pink Panther Records – Carlisle

Pink Pig – Earlstown

Planet of Sound – Ayr

Plastic Factory – Walsall

Playback – Middlesbrough

Play In – Swinton

Popscene – Portsmouth

PR Sounds – Devizes

Pulse – Horley

Quantum – Liverpool

Quarterdeck – Newquay

Quirks Records – Ormskirk

R&K Records – Newark

Range Records – Brownhills

Rayners – Bristol

Real Music – Glasgow

Reckless Records – London

Record Centre – Dorchester

Record House – (3 shops based around Bucks)

Record Rendezvous – Inverness
Record Savings – Banbury
Record Select – Wadebridge
Record Shop – Hastings
Record Store – Wisbech
Record Village – Scunthorpe
Redbridge Records – Canvey Island
Red House Music – Aberdare
Red Planet – Tavistock
Reel to Reel – Arbroath
Regal Music – London
Re-employ – Coventry
Re-Pete – Hythe
Replay – (3 shops based around
    Bristol)
Retroblue – Aberdeen
Return to Forever – Totnes
Reveal Records – Derby
Revo Records – Halifax
Revolution – Norwich
Revolutionary – Worthing
Revolver Records – Bristol
Rex Records – Ipswich
Reynolds Records – Ilkeston
Richard's Records – Ashton
Rhythm Records – Camden
Rhythm and Rhyme – Launceston
Rhythmic – Wallsend
Rival – Bristol
RMD – Coleford
Roccola – Pontefract
Round Sounds – Burgess Hill
RP Music – Thatcham
Salvation Sounds – Glasgow

Scorpion – High Wycombe
See Dee Jon's – Jersey
Sho 'Nuff – Bangor
Skandalous – Coalville
Sound & Vision – Barnstaple
Soundlee – Hayle
Sound Machine – Reading
Sounds Plus – Burton
Spin-A-Disc – (2 shops based in
    Northampton)
Stamford Music Shop – Stamford
Station Street Jazz – Bromley
Stephen Siger Music – London
Stereo 1 – Paisley
Sullivans – Swansea
Sundown – Walsall
Swales – Pembroke
The Bronx – Sheffield
The Music Quarter –
    Gainsborough
The Ska Shak – Ramsgate
The Stop – Peterborough
Top Sounds – Bishop Auckland
Track – Chesham
Track Records – Doncaster
Track Records – York
Tracks – Hertford
Trax – Christchurch
Trumps – Ilford
Tudor Tunes – Lichfield
Upfront – Barnstaple
Warrior CDs – Crystal Palace
What Records – Nuneaton
What's Going On – Birmingham

All those businesses – gone to the wall: all the effort that people put in to make things work.

The last shop listed sums things up. WHAT'S GOING ON?

Chapter 1

How it Began

What am I doing here? That was what I was pondering as my lungs filled with another cloud of cheese-and-onion flavoured dust. I had begun with such high hopes and had been certain that I would be a professional goalkeeper, starting off with Tranmere Rovers and, after a couple of seasons there, Liverpool FC would sign me and a career with England was the obvious next step. As a schoolboy, I had always played at county level and everybody had told me how good I was. Unfortunately for me, Tranmere did not see it that way and I was soon sent on my way, after playing youth-team football for them, with the impression that the dream was over and that it was time to find a proper job.

That is how I found myself working for Unilever, making the flavours for cheese-and-onion crisps. It was boring and monotonous and after an eight-hour shift I would be covered from head to toe in cheese-and-onion dust. This fine powder managed to make its way into every crevice of my body. Worst of all, no matter how much I showered and scrubbed and sprayed cologne, I could never rid myself of that cheesy smell. It did nothing for my self-confidence. I often found myself in a pub or club, talking to some girls, and somebody would pipe up with, "Can anybody smell cheese and onion?" resulting in my having to sneak off, embarrassed, to the gents to re-wash under my arms and re-apply the deodorant that I always carried around in my trouser pocket. Several girls actually thought that I was delighted to see them, only to discover that it was just the roll-on …

I had started to speculate on how I could escape this zombie-like existence and contemplated what I enjoyed. Sport and music were my two loves. I had already failed to make the grade in sport, so a career in music it had to be.

Little was I to know that two opportunities were soon to come my way. One evening, whilst glancing through my free local paper, *The Wirral Globe*, an advertisement caught my eye – 'For sale – 1,000 ex-jukebox singles – £200'. I was on the phone immediately – this was my chance to be the next Richard Branson and to start up my own business. I called the seller and he informed me that the singles included The Beatles, The Rolling Stones and The Doors etc. It sounded like a real bargain, so I arranged for him to call around to my house the following evening.

That day was occupied by dreaming of where I should open my first store and, more importantly, how I could broach the subject of asking my Mum for a loan. All new businesses need investment and mine was no different. My Mum was used to me borrowing the odd £10 and, as I only had £120 of my own, I hoped she would be equally fine about a loan of £80. (It did cross my mind that my prospective supplier would be wasting his time coming over if she refused. I got around that concern by speculating that maybe he might just take £120 for the lot, or perhaps I could just buy £120-worth.)

But, as usual, Mum did not let me down, especially as I was so enthusiastic about my new business opportunity. In fact, she also seemed keen on the venture, so I suggested that, rather than pay her back the £80, I would give her the equivalent in shares in my new, as yet un-named company. However, I quickly realised that she was not as keen as I thought when she said, "Just give me the cash when you have it."

That afternoon I must have visited the toilet four or five times, as I was so nervous. Soon there was a thunderous knocking sound. I opened the door. "Sorry for knocking so loudly but I've been ringing your bell for ages. I don't think it's working."

"No," I replied, "The battery has expired." When you're starting a new business every penny counts, and not having a battery in my bell was one of the sacrifices I was just going to have to make.

My supplier had turned up in a big white van and he asked me if I would help him to carry the singles in. They were packed in two large tea chests and were extremely heavy. We laid them down and I could not contain my excitement as I rummaged through the chests. I was like a child opening his presents on Christmas morning and, sure enough, there were all the artists he had mentioned.

"Boy, what a mug he must be to be selling all these singles for £200," I thought. At that age I had yet to learn one of the foremost rules of negotiation in business, which is not to show your hand. He could see from the fact that I was nearly wetting myself that I was sure to purchase this job lot. Trying to be shrewd, I offered him £180. "I'll tell you what, I'll take £190 and I'll throw in the tea chests for free," was his response.

"Done," I replied, ending my rather feeble first experience of negotiation.

"Not only have I bought all these singles," I contemplated "but, if I ever move into the tea wholesale industry I've already got a head-start."

I quickly ushered him out of the door, keen to see what other delights the tea chests held. As he left I apologised for not even having asked his name. "Don't worry," he replied, looking rather satisfied with himself, "it's Con". Perhaps at this point I should have smelt a rat, as he turned out to be Con by name and con by nature. As I unloaded the singles I placed them in neat little piles of fifty. It soon became apparent that I had a lot of duplications and that, in fact, many of the titles were in bulk.

By the time I had finished I realised that my bargain deal was not going to be the sale of the century. I surveyed the damage – 37 copies of a Rubettes single. It was not their number one single, 'Sugar Baby Love', but their dreadful, non-selling, follow-up release, 'Juke Box Jive', which probably got to as high as 99 in the charts. To add to my disappointment there were 25 copies of an unfamiliar Suzi Quatro record. This was a surprise to me, as I had presumed that all her singles had been hits. Then I noticed that many of the records at the bottom of the chest were scratched.

Well, I had no option other than to make the best of a bad job and on the following Saturday I set off to Ellesmere Port market in my car, with its bonnet pointing to the sky due to the weight of 1,200 singles in the boot. My initial objective was to make enough money just to pay for the repairs to the suspension on my car that I was surely going to need – and to meet as many Rubettes fans as possible.

My mate, Phil Burke, had come along to help me with the selling. He was a Burke in name only, and he had the gift of the gab, so I was confident that he could smooth-talk the people of Ellesmere Port into purchasing my stock.

As well as the 1,000 singles purchased from Con, I had also acquired a further 200 from a failed suicide bid. Let me explain.

Before my time at the food factory I had worked at a company called Bromborough Paints and Building Supplies. It was a dead-end job, requiring me to help drivers with deliveries of building materials. Customers would telephone our office and order bricks, sand, cement and other building materials, which we would load onto a lorry and deliver to the customer's house. Health and safety regulations dictated that if a load was more than a certain weight, the driver should have an assistant to help him unload the goods. One day, I went out with a driver called Starkey who was delivering some cement to a customer in Bebington. After dropping off the cement, Starkey told me that he just needed to pop in to see his girlfriend but would not be long. He was in the house for ages and I was beginning to wonder what my boss would say on our return, as what should have been a one-hour job had already taken more than two hours.

I was just about to start honking the horn when, at last, Starkey reappeared, carrying a huge box, and crying his eyes out. "What's up?" I asked. "She's finished with me," he sobbed. "Here, these are for you." He then passed me a box containing approximately 200 singles. "The memory of her is too painful, so please take them away. Every record reminds me of her."

I glanced through some of the records and looked at the titles – 'My Ding-A-Ling', 'Two Little Boys', 'Ernie (The Fastest Milkman in The West)' – and struggled to come to terms with how these songs could remind anybody of a girlfriend. Although still in no fit state to drive the lorry, Starkey started the engine and we moved off with him sobbing at the wheel. The conversation soon turned to suicide, and he told me that his life was not worth living without her. "Don't worry," I said, "there are plenty of other fish in the sea." My desperate attempts at compassion fell on deaf ears, as Starkey told me he did not want any other fish.

I struggled to keep my laughter in until, still sobbing, Starkey took a turn for the worse. "I am going to crash the lorry into the Rose and Crown," he announced, leaving me scarcely believing what I was hearing. I anxiously asked why. "I can't take anymore," was his distressed reply. This was rather worrying, as the Rose and Crown was less than a mile away and was situated on a T-junction at the bottom of an extremely steep hill.

As we approached the hill, the lorry began to pick up speed. "What are you doing?!" I cried in panic. There was no reply. "Starkey!" I shouted, but there was still no reply – he seemed to be in a trance and, in desperation, I shouted at him, "What about me?" Self-preservation had suddenly become top priority: the people relaxing in the Rose and Crown, sipping their lunchtime pints, with a lorry about to plough through the wall, did not enter my thoughts.

I opened the door of the lorry, thinking that jumping out was an option but, by now, the lorry was travelling too fast. "STOP!!" I screamed and, too late, Starkey suddenly slammed on the brakes. The lorry screeched and skidded right through the T-junction without, amazingly, hitting any other vehicles, struck the kerb and came to rest a couple of feet from the pub entrance.

Whilst it was skidding to a halt I had dropped the box of records and now my feet were deep in 7" singles. Starkey, meanwhile, had his head in his hands and was still crying his eyes out whilst slumped over the wheel. I leapt out of the lorry and realised that it had become a major traffic obstruction, blocking both lanes of the road.

Drivers had left their cars and began questioning me as to what had happened. I thought it best to say that the brakes had failed. One driver, noticing Starkey still slumped at the wheel, asked what was wrong with him. "He's still in shock," was my meek reply. Guessing that the police would be arriving soon, I jumped back in the cab, shook Starkey and told him that we had to get out of there pronto. In the movies I would have slapped his face, but under the circumstances it probably would not have been appropriate.

Starkey, at last, seemed to get a grasp of our predicament, stopped crying and started extricating the lorry. As the traffic was so close he was unable to do a proper three-point-turn but eventually, after what seemed like a thirty-three-point-turn, we moved off to the sound of one of the motorists shouting "Hey dickhead, you can't drive it with no brakes!"

On the way back to the depot Starkey asked me not to mention the day's escapade, as he was already on a final warning and feared that he would be sacked. I agreed to say nothing, because I felt really sorry for him and, in his current state of mind, I would worry for him if he lost his job as well.

He then suggested that I give him £20 for the collection of singles he had given me and I was taken aback. For a start, the singles were not worth that amount and, secondly, you do not ask for money for a gift. Eventually I agreed to give him a fiver for the motley collection. I never played any of the records that I bought from him and they stayed in their box for the next two years. Now, however, I could finally dispose of them for a profit, and every time I sold one I laughed as I remembered my experiences with Starkey.

Unfortunately, my first day at the market did not go exactly to plan. Phil Burke and I turned up at the market manager's office promptly at 7.30am, asked for a pitch, and he explained to us how things worked. The market had 60 pitches that were mostly occupied by regulars but, nevertheless, each week there would be some 'no-shows'. These would be traders who were ill, or on holiday or who perhaps could not be bothered to get out of bed if it was pouring down with rain.

The manager ushered us into a room around the corner in which about five other traders were already waiting in the hope that they too would be given a pitch. At 9am he picked two of these traders, seemingly at random, to replace the no-shows and, as the new kids on the block, we had no chance. "Sorry lads, try again next week," he told us. Crikey, all that effort for nothing and, worse, I was further in debt, having given Phil £5 and with petrol to pay for – not a great start.

The next few weeks followed a similar pattern. Each week Phil and I would load the car, drive to the market, and hang around for a while only to be told "Sorry lads, try again next week".

One thing which did soon come to my attention was that every week the market manager would allocate a stall to a buxom blonde lady who sold homemade cakes. I wondered whether her success was down to her natural assets, or because she had been coming to the market for longer than us, or perhaps Ellesmere Port simply had a shortage of cake-sellers. But, for whatever reason, she was always allocated a stall. Until, one week, I discovered her secret when I saw there, on the market manager's desk – a big cake! She was enticing him with Bakewell tart!

I was a quick learner, and I knew that I had to adapt this technique if my budding business was to progress. I engaged him in conversation. He was an old guy called Arnold (are there ever any young people called Arnold? It seems to be one of those names used solely by the over-60s). He was a friendly chap who told me that he admired us for turning up week-in, week-out, despite not obtaining a stall. He also told me not to give in, as one day we would be given one of his cherished stalls. I secretly felt he enjoyed the power of his job.

"Do you like music, Arnold?" I enquired. "Oh yes, I am a big fan of all music," he replied. "Well, I have got a thousand records in the car. What do you like? I'll give you a couple for nothing."

"That's very kind. Anything would do. In fact, I am seeing my grand-children tomorrow so maybe something they would like would be good." I went to the car and came back clutching a couple of singles for Arnold. He thanked me and asked, "Do young people like The Rubettes and Suzi Quatro?"

"Yes, I am sure they'll be delighted with them, because they have both had number one singles," I replied.

Arnold seemed genuinely touched by my gesture, and I had learned another important rule of business – not that the best way to get on is to bribe people, but that any idiot can sell products which people want, but to succeed you need to dispose of your overstocks and, although I had left that week's market without a single sale, I had managed to reduce my stock of Rubettes and Suzi Quatro singles.

This was not the only business lesson I learned that day. My finances were decreasing rapidly and I had to face facts. I could no longer afford to employ Phil, and after long deliberation I was forced to take the decision to let him go.

Each week after being rejected at the market, we would return to my house where we would review the business and warm up with tea and toast whilst watching *Tiswas*. This week, as we watched the programme my stomach was in knots. I could not concentrate on the Phantom Flan Flinger, Spit the Dog or even the gorgeous Sally James, who always got 100 per cent of my attention. How was I to tell my best mate that his services were no longer required?

I decided to soften the blow by presenting him with a parting gift of £10, but Phil still got the hump when I told him. Maybe I was being a bit insensitive, but some people just don't understand how difficult it is to run your own business. Sacrifices must be made and, sadly for Phil, it was inevitable that he was that sacrifice. I knew Phil was upset as he just got up and left. He did not even stay to watch Compost Corner, which was always his favourite part of *Tiswas*.

Eventually, on one snowy January morning, I got my big break. Because of the dreadful weather there were a fair number of 'no-shows' and I was given a pitch at last. Along with my stock I had also brought my homemade sign, reading 'BARGAIN RECORDS', which was the name I traded under. Needless to say, seconds of thought went into choosing that name. I also brought my cassette player and a collection of tapes of obscure Liverpool bands that I blasted out, much to the annoyance of some of my fellow traders, and resulting in Arnold requesting that I keep the noise down a bit. Despite the weather the first day was a success. Although the stall cost £6, I left with more than £12 in my pocket.

Also, throughout the day, several people had brought me LPs and singles to purchase, as I bought records as well as selling them.

During the coming weeks I noticed that two types of people came to my stall. The first was the genuine record collector, who was looking to buy new products and to trade in records they had tired of listening to. The other type was normally quite dishevelled, and would only trade in records for cash. It took some time for me to realise that they were probably on drugs and that their goods were probably stolen. After a while my conscience would get the better of me and I turned these people away.

One other thing that I found remarkable was the number of people who came over and asked what I was playing. I realised that none of the tracks on my cassette were for sale on the stall. There was only one thing for it – when I went home I put together a cassette of all my overstock singles and for the next few months Ellesmere Port market rocked to the sound of The Rubettes' 'Juke Box Jive' and all the other singles with which I had over-stock problems. It was a shrewd move, although there were times when I felt like smashing up the cassette player.

Eventually, I did manage to sell all my copies of 'Juke Box Jive'. If I total up all the CDs and records I have sold over the years, it must amount to millions of pounds worth of music, but no other sale has ever matched the feeling of elation I had when the very last copy of 'Juke Box Jive' left the market.

By now I had become a regular at the market. I think it helped that each week I gave Arnold one of my overstock singles for his grandchildren. This gesture delighted him but more importantly, it guaranteed me a stall. Arnold's grandchildren must have had the worst record collection in the land!

One night, whilst I was watching *Blue Peter*, they showed how you could make a fruit bowl out of an old LP record by moulding the vinyl into shape (after first getting your parent to help you heat the plastic). "What a great idea!" I thought. "I could turn all those old albums I can't sell into fruit bowls."

Of course, I needed to get a new sign – 'BARGAIN RECORDS AND FRUIT BOWLS' did not have the required cachet. That night I put a scratched album under the grill; moulded it into shape; and, sure enough, when the vinyl cooled I had manufactured my first fruit bowl. There was no stopping me, and by the end of the night I had a motley collection of fruit bowls to sell on Saturday.

One thing I picked up on was that the bowl on *Blue Peter* seemed to hold a lot more fruit than the ones I was making. It was an illusion – they had cleverly used grapes, cherries, strawberries and plums to fill their bowl whilst mine looked considerably less impressive with a banana, an apple and an orange in it.

The fruit bowls attracted a lot of attention and brought many people over to the stall. Most of them seemed to laugh their heads off, though one sale was particularly interesting. I had a particularly badly scratched Queen album, which I had melted. "Wow, a Queen fruit bowl!" the customer exclaimed, and gladly handed over his £1. He was genuinely chuffed with his purchase. I thought that perhaps I was going about this the wrong way – instead of using fruit bowls as a means of clearing out my overstocks, what would be the response if I produced limited edition fruit bowls of famous bands?

That night I took a scratched copy of The Beatles' *Revolver* album and produced what I believe to be the first ever Beatles fruit bowl. It did cross my mind that perhaps I should contact Apple (the Beatles management company) in case I was infringing copyright laws, but then I thought to hell with it, if they want to sue me it would be great publicity.

I made a small sign saying 'Limited Edition Beatles Fruit Bowl – Only £2', and by the end of the day (and after some heavy selling, like informing a woman that I was sure in years to come it would be a collectors' item) I had relieved myself of the Beatles bowl and of a Gary Glitter fruit bowl made from the unfortunately named *Touch Me* album. I often wonder if they still sit on somebody's sideboard somewhere in Ellesmere Port.

One young girl told me that she would like to surprise her boyfriend by creating a fruit bowl from one of his Led Zeppelin albums, saying that she would bring his album down the following week. I charged her £1 for the job and she happily collected it, but I was never really sure if this was an act of revenge, or if she genuinely thought her boyfriend would be thrilled to see his beloved Led Zeppelin album turned into a fruit bowl. Sadly she never came back to tell me.

Chapter 2

Does Elvis Costello Still Play Football?

I was so desperate to leave the food factory that, when they offered voluntary redundancy, I was in the personnel department before you could blink. After depositing my redundancy cheque in the bank I thought I would take a trip down to the local job-centre to see what else the world had to offer.

After looking through endless requests for cleaners or dead-end jobs like the one I had just left, something stood out like a diamond in a bag of nutty slack. Amongst all the dross was a job that was perfect for me – HMV, the UK's top record retailer, was looking for a sales assistant in their Liverpool branch. "Wow!" I thought. "What an opportunity!"

I was determined to show them that I was the perfect candidate and promptly hurried home to write my CV, something I had never needed in my previous job. I also completed and sent off my application form. A few days later, a letter from HMV landed on my doormat inviting me for an interview.

I did as much research as I could into Liverpool HMV and even popped into the store and had a walk around to see if I had any ideas on how I could contribute to improving it. On the day of the interview I was flummoxed. What should I wear? A shirt and tie? But, as I had never seen anybody working in a record shop wearing anything so formal, I decided on the smart but casual approach.

The interview went well and the manager, Paul Johnson, was quite firm, although I did seem to gel with him. He asked me to name all of the other record stores in town, which was not a problem for somebody who bought lots of vinyl and who would always shop around for the best value. Paul then asked me to rate the stores in order of merit. It was a tricky question and I bravely took the decision to be honest, rating HMV next to bottom of my list. Paul was surprised and told me that most people rated HMV in the top spot. I explained that my experience of the store was one of less than great service and unsmiling staff. I also went on to say that if he employed me all that would change, as I would be so happy you would not be able to remove the smile off my face with Ajax. Paul laughed, and I was later to learn that this had been an excellent answer, as the Liverpool store had not been performing well and he had been brought in to turn things around. In fact, in football terms, they were heading for the Nationwide Conference, being third from bottom in the whole HMV chain.

The next question threw me, as I had never been asked this in any previous interview, "Do you play football?"

"Yes" I replied. The questions then became more surreal.

"Do you play in the Wirral Sunday League?" Again the answer was yes, and then it was, "Are you a goalkeeper?" Blimey, I thought, Paul must be psychic, or the HMV football team needed an injection of fresh blood. He then explained that he had been playing a match on the previous Sunday; the score was 2-2, and with one minute to go his team were awarded a corner. The ball was floated towards him; he met it good and true and headed the ball towards the top corner. Just as he turned to celebrate what he thought was the winner, the goalkeeper had leapt up and turned the ball over the bar. "You were that bloody goalkeeper, weren't you? I knew I'd seen you before." He was correct. I was that goalkeeper, and we had a good laugh about it.

I knew at that moment that I had the job, even though Paul told me over 300 people had applied. It was a good feeling – even though my football skills had failed to land me employment in my preferred career, they had helped me to secure a position in my second choice. Sure enough, two days later Paul phoned to offer me the position of sales assistant at HMV Liverpool. I was delighted.

Whilst working in the factory I had spent my life wishing it away. I would look at the clock and think, "only an hour to break-time", "only three hours to lunch", "only eight hours till I get home", "only three days to the weekend", "only six months to my holiday". I was constantly wishing for the future. Working at HMV did not feel like a proper job and each morning I could not wait to start – no more clock-watching for me. Now I did not want the days to end. Although Paul worked us very hard I enjoyed every second of it, and on most days we worked twelve hours, making a big effort to lift our store up the HMV league table. Like me, most of the staff were new, all brought in to replace the previous team. I loved working on the counter and soon built up good relationships with lots of the regular customers.

This was in the days when CDs had just come out. I lost count of the number of customers who brought back CDs because they could not play them on their record player. The music industry had marketed CDs so that many people believed that you could eat your dinner off them and they would still be playable. This was a blatant untruth.

One day, a chap came into the store demanding a refund. He had bought a CD and decided to show his mate that you could do anything to it and it would still play. He had stood on his and skated it around his carpet before attempting to play it. Needless to say the disc did not play. He told me this tale and then expected a full refund but, of course, he left empty-handed — just another customer taken in by the CD hype.

One lady brought back a CD single by Kenny the Kangaroo, complaining that it jumped. "What did she expect?" we asked. "That's what Kangaroos do!" The humour was lost on her and she demanded a refund.

Often you had to be a bit of a detective. People would come in and ask for "that song off the radio", and then look surprised that you required more clues. "Well, it's a woman" they would say and that normally improved my chances of success by 50 per cent. I recall a lady who asked for "The Jogging Song" and, after numerous guesses, I realised it was 'Running Up The Hill' by Kate Bush. Another guy commented that he had heard a great song on the radio, and though he didn't know the title, he thought the name of the band was something like diarrhoea. I soon deduced that the band was in fact Dire Straits. I thought this was the daftest thing somebody had said to me until a young man asked after a single by Squeeze and he thought the title was 'Up The Back Passage'. Trying to suppress my laughter I suggested it might be 'Up The Junction'.

A few great characters worked at HMV, none more so than our two security guards, Liverpool's own version of the Keystone Cops, Eddie and Paul. It never ceased to amaze me how few people they caught, although, in Eddie's case, it was easier to understand. He was particularly over-weight. I lost count of the times that someone ran past me whilst I was serving on the counter with the whole of the Genesis section tucked under his or her arm, pursued in vain by a wobbling Eddie.

One day a young scally zoomed past me carrying a batch of Bob Marley LPs. "Quick, Graham, give me a hand!" Eddie shouted, and so we set off in pursuit. It soon became obvious that we would never catch the young thief. Suddenly Eddie had a brainwave, no doubt influenced by the American cop shows he was so fond of. He cupped his hands around his mouth and shouted in the loudest voice possible, "Hey, you with the Bob Marley albums, freeze!" Much to Eddie's surprise the youth failed to drop the albums to the floor and put his hands on the nearest wall waiting to be frisked, whilst an old lady standing a few feet away did drop her shopping and nearly had a heart attack due to the shock.

Each time Eddie failed to catch somebody he would analyse the crime, looking for reasons as to why the latest youth had escaped. By going on about it all the time he did not realise that he was just confirming what we all knew – we had the worst security guard in Liverpool. One day he asked me if I had any suggestions to help him apprehend more people, but my unsympathetic response of "lose weight and learn to run faster" was probably unhelpful.

In hindsight, I don't think I helped the situation with my choice of music. Every time he returned, panting from another unsuccessful mission, I would put the song 'Something's Wrong With Eddie' by Wah! on the turntable at full volume. Everybody laughed except Eddie. Due to Eddie's lack of success it turned out to be the most played record in HMV Liverpool that year, and I lost count of the amount of copies of that record I sold. One day Eddie politely stated, "Put that song on one more time and I will f****** force it down your throat," and at that point I thought it wise to stop promoting Wah!

After returning from lunch one day I was advised by Eileen, one of the young girls who worked at HMV, to go down to the basement because we had a problem. It was a bit of a shock when I made my way downstairs to be greeted by a foul-mouthed youth screaming abuse, surrounded by all of the male members of HMV staff. "Quick, give us a hand," Eddie bellowed and I joined the circle, only for the psycho thief to lash out at me with his feet. Apparently Eddie had somehow caught this guy stealing a Pink Floyd CD.

It never ceased to amaze me that the same artists were always stolen; Pink Floyd, Bob Marley, Genesis and Frank Zappa. Hardly a week went by without one of us noticing the whole section of one of these artists was missing.

It was typical of Eddie – why could he not have caught a little old lady with a Mozart CD stuck up her jumper, or a young kid? No, he had to apprehend somebody who made Genghis Khan appear calm and peaceful.

I then made a real mistake – maybe it was nerves, but I smiled. 'Psycho' came within an inch of my face and asked what I was smiling about. "Nothing," I replied.

"When I get out of this I will track you down, it will be easy to find where you live and I never forget a face," said Psycho. "You're dead," he shouted, but it was quite nice of him to offer me a choice. "Would you like me to strangle you then stamp on your face or would you prefer for me to slash your throat, behead you and kick your head around like a football?" Although I was spoilt for choice, I felt silence was the best option, since none of his suggestions for my imminent demise really appealed. After what seemed like an age the police finally arrived, handcuffed him and took him to their van. This didn't discourage him, and he was still lashing out and shouting abuse at the police. I felt safe in the knowledge that he would be put away for a while.

That evening, five friends and I had bought tickets to see Julian Cope perform at the Pyramid Club in Liverpool town centre – he was one of my favourite performers and I had seen him play on many occasions. You could also generally rely on him to do something odd.

When he played the Royal Court in Liverpool he got carried away dancing, failed to notice the edge of the stage and tumbled into the orchestra pit. It made no difference – he hardly missed a note as he leapt back on stage as if nothing had happened. Also, at a gig in Manchester, Julian noticed a trap door in the ceiling above the stage and thought it would be a great idea to climb up. It was a surreal sight to see the band keep playing whilst, out of sight to the crowd, Julian sang the next couple of songs from somewhere above the ceiling of the stage. The next verse reduced the crowd to tears of laughter. "Your singer's stuck in the roof and can't get down," he sang, whilst every now and again popping his head out of the trap door. Eventually a couple of bouncers came to help him down, but not before a batch of plaster had fallen from the ceiling, which resulted in cheers from the crowd.

We were all anticipating another great gig that evening, including one of my mates from HMV, Steve Wade, who had been part of the 'ring of fear' that had encircled 'Psycho' earlier in the day. After handing in our tickets we made our way to the front of the stage where, to my horror, standing with some equally psychotic-looking mates was the psycho who was unable to decide whether to behead me or slash my throat. I made Steve aware of the situation and told our mates we must leave quickly. One of them did not agree and expressed his opinion in a voice so loud that everybody including Psycho and his mates must have heard him. Steve and I scampered off and sadly left our other mates to watch the concert without us.

During this period I was fortunate enough to be able to go to about three gigs a week. I would spend most Fridays and Saturdays at a famous Liverpool venue called Eric's. These were exciting times, and I was able to see bands like Joy Division, U2, The Jam and The Clash before they really hit the big time.

The most memorable gig was a band called X-Ray Spex. The performance was to be recorded by the BBC for a documentary show called *Arena*, which was quite an arty show on BBC 2, a sort of *South Bank Show* for the working class. The queue to gain admission that night was bigger than usual. As we were waiting to get in, a lad in front of me was talking to his girlfriend whilst leaning against a black door. Suddenly the door opened, and he fell on his backside, which created much mirth amongst the queuing punters. After the laughter had died down it became clear that this door led into the club. Everybody waited to see who would be first to venture down the stairs into the darkened gloom.

I was at the front, and we gradually edged our way down. Although it was pitch black, we knew we were getting nearer because the noise emanating from the club was getting louder. As we reached the bottom there was another door, which we opened and, to our surprise, found ourselves in the kitchen of the club. The chefs (well, microwave assistants) looked horrified as the crowd surged through. We realised there was likely to be trouble, so we quickly went to the bar, bought a drink and drank half of it so it appeared that we had been in the club a while.

The security was slow to react, and we watched in amusement as the crowd snaked through the kitchen knocking pans and plates on to the floor. By the time the stragglers were coming down the stairs the bouncers had arrived and started dealing with them in a really violent way. What followed was an horrific hour as a team of security, accompanied by kitchen staff, attempted to identify the people who had got in free. It was impossible for them to really know, as literally hundreds had surged through the kitchen. Lots of arguments and a number of fights broke out as punters were manhandled out, and it appeared to me that it was just an excuse for the bouncers to mete out violence.

I also witnessed the violence of Eric's security when the Stranglers played the club. It was the hottest gig I had ever attended and I was at the front, jumping up and down. Halfway through the band's set I became desperate for a drink to cool me down, but was reluctant to lose my place at the front. I compromised by taking off my T-shirt. So there I was, topless, swinging my T-shirt over my head to create a welcome draught. The bouncer at the front did not take too kindly to being showered with my sweat. But, instead of saying to me, "Excuse me sir, will you please refrain from swinging your T-shirt above your head?" he just smashed me in the face. I did not fall back, as the crowd was so packed, but I thought he had broken my jaw. I was stunned for a few seconds, and as I gathered my senses, the first thing I noticed was the band's bass player Jean Jacques Burnel who was laughing at the incident. Needless to say, I went off The Stranglers after that.

In comparison, Eddie, our own security man at HMV, was mild-mannered and in no way violent, but he was famous for not catching thieves, whilst our other security guard Paul did, every now and again, apprehend somebody. One day I took a phone call from his wife who had the best excuse ever as to why he would not be coming in that day. "Sorry, Paul won't be in today. He's been arrested for armed robbery on the Liverpool to London train." I always thought of him as a really pleasant guy, and was taken aback to discover that he had been influenced by Ronnie Biggs. It turned out that he was part of a gang who had attempted to hold up the train. I never saw Paul again and he was jailed.

We were now down to just the one security guard, but Eddie continued to show me why he was in the wrong job. During that period the IRA was still active, and Eddie appointed me official bomb finder. When he asked me I burst out laughing, but no, he was serious, so each day I had to get on my hands and knees and search under the record racks for bombs. One day I crawled out amongst a sea of legs and looked up to find a load of my mates staring at me. "What are you doing?" they asked.

"I'm looking for bombs," was my reply, and it must have been five minutes before the laughter died down.

To help Eddie out, the manager asked Steve Wade if he would assist and do some security work. This was a masterstroke. Steve just dressed like the average student, which I suppose was badly, but he was soon rounding up thieves at an astonishing rate, much to the annoyance of Eddie. As Steve did not look like a security guard, people would thieve in front of him and, one day, a potential thief asked Steve if he would keep a lookout for the security guard whilst he was stuffing Beatles albums into a carrier bag.

Working at HMV you came across many celebrities. I will never forget the day Cilla Black did a personal appearance. The rep for the record company had arranged it with Dave, the assistant manager, who then completely forgot about it. He also forgot to mention it to any other member of staff. On the morning of the PA (personal appearance) the rep phoned up to speak with Dave to finalise Cilla's appearance. Dave did not let on that we hadn't promoted it and the rep was left with the impression that an army of fans would greet Cilla. In a mad panic Dave informed us, and we hastily scribbled on a white sheet of paper "Here today, signing copies of her new album at 12pm – Cilla Black", and put it in the shop window. It was now 11am, so we had an hour to promote her visit.

When Cilla arrived she was plonked next to me on the counter to sign albums for the army of fans who had gathered. The army of fans turned out to be two old ladies and Mr Adelphi, whose second home was HMV. He was never out of the store. He was in his late 50s and had worked at the famous Adelphi Hotel as a bellboy for years. He was delighted to meet Cilla, and I laughed to myself as he engaged her in conversation about his hero, Cliff Richard. Luckily, Cilla had stories to tell about Cliff, and it temporarily kept her mind off the complete absence of a crowd.

My feeble attempts at humour did not go down well with Cilla as I said, "Surprise, Surprise, I bet you would have thought more people would have turned up." She looked at me with a face like thunder – she was not turning out to be a lorra lorra laughs.

I could see the rep from the record company was embarrassed for Cilla but, luckily, Dave had a cunning plan. Suddenly six young people came to the counter all holding copies of Cilla's album. I recognised every one of them as HMV staff who worked in the stockroom. Cilla was pleased to sign the albums and have a chat, even though I think a couple of our YTS trainees probably had no idea who she was. Whilst this was going on I noticed Dave sneaking out of the store clutching a batch of albums. Just as Cilla was signing the last of the albums another group of youngsters suddenly turned up. Again, I recognised them. They were the staff from Burger King, which was next to HMV, and two of them hadn't bothered to change out of their uniform. They were soon followed by yet another bunch of youngsters brandishing Cilla albums and this time it was the staff of TopShop, HMV's other neighbours.

By the time she had finished I am sure Cilla had a completely distorted view of what her fanbase was, and she was no doubt convinced that she was appealing to a young audience. This PA caused endless headaches, as Dave had given money to everybody to purchase Cilla's album and then had to get them all to bring the albums back so he could do a refund. The rep had sold us Cilla's album on sale or return for the PA, so after her appearance we sent them all back. However, the record company refused to credit us, saying they were damaged stock, as there was writing all over them. Sure enough there was, but it was Cilla's autograph and she had written things like, "To John lorra lorra love Cilla xx". We put the albums in our sale at 50p as damaged stock.

Another embarrassing incident occurred when a man approached the counter clutching a batch of CDs and I immediately recognised him as somebody I knew, but could not quite remember how I knew him. I soon convinced myself that he was somebody I had played football against and this was our conversation.

Me: "Hi mate, how is it going?"

"Fine."

"Are you still playing?"

"Yes, I'm playing tonight."

"Is it under floodlights?"

"No, at the Royal Court Theatre."

At that moment I looked at his credit card, which said Declan McManus, and the penny dropped. It was Elvis Costello, and I had not recognised him as he was using contact lenses rather than wearing his trademark glasses. My face was crimson! I couldn't believe I had asked him if he was still playing.

Even more embarrassing was the day I persuaded Billy Bragg to do a personal appearance. Although I had seen him live a few times, he was still unknown, as he had yet to have anything released. I noticed he was supporting a Liverpool band called the Icicle Works and was also releasing a mini-album titled *Life's A Riot*. I felt that as he was going to be in town it would help sales if he came in and signed copies of his LP.

I gave Billy a call but he did not think it would be a good idea, so, using my persuasive powers, I convinced him it would be a success. I would put a poster up and play his album constantly to attract interest. Billy came in on a Saturday afternoon. He turned up and stood by me at the counter whilst his album blasted out but, unfortunately, Billy was correct; nobody was interested in his album.

He stood there for half an hour whilst the customers of HMV Liverpool mistook him for a shop assistant, asking him where the Genesis section was, or if we stocked classical? Billy took the embarrassment well and laughed about the situation. Just as he was about to leave, a young lad came bounding up to the counter and said to Billy "Hey mate – what's this playing?" I breathed a sigh of relief – at last, a fan. Billy replied "It's the brand new album from Billy Bragg called *Life's A Riot*, would you like a copy? "F*** off", he replied, "it's the biggest pile of shite I've ever heard", and with that he left the shop, leaving us stunned, though seconds later we both burst out laughing.

That evening at the Icicle Works gig, Billy told the HMV story. Six months later in an interview with *NME* he re-told it and one year later he did an interview with *Q* magazine and told the story again, so I am glad he got something out of that day. A year later, Billy's career had taken off, so I took a chance and gave him a call and he agreed to do another PA. This time he turned up, along with Andy McDonald, MD of Go-Discs (Billy's record label), and Andy Kershaw from Radio 1. As well as doing a signing he treated the crowd to an impromptu concert.

Another character I will never forget from HMV is Pete Lie, although he wasn't Chinese and Lie wasn't his surname. Lie was just what he did, day in and day out. He seemed to have met every celebrity who had ever lived and many who were now dead. He had been to every destination in the world and even claimed he was 179th in line to the throne. He had managed to achieve all this and he was only 23. Exasperated by this conveyer belt of untruths, Steve bought a large diary and suggested that we keep it in the office and each day fill it with the lies from that day. Amazingly, Pete never knew about the existence of the book and seemed delighted as members of staff asked him about his life. He thought they were just interested in his tales, when in fact they were just looking for more material for the book. After a year, the book was full and we started Volume Two. Unfortunately this great work of fiction was never completed, as Pete was offered a job working for a record company. No doubt they had been impressed by his tales of how he had single-handedly transformed HMV Liverpool into one of the top record shops in the country. When anybody left the store we would normally purchase them a small gift but, in Pete's case, we presented him with the Lie Books, Volumes One and Two. To be fair to him he took it in good humour and, looking back, it is a pity he felt the need to fib as he was an interesting and funny person in his own right, but you just never knew when he was telling the truth.

Chapter 3

Give it Rice

One day I noticed an advertisement in the *Liverpool Echo*. It read 'Liverpool rock band requires manager'. Immediately, I recognised an opportunity to make further in-roads into the music industry. I phoned the number in the ad and it was answered by the band's singer/guitarist John Byrne. He told me that the band were called The Cherry Boys and invited me over to his house, in an area of Liverpool called Old Swan, for an interview. Next day, I travelled into town and purchased their one and only single, 'Man To Man, from Probe Records. I played the song until I knew every word and read the sleeve notes until I could recite them from memory.

Luckily, I had also seen the band perform. Every summer in Liverpool local bands would perform free concerts in Sefton Park and often six or seven acts would play in one afternoon. I vividly recall The Cherry Boys performance – the band had dressed in white clothes, and after they finished their set they leapt from the stage straight into the lake, which was in front of the stage, much to the amusement of the crowd. The boys were covered in mud and I feared that even Persil would not be able to clean those clothes. As I laughed at their antics little was I to know that in a few weeks they would become a major part of my life.

Whilst the band was on stage, I nearly purchased the dearest cake ever when a Rastafarian approached my mates and I and offered us a slice. We had brought a picnic and plenty of alcohol and just fancied a piece of cake to finish off, so I said we'd have a piece. As he wrapped it, I asked him how much he wanted and he replied that it was £2. I couldn't believe he was asking so much for a small piece of cake. "What's in it, gold?" I enquired.

"No, cannabis." I turned down the cake, thinking I could buy two whole gateaux for that price.

On the night of The Cherry Boys interview I was very nervous. Maybe this was how Brian Epstein felt when he was offering his services to The Beatles, I thought. As well as John, Keith Gunson, the bass player, conducted the interview whilst the band's other two members, Howie Minns, simply the best drummer I have ever seen (should Paul McCartney or Brian Wilson be reading this, get in touch and I will give you his details), and Jimmy Hughes, who was a bit of a one man band, normally playing rhythm guitar and keyboards as well as singing a few songs, decided they had better things to do. The boys seemed more nervous than me, but I was confident that I had impressed them with my expert knowledge of their record. I mentioned that I had my own business, Bargain Records, and I discovered, during the course of the interview, that they were huge Beatles fans. They were impressed when I told them that I was also involved in selling limited edition Beatles products, though it was probably a wise move not to expand on this subject in case they found out that it was Beatles fruit bowls.

The interview went well and they informed me that they would get in touch the following day, because they had a number of other people to see. As I stepped out of the door I was more than hopeful of getting the job. The following evening John rang and informed me that they would like to offer me the position. I was overjoyed. He mentioned that my first gig as manager would be on Friday, at a pub in Liverpool city centre called The Dolphin. There we could discuss the terms of my contract and I could explain my vision of how The Cherry Boys would conquer the globe. In the meantime John asked if I would ring some guy in London who organised gigs to see if he could offer us anything. His name was Harvey Goldsmith.

For the next couple of days I rang Harvey non-stop and must have made over thirty phone calls. Each time his secretary answered I could hear the lethargy in her voice, as she was no doubt thinking, "Oh no – not you again". It was interesting how many excuses she came up with for Harvey not being able speak to me. He was either on another call; in a meeting; out to lunch; out for dinner; out for tea; out for supper; out for some fresh air; or just out. In hindsight, perhaps Harvey was busy with Pink Floyd, Queen or The Who and just did not want to waste his time speaking to a cheeky Scouser.

Upon arriving at The Dolphin I was accosted by John. He asked how I had got on with talking to Harvey. "Very well", I replied, "I have to put a tape in the post to him". I did send him a cassette of Cherry Boys songs, but to this day he still has not got back to me.

The pub seemed quite crowded, but I couldn't see the band's equipment and John informed me that they would be playing in a room at the back of the pub. I was very nervous and told John I just needed a Jimmy Riddle and would follow him through. Upon attempting to enter the room I was stopped by a lad on the door who demanded 25p to get in. "I'm the band's manager," I replied. It sounded really good – I had arrived in the music industry. Sadly the 25p entrance fee had clearly put off the good people of Liverpool from coming to our gig, as the audience consisted of just twelve people. To be fair to the band they gave it 100 per cent and the twelve people in attendance were obviously hardcore fans, as they cheered enthusiastically and seemed to know the words to every song. Just before the penultimate number Keith announced, "Ladies and gentlemen, I would like to introduce you to our new manager, Graham." He then introduced me to every member of the audience and told me all their names and how they were related to the band. It turned out I was the only member of the audience who was not either related, or having a sexual relationship with one of them.

After the gig was over we sat down and agreed terms. The band would pay me 15 per cent of any money they received for anything that I arranged – gigs, record deals and the like. We talked through my plans and, no doubt, I would continue to try to develop a business relationship with Harvey Goldsmith whilst attempting to attract interest from record companies and TV. The band had given me a cassette of some of their songs and the more I listened to them the more I appreciated that, with a bit of marketing, and a little bit of luck, there was no reason why they could not go far.

One track on the cassette, entitled 'Kardomah Café', was truly outstanding, yet I had not heard the boys play it live and I asked John why. He replied that the song required him to sing, play guitar and mouth organ simultaneously and he found doing all three near impossible. I immediately booked them into a rehearsal studio for a day with the sole aim of mastering the song so it could be sung live. By the end of the day, they had produced a tremendous version of the track that became the highlight of the group's live performance.

Next I had to think of ways to attract the attention of the press. I had noticed during their performances that Keith, the bass player, kept shouting, "Give it rice!" This was his way of motivating the band to really rock.

For the next gig I bought a bag of rice and gave it to Janet and Mo, who were two band member's girlfriends, and told them to throw the rice at the band every time Keith shouted, "Give it rice!" The turnout for the next gig at The Dolphin was vastly improved. I had phoned every single person I could think of to come down to see my new band and my brother, Colin, had also brought a large group of mates. The atmosphere was far better than usual. 'Kardomah Café' went down fantastically and everybody cheered each time Keith screamed, "Give it rice!" and was pelted with hundreds of grains.

Word about the band that gave it rice quickly spread around Liverpool, and by the following week The Dolphin was full of people waiting to see the hot new group. Like the previous week, I had nipped down to the shops and bought another bag of rice, but I need not have bothered — it seemed like every person there had the same idea. Every time Keith shouted, "Give it rice!" the band were hit with a hailstorm of the stuff. The gig was a huge success and that night we left The Dolphin looking like a Christmas scene, vast quantities of rice covering everything.

The next day I received a phone call from Mary, the manager of The Dolphin. "Graham I am banning The Cherry Boys from The Dolphin."

"Why's that Mary? A few weeks ago the band were playing to nobody and last night it was packed!"

"It may have been packed, but all that rice has knackered my Hoovers and we are reduced to brushing the stuff up. I'm not prepared to risk my Hoovers, so you're banned."

This was music to my ears. I promptly phoned up the *Liverpool Echo* and spoke with their rock critic, Peter Trollope, who was intrigued by the band who 'gave it rice' and destroyed vacuum cleaners in the process. I could tell I had Peter's attention and suggested we do a feature in the paper. Peter agreed, and the next day we met him, and a photographer, outside The Dolphin. The photographer took photos of the band looking glum outside the venue that had helped us receive such great publicity.

Peter interviewed the band and first of all asked where the name came from. Immediately John launched into this incredibly long and boring story on how Japanese male virgins were called 'cherry boys', and as the band was so young and innocent Noddy Nowler, a Liverpool record producer, had suggested the name. I had a word with John and told him that in future he should just tell everyone that his name was John Cherry, which would be a much simpler explanation so, from that day, John Byrne became John Cherry.

The interview went well and two days later the band's story was featured in a half-page article, which included the epic quote from Mary, "We all loved The Cherry Boys. They are great lads, but after their last gig the rice has jammed two of my Hoovers." The publicity fuelled the band's momentum and we were soon packing out venues all across the city, going down a storm wherever we played.

The only downside was that the rice phenomenon was becoming bigger than the band's music, and we were getting more venues refusing bookings because of the mess we generated. We reluctantly had to appeal to fans to stop bringing rice to gigs.

At one gig at the Pyramid Club I turned up and heard the bouncer ask a group of fans if they were they carrying rice. After they said no, the bouncer fleeced them and, amazingly, as fans were entering the gig they were being searched for rice. I'm sure that in Liverpool people were used to being stopped and searched for knives and drugs, but rice?

Most Liverpool bands received their first national exposure via that champion of new music, the late John Peel, and The Cherry Boys were no different. In an attempt to attract his attention I forwarded him a copy of a demo cassette the band had recorded, named 'Give It Rice'. I packed this inside a real bag of rice, enclosing the feature from the *Liverpool Echo* and a letter to John which ended, "The next time you come up to Liverpool, give me a ring and I will take you for a drink".

A few days later the phone rang. "Hi Graham, this is John Peel. Do you fancy that drink?"

At first I thought it was a joke, especially as Keith from the band did a superb impression of Mr Peel. "Is that you Keith?" I asked.

"Graham, it's John. Are you coming out or shall I call somebody else?" I could not believe it – John Peel was asking me to meet him for a drink!

We arranged to meet up at a well-known Liverpool pub, The Grapes, in Matthew Street. "I will be wearing a black coat, with a Cherry Boys badge on my lapel so you can recognise me". I added foolishly.

"How about you just introduce yourself to me?" John replied sardonically.

I arrived at The Grapes 45 minutes early. I definitely could not be late for this. I ordered a beer and ten minutes later I was back at the bar ordering a second. My nerves had made me gulp the first one down so quickly that I decided that, rather than drink the next pint, I would just stare at it. The next half-hour was spent nipping to the toilet and coming back to resume the task of staring at my pint whilst waiting for John to arrive.

Eventually he arrived, and no sooner had I introduced myself and bought him a drink than he was telling me lots of remarkable stories of things that had happened to him over the years. He was exactly as I had imagined him from hearing him so many times on the radio. John was a fabulous raconteur and I could have listened for hours but, as always, he was on his endless search for new talent.

He asked me if I would like to come with him to check out a couple of bands that he had heard good things about. The first group we went to see were a then-unknown acapella band called The Christians, who were very impressive and later went on to become extremely successful. The second band was less remarkable and left so little impression on me that, to this day, I cannot remember its name.

It amazed me just how many people approached John with cassettes of their music and, by the end of the evening, he had filled his pockets with a variety of recordings. I can only presume that there were lots of people walking around the country carrying cassettes on the million-to-one chance that they would bump into John Peel.

The evening was thoroughly enjoyable. At its end, John told me that he was going to a village named Burton to meet his friend and producer, John Walters the next day. He invited me along and, of course, I jumped at the chance.

At lunchtime I travelled down to Burton, which turned out to be the village where John grew up and was only a few miles from Bebington, where I lived.

John was in a nostalgic mood and reminisced about his childhood whilst, needless to say, John Walters also had a wealth of stories – after a few hours in his company I could understand how he made the transition from producer to broadcaster.

I felt very privileged to be in such amusing company and I did manage to contribute to the laughter by bringing up tales of my disasters at the food factory. As John left, he told me that the BBC would be in touch to give the band a session and he also said to give him a ring whenever I was in London and I could sit in on his show. Wow, who would believe it?! Six weeks after I took over managing the band, when they were playing to a crowd of relatives and sexual partners, they would be broadcast on Radio 1. I couldn't wait to phone them.

Sure enough a letter soon arrived from the BBC and two weeks later we headed down the M1 to Maida Vale to record four songs for the *John Peel Show*. The producer of our session was Dale Griffin, who had been the drummer with a band called Mott the Hoople, which had been my favourite band when I was a schoolboy. In fact, I had a picture of them on my bedroom wall, which my Mum had bought for me as a Christmas present, though, at the time she could not understand why the shop assistants all burst out laughing when she asked for a Dr Hoople poster.

The session sounded great and, when we finished, Dale kindly stayed for a drink and told us stories of his days with Mott. I cringed when John asked what advice he would give a band starting off in the industry and Dale's reply was to watch your manager. It seemed that every manager Mott had employed had ripped off the band and, after ten years of success, he was left with very little money when the band split up. "No offence, Graham," he said.

When The Cherry Boys session was aired on Radio 1, John Peel told the story of how he had received the band's cassette in a bag of rice, which was what had attracted his attention. Later John told me that doubtless it was this story that had inspired another band to send him a cassette enclosed in a plastic bag inside a prawn curry, which, almost inevitably, spilt all over his trousers when he opened the package. Sadly for the band the curry had also found its way into the cassette itself.

After the John Peel session was broadcast I was inundated with letters and phone calls, most of them raving about 'Kardomah Café'. One of the calls was from a chap from Warner Chappell, a music publisher called Jeff Chegwin, asking if we could do a deal. Jeff was the brother of Keith Chegwin, the TV personality, and also of Janice Long, the stalwart of Radio 2. Janice, who was working for Radio Merseyside at the time, had tipped off Jeff about how good 'Kardomah Café' was. Over the next few years Janice championed the band all the time and we will always be grateful for the support she gave us. I recall that in an interview with *She* magazine, after she had started work at Radio 1, Janice was asked what she kept in her handbag, and she replied that she carried a tape of 'Kardomah Café' by The Cherry Boys to remind her of Liverpool.

Regrettably for Janice, Keith, a member of the band, had fallen madly in love with her. Every time we passed Radio Merseyside Keith would pop in and gather a batch of photos of Janice. What he did with them I really don't know, but it inspired Howie to play a trick on him. We were on our way to do a gig at Salford University when Howie asked Keith about his feelings towards Janice. Keith poured his heart out, but then went on to explain what he would love them to get up to should they be alone. Unbeknownst to him, his outpourings of love were being recorded. That evening, as they did at every gig, the band took the stage to the sound of the theme from *Thunderbirds* and, halfway through, the theme music was interrupted by the sound of Keith expressing his feelings for Janice in a most inappropriate manner. The students of Salford didn't know what was going on. I thought the gig was about to become a brawl, with Keith brandishing his bass guitar above his head, but luckily the rest of the band started the first number to defuse the situation. Needless to say, the atmosphere between bass player and drummer was tense for the rest of the evening.

By now the band were receiving offers to play bigger venues. Aberystwyth University phoned me and asked if we could perform there the next day, as the band that they had booked had pulled out to appear on a BBC programme called *Pebble Mill at One*. This was hardly rock 'n' roll, since *Pebble Mill* was less exciting than the test card and aimed at pensioners. Talk about selling your soul! As the money was good we were happy to oblige, and the gig went well.

We left the University around 1am for the long journey back to Liverpool. It was a cold, snowy January night and I was worried that our hired van, which had been very temperamental on the way there, might not make it back. My fears came true when, in the middle of absolutely nowhere, the van shuddered to a halt.

Most members of the band were sleeping, so I said I would try to get some help. Why couldn't mobile phones have been invented a decade earlier? I walked for half an hour without finding a phonebox and then came across an isolated cottage. No lights were on, so I presumed everyone was in bed, and who could blame them since, after all, it was 3am?

I knocked on the door for quite a while before I heard the sound of a window being opened. "Hi", I shouted, "we've broken down. Can I use your phone please?" It was at this point that I noticed he was pointing a shotgun at me. "Get off my land or I'll shoot your balls off." I started to repeat myself when he interrupted me, by threatening me again, only this time much louder. I felt that my manhood was important to me, so I decided to flee the scene. After departing the farm I re-joined the road to try to find a phone, and reflected on whatever had happened to the Welsh claim that there would be a welcome in the hillside.

Eventually I came across a phonebox, called the AA and headed back to the van. When I got there, I found that John had started a fire to keep everybody warm. John was unlike anybody I had ever met. Most lads have hobbies like football or rugby, but his was pyromania! He would start a fire anywhere. I asked what he had used to get the fire started. "Just all the waste paper we had in the van", he told me.

"Did you notice a white envelope that was on the dashboard?" I asked.

"No", John replied, "there was just a load of waste paper there." John had started a fire using a £400 cheque from Aberystwyth University that was inside the white envelope. Needless to say, I did not need the heat from the fire, because my blood was boiling! Luckily for me the University were understanding and issued us with another cheque.

Our next gig also turned out to be an adventure. We were to support a band called Black Slate, who were riding high in the chart with their one and only hit 'Amigo'. The problem for us was that they were a reggae band, and a more unsuitable support act than us would be hard to find. The other problem was that it was at the University of East Anglia, which wasn't exactly local to Liverpool and involved a long, cross-country journey. Needless to say the band went down like a eunuch at an orgy.

Something I had not told the band was that I had a temporary cash flow problem and had set off with less money than I usually carried. I did not see this as a major problem, as by now I had produced a range of Cherry Boys merchandise – badges, T-shirts, cassettes and the like, which normally brought in about £50 worth of sales. What I hadn't taken into account was that we wouldn't be able to sell our products that night, as most of the crowd were Rastafarians with no interest in our music. Of course, just when I needed our money in cash, the University paid us by cheque and, after I had bought the band some food and drink, it became apparent that I didn't have enough money for the petrol to get us home. I asked the band to lend me whatever they had, but none of them carried money, and my appeal raised a measly £3. I set off for the long journey home and left the band to sleep.

With still more than a hundred miles to go the dial on the petrol tank had reached zero and, with no money left, it called for drastic action. I stopped at the services and thought of two options. One was to wake the band up and see if they would busk in the services. As it was 5am, and not many people were around, I felt option two would be the best bet: I would grab some merchandise and approach people eating their break-fasts and flog them products they didn't want. I planned to approach them and say, "Excuse me sir, we are a poverty stricken band from Liverpool. We have run out of petrol and need to get back, but we have no money. Would you be prepared to purchase our merchandise at a greatly reduced price? In years to come I can assure you these will become collectors' items."

Well, the Great British public responded in style and in no time at all I had enough not only for petrol, but money left over to buy the band breakfast. One kindly gentleman bought four T-shirts for his grandchildren. I failed to mention that all our T-shirts were one size (large) so hopefully they may all have grown into them by now. Hardly anybody had refused to purchase something upon hearing my sob story. Maybe this was a new way to break the band – I could just tour the services of the UK and sell merchandise.

These were busy days for the band with two or three gigs a week, but an opportunity arose for me to publicise them further. Radio Merseyside were having a poll for the best current Liverpool band. As it was in the 80s the votes were to be cast on postcards, as opposed to the Internet. I bought batches of them and, along with the band and every friend we knew, got people to fill in a postcard with a vote for The Cherry Boys. So as not to create suspicion it was important to try to make the postcards different in some way, so we did things like adding comments or putting requests on the cards.

We heard on the grapevine that another local band, The Icicle Works, were also hyping the poll, which resulted in me purchasing a second batch of cards.

On the night of the awards everyone who was anyone in the Liverpool music scene was represented. We had some stiff competition from the likes of Frankie Goes To Hollywood, Echo and the Bunnymen, Wah! and China Crisis, who had all had recent chart success. Janice Long announced the results in reverse order and it was like being at Miss World. Third was a local band called Cook The Books who lived up to their name, as they too had obviously hyped the result. We all glanced at the Icicle Works and they stared back. Who had hyped the best? Soon Janice announced the Icicle Works as runners up and they were gutted. I will never forget the look on Bill Drummond's face when The Cherry Boys were announced as the best Liverpool band. Bill was manager of Echo and the Bunnymen, and later became famous as a member of £1 million-burning band KLF. He could not hide his disgust at his band not being in the top three. Janice invited The Cherry Boys on stage to receive the award and asked Keith how he felt. "With my hands," was his quick reply. Winning the award made my job so much easier, as I was able to obtain more money for gigs and it was easier to get record companies to listen to us.

By now we had signed a publishing deal with Jeff Chegwin at Warner, Janice Long confided in us that she had been offered a job at Radio 1 and we had a record deal on the table from Satril Records. They were not the biggest label in the world, but at the time of us signing they had the number two single in the charts. Alarm bells should have rung in my head when I realised the record in question was 'The Birdie Song' by The Tweets, which nowadays is in everybody's top 10 worst ever records. A man called Henry Haddaway owned the label or, as we knew him, Henry Hadditaway, because every time we met up with him he seemed to have a different woman in tow. We recorded a magnificent version of 'Kardomah Café' and the label decided to release it on cherry red coloured vinyl later that summer. The band embarked on more dates, and we were all buoyed by the offer of another Radio 1 session, this time with Kid Jenson.

Just two weeks before our release date we received some mixed news when Janice Long told us that she was taking maternity leave. We were, of course, delighted for her, but the timing for us was unfortunate – the DJ who championed us would not be working at the single's release. The record received fabulous reviews and was well supported by John Peel, Kid Jenson and, of all people, Gary Davies. For six weeks it hovered just out-side the top 75, but in our hearts we knew the single would have charted with Janice's help. At that time she had a prime-time show on Radio 1, and without her help, the band wouldn't have got where they were.

Two people who slated the record were George Michael and Paul Young. Radio 1 had a show called *Round Table*, which reviewed the latest releases. Working in HMV, I knew the record label of each new release and I realised that the show was very political. George and Paul were both on Sony Records, and any release on Sony was praised as if it was the new 'Bohemian Rhapsody', whilst they also praised any single by a well-known artist, who at some point might be able to further the reviewer's own career. Of course, all the records couldn't be praised, so normally the new bands on small labels were the ones to receive bad reviews. I had listened to the show for years, and as soon as I heard that George and Paul were reviewing that week's releases I predicted with amazing accuracy what kind of review they would give. Recently I visited a record shop where, for years, the owner had also booked gigs and I asked him who was the best and worst artist he had ever booked. I allowed myself a wry smile when he announced that the worst performance he had ever seen was by Paul Young, who had completely lost the voice he once had.

To help finance the band John, Keith and Howie often did gigs under the different name of Take 3. They were essentially a Beatles covers band and they played the social clubs of the North West. This was a different world exactly like you see on Peter Kay's *Phoenix Nights*, which captures the madness of those clubs so well. If I had no plans on a weekend I would often go down and offer moral support. The band referred to these gigs as 'Elsies' due to the fact that most women there seemed to be called Elsie, Doris, Mabel, etc. The average age of the audiences was over 50.

At one gig in Huddersfield I recall that the band were halfway through the Beatles classic 'Let It Be' when the MC (master of ceremonies) stood up and started ringing a large hand bell of the type that teachers used to tell you that playtime was over. "Now then lads, just have a break for a minute, as the pies and peas have arrived." It was as if he had said they were giving out free money at the back of the hall. Everybody left their chairs and a mini stampede started as they rushed to get their pies and peas, leaving the band flabbergasted on the stage, having sung only half the song.

At one Elsie gig I arrived and found the band in a tiny dressing room, which was made smaller by the presence of two large bingo machines. At these gigs the band would normally play a set and there would then be a break whilst the audience played Bingo, after which the band would come back and do a second set. The prizes they played for never ceased to amaze me. The first time I attended an Elsie gig the MC announced: "Tonight the prize will be a joint". It took a while for me to realise that they were playing for meat, not cannabis.

This night the band had been getting a hard time from the MC, who insisted they do a shorter set. In revenge they came up with a cunning plan, which was bound to entertain the four of us, but guaranteed to ruin the MC's night. We decided to take ten bingo balls out of the bingo machine in the corner and put them in the machine near the door, which was the one they would use in the interval. As soon as the band finished their first set, the MC and a helper wheeled the bingo machine out and on to the stage. He then started calling out the numbers: on its own number 4, two little ducks 22, Maggie's Den number 10, two fat ladies 88, on its own number 4. "Hang on," came a shout, "we have already had that one." The MC was perplexed, but decided to carry on with the game, but when another number was repeated, you could sense a minor riot was about to happen. Soon a third number was repeated, and the MC announced he was abandoning bingo for the evening. Well, there was a blue rinse riot as pensioners stormed the stage, some complaining that they were only a few numbers away from winning the joint, whilst others were asking what was going to happen to the joint and the rest of them were demanding their money back. Eventually calm was restored and the MC came into the band's dressing room snorting with rage. "It was you, weren't it?" he snarled. Of course we denied all knowledge.

It soon became apparent that the band could no longer continue doing Elsie gigs, as more offers of supporting bigger bands and TV action came our way. Although 'Kardomah Café' had not charted as we had hoped, it had received rave reviews and even made number eight in the Spanish chart (it looked strange when I was given a sheet showing the Spanish chart, with Michael Jackson's 'Thriller' at number nine). I argued with the record company about doing a Spanish tour, but Satril were not known for spending much on support. One bit of promotion they did do was to produce thousands of cherry shaped jelly sweets that were to be given away by the record company sales rep to shops, to encourage them to promote the record.

A company called Spartan, whose name summed up their efforts, distributed the 'Kardomah Café' record. The rep who called into HMV was Sid and, at first, I didn't let on that I was the manager of the band so I could see how he was promoting the record. "Hey Sid, how is The Cherry Boys' single doing?" I asked.

"Fantastic" came the reply, "they have given me all these cherry sweets to give away, would you like some?" I accepted his offer and then Sid went on to tell me that his kids had never eaten so many sweets in their lives and his son had developed a nice little earner to boost his pocket money by selling the bags of sweets at school. At this point I felt it wise to inform Sid that I was the manager of The Cherry Boys and the money used to purchase all those sweets for his son would no doubt be deducted from our royalties. Sid was mortified and asked me to not tell his bosses. I agreed, as long as he phoned me up every couple of days to tell me how well the record was selling – I felt this would put a bit of pressure on him.

To promote the record, the band were gigging most days, and on one warm Saturday we were down to play at a festival at Norward Abbey in Yorkshire, at which Tom Robinson was the headline act. When we arrived the promoter showed us to a small caravan, which was to be the changing room for us and about ten other bands. I felt this was a poor show and went on the lookout for alternative facilities. I soon found a much larger caravan and ushered the band in. This was more like it – there was a fridge full of food, wine and beer, and the boys soon made themselves at home tucking into it. Soon a tall well-spoken man arrived and politely said "Excuse me gents, I think this is my caravan."

"Who the f*** are you?" John enquired.

"Err, I'm Tom Robinson," the man replied. Sadly for Tom this meant nothing to John, who's music knowledge ended with the Beatles splitting up. "I don't care if you're Robinson Crusoe, we were here first so f*** off," was John's response. I stood in the corner cringing before security came and escorted us back to the tiny caravan.

Over the next six months it was all action. The band supported A Flock Of Seagulls or 'A Flock of Haircuts' as we called them on their UK tour. Although they were also from Liverpool they never mixed with us, and at every gig, like most support bands, we were given an abysmal light show and dreadful sound. I learned an early lesson: if you wanted a sound where you could understand what the band were singing, or a light show that used more than one colour, you had to bribe the operatives. I realised I was paying out more in bribes than we were earning for the gig.

After touring with the Haircuts we did some dates with Level 42. The band's main man was a genius called Mark King and we used to watch him do the sound check on his own. He would play every instrument whilst the rest of the band was probably down the pub.

One support slot that never came off was with The Eurythmics. Both members of the band, Annie Lennox and Dave Stewart, had previously been in a band called The Tourists, who I had really enjoyed. When they released their first single as The Eurhythmics it had only just scraped into the top 75, but I had a feeling they would be big.

I had heard on the grapevine that they were planning a tour, so I tracked Dave Stewart down and asked him if we could support them. Dave asked me to send him some details and a copy of our record and to follow it up the next week. When I called Dave again he told me how much he had enjoyed the record and after that we spoke about twice a week. He agreed for us to support and kept me informed of the gig dates. So that I would be able to attend every show, I booked my holiday from work. Ten days before the tour started Dave phoned me to tell me that the record company, RCA, had offered him £2,000 if he allowed one of their acts, One The Juggler, to support The Eurythmics. Unless I came up with the cash it was curtains for us. There was no way I could have raised that sort of money and since then I have followed their career with interest, hoping deep down that they would fail. Instead, they became one of the most successful bands of the last thirty years.

The release of The Cherry Boys second single, 'Shoot The Big Shot', came in 1984 and, to coincide with the release, I lined up a 25-date UK tour. It was fair to say the band were big in the North West, but in the rest of the country they could be best described as a cult band. Most of the venues were universities or small clubs and the difference that we were paid for gigs on this tour was amazing, from the lowest at £100 to the highest at £600. It all depended on what I could negotiate. Ticket prices for each show varied between 75p and £4 and, of course, gigs charging 75p tended to be sold out whilst £4 gigs tended to be for die-hard fans only. Often in these cases I had oversold the band and the venue would have to take a loss.

At Warwick University the social secretary had organised the gig, and just two days before he phoned me to ask that we cancel the gig, saying he would still pay us the £400. Only 20 tickets had been sold, and if the gig went ahead they would have to employ bar staff, security etc – it was cheaper to call the gig off. My view was that the 20 people who had bought the tickets were die-hard fans, and if we cancelled they would no longer be fans. I could tell he wasn't happy with my explanation, but I told him we would be there. Next day the phone went again and this time he offered me £500, but the answer was the same. I did not attend the gig, but the band said it went well. They had a huge PA and lighting rig and the audience had plenty of room to dance in the huge hall. In total around 40 people came, and taking into account that they would have sold £160 worth of tickets, and we were paid £400 before all the extras, it was no wonder he had tried to cancel the gig.

Ten years later I started working with a likeable chap called Steve Bunyan. We got talking and I asked him how he had started in the music industry. He told me that his first job was booking the bands at Warwick University, so I asked him how he had gotten involved. Steve explained that the previous year the University had booked some really dodgy bands and lost quite a lot of money and he felt he could do a better job. He campaigned for the role with the slogan 'Better Bands With Bunyan'. With his catchy phrase Steve won the vote and was duly elected as social secretary at Warwick University. It came as no surprise that he would end up working in the marketing side of the music industry years later. I asked him what bands he booked and was impressed by his answer of REM, Motorhead and Killing Joke. Steve then started telling me about the dodgy bands Chris, his predecessor, had booked. I laughed along at this list of failures and one hit wonders until he said the biggest disaster had been a band from Liverpool called The Cherry Boys. I tried not to look too shocked whilst choking on my beer. Steve started telling me about their manager, who had convinced Chris that he was booking the new Beatles. Chris had even offered him £500 for The Cherry Boys not to turn up, but the manager had turned that down and insisted on playing to an empty hall.

"He was mad." At this point I felt it was only right that I should introduce myself as that mad manager whom had cost Warwick University so much money all those years ago.

During that tour I drove the band to as many gigs as possible and, if I couldn't attend, my brother would replace me. We would always meet at the Mersey Tunnel where the band would park their cars and we would all head off together in a hired transit van.

One day I had arranged a gig at Treforest Polytechnic, and when Keith arrived he informed me that he didn't have his amplifier. I asked why and it turned out that Keith's van was filled with rubbish, so he had tied his amp on to the roof rack and disappeared for a drink down the pub with his mate. Keith lived in Kirby, and anybody could have told you that the chances of the amp still being there upon his return were about 50/50. Needless to say, Keith was unlucky and there was no sign of the amp.

There was no way we could perform without his amp, so I suggested we drive into town and purchase a new one, and then drive on to Burtonwood Services on the M62. Keith could leave his van there and we could all head off together. The first part went to plan as Keith bought a brand new amp for £80, but little did we know that it had a lifespan of less than twenty minutes. We set off to Burtonwood with Keith's new amp tied on to the roof rack. We were behind his van when suddenly, without stopping, a car came out of a junction. I slammed on the brakes and, luckily, stopped. Unfortunately Keith was not so lucky – when he slammed on his brakes the amp did not stop. Instead, it flew off the roof rack and bounced on to the other side of the road. It had been badly damaged by its fall, but a large lorry soon put it out of its misery by smashing it into thousands of little pieces.

It was obvious that we were never going to get to our gig on time so I phoned the venue, who where very good about it. When we eventually arrived we were greeted by a big poster saying that The Cherry Boys' gig was delayed due to them breaking down on the motorway. I couldn't tell them that the real reason we were delayed was due to Liverpool's answer to Frank Spencer losing two amps in a day. I was unaware that Keith would soon eclipse this achievement.

We did a gig at the Rock Garden in London and Keith arrived with his equipment crammed into his sister's mini, which was a change from the van he normally turned up in. "Where's the van?" I asked.

"Oh, I wrote it off when I hit a wall and my sister has lent me her car." A week later we were waiting at the Mersey Tunnel for Keith and there was no sign of him. I phoned his house: "Why aren't you here?

"Well, I need you to come and pick me up, as I have no transport."

"Why can't you borrow your sister's car?" I asked.

"Well," came the reply, "you know after the Rock Garden gig? Well, I think the LSD I took hadn't worn off by the time we arrived back in Liverpool, because as I was driving back home in my sister's mini I saw a herd of elephants charge towards me, and I swerved to avoid them and crashed the car into a wall. It's a complete wreck and my sister is furious with me."

"We need to leave soon," I reminded him, "and we don't have time to drive back to Kirby. Can't you get your dad to give you a lift down?"

"No," Keith replied, "he's out, and I've already asked him and he said over my dead body."

"What about a taxi?"

"No money." Exasperated, I told him to get down here ASAP, and I didn't care how. Keith told me he would be down within the hour and was going to phone his mates to see if any of them could help. An hour later he turned up in his dad's vehicle. "It was good of him to lend you the car," I said.

"He hasn't," was Keith's reply, "I've left him a note, but I know he will kill me when I get back."

That night's gig was in Leicester and on the way home I reminded Keith that, as he had to drive his dad's car back to Kirby, it might be a good idea to give the LSD a miss. Sadly I was too late – he had taken a tab five minutes before and I shook my head in disbelief. On the way back from Liverpool I could hear the shouts of the band as the hallucinations kicked in and often it was quite funny to listen to them all being off their heads. Frequently they would advise me to miss the pixie or space creatures they thought they were seeing on the road ahead.

Upon arrival back in Liverpool I could tell Keith still hadn't fully recovered, but he was insistent that he was fine to drive his car back to Kirby. He hadn't gone two miles when he crashed into the back of a parked car and had to be towed home.

That evening we had another gig, and this time we had no choice but to pick Keith up, because now his family were devoid of any transport. Arriving at his house we were greeted by what looked like a scene from the pits at a stock car meeting. On his drive was a smashed up mini, a smashed up van, and parked outside on the road was his dad's smashed up car.

Keith was pretty distraught about the situation, but it was soon about to get even worse. Howie thought it might be a good idea to put an advertisement in the *Liverpool Echo*. Along with Keith's phone number, the ad read, 'Seeking parts for your car? Then look no further. Call Keith's car spares – all makes catered for'. Well, we all underestimated the popularity of the *Liverpool Echo*, as the phone rang non-stop for weeks with people asking for clutches, tyres etc. Keith told us that two years later they still received the odd car enquiry.

By the beginning of '85 the band were beginning to lose their enthusiasm. Howie had a bad accident when he slipped in a phonebox and, as he tried to save himself, he put his hand through the glass pane, severing tendons in his arm. It meant that we were without a drummer for a long time and although we tried a stand in, it just wasn't the same. 'Shoot The Big Shot' had not sold as well as 'Kardomah Café' and even though I had obtained a couple of TV appearances and Radio 1 sessions, we had lost our momentum. Frustration with the record labels lack of commitment didn't help, and the band decided to split.

John ended up in a Liverpool band called The La's who had a big hit with 'There She Goes', an absolute classic. Howie and Jimmy formed Exhibit B, who I managed. We released two singles, 'Who Killed The Smile' and 'It's Hypothetical' and an LP titled *Playing Dead*, which all received great reviews. Amazingly, a CD version was released in Japan eighteen years later after a top Japanese band, Flippers Guitar, sampled one of the band's tracks, 'Excerpt From A Hippy Opera'. Meanwhile, the other member of the band, Keith, continued to crash cars.

After Exhibit B Howie went on to join the Macc Lads, the lewdest band on the planet and probably Macclesfield's biggest contribution to the UK economy. He also established himself as an alternative comedian with an act called Eddie Shit. Check him out on YouTube. The gist of his act was to sing rather crude versions of famous songs with lyrics about toilets and bodily functions: 'Bohemian Rhapsody' became Bohemian Crapsody; '24 Hours From Tulsa' became 24 Hours On Toilet; 'Light My Fire' became Light My Fart; 'Message In A Bottle' became Massage In A Brothel – you probably get the idea!

Whilst performing as Eddie, Howie dressed as a Victorian strong man with slicked-back hair, false moustache and a pink lycra suit. On tour with the Macc Lads, Howie would do the support spot as Eddie Shit, with most of the audience oblivious to the fact that Eddie Shit was also the band's drummer. This led to one of the funniest stories I have ever heard. For one tour the Macc Lads had a new roadie who became a big fan of Eddie Shit, unaware it was Howie. After one gig Howie arranged a fantastic stunt. The roadie was called Sandbach, due to the fact that he had tattooed on his neck, 'If lost return to Sandbach'. Next to this was an arrow pointing the way (Sandbach is a Cheshire town). He started talking to Howie about how funny Eddie Shit was and Howie stopped him in his tracks by saying that one of these days he was going to kill that Eddie Shit. "Why?" asked Sandbach. "Well, a few years ago he had underage sex with my sister and I've never forgiven him." Sandbach, who was no mastermind, was genuinely shocked. Howie then got Keith from The Cherry Boys to dress up in one of Eddie Shit's outfits and meet him at 1am at Knutsford services. He was to bring a bag of pig's blood and leave the bonnet up on his car to give the impression that it had broken down. The Macc Lads were in on the stunt, so one night, after a gig, they pulled into Knutsford services under the pretence of needing petrol. "Stop!" Howie shouted, "there's that bastard Eddie Shit". He then proceeded to pull a large knife out of the glove compartment, leapt out of the van and shouted that he was going to kill him. Howie leapt on Keith, and after much rolling about he left Keith feigning dead and lying in a pool of pig's blood. Howie jumped back into the van and shouted to get out of there quickly. Sandbach was visibly shocked and shaking after witnessing what he thought was a murder. Howie passed him the bloodied knife and told him to dispose of it. In panic Sandbach wound down the window and threw the knife out of the window on to the hard shoulder of the M6. "What have you done that for?" Howie barked.

"Well you said get rid of it".

"Yes," Howie said, "but I didn't mean for you to throw it out of the window. It's got your fingerprints all over it you dickhead."

By now Sandbach was crying with terror, convinced that he was on his way to a lifetime in jail. When they arrived back in Liverpool, Sandbach was dropped off, with Howie telling him to lie low for a while. It transpired he didn't leave the house for a week.

When Howie played a trick it normally involved lots of planning, and this one was no different and things were going to get even worse for poor Sandbach. Utilising a contact at the *Liverpool Echo*, Howie was able to get a spoof page of newsprint with the headline, "COMEDY PERFORMER MURDERED AT KNUTSFORD SERVICES". He stormed around to Sandbach's and showed him the headline. Sandbach, of course, hadn't left his house or answered the phone since the incident. After a week of torture the boys finally confessed to Sandbach that it was a hoax, as they had begun to worry about his health, and, after much swearing, he eventually saw the funny side of the joke.

You would have thought that Sandbach would have learned his lesson but, like a mug, when the Macc Lads were looking for roadies for their next tour he quickly volunteered his services. It wasn't long before another joke was planned. The band used two roadies on this tour, the other being an extremely friendly chap called Al who was known as Al O'Peesha, due to his lack of hair. Al's friendliness unnerved Sandbach so much that he asked Howie if Al was gay. Quickly sensing an opportunity for some fun, Howie told Sandbach that he was, and that Al had told him how much he fancied Sandbach. Sandbach was anxious, and Howie quickly approached Al and told him to play along with the joke. Al was straight, and was being friendly with everybody because he was the new boy and wished to make a good impression. That evening, after the gig, the band went back to the hotel and Howie had booked a room with one double bed, just for Sandbach and Al. The boys retired to their rooms, the band having two rooms with single beds. Soon there was a knock on the door. Howie answered and found a distressed Sandbach, who asked if Howie would swap rooms, as he did not fancy a night sharing a bed with Al. "It's not me he fancies," Howie retorted, and quickly shut the door. It turned out that Sandbach slept on the floor and kept his trousers on.

For the rest of the tour the same thing happened every night. Sandbach and Al would share a room with Sandbach sleeping on the floor. On the last night of the tour the band and Sandbach all got drunk whilst Al just had a couple, as he had to leave early in the morning. The band encouraged Sandbach to drink a few too many and of course the inevitable happened; he passed out. The band carried him to his room and put their cunning, if somewhat cruel plan, into action. After laying him down on the bed they removed his trousers and underpants and, wearing a surgical glove, Howie smeared Sandbach's anus with Deep Heat cream just to give that hot, burning sensation. Next they placed a used condom in the bed, and Al slept on the floor leaving at 7am to catch a train back to Manchester.

The next morning a clearly distressed Sandbach came down to breakfast, where Howie was the only member of the band up. "Are you OK?" he enquired.

"No," Sandbach replied, "I've got a real pain in the arse." For the next few minutes they sat in silence eating their breakfast. Eventually Sandbach broke the silence by asking Howie if he could tell him something in the strictest confidence. "Sure," Howie replied. "Well, I think Al raped me last night whilst I was asleep. I found a condom in the bed and my arse is in agony. What do you suggest?" Howie advised him to say nothing, as it would only bring embarrassment. It was advice that was ignored. As each member of the Macc Lads resurfaced and came down to breakfast, Sandbach would tell them how he had been raped the night before and all of the band feigned shock at hearing this revelation.

After heading back to Macclesfield and dropping Sandbach off, Howie put part two of his plan into action. Contacting his friend who worked in Alder Hey Hospital in Liverpool, he asked him for some headed paper. He then sent Sandbach a letter asking him to come in for an AIDS test, saying that Al had tested positive, and they were writing to all his previous sexual partners and advising them to make an appointment as soon as possible. At the time this seemed very funny, but the joke soon backfired in a most spec-tacular way. Unbeknownst to Howie, Sandbach's elderly father was being treated at the local hospital, so when the letter arrived he thought it was for him and opened it. Needless to say, he was shocked and confronted Sandbach about what he had been up to. No doubt it was a stressful day for them both, and it was only after they had phoned the hospital to speak to the bogus con-sultant whose name appeared on the letter that the penny dropped and they realised that it might be a hoax. Sandbach suspected he knew who might be behind it. When Howie heard how Sandbach's father had opened the let-ter, he confessed and, Sandbach never roadied for the Macc Lads again.

* * *

After The Cherry Boys split up it was time for me to make a decision about my own future. HMV were keen for me to go into shop management, but that would mean moving away from Liverpool, which would have made it very difficult for me to continue managing bands. The pay as an assistant was not really enough, but I was keen to stay in music and was not sure what else I could do. I was confident I could sell CDs, but working for a major record company had no appeal.

At HMV we were visited every week by various reps and none of them impressed me. They all told you what the company wanted you to hear. Every new single was great and every new band was going to be massive. "How could they have any credibility?" I thought, and it crossed my mind how many lies they must tell in the average week.

In those days the chart was open to corruption and manipulation. It was compiled each time a sale was made, by manually keying in the catalogue number of the record being sold into a terminal. The data was then collected by a company named Gallup, and the information used to compile the charts. Even though it was HMV policy for us to enter each number, often, to save time when you had a large queue at the till, you wouldn't bother. Almost without exception all the sales reps would try to bribe you to put extra catalogue numbers of their artists into the machine to get their records up the chart. We were given free T-shirts, records, concert tickets etc as incentives.

I pretended to have good relationships with all these other reps, as it was in HMV's interest, and mine. When they wished to promote an artist they would offer us a buy-one-get-one-free deal on that artist's records. Depending on how desperate they were, we might be offered buy-one-get-two-free or buy-one-get-three-free, and in some rare cases buy-one-get-five-free. It was a dreadful system, but the incentive for us was to sell the free product, since on each record we sold every penny, apart from the VAT, went to the company. Therefore we would sell the record cheap or put it on the counter and give it plenty of in-store play. This meant that records from the smaller companies had little chance of charting, as they could not compete on promotion. Although I loathed the system, I knew that my own band had attempted to influence stores with free cherry sweets (or we would have, if our sales rep had given them out instead of giving them to his kids). I knew I had no interest in working on that side of the business and can honestly say I never once put in a number of a record that hadn't sold.

Most sales reps called twice a week and would always ask the sales assistant to put in a few numbers, whereupon they would give us a freebie. I would always take the gift and then, as requested, type in the catalogue number. I would then press the cancel button instead of enter.

One rep always gave me a sheet with three numbers on that he required me to enter at regular intervals. As soon as he left the store, the paper would go in the bin. If this happened in our shop then I've no doubt that most other stores were offered the same bribes. It is hard to believe this system was an improvement on the previous one, where dealers wrote in a book the catalogue numbers of the records sold and once a week they would be phoned up to read out the total of their sales. A couple of shops admitted to me that they would let the sales rep fill in his totals himself. It was a system entirely open to abuse. To combat fraud, Gallup later collected the data through the dealer scanning the barcode, which was a major improvement and made fraud a lot more difficult.

Chapter 4

The Man with the Van

One sales rep who called into HMV and who did not ask us to fix the chart was a man named Alan Whittaker. He worked for a company called SP&S who specialised in selling deleted records.

Alan would travel the North West in a large Mercedes van full of CDs, LPs and cassettes, visiting the record retailers and offering product that was ideal for promotions and sales. Record companies deleted product when it was no longer worthwhile keeping it in their warehouses, so that on Alan's van would generally consist of titles from between three and twenty years ago. When companies deleted product they would sell them off cheap to companies like SP&S, then in turn SP&S would sell it on at a bargain price to the shops, who, in turn, would sell it cheap to the general public.

All in all it was a very green system, which meant that most records would be recycled. Unfortunately there were a couple of major record companies who preferred to crush their unsold records rather than offer them out to a deletions company. This was a real pity or, in the words of the late, great Ian Dury, 'What a Waste'.

Alan would call on HMV once a month and I always enjoyed rummaging through the van and discovering all these long lost classics at bargain prices. It was a real Aladdin's cave. One day Alan mentioned that he was moving on to a different job at SP&S so there was a vacancy in van sales. Wow, this is perfect for me, I thought. Alan gave me the number of his boss, a man called Malcolm Mills, who would later play a major part in my music career. I phoned Malcolm and told him to look no further as I was the man for him. I was invited to an interview in Manchester, which seemed to go very well. Malcolm was a real music fan and seemed incredibly positive and enthusiastic and I knew straight away that I could enjoy working with him. The next day Malcolm called me up and offered me the job. I must have been a cocky so and so in those days as, when he told me, I replied, "Wise move".

I was very sad to leave HMV. My period working there was one of the most enjoyable times of my life. I had made some great friends and even met my future wife there. But it was time for a new challenge and the opportunity to earn some money. One of the great appeals of working for SP&S was that you were paid a commission of 10 per cent of your sales. Therefore, if I sold £500 worth of stock I earned £50. I found it a great motivation to be able to see each day how much I would earn.

On the day I started work I was invited down to London to pick up my van and for some training. SP&S were based in Stratford, in London, in an area full of fruit markets. You could smell the sickly odour of rotting fruit everywhere, but it was a vast improvement on cheese and onion. I was to stay in London for three days and on the first two I was to go out with another van salesman called Neil Kellas. The only flaw in this idea was that Neil was the classical rep and the only product he had on the van was classical. This wasn't much use to me, as I wasn't really interested in classical music, and when I had my van, I wouldn't be stocking much of it. I learned three things from Neil – that classical customers are snobby and didn't appear keen to engage in conversation with cheeky Scousers, that London's a bugger for parking and that, most of all, I was flabbergasted at how much of this classical music Neil was able to sell. I changed my mind about my van. I was going to stock lots of classical!

The next day I was given my new Mercedes van and told to pick stock out of the warehouse and fill it up. This was quite a daunting task as there were over thirteen thousand different titles. One thing was for sure and it was that I was going to devote a fair bit of space to those top-selling classical boys, Mozart and Beethoven. Other than classical I felt I had a good knowledge of music so, as my area was the north of England, I concentrated on filling my shelves with lots of bands from Liverpool, Leeds, Sheffield, Manchester and Newcastle. It was 5pm when I finally finished putting the stock on the van and I was ready for my baptism of fire, driving through London in the rush hour in a vehicle five times larger than I had driven before. I just hoped to get back to Merseyside without an accident. I asked Steve, who was the transport manager, if he had any advice for me. He told me it was just like driving a car, except bigger, and that I could impress all the girls by telling them I had a Mercedes. Of course I wouldn't mention that it was forty feet long and the cab was so high off the ground that they would probably need a rope to climb up. He also told me not to change the channel on the radio as it was set on Capital and it was very good. With Steve's words of wisdom ringing in my ears I was on my way and by the time I reached home it was nearly midnight.

Earlier in the day I had phoned the customers of Sheffield and booked appointments for the next day. Perhaps I was over enthusiastic, or maybe I hadn't quite grasped how long it would take me to get to Sheffield, but I set my alarm for 4.30am and I was on my way by 5am. Of course there was no traffic about at that time of morning and I whizzed there, arriving at 6.45am, two-and-a-quarter hours before the first shop opened. I popped into a greasy spoon café and had breakfast and bought a paper but still found myself outside my first appointment, at a shop called Bradleys, at 7.30am.

Time dragged and I could not wait to start selling. Malcolm, my boss, had explained to me that he expected me to sell around £500 worth of stock per day. Eventually the shop opened and I walked in and introduced myself to Ian, the buyer. "Blimey," he said, "did you wet the bed or something? I didn't expect you this early." I did not tell him that I had been outside since 7.30am.

Bradleys was a shop that specialised in classical, so I launched into my sales pitch by telling Ian all about those top blokes, Mozart and Beethoven, and how much stock I had. Ian perused the racks, but did not seem overly impressed by my Mozart and Beethoven selection. He explained to me that both these composers had written hundreds of pieces of work, some brilliant, some average and some that just don't sell. It turned out I had stocked my van with all the titles that just don't sell. When he finished I totalled up his order and it came to a measly £40 – not a great start.

After that, I travelled to a store called Kenny's where, once again, I gushed with enthusiasm about those top blokes Mozart and Beethoven and told Kenny about my superb classical selection. Maybe the large quiff on his head, plus his black leather jacket, should have given me a clue that his was a specialist rock 'n' roll shop. It taught me a good lesson: always look around the shop before announcing who you are, then you have an idea of what they stock. Kenny's order was a 100 per cent improvement on Bradleys, but it was still only £80, and I thought it was going to be difficult to reach the £500 target.

After a visit to HMV, where I had expected big things, but instead got a poor £100, I headed off to my final call, a chap called Barry Everard who owned a shop called Record Collector. After keeping me waiting for a while Barry came on to the van and was most apologetic. Barry had previously been a manager at a Virgin Records store and kept me amused with lots of tales from the music industry. He was incredibly methodical and read the sleeve notes on nearly every album he pulled out and, in most cases, put back. Those he did not return he made a small stack of on the floor of the van.

As I had 4,000 CDs, cassettes and LPs on the van I guessed I was going to be with him for a long time. After three hours I offered to get Barry a drink and a sandwich, as he looked as if he was flagging. Although the pile of records he pulled out appeared small, I was grateful for each one, as I was edging closer to my target. Barry had to take a break to shut his shop and eventually, at 7.30pm, Barry announced that he had looked at everything. I looked at the small quantity of stock on the floor and thought, in frustration, "I've sat in this van for five-and-a-half hours for that tiny collection". Then Barry picked up his stock and started giving me quantities. He wasn't just taking single copies, he was asking for between ten and twenty five of each title. I was ecstatic, not only had I smashed my target but I could see pound signs in my eyes. In all Barry had purchased over £800 worth of stock and on my first day I had doubled my target. It had been a long day and, although I didn't get home until 10.30pm, I felt that I was going to enjoy working in van sales.

Over the next few weeks I worked extremely hard and was always at a store for opening time. I never had a lunch break and I would just live off bananas. One of the perks of the job was that I could stay out at a hotel if need be, the company would pay for it and I could also claim an evening meal on your expenses. One of my first experiences of eating out alone was in quite a posh restaurant in York. For starter I ordered crudités and for the main course I went for a cheese soufflé. The waiter brought me out some strips of vegetables and, not long after, he brought the cheese soufflé. He placed a small burner on the table and the idea was that the burner would heat the soufflé mixture until it rose. After I finished the starter, the soufflé still hadn't risen. I messed about with the burner, but unfortunately turned the flame off, so I called the waiter over and asked him to re-light it. I read my magazine for half an hour and the soufflé was still not showing any signs of rising. I presumed it was due to me accidentally turning the heat off. Once more, I attempted to turn the heat up, but only succeeded in extinguishing the flame. I called the now-exasperated waiter over to re-light it again. Twenty minutes later, nothing had happened and I was beginning to lose interest in this dish. I noticed the waiter clearing all of the other tables and I was the only person left in the restaurant. The waiter approached me and informed me that they were hoping to close in ten minutes and asked whether I have any intention of eating my food. I informed him that I was still waiting for my soufflé to rise. "Sir," he replied, "that is not a soufflé, it is a warm cheese dip and the idea is for you to dip your crudités into it. The chef has been waiting one-and-a-half hours for you to finish so he can cook your soufflé." I was too embarrassed to stay and departed into the cold night, still starving.

Over the next few years I was fortunate to eat out in restaurants and stay at hotels three or four nights a week. The advantage was that I could be at the shops at 9am and often I was able to see customers after they had closed, thereby maximising the sales opportunities – as I was being paid commission, this was in my interest.

One evening I arrived at a hotel in Hull and by the time I checked in it had gone 11pm. I went to my room, opened the door and before I switched the light on I hurled my heavy briefcase on to the bed. "What the f***?" a man screamed, and as the light came on he bolted upright in the bed with blood pouring from his nose. Unfortunately for him the hotel had double booked the room and he was asleep when my briefcase caught him squarely on the nose. I apologised and quickly departed the scene. I think he was in such a state of shock that he didn't respond or maybe he did say something, but I was unable to hear him, as he had the white sheet around his nose. By the look of things the sheet wasn't going to remain white for long.

Even more memorable was the night I checked into a B&B in Greenwich. I used to stay in south London once each month, because I had to visit our head office in Stratford. The landlady showed me to my room and explained that the toilet wasn't in there, but on the landing outside. I left my bags in the room, walked into the centre of Greenwich and went for an Italian meal and a few drinks. Upon my return, I watched a bit of TV before retiring to bed. At about 2am the drinks began to take effect and I woke up anxious to go the toilet. Remembering that the toilet was on the landing and, just wearing a T-shirt, I made my way there. Not wishing to wake the other guests, I didn't bother to turn on the light on and I turned the handle of the bathroom door, desperate to empty my bladder. As I entered there was a piercing scream and a naked woman leapt off the toilet seat, screaming. In shock, I fell backwards and bashed my head on the back of the door. It took a few seconds for me to realise what was happening: I was on the floor with my tackle hanging out, and towering above me screaming to get out was a naked woman who I recognised as the landlady of the establishment. I didn't need to be asked twice and fled to my room and locked the door. My heart was beating so fast I thought my chest might explode. The two things I failed to understand were why she failed to lock the door when she visited the toilet and how on earth I hadn't wet myself. The next morning both of us were waiting to see if the other was going to comment on the evening's proceedings. I was very tempted to say, "I don't recognise you with your clothes on," but bottled out. I gulped my food, because I wanted to get away as soon as possible, and spent the rest of the day suffering with indigestion.

Greenwich was my bogey town. I always struggled to find suitable accommodation there and I would not have felt comfortable staying with the naked landlady again. I had heard that British Telecom had a new service called Talking Pages, which would put you in touch with a recommended business. It was perfect for finding plumbers and electricians and it could also advise on accommodation. I called them up and asked if they could suggest anywhere to stay in Greenwich. They had only one place listed, but that was fine for me. I rang the establishment and booked a room for that evening. Arriving late, I knocked on the door and the softly spoken owner, who whispered to me, "You must be Graham," opened it. He told me that breakfast was from 7am and showed me to the room. I was taken aback by the decor of the room – everything seemed fluffy and floral, and a pink dressing table and a pink bedspread had pride of place. The owner introduced me to Edward, who was the teddy bear sitting on my pillow. "Pleased to meet you Edward," I said, rather uncomfortably.

The owner told me his name was Roger and if I wished I could come down and have a chat with the rest of the guests, but I told him I was tired and would see him in the morning. Next day I went down for breakfast to be greeted by the sight of nine men all sitting around a huge wooden table. "This is Graham," Roger announced, and one by one the men stood up, shook my hand and introduced themselves to me. I was slightly uncomfortable, because I had never stayed in such a friendly place. I found it a struggle to eat much breakfast as all of the gentlemen kept asking me questions about myself. I was too polite to say, "Can you just shut up, as I am trying to eat." The penny finally dropped when one of the men asked if I had a boyfriend? "Is this a gay hotel?" I asked Roger.

"Well, it is a happy hotel," he replied, much to the amusement of the other guests. He asked me how I had heard of the place as nearly all their guests came via recommendations and I explained that it was through BT's Talking Pages. "Wow," said Roger, "we signed up for that service eight months ago and you are the first person who has come through their recommendation." I told Roger that I was happily married, and they all burst out laughing. I didn't know if I should take it as a compliment when one man said it was a pity.

Another conversation I will never forget occurred when Herman, the boss of Hermanex, one of our biggest suppliers, paid SP&S a visit. A man called Peter Harris was my immediate boss, and he felt it was a good idea for Herman to have a look in one of our vans. The two men stepped on to my van and Peter introduced me to Herman. "This is Graham," he announced, "our best salesman." He went on to say that Herman had a few new lines we were thinking of trying. Herman asked me if I could sell vacs – I knew we were looking at stocking new lines but this sounded quite a diverse move. "Well," I replied, "I reckon I can sell vacuum cleaners, electric blankets, toasters, baked beans, anything. I'm a natural salesman." There was silence for a few seconds whilst the two men digested my answer. Herman was Dutch and maybe, due to his thick accent, I had misheard something. The silence was broken when Herman announced that he had thousands of vacs in his warehouse.

I replied that I thought the biggest problem was space, as I could probably only fit about 20 in my van. Again there was silence, with both men having a puzzled look on their faces. It was one of those situations where you know something's wrong but I could not figure out what it was. "Are they Hoovers?" I enquired. At this point the penny dropped with Peter, who started laughing. "Graham, what Herman is saying is, can you sell Wax?" This left me more confused. "What, candles?"

"No, the *band* Wax." And he then pointed to a CD in the rack behind me by a group called Wax. They were a band formed by Graham Gouldman, formerly of 10CC, and Andrew Gold. The album hadn't done as well as everybody expected, so there was a lot of unsold stock in the market and Hermanex had thousands of unsold copies in their warehouse. Herman just wanted to know if I could sell them!

Things were going well for me regarding van sales, but I was still finding my feet with some of the more eccentric customers, of whom none were more so than a place called Church Street Records in Manchester. I knew this customer spent a lot of money, but nothing could prepare me for what happened on my first visit. I turned up to discover that it was a collection of wooden racks out on the pavement with a timber roof, which was there to stop customers getting wet in the rain. At the end of this collection of racking was a garden shed. Inside were two men, and I asked if Tony, the owner, was about. "No, Tony is not in today," the taller man told me. I asked the gentlemen when he would be in, and asked their names. The taller gentleman told me he was Paul and that he was Tony's identical twin brother. He then introduced me to the other man, a hunchback of Notre Dame look-alike, called Bernard. He also had quite a large belly, therefore I christened him 'Hunchback Tofront'. As I had come all that way, he enquired whether I would like some hot chocolate. He sympathised with me for missing Tony, but assured me that if I called back at the same time next week, he would be there. Bernard passed me the drink, which was the weakest hot chocolate I had ever tasted, but I felt it would be rude to say anything. We chatted for a few minutes and then I announced that I should go and would call back next week. "You haven't finished your drink," Paul shouted, so I went to gulp it down. As I drank, I choked when a huge lump of congealed powder went down my throat. It was clear that the drink had never been stirred.

Paul and Bernard had burst out laughing as I choked and, over the coming months, I realised that offering people a drink was just a big joke to them. They never had one themselves and, although there was a tea and coffee machine, if you asked for one of those beverages, they never had any. The only drinks they ever had were hot chocolate or soup. They would never do business until you had finished your drink. It was like some strange initiation ceremony in which you had to drink this warm water, followed by a congealed lump, whilst this pair of nutters stared at you until the cup was empty.

The next week I turned up to be greeted by Paul. "Hi," I said, "is Tony in today?"

"I am Tony," he replied. Crikey, I thought they *are* identical. Bernard offered me a hot chocolate, which I politely declined, but Tony insisted and told me that it would be rude to turn down his kind hospitality. After I had suffered the drink Tony came out to my van and, like a whirlwind, just pulled out piles of records and CDs and threw them on the floor. Many of the LPs were falling out of their sleeves and numerous CD cases were smashed.

After only a few minutes he announced that he had spent enough and, with that, leapt off the van leaving me to sort out the wigwam-shaped pile in the middle of the floor. When I raised the invoice he had spent over £500, so it was well worth putting up with his eccentricities for an order that large. I dropped his stock off into the hut and Tony told me to watch something before I left. With that he picked up a large megaphone, crept up behind a customer and, at the top of his voice, shouted through the megaphone, "BARGAINS BARGAINS!" The poor customer jumped out of his skin.

Tony came back laughing his head off. "Don't you lose lots of customers doing that?" I asked, whilst stifling my laughter.

"Of course I do," he replied, "but it's worth it for the laugh." Over the next couple of years every visit would end with him getting his megaphone out and scaring another poor customer witless. It's a bit sad, but it used to be my highlight of the day and, amazingly, I never witnessed one customer resort to violence. One thing that struck me about their operation was the lack of security and I asked Tony if he had problems with thieving. "Yes," he replied, "but I don't do anything about it."

"Why not?" I enquired. Tony then told me a very sad tale about how, when he first started, he caught a lad stealing some records. The youth begged Tony not to call the police, but Tony felt he had no option. The police took the youth away, and Tony thought nothing of it until he was informed the next day that the youth had hung himself in a cell at the police station because he was terrified of what his parents would say. Tony told me that nobody's life was worth a few records and, these days, if he noticed anybody stealing he would ask them to put the records back and threaten them with the police, but never call them.

I visited Tony at least once a month and became convinced that his twin brother, Paul, never existed but, each time I mentioned it, Tony would get upset and insist that Paul also worked on the stall whenever he took a day off. One day Bernard took me aside and told me what I already knew. Paul didn't exist, he said, Tony just wanted to check me out before he started buying from me and that was just his way of doing it.

The most amazing store I visited was based in Wakefield and called EGS. It was run by a charismatic couple called Alan and Carrie Parkin who reminded me of Angie and Den Watts, from *EastEnders*, because they fought like cat and dog, although I felt that deep down they loved each other. On my first visit they pulled huge amounts of stock out of my racks. I thought they were just making space and started putting the stock back. "What the f*** are you doing?" Alan shouted. "We want all that." I was delighted when he had finished, because the total of the invoice was £1,200, my commission was £120, and I knew that I needed to look after this customer. As I was finalising the invoice Alan came over and handed me a package and said, "No need to do an invoice, keep that, there's £600 in there for you." I was shocked and explained to Alan that I didn't work like that and, if he still wanted the stock, I had to invoice him. Alan told me that it was years since he had met somebody like me. "What do you mean I asked?"

"An honest record company rep," was Alan's reply.

I soon learned of the corruption that went on. One Friday I called at EGS and there was a queue of record company reps. In those days reps were meant to give away thousands of pounds of free stock to shops which, in a way, was bribery designed to manipulate the chart. To explain – if a shop bought a single for £1.50 they would sell it for £2.99, but if a record company rep gave them a free copy of the same title the retailer could discount the single and would sell it for £1.99. Often the reps would give them three free copies, enabling the retailer to sell them for 99p, which gave the major record companies a huge advantage over the small indie record companies who could not afford to indulge in such practices. Put yourself in the position of the consumer – would you buy a single at 99p or £2.99? It was clear to me that all the free stock was not given away, as boxes of the stuff were being handed over to Alan in exchange for wads of cash. From that day I had no respect for any reps from the record companies.

Over the years Alan became my biggest independent account and although I never did a dodgy deal, I always phoned him with anything of interest and he would buy big.

One day Alan announced to me that he was retiring to Portugal and had employed Elaine, who had been the MCA rep, to run his business whilst he was out of the country. I had dealt with Elaine when working at HMV and had met her a number of times. I knew it was not Alan's shrewdest move – at this point he had four stores, one each in Wakefield, Huddersfield, Bradford and Barnsley, and I worried for Alan, feeling he would live to regret this decision. It was soon clear that things were going wrong and I was hardly doing any business with EGS. A year later Alan returned from Portugal and EGS was in a mess with none of the record companies supplying him.

Alan tried to rescue the situation, and I provided him with all my best stock, remembering all the business he had given me. A couple of the other reps, notably Dave from Impulse (who later opened Pendulum Records), also tried to help him, but most of them had found another shop to sell their free stock to. Eventually EGS lost the battle to keep going and the strain ended Alan and Carrie's marriage. I will never forget the reaction of other reps when EGS closed its doors, because they seemed to be gloating and their attitude was that Alan had got his come-uppance. Myself, I felt that they all had short-term memories and they had forgotten how they had taken his money for years and all the great parties with free drink and food that they had been invited to. It taught me that loyalty in life is very rare. A couple of months later I called Alan just to see how he was getting on and he invited me down for a cup of tea. It was incredibly sad to see that he was living in a tiny cottage when one year earlier he had lived in a massive house with acres of land with stables and horses. I admired Alan, he was a real character who just took advantage of other people's greed but, sadly, he took his eye off the ball.

After four happy years working with SP&S the company unexpectedly went bust. They owned a pressing plant and their largest customer had folded, owing them £600,000. It is hard to believe how a business can allow that debt to mount up, but the knock on effect bankrupted the company.

Chapter 5

The Most Dysfunctional Family in Pop

I soon found work with another van sales company that sold deletions called Panther Music. Trevor Reidy and Aniff Allybokus owned Panther. Trevor was the drummer in cult band The Monochrome Set, whilst Aniff was the financial brain behind the business. The only problem for me was that the vacancy was for a van sales rep in Scotland, but my then-wife Rachael and I packed our belongings and headed north where we purchased a one bedroom flat in the centre of Glasgow. I loved Scotland, and people were fantastic, but the only problem was the weather. It was either raining, about to rain, or had just stopped raining for a while.

At first Panther was a great company to work for, but they were soon to make a calamitous mistake. A company who had a van sales team selling 12" dance singles had gone bust and Panther took the decision to employ the staff and start their own Panther Dance operation. It was a disaster. The problem with dance music was that the music was fashionable for just a couple of weeks and then those fans moved on to the next release. Therefore, if the dance sales people didn't sell the 12" singles straight away, the stock became obsolete and too much money became tied up in non-selling stock that had no value.

Something I will always remember Panther for is the fabulous Christmas parties they held, but there is one party I cringe about whenever I think of it. The sales manager at Panther was an ex-Our Price employee called Phil Edwards. I was amazed that Phil had reached this position and put it down to his talent for creeping up. He had the manner of a traffic warden and introduced pointless paperwork for us to fill in. He had previously been our rep for the Midlands and in football terms he was our Derby County;

always bottom of the sales table. This made his appointment all the more bizarre. He took me out on his van one day to offer me tips on selling, but during two years of working together I had never known any month when he had achieved more sales than me. Thus I was slightly insulted.

He certainly had an unusual method of selling. He would lecture the customers on titles they should buy. Then, when they did buy them he would spend the next few minutes praising their choices and tastes in music. I tolerated Phil and tended to ignore most of what he said. In fact if Ricky Gervais had met him he would have written a sitcom called *The Van Salesman* instead of *The Office*. However, our relationship became unworkable after an incident at that one particular Panther Christmas party.

Panther always threw a good bash and this particular year they really pushed the boat out. The visiting staff were put up in the top London hotel where the party was taking place. I arranged to meet Rachael at the hotel as she was getting the train down. When she arrived she knocked on the door of the room she thought I was in. A lady answered, and it was obvious that she was not best pleased, because she was taking a shower at the time. She made it clear that nobody called Graham was in the room and shut the door.

Rachael told me this story when I finally arrived. I then showered and got ready before going down to join the rest of the staff. We entered a beautiful ballroom and everyone was dressed smartly. Phil was surrounded by the other sales reps and beckoned me over to join them.

He asked how the room was and I said that it was fine. I then went on to tell him about our unfortunate start and how Rachael had knocked on the wrong door and asked for me, but this miserable cow had told her where to go. In hindsight, I do recall at this point feeling a gentle tug on my trousers. Just as I was finishing this tale Aniff came over and asked about our rooms. I quickly started re-telling the miserable cow story, but my new version had changed the miserable cow to an old bat. By now the tugging on my trousers had been replaced by some gentle kicks. By the time I had finished the tale for a second time the kicks had become something Roy Keane would have been proud of. I realised they were coming from Rachael. Everybody had been laughing about my tale, or so I thought, but Rachael had a face like thunder. When I looked at the lady opposite she had a face on her that made Rachael's look positively delirious. Yes, the miserable cow/old bat was Phil's wife, and it's safe to say that our relationship went downhill from that moment onwards.

One good thing to happen at Panther was that I met a person called Steve Kersley. He worked in our accounts department and had quickly established a good reputation as somebody who knew what he was doing. Steve is now Managing Director at Proper Distribution, where we still work together, and here is the tale of how we got to know each other. Steve was lumbered with the poisoned chalice of organising a tour for the most dysfunctional family in soul, The Jones Girls. My role was to line up a couple of personal appearances at the HMV branches in Liverpool and Manchester and this is the story of that ill-fated tour.

The Jones Girls were three sisters (Shirley, Brenda, Valerie) who had some success on the legendary Philadelphia International label in the 70s. 'Nights Over Egypt' was their biggest hit. A man called Richard Satnarine ran the dance department at Panther and, despite the company being skint, he managed to persuade Aniff, the owner, to set up a label called ARP (I do not recall what it stood for, but Arseholes Ruining Panther would have been apt). Their first two signings were The Jones Girls and a UK act called Kreuz, who were part of the very short-lived UK New Jack Swing Movement. The Jones Girls' release was a comeback album called, amazingly enough, *Coming Back*.

By this stage, the early 90s, Aniff had really lost the plot and was seduced by the glamour of having his own label. Richard was a hustler who got momentarily lucky. Despite Panther having no money Richard spent a fortune on The Jones Girls project, including £50,000 to fly the girls in to record the album and securing Soul II Soul's Jazzie B to produce two of the tracks.

When the release came around Panther were broke and needed the album to make some money. We set up a promotional trip that involved a nightclub appearance and an in-store signing at an indie in Manchester, a PA at HMV Liverpool and we were to round off with an appearance at the 291 Club at the Hackney Empire before a big show at the Hammersmith Apollo later in the week. Steve was deputed to go on the trip because, by this stage, he was about the only person trusted by all the warring factions, namely Aniff, Trevor and Richard. Steve felt hopelessly out of his depth, because his entire music industry experience consisted of one years' warehouse work and two more as a wannabe accountant. He hired a van, and set off to pick them up from the Royal Garden Hotel in Kensington. After what seemed like an interminable wait, they finally appeared together with their manager, a lovely ex-CBS New York employee called Myrna Williams. They were just pulling off the forecourt when a member of staff came running after them waving a bit of paper. That was when the problems started...

It turned out that Brenda Jones had a drink problem, and the bit of paper that the receptionist was waving was her room service bill, which was prodigious given that the night before she'd drunk the entire contents of the mini-bar. She was skint and chaos ensued. It transpired that this was The Jones Girls' last shot at making a record and Brenda had promised her mother, who was back in the States, but obviously wielding the power, that she'd behave herself. The oldest sister, Shirley, was beside herself with rage, whilst the cash float Steve had been given for the trip disappeared before they even got underway. The bickering continued as they drove through the Kensington traffic, but they had not gone far before it was decided that the disgraced Brenda should be taken back to the hotel to be left behind. There followed a somewhat difficult phone call with the hotel as Steve established that the person who had just tried to leave without paying would be returning and could they empty the mini-bar before she got to her room?

They set off again, a number of hours late, and so the Manchester in-store was cancelled. They arrived in Manchester without further mishap and got to the nightclub. At this stage Steve received a phone call from the night manager at the Royal Garden telling him that Brenda was in the hotel bar and asking could she be served! No! Thankfully Steve's memory goes blank at this stage, but he did recall that a friend of Shirley's, who was also on the trip, stood in for Brenda at the nightclub.

Next morning they were sitting in the van waiting to leave to go to Liverpool – and waiting and waiting. Eventually they learned the cause of the delay. Brenda's problem was alcohol, but Valerie's was pills, and she was a total zombie. They managed to get her into the van but she sat there totally out of it. The word was that without Brenda she couldn't cope.

So they set off for Liverpool where Steve seemed overly pleased to meet up with me, as he was totally freaked by what was going on. The future of the company rested on the success of this act and Steve had mislaid two-thirds of them. Steve tapped me for some more cash and I gave him every penny I had. The band did the in-store signing with Myrna deputising for the slumped Valerie, who was left in the van, so the few Philly Soul fans who had turned out were a little unfortunate in that there was only one Jones Girl signing album sleeves, along with two imposters.

The journey back to London was not a happy one. Shirley went off to Hackney to prepare for the 291 club show, which was televised in the London region. Myrna took Valerie somewhere whilst Steve went back to the Royal Garden to check on Brenda. The situation that greeted him there placed even more demands on Steve's powers of diplomacy. The hotel management was anxious to find out from him how soon she would be leaving. Meanwhile, in the privacy of her room Brenda left him in no doubt that she would go to any lengths to persuade him to fill the mini-bar. As she advanced on him, whilst removing her clothing, Steve stammered something to do with his dad being a vicar and not approving of such things.

The rest, thankfully, is a blur, although they did pull themselves together to do the Hammersmith show. It almost sold out, as I recall, so they were pretty popular. The album went in with a bullet at number seventy-six and within months we were all out of a job. Ironically, Steve ended up in PR where the promotional trips in which he was involved occasionally got hairy, (wrestlers getting thrown in jail in Kuwait) or difficult (Mica Paris), but never, ever, as bad as The Jones Girls.

Despite the debacle with The Jones Girls, I had no idea how bad the company's finances were. Being based in Glasgow, I didn't see the end coming. I returned from holiday to find that whilst I was away the company has gone bust. The liquidators contacted me to ask if I would help to value the stock that was left, and to see if I could help to dispose of it. I recall walking around the warehouse helping with the valuation. When we came to the 12" section I was informed that we had 40,000 12" singles, for which we had paid on average £2 per unit. Did I think we could get £1 per unit? I laughed and said I reckoned we could sell them for 2p per unit. The liquidator burst out laughing and said, "Come on, Graham, you must be joking – how much can we really get?" I thought about it for a minute and realised I was wrong with my initial valuation, the true value was probably 1p per unit and, sure enough, we eventually sold them all at that price.

As I left the empty warehouse for the last time, I felt a great sadness because there were some great people working there and the company should have been a big success. Little did I know then that some of those great people I worked with at Panther would join me at Proper Distribution several years later.

Chapter 6

Proper Music

After the demise of Panther, it was time for me to review my future prospects.

I had been working for two 'overstock' companies, both of which had gone bust because of over-involvement in other projects – SP&S had failed by investing in a pressing plant, whilst Panther had invested heavily in dance music without really understanding the market.

Aniff Allybokus and some of my friends from Panther – Gary Harries, Rob Hutchison and Dave Webb – started a new company, called North West, and were keen for me to join, but I was sceptical of its chances of becoming successful with Aniff at the helm. Instead, I was about to put into action a plan to work for myself buying and selling overstock CDs when I received a phone call from an old friend, Malcolm Mills. He and I had enjoyed working together at SP&S and it is fair to say he has had a major influence on my career in the music industry.

Malcolm has had a fascinating history in the music business. His father was a jazz drummer, so it was only natural for him to follow in his footsteps. As a teenager he saw artists of the calibre of Duke Ellington, Count Basie, Woody Herman, Stan Kenton, Coleman Hawkins, John Mayall and Eric Clapton. Malcolm started playing drums in bands at the age of thirteen.

One of the best moments of his life was when Drum City, the country's leading supplier of drum kits, displayed in its window a set of drums that had belonged to Sam Woodyard, Duke Ellington's drummer. Sam had recently signed a sponsorship deal with Premier Drums and so had asked Drum City to sell his old kit for him. Malcolm raced home to tell his father, who immediately went and purchased the kit for his son.

Forty-five years later that gold, double-bass drum kit still sits in our studio at Proper Records. All that young Malcolm ever wanted to do was to play drums, but, after he left school in 1966, his first day-job was at Liberty's department store in London, where the staff entrance opened on to Carnaby Street.

These were the Swinging Sixties, and Malcolm was living life to the full. When he wasn't playing a gig himself, he was spending all his wages watching bands.

Following the example of a number of friends, he then joined a staff agency who supplied temporary staff to Phonodisc, an Ilford based company owned by Philips, working the night shift as charge-hand for a team sorting records.

One night, their job was to remove all of the deleted albums from the warehouse and to load them into a 40-foot truck. It was a huge job and took them two days to finish. When it was completed, Malcolm sent his team home; personally sealed the truck; completed the necessary paperwork, obtaining the driver's signature; before sending the truck on its way to the deletions company.

The next day, Malcolm went to work and was immediately hauled into the manager's office and grilled about what had happened during the previous shift. Malcolm recounted the events of the night and went to confirm them by producing the signed paperwork from his drawer, which was empty. Malcolm immediately knew he was being stitched up – the lorry had gone missing and the managers were looking to place the blame on him. There were some really dodgy people working there, including a few East End families nobody would want to cross.

Under the circumstances, he felt the best form of defence would be to attack – declaring that he had done nothing wrong, he suggested that the police be called to sort out the situation. For some reason, his bosses were reluctant to take up this option. The police were never called; the lorry and its contents were never found – it was time for Malcolm to move on.

In the early 1970s, Malcolm was the manager of Maurice Placquet's famous music store in Shepherds Bush. He needed a spare part for his drums and visited Drum City in Soho to buy it. The sight that greeted him was downright depressing – the staff were all playing in an impromptu jam session. He, a potential customer, stood around for ages and nobody approached him to ask if they could help. Malcolm left the shop, found the telephone number of the Drum City area manager and called him, arranging to meet in a local pub.

Malcolm informed him that Drum City needed Malcolm Mills. He recounted what he had seen and guaranteed that he would increase Drum

City sales. He began work the next week and, true to his word, he turned around the shop's fortunes, partly by instilling into the staff the simple truth that selling drums was their real job.

Malcolm had a fabulous time at Drum City but, simply by working there, he was constantly being tempted by bands offering drumming jobs. He resisted until just before Christmas 1975, when an offer of big money for a Christmas season in the Canary Islands proved too attractive. He was planning to get married the following year, and the prospect of coming home with his pockets bulging with pesetas held great appeal, despite his bride-to-be, Miriam, not being overly keen on the idea.

Predictably, problems arose early on. The band were heavy drinkers, further complicated by the fact that two members were also ex-boxers. On their first night away they got smashed and ended up in a massive brawl, inflicting facial injuries on each other. For its first gig the band took to the stage looking more like escapees from the local hospital than a professional band.

During a subsequent period with Vixen Records (working, appropriately, for Mr Fox) as telesales manager, where he revelled in the role of selling imports to record shops, Malcolm felt that this was his future. Sadly, it was not to be and he soon left, after an argument over nothing more serious than the cost of sending a telex to America.

Malcolm arrived home and announced to Miriam that he was going to start his own importing and sales business. Fortunately, and as always, Miriam offered him her unstinting support. He called his company Cruisin and it was based in his back bedroom.

During his time at Vixen, Malcolm had built a list of sales and purchasing contacts. He imported 'cut outs' from America. (When US record companies deleted titles they clipped the LP sleeves to indicate that the album was a deletion. They would then sell on the stock, without any obligation to pay artists' royalties).

Malcolm would drive to Heathrow each week to collect his stock and would then head straight down to the West End to sell it from the back of his van to his retail customers. Business boomed. He was a top salesman but, sadly, not a top debt collector.

Harlequin Records, a well-known chain of London shops, was his biggest customer. Unfortunately, his big problem with them was obtaining payment. Being a one-man-band, it was difficult for him to exert pressure on their accounts department. They continually denied that they had received most of his invoices. It took months before he realised that the staff in many of their shops were destroying his invoices and keeping the stock for themselves. In those days record shops did not have computers, so stock control was difficult. Frustrated, Malcolm wound up his company, having learned some harsh lessons.

Whilst pondering his next career move, he went to his local pub one lunchtime to drown his sorrows – a couple of pints would help him to ponder. Whilst there, he started telling his story to a bloke who traded on a market stall. Malcolm explained that he was skint and that he was really worried about being able to afford the approaching Christmas holiday. The only asset he owned was a house full of records.

The market trader offered to help Malcolm out by selling his records on his stall over the Christmas period. The two men came to an agreement within which the trader would deliver half of the money he had taken each week from selling Malcolm's albums. Any stock he had remaining after Christmas would be returned. Malcolm queried whether, as he was a bit short on the cash front, there would be any possibility of an up-front sub. The trader explained sweetly that he also had a bit of a cash flow problem but, as a mark of his integrity, he was happy to deposit with Malcolm the gold sovereign ring, which had been given to him by his grandfather. Malcolm was overwhelmed by the man's sincerity and placed his total trust in his new-found mate, allowing his records to be taken away and telling his new buddy to keep the ring.

The two new partners shook hands on the deal and the trader informed Malcolm that he had his big white van outside and was able to collect the load of records there and then. (In the early 70s drinking and driving was not perceived to be such a heinous crime as it is today – do you remember the Mungo Jerry classic number one 'In the Summertime', which included the line 'have a drink, have a drive'?) The two men promptly set off to Malcolm's house and cleared it of every single record.

At this time Malcolm's wife, Miriam, was working at Beano's, the world-famous second-hand record shop in Croydon. Suddenly a stranger turned up in a big white van full of records he was happy to sell at second-hand prices. Miriam recognised immediately that the records were Malcolm's stock (they had, after all, been in every room of their house) and presumed, reasonably, that they had been burgled. She instructed shop-owner Dave Lashmar to keep the man talking whilst she rushed home to get Malcolm. When she arrived home shouting that there was a guy in the shop with all their records, Malcolm calmly told her not to worry and explained his deal with the trader to get them some money in for Christmas.

"So," Miriam questioned, "why is he trying to sell them to a second-hand shop then?"

Malcolm raced to Beano's to confront his erstwhile business partner, who claimed he was simply trying to get Malcolm a bit of ready cash by selling some of the records quickly. A furious Malcolm explained that if he wanted to sell them to a second-hand shop he could have done that himself, and that the deal was off.

Miriam was thrilled, and relieved that, thanks to her intuition, she had averted a domestic financial disaster. They reloaded the van and headed back home. After unloading again the trader suggested they go down the pub – a decision Malcolm was soon to regret. (If he has a fault, it is that he is too trusting and never was this more evident than during the events of the next few hours).

It took only a few drinks for the trader to persuade Malcolm that the Beano's episode was a genuine mistake. A few more drinks convinced Malcolm that he had made a lifelong buddy and, incredibly, he agreed to the original deal all over again.

So, the two inebriates went back and cleared Malcolm's house for a second time. When Miriam arrived home to an empty house, she was shocked and demanded to know where all their records had gone. Malcolm confidently explained that his new trader mate was, in fact, a diamond geezer who had only wanted to sell a few records to Beano's for a quick cash injection.

Miriam demanded his address, as she was certain that he was a conman. Malcolm sheepishly admitted that this was one small detail he had overlooked but, not to worry – he had been assured that the bloke traded on East Street market every weekend.

Of course, their frequent visits to the market were completely fruitless – neither the trader nor the records were ever seen again. Christmas came rolling round with nothing in the Mills household, and their only present was from the gas board, who cut off their supply. However, the really incredibly point of this story is that, 34 years later, Malcolm and Miriam are still happily married.

For the next few months Malcolm kept body and soul together by doing a few odd jobs, but his desire to get back into the music industry never waned. An entry in the music directory for a company in Stratford called SP&S, which sold deleted LP's, caught his eye. He phoned the Chairman, George Harris, and told him that SP&S needed him and that he was less bothered about salary than the chance to prove that he could make money for the company.

George's brother, John, offered Malcolm a job, and from that point he quickly rose through the company to become Sales Director. It was at this juncture that I first crossed his path when he took me on as a sales rep.

Malcolm has always been full of praise for the Harris family and regards the time he spent with SP&S as amongst the happiest days of his life. Unfortunately, in 1987, the company folded. I moved on to Panther whilst, after a short while, Malcolm set up a company called The Sale People, which provided stock periodically for only one customer – HMV. Four times a year he would ship out thousands of CDs and cassettes to HMV's stores and one month later they would return all their unsold stock.

Two issues needed managing – to keep the sales offers looking fresh Malcolm had to put in lots of new titles each sale and he also needed to re-cycle all the returns productively. The latter was where I could help. Over time, the HMV returns started to pile up and become a problem, so Malcolm got in touch with me again.

He and I, together with our wives, held a meeting and decided to form a new company – Cee Dee Sales (looking back, I realise that it was an awful name, especially when some wags spelled it Seedy Sales – I did actually receive one phone call asking if we stocked porn). The company's objective was to shift HMV returns in quantity.

Malcolm printed a complete stock list and off I went to sell his entire stock of redundant product to the record shops of the UK. Those were the days before the Internet so, armed with every page that listed record shops from all of the Yellow Pages that I could scavenge from the local library and an old customer listing from Panther, I set off on a one-man sales campaign across the whole country.

When I look back I realise that I must have been mad, but when you are trying to establish your own business you have to give it your best shot. Four Sundays out of five I would leave home and travel to Scotland, the North East the North West or Cornwall, where I would work all week before returning home.

Meanwhile, Rachael was working in our spare bedroom, faxing customers with lists of bargains that we had compiled from the stock sheets. The orders she took would be forwarded to The Sale People who would dispatch them from their London warehouse.

Of course, this arrangement led to some incongruities, as I was giving my customers the impression that we were an exciting new company with lots of brand new stock – I could not really admit that we were a husband-and-wife team selling reject stock from our spare room, equipped with only one phone and one fax line. Inevitably, there were several times when customers called up and overheard our baby son crying, so that Rachael would have to excuse herself, saying that she had had to bring the child into the office because of childminder problems – the real problem being that we had no childminder.

Despite everything, within a short time we had built up a large customer base and Cee Dee Sales was making more money than The Sale People. We were working long hours just to cope with the volume of sales and, ultimately, we took the decision to wind up The Sale People and employ its staff within Cee Dee Sales. Over the next couple of years we were successful at selling overstock CDs to independent shops but, for all our hard work, profits remained small.

Then, one day, Malcolm told me that he had spotted a gap in the market, which he wanted to exploit. He had noticed that were only two different types of CD boxed sets – one was very expensive, usually containing four CDs of contemporary material and a quality book, retailing at around £30; the other tended to be more cheap and cheerful, also containing four CDs, often of old jazz recordings or retrospectives by bands from the 50s and 60s re-recording their old hits, which retailed at around £10.

Malcolm's idea was to put out boxed sets of quality recordings with quality books, but retailing around the £15 mark. All the recordings would need to be out of copyright so that we could keep the prices low. We named these sets 'Proper Boxes', as they were designed for people who liked proper music.

The first release was by jazz drummer Gene Krupa, and sales far exceeded our expectations. More releases followed quickly, and it was soon clear that the record-buying public could not get enough of these quality bargain boxes.

Around this time a company called Direct Distribution came into my life. It was based in North London and was the biggest supplier of folk CDs to UK retailers. Its Managing Director, Richard Porter, suggested that we merge our two companies together to create a real force in specialist music distribution. I had a few initial reservations but, ultimately, Malcolm and I deemed it to be a good idea.

Bizarrely, I had once met Richard and his key accounts manager in a shop in Somerset and they introduced me to a sales technique that I had only ever witnessed before being practised by double-glazing salesmen. The technique required them to keep talking in a constant monotone to the point where the customer could take no more and they would place an order simply as an act of survival. The shop in question contained an integral café and I was able to sit and watch this far-from-dynamic duo trying to out-drone each other – just as one finished, the other would start. Unfortunately, I could not have realised at the time the implications of working alongside this monotone double act.

Anyway, we decided to merge our two companies together and call the new company Proper Music Distribution. Malcolm became Chairman, with responsibility for developing our own label, Proper Records, so that we would have more product that was exclusive to us; Richard Porter was to run the company on a day-to-day basis; whilst Tony Engle, who owned Topic, Britain's biggest folk label (and who would be a major asset), was brought on as a director. A great lad called Phil Harding was appointed Export Director. John Glockler, with whom I had worked at SP&S, and myself then completed the Board of Directors.

Merging two companies was more difficult than I ever imagined. It soon became clear that we were not gelling as a team and that Richard was a Managing Director who I felt could neither manage nor direct. He was also excessively loyal to all of the people he had transferred in from Direct, supporting them in every decision, to the point where ex-Cee Dee Sales staff soon started quitting.

These were not good times – Richard and I seemed to clash over everything, and I was still working away four or five nights a week. I found it extremely difficult to work so hard with so little appreciation.

Malcolm, meanwhile, did his best to bring people together. He even took all the staff to the Brit Awards, which was fine, though it would probably have been cheaper to take everybody to Spain for a week.

He also hired a table for us at the HMV Football Extravaganza, which was a memorable event for a number of dubious reasons. Firstly, the guest of honour was George Best who, when invited on to the stage by host Rodney Marsh to give a talk, fell flat on his face as he approached and needed to be helped away. We never did get to hear him speak.

Secondly, Malcolm chose to perform his famous party trick on our table, which sat ten people. He managed to whip the tablecloth away whilst leaving all the cutlery, crockery and glasses still standing. Everybody was mightily impressed – except the waiting staff. For the rest of the evening Malcolm was pressured by lots of people who had not witnessed the trick to perform it again for their benefit. Unable to resist a challenge – vanity played no part in this, I'm sure – Malcolm agreed to a repeat performance ten minutes later at a table in the corner and out of sight.

When he made his way across to the corner it appeared that word had got out and it seemed like the whole room of people had gathered around the table. Malcolm made his way through the crowd, knowing he had to be quick, or the staff would realise what was going on and stop him.

Everybody went quiet as he took hold of the cloth with a firm grip – whoosh! Malcolm yanked the cloth, but as he pulled he bashed his arm into somebody who was standing too close. The result was a mighty crash and the sound of glasses smashing. It was time for us to make a hasty departure.

Not to be outdone, Richard also had a personal party trick. At both the Brit Awards and the HMV function he had thought it really funny to walk around with a silver ice bucket on his head. It was the only time in my life I had wanted to kick the bucket.

My favourite Malcolm Mills story is how he first met Paul Riley, who is now Commercial Director of Proper Records, at a Jimi Hendrix gig, back in 1967. Paul has played a huge part in the success of the Proper Music group of companies since he joined Malcolm in Proper Records during the mid-90s. Immediately prior to this he was at Demon Records and was recording and touring as bass player for Nick Lowe on the *Impossible Bird* album.

Paul has an awesome range of skills, which have been employed in almost every aspect of the group's development and growth right from the moment he first came in to 'help out' with designing a royalty accounting programme. He is a renowned musician and sound engineer, whose ability and willingness to turn his hand to absolutely anything has been a key factor in the development of the company.

It was Hendrix's first UK visit, and one of his earliest dates was at The Star in Croydon. As a venue, The Star was far too small to cope with the audience attracted to this gig. It had a low stage, behind which stood a set of French windows through which the band would enter.

A beaded and kaftan-wearing Malcolm was first in the queue and, when the doors opened, he bagged his position right in front of the stage. This was at a time before fire regulations were strictly enforced and The Star took the opportunity to cram in as many people as possible. Soon Malcolm found that the only way to avoid the crush was to make his way on to the stage, where a guy in a herringbone overcoat with big hair soon joined him. This was Paul Riley. The two men started chatting, but the entrance of The Jimi Hendrix Experience through the French windows cut short the conversation.

The band started up and the two men remained onstage throughout the performance. Hendrix had to play around them as they were standing inches from Mitch Mitchell's drum kit. Despite abuse from the crowd due to his flowing kaftan blocking their view, Malcolm was onstage for the whole gig, acting as an unofficial cheerleader and leading the applause after each song. The atmosphere was electric – everybody there was aware they were witnessing a truly remarkable talent.

Even so, although it was the most memorable gig of his life, Malcolm left thinking somewhat less of Jimi Hendrix, the person – as the gig finished a stunning looking girl handed Jimi her white handbag and a pen, asking him for an autograph on the bag. Hendrix smiled, took the bag from the girl, opened it and, mean-mindedly, tipped out its contents before handing it back.

A couple of weeks later Malcolm auditioned for a band needing a drummer. The bass player in the band was Paul Riley, the herringbone overcoated guy with the big hair whom he had met at the Hendrix concert. How could that band deny him the job after he was introduced as a musician who had been onstage for a full gig with Hendrix? They have been firm friends ever since.

Paul is somewhat known for keeping himself somewhat to himself. Never was this more evident than the day he came in to ask if he could he borrow some Carl Perkins albums.

Nobody thought any more about it. However, when the next edition of the rock 'n' roll specialist magazine *Now Dig This* arrived at the office, there, on the front cover, was a picture of Carl Perkins playing at the Jazz Café. The accompanying musicians in the background included guitarist George Harrison, who had enjoyed minor success with a noted Liverpool combo, keyboard player Geraint Watkins and bassist ... one Paul Riley.

We were astonished by the fact that Paul did not see fit to mention the gig – though he was gracious enough to thank us for the loan of the Carl Perkins CDs.

A seminal moment in the history of Proper was the day I received a phone call from Steve Kersley, with whom I had worked at Panther Music. Steve explained that the team, which had moved from Panther to North West Music, a similar company selling import and overstock CDs, had become disillusioned and were thinking of starting up their own independent venture. I responded by doing my utmost to persuade Steve to abandon this plan and to come and work with us at Proper.

I spoke with Malcolm and gave him my view that signing up this team of good people could revolutionise our business. I was delighted when he and

Steve came to an agreement that the whole team of Steve, Gary, Rob and Dave would join Proper Music.

Especially pleasing was the opportunity to work again with Rob, as he and I shared a special bond, forged in the unlikeliest of circumstances. During the 1990s, I was working as a van salesman for Panther and Rob was the manager at the Our Price record shop in Newcastle. Everything we sold to Our Price was on sale-or-return terms, so when I turned up one day at the store's loading bay, underneath a vast shopping complex, I was not surprised that Rob had several boxes of unsold CDs for me. I had just picked up around ten boxes of new stock and there was no obvious space to put the returns into the back of the van, so I asked Rob to leave them on the ground by its back door. The van doors were open, so I could easily keep an eye on the returned stock and, after all, we were in a huge underground delivery area, which was deserted.

Rob then spent half an hour or so selecting new stock, and when he had finished I wrote out his invoice and turned to sort out the two boxes of returns by my van. They were gone. I could not believe it. Somehow, two large boxes of CDs had vanished from under our noses. Rob was convinced that he would be sacked – even though the fault was clearly mine. I can still recall him enduring a difficult phone call with his area manager, and what was striking was that he did not blame me – even though I was the utter plant pot who had told him what to do.

Rob was, and is, a trusted friend.

It was fantastic to be working again, in Proper, with my old mates. Their enthusiasm and work ethic was a breath of fresh air. Every day was good fun and every night they were the last to leave the building.

However, instead of being delighted by the new arrivals, Richard seemed to resent how hard they worked. I had thought that their evident zeal would inspire the staff that had come over from Direct, but instead it divided the company further.

Subsequently, Richard had appointed ex-Direct staff in the key positions at Proper – head of jazz, head of folk, head of country and key accounts manager. Meanwhile, from my position in sales I began to notice that we seemed to be out of stock of so many titles, and that our sales had become very disappointing.

It turned out that Richard was intent on starting a new company, Cadiz Music, and on changing his name to Richard England.

He quietly informed the ex-Direct staff of his intentions and they had all agreed to leave en masse to join his new operation. In the meantime they were working only half-heartedly and Richard was busy contacting all of our supplier labels to persuade them to transfer their business to his new company.

Several labels thought that this was beyond the pale and called to let us know what was going on. Richard was confronted and immediately resigned. He left, taking eight key members of staff with him.

The next few months were difficult as we steadied the ship, everybody pulling together to keep the show on the road. We desperately needed some new, knowledgeable staff. Luckily, Steve Matthews, who had worked for Sony for twenty years as their key accounts manager, had just been made redundant. We snapped him up, and it turned out to be an inspired move. Other great signings included Fran Courtney as Head of Buying; Brian Showell, who took over the running of jazz; Esther Tewkesbury, who brought in some great world music labels; Ian Green in telesales; and Jon Hughes was put in charge of imports, helped by Ben Edwards, who later moved to EMI. Proper will always be grateful to all those labels who stayed loyal to us in difficult times and gave us the chance to put things right.

In hindsight, I believe that Richard and his crew leaving was the best thing that could have happened to us. Proper has since gone from strength to strength. We now have excellent staff, who have moulded themselves into a terrific team, pulling in the same direction and trying to give talented musicians the chance to get their music heard and understood.

During the last few years we have distributed music by artists of such stature as Alison Krauss, Jamie Cullum and Dolly Parton, whilst our own record label, Proper Records, has had success with artists including Richard Thompson, Nick Lowe, Joan Baez, Little Feat and Andy Fairweather-Low. We have also released more than 150 different titles in our successful 'Proper Box' series.

We realised that critical magazines, such as *Mojo* and *Q*, could not be expected to review all of our releases, and so in 2007 we started our own magazine *Properganda*. In 2008 over 200,000 copies were distributed to record shops and at all the top music festivals.

In 2007 and 2008 Proper was a nominee for 'Distributor of the Year' – a fantastic achievement, given that we have a market share of under 1 per cent and generally have only two top 40 albums in any given year.

In 2008 I am proud to say that Proper:
• Distributed more than 2,000,000 albums.
• Distributed across almost 48,000 titles.
• Sourced from 421 suppliers to 721 retail accounts and into thousands of outlets.

- Ran a TV advertising campaign with a week one budget of £50,000. We also spent £50 advertising in the *English Folk Dance and Song Society* magazine – and covered pretty much everything else inbetween these two extremes.
- Received its fourth Mercury nomination in four years when, by rights, it should be lucky with a nomination once per decade. It also distributed the BBC folk, jazz and world music 'Albums of the Year'.

We are able to do this because we are an independent company based in a building that we own in London SE26. The people who work for the company also own the company. We employ fifty people – twelve in sales; six in product management; five in marketing; six in admin; and twenty-two in operations.

The ethos of the company is great – we are all in the warehouse when it's busy. We know when we get it wrong, because retailers are not afraid to ring up and tell us. Generally, though, it seems to work.

As the industry marches in one direction, we are happy to go down another. Whilst many of our releases are now available digitally for download, our sales of physical CDs have increased significantly. In circumstances where our artists, our labels and our retail customers depend on CD sales – and where they still represent 95 per cent of the total music market – we figure that it is obvious what medium we should be concentrating on, however unfashionable that may seem to some.

So, Proper stocks 48,000 titles – not even EMI have to cope with that amount of grief. About half of those titles are our own exclusive lines and the remainder is chiefly product unavailable elsewhere in the UK. On 16,000 of those titles we sold just one unit last year. We did not make money on those sales but, unless there is one mad punter out there with 16,000 obscure albums on his shelves, the chances are that thousands of happy customers have been able to track down exactly the album that they are looking for – and via a retailer they will now probably return to.

Without exaggeration, the company is focused on quality. The music we represent consistently generates critical acclaim and awards way beyond its market share. The pride we take in representing this music is matched by a quality approach to service for retailers – and beyond, because we understand that we have a responsibility to help sell the music all the way through to the eventual listener.

We know that the future for retail stores will be difficult, but Proper intends to be around to support them in any way we can. It is my belief that there will always be music fans who prefer a CD to a download, and so there will always be a market for us so long as we keep adapting to people's buying habits.

We are all older, wiser and with a bit more hair on our arses, but our enthusiasm is undiminished and we all love what we do because, deep down, we are all MUSIC FANS.

Chapter 7

The Final Journey

Having spent twenty years on the road, and in that time visited over a thousand different record shops, people often ask me what are the best and the worst shops I have known. The first part of the question is difficult, as I am spoilt for choice. The second part is easy. It took me all of ten seconds to select the shop to which I can grant the accolade 'The Worst Shop'.

One day whilst working in Bolton, I stumbled upon a shop I had never seen before, called Sounds. I popped in and introduced myself to Craig, the seventeen-year-old owner. He informed me that he had recently left school and that his dad had asked him what he wanted to do with his life. When Craig told him that he would like to run his own record shop, his father, obligingly, stumped up the funds.

A succession of customers then interrupted our chat. The ensuing conversations illustrated both Craig's business acumen and his aptitude for customer care.

Customer: "My stylus seems to be faulty, as all my records are jumping."
Craig: "Bring it in and I will have a look at it for you."
Customer: "I have it with me. I think it's bent."

Craig spent the next two (interminable) minutes holding the stylus up to the light before confirming that it was bent and handing it back to the customer.

Customer: "Do you have one in stock?"
Craig: "No."
Customer: "Can you order one for me?"
Craig: "Sorry, mate. This is a record shop; not a hi-fi dealer."

The disgruntled customer left, whilst I quietly explained to Craig that record shops stocked basics, like styli.

Another customer came in and asked Craig if he had anything by the Halle Orchestra. (As the Halle is Britain's longest-established symphony orchestra and is based in Manchester, a mere ten miles from Bolton, you would have expected Craig to be aware of it.)

"Of course I have mate," Craig responded, as he plonked a copy of *Bill Haley's Greatest Hits* on the counter.

The classical customer looked at Craig in disgust. I was not sure if it was due to a dislike of being referred to as 'mate' or to Craig's ignorance of the Halle Orchestra. "It is the Halle I am after," the customer insisted.

"I think you will find that it is pronounced 'Hay-lee'", replied Craig, knowingly.

Shaking his head, the customer started to make his way out of the shop. In a last desperate attempt to procure a sale, Craig started to read out the track-listing from the Bill Haley CD, "Hey mate, all the hits are on this – 'Rock Around the Clock'; 'See You Later, Alligator'…" But, to no avail – the customer had gone.

Then, just as I thought things could not get any worse … they got worse…

The next unfortunate customer came in and purchased a CD for £3.99. Craig took the proffered £5, but then shut the till without giving any change. When the customer pointed out the error, Craig, for some reason, could not get his till to open. A full ten minutes elapsed, with Craig frantically bashing every possible combination of buttons on the till in an attempt to open it.

When he was reduced to trying to force it open with a screwdriver, the customer called him an idiot – to which Craig responded, "Tell you what, mate – why don't you try and f***ing open it?"

To calm the situation I gave the customer £1.01 from my own pocket and told Craig to repay the money when he got the till open.

Sadly that time never came. Half an hour later, the till was still shut. I promised Craig I would call on him the next time I was in the area – I had spent more than an hour with a customer and had achieved sales worth minus £1.01, but the comedy value had been worth every penny.

Predictably, when I next checked out the store, it had closed … perhaps Craig never did get that damn till open.

From the worst record shop, to my personal fifty best. Throughout the summer of 2008 I took it upon myself to undertake my last tour of the finest independent stores in mainland Britain, to hear the tales of the owners, and to discover why their competitors have been closing at such an alarming rate.

When I look at a map of the UK and picture where the independent shops are, it is clear that the majority of stores are in towns, as opposed to cities. Most are not on the high street. Many are tucked away in hidden side streets, relying on regular customers rather than passing trade. Usually the ones that survive own their property. It is incredibly difficult for an independent shop to survive whilst paying city rates and rents.

As I live in Chippenham, Wiltshire, I thought I would start my journey by visiting the stores of the South West. First call was Acorn Records in Yeovil.

In many ways Acorn Records is a unique store. Surely it must be the only record shop in the world where the all-time bestselling CD is *The Best of the Wurzels*. Another claim to fame is that it has probably the oldest record-shop assistant in the country in the shape of the evergreen 80-year-old Mavis Slater.

It was formed by two friends, Chris Lowe and Rob Bacon, who opened the doors of their first shop in 1973. Chris and Rob had met at North London Polytechnic and, following their studies, Rob started working for a fire extinguisher company in Bristol, whilst Chris found work in a timber yard in Yeovil. Chris paid a visit to Bristol, and called in on his friend for a few drinks. Rob had a business diploma and Chris had a degree in English, French and Philosophy, so understandably conversation soon turned to the fact that a fire extinguisher company and a timber yard were probably not the best places for their respective talents. As the night wore on and the drink flowed Rob suggested that they should open a record shop. The two friends agreed on the plan, stating that tomorrow they would find some premises.

No matter how mad it seemed, the next day Chris went looking for a property whilst Rob contacted the UK record companies and told them they had a small amount of cash and wished to purchase records. Between them they begged and borrowed to get them started. Chris found a site in Princes Street, Yeovil, and purchased some glass counters from a sweet shop that had closed down. Rob purchased the LPs and the next few weeks were spent preparing the shop for the grand opening. Chris suggested that the shop should have a name that began with 'A' so they would be at the front of the phone book and, after bouncing names beginning with that letter off each other, they settled on Acorn. The night before opening they worked until 2am getting the shop prepared. Even the police paid them a call to find out what was going on, with Chris having to explain why he was up a ladder at 1am putting up sticky letters that spelt the name Acorn above their shop.

The next day, Friday 7 December 1973, Acorn opened its doors for the first time. For the first hour Chris and Rob stood there wondering if anybody was ever going to walk through those doors. After more than an hour a man came in and looked through the racks, before picking up a copy of the soundtrack to *O Lucky Man!* by Alan Price. He bought it and the shop was up and running. Throughout the day a steady stream of customers paid the store a visit.

One of the shop's earliest customers was the singer and musician Georgie Fame. When he walked in, the staff could not take their eyes off him. It wasn't because they were in awe of having such a famous person in the shop – it was due to his having his flies wide open and his tackle bulging through some bright underpants. The staff looked at each other to see which one should tell Georgie. The policy of 'say nothing' was adopted and Georgie bought his LPs and went back into Yeovil town centre, his flies still wide open.

For the next year or so the two friends had a great time with their relaxed approach to business. The shop opened whenever one of them got out of bed; there were no set hours and often they would close at lunchtime to go to the Glovers Arms for egg and chips and a couple of pints.

Business picked up and became good enough for them to move to larger premises in Glovers Walk, where the business is still trading. As they were expanding, they needed to take on extra staff. Their main rival in Yeovil at that time was a store called Radio House, which mixed selling electrical goods with records. When that store closed down Chris wasted no time in approaching its record department manageress, Mavis Slater, to come and join them at Acorn. At this point Mavis was a mere whippersnapper, aged around fifty. She came with quite a reputation. One of her sons was a member of the 70s cult band, Stackridge, which had charted with a couple of singles. Every pub in Yeovil knew of Mavis, not because of her drinking habits, but because of her insistence that a Stackridge record had to be on the pub's jukebox. Mavis immediately made an impact on the shop, installing some much-needed discipline. No more late openings and no more closing at lunch for egg and chips!

Mind you, Mavis did not get off to the most auspicious of starts. One of her regular customers from her days at Radio House, an elderly gentleman, called in to order a classical record. Chris explained that they were a rock shop and didn't stock classical music (they do now). Mavis took over and told the gentleman that she would order his classical LP. The weeks passed and the gentleman never came back for his LP. Eventually, Chris asked Mavis to track him down so that the shop could sell its one and only classical album. Sadly, Mavis found out that he had died and had never had the chance to buy or listen to his album. It was years before Acorn finally sold the album, in a sale for 50p.

Chris recalled that the most exciting day the shop ever had was the release of the Sex Pistols' classic album *Never Mind The Bollocks*. They played the record in store all day, and all of the 50 copies they had ordered sold in a few hours.

With the shop running smoothly, Chris applied for a job as sales rep with Virgin Records, hoping to learn more about the record industry from the other side of the counter. It is hard to believe that he was given the job, as surely it was a conflict of interests to have a record-shop owner selling to other shops. Chris spent his time well, visiting other stores and learning from their experiences. He spent only 18 months with Virgin, as he wanted to get back to being full-time in the shop, to put the ideas he had picked up on the road into practice.

One system Chris wanted to introduce at Acorn, having noticed it at another shop, was to install a shrink-wrap machine, which covered the album sleeve in a plastic coating. Before going through the machine a security tag would be inserted, so that should anybody try to leave the store without paying, an alarm fitted in the shop's doorway would sound. This system would replace master-bagging the albums, a laborious process where the retailer removes the record from the sleeve and stores it behind the counter. The empty cover is then put back in the rack for customers to look through. The problem with that system was that sleeves would often get a bit tattered, especially if the record did not sell quickly. They decided to go ahead with it, despite the massive job of removing thousands of LPs from master-bag to shrink-wrap all of them.

Chris and Rob decided to close the store for a week so that it could be completely refitted, but in that week they made a calamitous mistake. After spending many hours wrapping the LPs, Rob decided to test the new system. Sadly, they had been sold a faulty batch of 10,000 security tags. Thus, thousands of LPs had to be reopened so that the faulty tags could be removed. The tag company supplied them with new tags the next day.

Needless to say, this time they checked that the tags worked before inserting them and re-wrapping the records.

A few years later, events at Acorn took a turn for the worse. The partners decided to expand and took the decision to open a second shop in the seaside town of Weymouth. As is often the case when you expand, it is crucial to get good staff, but no matter who they had running the store, they could not make this venture profitable. After two unsuccessful years they took the decision to close and abandoned further plans for expansion, vowing to concentrate on giving the people of Yeovil a fantastic record shop.

Worse was to follow when, ten days before Christmas in 1992, the store was burgled. The thieves broke down the back door and removed every single CD from the shop bar one. Left in the rack was a single copy of Paul Young's *No Parlez*. Maybe the thieves had taste. The shop was left with only the vinyl and cassettes. To the credit of the record industry, everybody rallied round and the store was closed for just one day. Chris phoned all of the record companies and asked them to send their thousand bestsellers. Every single company got the stock to them next day, and with the help of friends and family the shelves were full again. The police never found the criminals, but Somerset car-booters probably had a field day.

The worst, and saddest, setback was to follow in 1995, when Rob was diagnosed with a terminal illness. He was incredibly brave and continued working until just a few months before his tragically early death on December 15 1996. It was especially sad since Rob, with his usual sardonic humour, had vowed to stay alive until the New Year. He was a retailer to the end and didn't want to cause problems by pegging out at the busiest time of the year. He nearly made, it and is still sorely missed.

Things were understandably tough for the next couple of years. One day Chris was working on his own, attempting to serve a large queue, when one of the customers, who was also a close friend, said to him, "You need some help". With that, Anna Wood joined Chris behind the counter to help out for five minutes. Twelve years on and she is still working there as part of his loyal team. Anna is a real dark horse – she is reminiscent of a favourite attractive aunty, when in fact she has lived the rock 'n' roll lifestyle. She started her career in music selling merchandise for Joan Armatrading, before graduating to touring the world, handling the merchandise for the likes of Thin Lizzy and Elton John. In fact, I am surprised she hasn't written her own book. These days Anna's son, Ben, has been added to the staff and works part time when not touring with his band.

One of the saddest, yet funniest, things that ever happened occurred on a very grim day at Acorn. I turned up at the shop and noticed how quiet it was. Normally, I'd be greeted by Mavis complaining that I'd been selling them too many box sets. On this day the shop was silent. "Where's Mavis?" I enquired. Chris explained that earlier that day Mavis's husband, Dixie, had collapsed and died whilst working at his gardening job. Mavis was out shopping when Chris took the phone call telling him of Dixie's death, leaving him with the task of informing Mavis upon her return. Chris tried to break the news gently. He took Mavis to one side, put his arm around her and quietly told her that he had some really bad news; Dixie had been found dead in his employer's garden. She rested her head on his shoulder for a few moments and then looked up to utter the immortal words: "But I've just bought the old bugger some fish for Thursday".

It just goes to show that even in our saddest moments you can find humour. There was more to follow at Dixie's funeral. Mavis's son, Mike, noticed that the headstone on the grave adjacent to the one in which Dixie was to be buried was for a lady called Alice. "Look," he said, "Dad will be living next door to Alice". Mavis's reply was priceless, "Living next door to Alice. Who the f*** is Alice?" I laughed so much when I heard this tale, though I appreciate it will be lost on anybody who has not heard the Chubby Brown and Smokie hit 'Living Next Door to Alice (Who the F*** is Alice)'.

Acorn is situated close to the bus station in Yeovil, and next to the store is an escalator that takes people up to another shopping area of the town. On one occasion, when I was in the store, a man popped his head around the door and shouted, "Escalator off". He made me jump and I asked Anna who he was. "Oh," she replied, "that's Escalator Man. We don't know his name, and he has never bought anything from us, but he just likes to inform us when the escalator is off".

On another day, a lady popped in and asked if they had any 'String'. Chris searched the database on his computer, and although he knew of bands like String Driven Thing and The Incredible String Band he could not find a band called 'String'. "Are you after Sting?" he asked.

"No, string," the woman replied. Chris asked the lady if she had any more information on 'String'. "It's for tying up a parcel", was the reply.

It will be a sad day when Mavis retires, but I fear that day might not be too far away.

I asked Chris if his would be one of the 'Last Shops Standing'. He'd like it to be, but the huge downturn in business and the imminent end of the lease are starting to make retirement look like a more attractive proposition to him.

I hope the people of Yeovil will appreciate and support Acorn in its final years. It will be a sad day for the town when this gem of a record store finally calls it a day.

* * *

From Yeovil I travel south, through the winding country roads of Somerset into Dorset, to meet Chris's good friend Piers Garner, owner of Bridport Record Centre. The two friends speak regularly about music matters. Piers became involved in music when his brother-in-law, Andy Bell, phoned him to say he had taken out a lease on a new shop. Andy already had a Spar-type mini-market, but he wanted a record shop, and asked Piers if he would be interested in running it. At the time, Piers was studying law at Sheffield, but had, however, become disillusioned and was desperately seeking an alternative career path. He packed his bags, headed to Bridport, and in 1979 the Record Centre opened.

Piers married Stephanie in 1980, and since then this dynamic duo have run the store. The first thing you notice as you enter are the bongos, guitars and ukuleles hanging down from the ceiling. Piers and Stephanie work on a raised platform at the far end of the store, looking down on their kingdom below. I often leave the store with neck ache because of that raised platform – standing on the shop floor my eyes are level with their stomachs so I am constantly having to look up to them. As with most stores, when they recognised that the CD industry was in decline, they realised that to survive they would have to diversify. After visiting a stand at a music industry conference they took the decision to stock musical instruments. It proved to be a sensible move – one which, I am surprised to observe, only a few stores have taken. Musical instrument companies often supply their goods on consignment, so the retailer pays only for what it sells. In recent years I have noticed how much more space has been given over to instruments and how much less to CDs. Piers has even been known to bring out his ukulele and give the customers a tune – always a handy tactic to employ at closing time when looking to clear the shop!

One great thing for record-store owners around that time was the fact that they did not need to buy many clothes. In fact, Piers did not buy a T-shirt for ten years – he simply wore the free clothing dished out by the major record companies. He recalled how one day he came into work wearing his REM leather jacket; a *Now That's What I Call Music!* sweatshirt;

his Joboxers boxer shorts; and his Swing Out Sister Ray-Ban sunglasses. After work, he returned home to watch his Sony-donated TV. Each Christmas, record companies gave gifts to dealers to thank them for promoting their artists.

What chance did independent record companies have? No wonder so few indie acts made the national chart, as small companies did not have the money or resources to bribe their way into it.

The reference to Joboxers reminded me that their song 'Boxerbeat' turned out to be Bridport Record Centre's most profitable record ever. When it was released, RCA must have thought that they had found the new Queen and the next 'Bohemian Rhapsody', as the promotional hype they put into this song was phenomenal. On the week of release the rep came in and gave Piers a counter display with six free singles, which Piers priced at 99p. Here is what happened over the next two months:

Week 2 – The rep asked Piers if he had sold any copies, to which Piers told him he had not. Regardless, the rep gave him another six copies.
Week 3 – The shop had sold one copy. Once again they were given another six singles for free.
Week 4 – They had sold a further two copies, and were given six more for free – and by now the single had charted, so you would think that RCA would no longer need to be giving the record away.
Week 5 – The single now peaked, with Piers selling a record three copies but, of course, the shop received another six copies free.
Weeks 6/7/8 – The single continued to trickle out from the shop, and each week it was given another six free singles.

In total, the shop received 48 free 7" singles of 'Boxerbeat', which meant that for no outlay whatsoever they had managed to recoup £48. If this exercise had been repeated in every chart shop, it is anybody's guess how many records were given away. I am sure Joboxers' royalty statement would have made interesting reading.

During this period I had my own Joboxer experience. I was managing The Cherry Boys when I received a phone call from an Oxford College asking if we would play at their May Ball. The money they offered made it impossible to refuse. It would be a great experience, and on top of this we would be supporting Joboxers who, thanks to their record company's bribery, were in the top 10 singles chart. We arrived at the college mid-afternoon and were escorted to our makeshift changing room, which turned out to be one of the study rooms, full of books, with a large balcony overlooking the courtyard below. We were assigned two students to look after us, to supply us with anything we wanted and to make sure we behaved ourselves. It turned out that four bands were playing, and that we were to go on last after Joboxers had finished their set.

It was then explained to us that after our soundcheck we would be confined to our room until it was time to perform. Although they supplied us with champagne and fabulous food, it soon became very boring and the band spent their time on the balcony watching the events below. Young students were dressed in their finest – girls in beautiful ball gowns and boys in tuxedos.

The sound of posh accents filled the air – with the odd upper class twit impression emanating from the balcony. Eventually, one of the band's minders asked the band to 'stop taking the mickey', or we would get no more alcohol.

By the time The Cherry Boys were due to come on it was 2am, and after a night of drinking, the audience were either paralytic or lying on the floor, comatose. Unfortunately, the band were in a similar physical state, having drunk free champagne since 4pm. The band produced their worst performance, culminating in a hideous version of their best song, 'Kardomah Café'. The song features a beautiful harmonica break performed by the band's vocalist, John, who also plays guitar on the song. This night, however, it sounded like somebody jumping up and down on an accordion. As the band staggered off stage I asked John why it sounded so bad. It turned out that he had put the harmonica the wrong way round in its holder and had to suck the harmonica instead of blowing it!

As well as owning one of my favourite stores, Piers Garner can claim to be my most knowledgeable customer. I recently had to sell a three-CD box set called *Name That Tune*, which played introductions to 500 pop songs from the 60s up to the modern day. The CD plays them in batches of twenty and, out of sixty shops visited, Piers was the only one to achieve twenty correct answers. The store that got only five correct will remain nameless – other than to say it was in Bath and features in this book ... I have, however, no wish to embarrass it, so its name will remain a secret!

Piers's knowledge came in handy the day a lady asked for the new Julian Glasshouse CD. Never having heard of Julian Glasshouse, Piers asked if the lady had any more details. She told him that Julian was Italian and good looking. Piers asked her if she meant Julio Iglesias. "That's him", she replied. I was most impressed with how he had worked that out – taking into account the misleading clues: he was not Italian; he was not called Julian; and he certainly was not named Glasshouse.

The first couple of years of the Record Centre's trading were a learning curve, and the business trundled along, making a small profit. However, things changed the day that Gallup contacted them to ask if they would like to become a chart shop. This meant that data from their sales would count towards chart figures.

Suddenly, the next week was like Christmas: reps from all the major record companies – EMI, Sony, BMG, Warner and Universal – all turned up at the shop and showered Piers with gifts and free stock. Bridport Record Centre had never previously encountered a rep, so they assumed that Gallup had informed the record companies of those shops which had become chart shops, so that they could get reps out to bribe them.

Piers told me about some of the deals they were given in order to promote specific artists: for example, when Warner was breaking Prince, they offered the shop a free 7" leather single carry-case, each of which held 50 records, for every Prince record that was sold.

As Piers knew several DJs, and was able to sell the cases to them for £4.99, he took advantage of this 'offer'. Soon it was hardly possible to move in the shop without tripping over 7" single carry-cases. Of course, Warner's generosity paid off, and Prince became one of the world's bestselling artists. However, things have now come full circle, with Prince recently giving away his album for free in *The Mail on Sunday* newspaper.

I asked Piers if he thought that the Bridport Record Centre would be one of the 'Last Shops Standing'. "Of course", was his reply; "I will just purchase more musical instruments and fewer CDs".

The Record Centre is one of the stores that has benefited greatly from getting regular visits from sales reps. However, times are changing, and many shops now receive no visits at all and have suffered as a consequence.

I believe that the reduction in the numbers of sales reps on the road has had a major impact on the demise of the independent record shop. Throughout the 90s most stores received visits from around seven companies each week. Some would call two or three times in that week, whilst others would call just the once. On top of this, there was a second wave of reps who would call monthly. This attention generated a positive exchange of information – reps would inform independent shops of what was happening with their artists; the promotions that were in place; and the special offers that were available.

Nowadays, stores are out of the information loop. It was because of reps that shops were privy to what titles were selling well in other stores. Now the shops receive information solely by blanket e-mail, and if they are to believe every e-mail they receive, then every CD release is a sure-fire success.

Reps also carried stock that the shops could buy, along with a collection of free stock to be given away, ensuring that a company's artists were displayed in prominent positions in the store. They would also supply display material and posters. Best of all, they were able to offer deals on the CDs they sold, thereby giving the independent stores an opportunity to buy at a lower price.

In the past record companies had deemed it important to look after record stores, as all of the top independent stores were used to collect data for the charts. The most pivotal day in the decline of independent record shops was when Asda was invited to contribute their sales data to the chart ratings. Soon the other supermarkets followed, and simply through their sheer buying power the balance of attention was shifted decisively – record companies no longer needed to court independent shops, but they needed the support of the supermarkets.

Soon, downloading also counted towards chart statistics, which further diminished the influence of independent shops and their relative importance to record companies.

* * *

From Bridport, I head east to the beautiful Dorset town of Wimborne, home of Square Records. Opened in 1974 by Roger Holman, the shop was originally an electrical goods retailer. Roger decided to utilise some empty space by selling cheap LPs, and by 1978, Roger recognised that he was making more profit from record sales than from electrical equipment and took the decision to open a separate record shop. His shop has now grown into one of the best independent record shops in the country. The shop has always been a family business, with Roger's wife and daughter working there. His son, Paul, a professional musician who played in the cult 90's band The Lemon Trees, also helped out.

The Lemon Trees have had a colourful history. After having five top 75 singles taken from their debut album *Open Book*, they spent two weeks in a château in France recording their second album. Then, just before its release, MCA dropped them, and informed them that they were a million pounds in debt – as well as the time spent in France, they had also shot two lavish videos, one of them in LA.

The band featured a young Guy Chambers, who has since made his fortune writing songs with Robbie Williams – the number one single

'Angels' being his greatest success. Another hit for Robbie was 'Lazy Days' – an old Lemon Trees number, which Paul had sung originally.

Of the other members of The Lemon Trees, drummer Jeremy Stacey is now with Sheryl Crow's band, whilst guitarist Paul Stacey has produced The Black Crowes.

Working part time fitted in well with Paul's work pattern and lifestyle. By 1987, he had accepted that he was not going to be the next Jimi Hendrix and the family business passed into his hands, leaving Roger to concentrate on the electrical business. With the help of his other sons, this soon expanded to embrace three shops.

The reason the shop is still trading is because of the support of the local community. It always surprises me, when I visit, how the shop acts like a drop-in centre – people calling in; having a chat; then leaving without purchasing anything. The shop has a friendly atmosphere – helped along by the long serving staff: Paul's sister Julie, Leeds United fanatic Rob and Kerrie, who works part time whilst also studying at Southampton University.

The shop is neat and tidy, with numerous posters supporting local events on the door and in the window. The first few years were fantastic for Paul – back then independent shops played an important part in getting artists into the chart. In addition to giving away lots of freebies, the major record companies offered great prizes for the best window display. Square Records soon established a solid reputation for winning these competitions, thanks to the talent of one of Paul's artistic friends, who helped to design some amazing displays. They won a holiday in Memphis, which was offered to promote the Marc Cohn single 'Walking in Memphis', by making Mississippi mud pies to serve to customers, painting footprints on the floor and building a set of Elvis Presley gates to adorn the shop. Other prizes included a trip to Europe to see Elton John, a Les Paul guitar valued at over £500, a leather jacket and a pair of Ray-Ban sunglasses.

Paul was phoned by one rep and was told that if he could help the Swing Out Sisters record 'Breakout' reach the top 5 in the forthcoming week's chart, he would be rewarded with a pair of Ray-Bans. Sure enough, Swing Out Sister made the top 5 and lots of record-store owners looked cooler than usual in their shades the next week!

The most blatant case of hyping a record I ever came across was when I was working at HMV and 'Caravan of Love', by The Housemartins, was released. The HMV rep came into the store and handed me a Ladbrokes betting slip. It was for a £1 wager, at odds of 33/1 that the Housemartins'

'Caravan of Love' would be Christmas number one. The rep told me they had placed 500 £1 bets and he was distributing them to record-store staff. The incentive was blatant; if The Housemartins made it to number one, I would pick up £34. I am sure lots of record-store staff keyed in a few extra numbers and, as my wages were only £69 per week, £34 would have been handy. However, I was dismayed by the nature of the bribery ... and I often wondered if the band had any idea what was going on, as the money would certainly have come out of their royalties and surreptitiously charged to 'marketing'. The days of such bribery and fantastic prizes for window displays have long since passed.

Paul once related to me the tale of the worst day in the history of Square Records. A customer had ordered a Doors record, and when he arrived to collect it the album was, unfortunately, out of stock. The customer did not take this news at all well and stormed out shouting that the store was rubbish – a word which, no doubt, influenced his next move.

It was refuse-collection day in Wimborne, and so there was lots of rubbish piled up in black plastic sacks on the streets. Suddenly the man returned, shouting, "Your shop is rubbish!" and at the same time hurling a bin bag full of rubbish through the doorway, all its contents spewing out over the floor. As the staff started clearing up, two more bags were thrown in and, seconds later, another two followed.

Paul felt it wise to lock the door for the sake of the safety of his customers. He then phoned the police who, believing it to be no more than a minor disturbance, turned up 40 minutes later. By the time they arrived the irrationally enraged customer had piled up so many black bin bags against the shop windows and door that it had started to go dark in the store.

Having used up every bag in the road, he started fetching them from surrounding streets, to the point where he eventually managed to totally obscure the daylight in the shop. The customers whom Paul had locked in thought it was very amusing but, after a while, he sneaked them out of the back door. When the police arrived and took away the mad, disgruntled man all of the local onlookers who had gathered to watch events unfold were disappointed – but none of them had intervened.

Paul told me that his only problematic customers were the two types that hum: the first comes in to hum a tune and expects him to recognise it immediately; and the second is his regular customer, who clears out the shop by humming in a stinky sort of way. Most shops seem to have one smelly customer – I often wonder if they are rationed to one per store, as I have never heard of a shop bemoaning two smelly customers.

Square's whiffy customer, whom they referred to as Mr Smelly, was a huge Showaddywaddy fan. Whenever he came in, the staff would decant themselves into the back room, leaving the slowest at the counter to serve him. One day he asked for 'A Little Piece of Soap', which was the title of the new Showaddywaddy single. The back room staff all burst out laughing for the next two minutes. Mr Smelly was bemused, as were the other customers, but laughter is infectious, and soon the whole shop was rocking to the sound of laughter. Mr Smelly walked out with 'A Little Bit of Soap', but sadly it wasn't the soap that he really needed!

My own experience of smelly customers occurred whilst working at HMV. A thoroughly pleasant, if somewhat whiffy, young man always engaged me in conversation after he had purchased his CDs. One day he informed me that he was planning to go to university, but could not decide where. "How about the University of Bath?" I suggested. The irony was lost on him, as he told me it was too far away.

Other eccentric customers at Square included the lady who would come in and ask for Richard Claydermouse instead of Richard Clayderman. However, the most bizarre customer is the man they have christened 'Mr Alsop', because every three months he purchases seven Alsop head cleaners for his cassette players. They have never known him buy anything else, and the fact that he only ever dresses in purple has added to his mystique. Paul's computer records indicate that every three months they have sold seven Alsop head cleaners, whereas other sales were virtually non-existent. In fact, since 2005, his sales of Alsop head cleaners have been: Mr Alsop – 42; the rest of the entire population of Dorset – 1.

I am surprised Alsop has not rewarded Paul with a holiday, as he must be their best customer. I had to laugh when he informed me that buying in sevens ran in the family, as Mr Alsop's dad used to come in and purchase seven styli at a time.

Another idiosyncratic character is the customer they have christened Mr Bin Laden, because the terrorist attack of 9/11 has become virtually his only topic of conversation. Not only does he regularly offer his latest conspiracy theory to the staff, he also engages complete strangers on the topic whilst they are browsing through the store's racks. You would have thought that, by now, he would have moved on to some other great world event, but every week he arrives with yet more 9/11 tales. He also has a wild taste in music and asks for the most unusual things – recently he enquired if they had any tango music from Mongolia...

The shop's most frustrating customer is a lovely lady called Sue. She is an extremely likeable and friendly lady who pops in most weeks for a chat with both staff and customers, as she has an opinion on almost every topic. The only downside to this is that, in all the years she has been frequenting Square Records, she has yet to make a single purchase. This has become a standing joke and, despite the best efforts of all the staff, she is still a Square Records virgin. To make matters worse, one day when Sue was in the shop, Paul was chatting with his niece, who works in HMV Poole, and he remarked to her how Sue had been coming in for years and had never purchased anything. "But that's amazing," said his niece, "because I served her last week in HMV. She bought a DVD". Paul was astonished – Sue lived in Wimborne and had never bought a thing from his shop, yet travelled all the way to Poole to shop at HMV.

A few years ago I noticed a photo book on the shelves of the shop that contained beautiful pictures of Dorset landscapes. Paul informed me that his dad had written the book and was also responsible for all of the splendid photographs. I remarked that I regularly visited Wells, a shop in Southwold, whose owner, Richard, was a talented photographer, and which successfully combined selling CDs with selling fabulous photographs of the town's beach huts.

I suggested to Paul that it might be a good idea to display his father's work in the shop. Paul agreed, and the following week he put some of the photographs in the window. It was a wise move, as photograph sales were soon making a significant contribution to revenue. Now the whole of the back of the shop features his father's work, but memories are short – recently, Paul mentioned to me that shops need to diversify to survive, and he was really glad that he had thought of displaying the photos in the store. I gently reminded him of the conversation we'd had on this subject a few years earlier.

I asked Paul if he felt that Square would still be here in five years' time. He was confident that, as he owned the building, he would survive. A customer had recently remarked to Paul that it was lovely to come into a quaint, old-fashioned record shop … and that is how it will still be in five years time – a "quaint, little, old-fashioned record shop!"

* * *

The following day I visited those shops which are all within a 50-mile vicinity of my home. First, I set off to visit a unique shop – Changing World Music – in a town which every music fan in the country is aware of – Glastonbury.

As you would expect from Glastonbury, Changing World is a mysterious and magical store. Decorated in bright colours and based at the back of the bookshop Gothic Image, the famous and first ever New Age bookshop in Glastonbury High Street, it has a real New Age feel. David Hatfield is the shop's buyer and visionary, and looks as if he has just stepped out of a *Lord of the Rings* movie.

David has had a colourful life. He started off working in The City by day and playing bass in various bands at night. Being an artistic type, David soon packed in the day-job to hire a little studio in Leigh-on-Sea, Essex, and work for himself as a freelance designer.

Then, his life changed on the day a lady walked into his studio and asked him if he would display her pottery in his window and be prepared to sell it for a commission.

David agreed and, to his surprise, it sold really well. Consequently, he pondered on what else he could sell and, as he was a musician, decided to give music a go, without realising just how un-cooperative major record companies could be. To obtain a credit account, they required him to spend as much as £2,000 with them in advance! He realised that there was too little space for such a large amount of stock in his small studio and so together with a friend, Dave Lawrence, he came up with a clever plan.

To obtain their first credit account, they ordered 250 copies of the new David Bowie album, *Diamond Dogs*, from RCA. They then advertised the album by putting a flyer in a student magazine, offering it at cost price. This was how his first account with RCA began. He then went through the same procedure with the other major record companies until he had opened accounts with all of them.

This was the start of Projection Records. Mail order soon became so successful that David could no longer operate from his studio, so he rented The Old Custom House – a large, ramshackle two-storey building on the Old Leigh waterfront, which became the HQ of Projection Record Distribution. From here he ran mail order, direct retail sales to the public and a specialist folk/blues and jazz wholesale distribution service.

As David was also playing with a variety of bands in the evenings, he dropped his design work. Instead, he started playing at music festivals and, while doing so, noticed a niche business opportunity. After approaching the festival promoters, he was soon running record emporia at their festivals and this soon became his main source of income.

David was also still in great demand as a double-bass player – in fact, for twenty years, he was the resident double-bass player at the Cambridge Folk

Festival, performing with such prestigious acts as Arlo Guthrie, Peter Rowan, Flaco Jimenez, Mark O'Connor, Bill Keith and Jim Rooney.

David then approached Tony Engle of Topic Records (now a Director of Proper Records) to secure supply of Topic's entire catalogue. For his first festival in Bracknell, Tony gave him a complete set of LP sleeves from the whole Topic catalogue. Incredibly, David simply displayed the sleeves, and when people wanted to buy an LP (vinyl was the only medium in those days!) he told them that he did not keep stock on site, but if they paid for the LP and left their address, he would post their purchase on to them – mail order from a field! He must have been some salesman, as he sold over £500-worth in this fashion!

Things were looking promising for his business and so he opened another outlet in Southend-on-Sea. He also invested money in a new label venture called Waterfront Records. This label released albums by the likes of The Chevalier Brothers, Flaco Jimenez, Peter Rowan, Martin Simpson, Eddie and The Hot Rods and Wilko Johnson. Waterfront was distributed by Rough Trade. David was actually the man who came up with the name for, and was a founder member of, The Kursaal Flyers. The band had some success with the Mike Batt produced 'Little Does She Know', a top 20 hit in 1976.

David is a great salesman, but he is first to admit that he is no accountant. Consequently, when the VAT man demanded a large chunk of money, he found that he had serious cash flow problems and so took the inevitable decision to gradually wind up his business interests in Southend. The next couple of years were difficult, but David managed to get back on his feet by concentrating on the festival business.

This included receiving some help from Fairport Convention. The band was doing a festival in the grounds of Broughton Castle and David was asked if he would help sell records there. This proved to be a success and so the band asked him if he would like to sell at its annual festival in the village of Cropredy, which he did then and still does every year. This, in turn, led to his selling at the Sidmouth Folk Festival. As the folk scene seemed to be so vibrant in the West Country in 1989, he moved to Somerset and struck up a strong relationship with WOMAD (World of Music and Dance). Together with Dave Longley, he opened the Womad Shop in Crewkerne. As the name implies, they specialised in world music and they used the premises to expand their festival activities. By 1990, Projection Records were selling at 30 different music festivals every year and had established a CD shop at The Glastonbury Festival, on the Field of Avalon, that still trades each year.

However, the festival business simply grew too fast, with David focusing on sales to the detriment of the accounting side of the business. Eventually, this resulted in the business's demise. Sadly, in 1995 he was declared bankrupt, after having run Projection Records for more than 20 years. It had made a big name for itself on the roots music scene, in terms of retail, distribution and festivals. David actually set up the original folk/roots sections at HMV Oxford Circus; Tower Records, Piccadilly; and the Virgin Mega Store.

After a year away from the music business, his partner, Susan Malleson, helped David to bounce back by setting up Changing World Music. In 1999 they started renting the backroom in the Gothic Image bookshop. Here, David could sell the music he loved. Susan's daughter, Rowan, has been managing the shop since the day it opened.

David is also now playing music again, with his own band Three Tuns O'Grass, and displays his bass-playing skills with Chris Jagger's Acoustic Trip. Recently, at Chris's birthday party in The Glastonbury Assembly Rooms, he played bass whilst Mick Jagger performed – not many people can claim to have played with a Rolling Stone!

If you ever find yourself in Glastonbury, Changing World Music is a must to visit, with full racks of world, folk, roots, dub, beats, trance, ambient and fusions, as well as the huge New Age selection. It is also worth checking out another project that David is involved in – a little shop called The Summer of Love, which is packed full of psychedelic music and country rock from the halcyon days of the 1960s and early 1970s and which is tucked up a little alley behind the high street.

*   *   *

I stayed in Somerset for the second call of my day. All music fans visiting the county should make a diversion to Frome to call in on an Aladdin's cave of a store – Raves from the Grave.

It is situated in the old town on a medieval street full of interesting shops, and I am confident it is the only record shop in the world that has an open leat running across the front of the store. A leat is an artificial watercourse – a bit like a stream. During my years of calling there I have twice tripped over it and ended up with my foot in the water. On one occasion I noticed an ambulance crew attending to somebody there, so it seems that I am not the only accident-prone one around. In fact, I understand 'watching the tourists fall down the leat' is an established local pastime.

Raves from the Grave is the sort of shop that you feel you remember from childhood with piles of stock everywhere. It never ceases to amaze me that the staff seem to know where everything is located. There are boxes under the counter and a back room full of videos. Raves from the Grave is certainly the only store I visit these days that still takes a three-figure sum on video sales each month. It is a shop that I enjoy visiting as a customer – there are always some collectable classics amongst the boxes.

Raves from the Grave have an astonishing amount of stock: 53,000 LPs, 27,000, 7" singles, 24,000 CDs, 7,000 DVDs, 4,000 videos and about 10,000 greetings cards, a consequence of owner Richard Churchyard branching out into a greetings card shop. This, unfortunately, did not work out, so Raves now helps to offload his leftover stock.

However, the silver lining to this piece of misfortune is that Richard has now turned the card shop into a vinyl-only shop, which is doing a fantastic trade. Vinyl is seeing real market resurgence, and the shop has many regular customers who travel miles to look through its superb collection. Without doubt his biggest customers are Japanese vinyl dealers, who regularly spend hundreds of pounds at a time.

Richard was a shop manager at WHSmith in Notting Hill Gate when he decided that corporate life was not for him. He looked for a town without a record shop already in place, and finally settled on Frome. Raves from the Grave opened in 1997. Richard tells me he has never regretted the decision and, despite being skint, has never been happier. In addition to running his shop, Richard also plays in a number of local bands, of which the most famous is an Abba tribute band called S.O.S. He plays the part of Benny, playing the keyboards in his white suit. The band has had significant success, playing Glastonbury and touring Germany and Poland. Any Abba fan should pay the shop a visit, as his collection of Abba stock is unrivalled.

Another band that he is a member of is Pretenders 2. The band features Raves from the Grave staff member Nicky on lead vocals. Other members of the long-serving team are Simon, who combines working in the shop with teaching guitar and saxophone, and Andrew, who runs the vinyl shop and does the administration.

The shop counts Van Morrison and *Wicker Man* director Robin Hardy amongst their regular customers.

Another regular is Porn Man. I assumed he was somebody who came in and asked for dirty DVDs, but it turns out that most weeks he comes in to buy a few CDs, then a week or so later, he returns to sell them back to Richard, so he is really 'Pawn Man'. His CDs are then put in the second-hand section, from which he will often re-purchase them when his cash flow improves. For one band – Overkill – he has bought/sold/re-bought their catalogue three times over.

Some of the more unusual requests Raves have had to sort out include customers looking for music by Ernie Stubbs (Ernest Tubb); Ralph Horris (Rolf Harris) and those kings of electronic progressive rock who, doubtless, enjoy the occasional steak meal, Barclay James Harvester.

One late afternoon I called on Richard, and he was playing the worst CD I had ever heard in my life. Two customers were laughing their heads off at how bad it was. Richard told us that he put it on at closing time to clear the shop. After the laughter died down, Richard asked me if I, too, felt that it was the worst piece of music I had ever heard. I replied that, in 20 years of selling music, I could safely say I had never heard anything as bad.

When I asked who was playing, Richard told me it was a band called Lemp Bek ... and that I had sold him the album the previous month whilst telling him it was going to be the next big thing in modern jazz! Damn – the laughter started up again.

I learned a lesson that day – do not make claims about anything until you have heard the material. I did explain to the assembled throng that my company releases about 60 CDs each month, and that I cannot listen to all of them ... but I acknowledged that it was a pretty feeble excuse.

I genuinely feel that Raves From The Grave will be one of the 'Last Shops Standing' as, quite possibly, there is still 20 years of stock currently in the shops and in storage. Richard also needs to get rid of all of those greetings cards. If you do pay him a visit, here is a top tip – ask him for a complimentary greetings card with your purchase. I am sure he will oblige.

* * *

From Frome I travelled the short distance to Trowbridge, a town renowned for its annual folk festival – the Village Pump Festival. It was there that I called in on probably the only independent record shop that I have ever dealt that has felt no need to open accounts with the major suppliers EMI, Sony BMG, Universal and Warner.

Brian Ottway, of the Trowbridge-based Sounds Interesting, has been one of my most remarkable customers. Born and brought up in Gravesend, Brian came into the music industry whilst rising through the ranks of the banking world. When he was still a teenager, and whilst working at the local NatWest Bank, Brian took the bold decision to hire the Woodville

Hall – the town's largest venue – and started promoting bands like Barclay James Harvest, Blodwyn Pig and Gentle Giant to play there.

Shortly after, Brian was headhunted by the Bank of Montreal and was offered an opportunity to work in Canada. It was a difficult decision for Brian as, deep down, he quite fancied taking on Harvey Goldsmith in the world of promoting concerts, but the financial offer combined with the excitement of working in a new country appealed to him.

Brian worked at the bank for eight years before the lure of rock promotion proved too compelling. He successfully went into business in a nightclub in British Columbia, promoting up-and-coming comic talent as well as rock artists such as Donovan and Long John Baldry. During this period, Brian required that every band that played at the club should sign a copy of its latest CD for his own collection and to remind him of each gig. After six years, Brian had amassed an impressive collection of these signed CDs. However, one night, the club was burgled and his collection, along with that night's takings, was lost. Using the local press, Brian appealed to every band that had played at his club to send him an autographed CD to replace his stolen collection. The national media picked up on the story, and during the next few months he was bombarded with hundreds of signed CDs. After a while he counted up the CDs and realised that he had been sent more than one thousand – many from bands which had never set foot in the club.

When both of his parents fell ill, Brian decided to sell his business and return home. After several months back in England, he realised that he needed to resume earning money and an advert in the *Daily Mail*, for selling franchises to service corner shops and petrol stations with cheap CDs caught his eye.

The idea was that Brian would leave a counter display full of cheap CDs at each outlet. Each month he was to call in and collect the money for CDs sold and replenish the stock – it seemed straightforward enough.

Brian met with the management of the franchising company, Music World Ltd, who agreed that, in return for an investment of £7,000, he would be provided with 60 outlets and a selection of bargain CDs. These CDs were of extremely low quality, and although they were performed by some famous-name bands, they often featured only one member of the actual band and were not original recordings.

Unfortunately for Brian, after investing he only received twenty confirmed outlets and, even worse, Music World went into administration three weeks later. Brian's house was full of CDs that he needed to shift –

and quickly. He and his wife, Susie, toured Wiltshire in an attempt to convince more outlets to stock his cheap CDs. His house was looking less like a home and more like a mini CD warehouse.

Drastic action was called for. Brian hired a tiny shop in town – the rent was only £100 a week. His daughter, Angela, was studying A-levels by correspondence course to obtain a place at university, and, as she was studying at home, Brian installed her in his new Trowbridge shop where she could attempt to learn whilst selling CDs. The shop opened just in time for Christmas 2000.

It soon became obvious to Brian that trying to find new outlets for his CDs was like flogging a dead horse, so instead he tried his luck at local markets. After a few successful weeks' market sales, Brian soon realised that he was selling through his stock and that he would need fresh product. He opened accounts with Proper, Gold's and Midland Records, and to this day has traded without ever purchasing from the major suppliers – now, I am the only rep who ever visits him.

Sounds Interesting soon outgrew its original site and moved twice before settling at its current location. It is one of the independent shops that has embraced Amazon.com and has its own page on their website. It is classed as an Amazon partner, and significant sales can be generated each month in return for a small fee. The way the system works is that, if somebody orders an item on Amazon.com that is out of stock, Amazon lists its partners who stock that item, and they can then fulfil the customer's order.

Brian told me about the worst purchase he ever made – he was offered, and took up the offer of Danielle Steel DVDs at an amazingly low price. He sunk £2,000 into this offer and, that same evening, sitting at home watching TV, an advert drained the colour from his cheeks – "Starting tomorrow in the *Daily Mail*, collect the first in a series of free DVDs by Danielle Steel". To this day he is still trying to get rid of the job lot that he bought.

The *Daily Mail* is no longer Brian's newspaper of choice. Along with their sister paper, *The Mail on Sunday*, they have created an immense amount of problems for independent record shops, as they are foremost in the recent trend of giving away free CDs and DVDs. These giveaways are known as covermounts.

The biggest bombshell of this kind came on 24 July 2007 when the music industry was rocked on its heels. *The Mail on Sunday* announced that Prince – one of the most famous artists in the world – would be releasing his new CD *Planet Earth* as a free covermount with that week's newspaper.

Paul Quirk, co-chairman of the Entertainment Retailers Association (ERA) said that the giveaway "beggars belief ... It would be an insult to all those record stores who have supported Prince throughout his career and would be yet another example of the damaging covermount culture which is destroying any perception of value around recorded music."

"The Artist Formerly Known as Prince should know that with behaviour like this he would soon be the Artist Formerly Available in Record Stores. And I say that to all the other artists who may be tempted to dally with *The Mail on Sunday*." By not uniting and telling Prince that he risked not being stocked in UK record stores, it just encouraged more artists to go down the covermount route.

Lenny Kravitz recently released new tracks and several greatest hits via *The Mail on Sunday*. So did McFly, and it is hard to believe that *The Mail on Sunday* readers are McFly's target audience. Ray Davis from The Kinks released a solo album through that well-known CD distributor, *The Sunday Times*. Artists of the stature of Paul McCartney and David Bowie are joining the covermount culture, so shops are right to be worried. Are we to reach a position in which the big five distributors are Universal, EMI, Warner, Sony and *The Mail on Sunday*?

In September 2008 the *Daily Mail* came up with the ultimate promotion. On twelve consecutive days they gave away an original 80s album. It started off with Spandau Ballet's album *True*, and then over the course of the next eleven days readers could obtain albums by Culture Club, Terence Trent D'Arby , Paul Young, Bonnie Tyler, Haircut 100, Marillion, The Human League, Dexy's Midnight Runners, Adam and the Ants and Simple Minds. To obtain the CD, customers simply had to cut a voucher out of the newspaper and take it to Tesco or WHSmith and redeem it for the album. So the value of those CDs is now the same as a Tesco carrier bag. In October of the same year *The Times* and *The Sunday Times* raised the bar higher by offering six seminal albums free:

- The Doors – *Strange Days*
- Love – *Forever Changes*
- Joy Division – *Closer*
- The Jesus and Mary Chain – *Psychocandy*
- New Order – *Power, Corruption & Lies*
- Echo and the Bunnymen – *Ocean Rain*.

The titles featured in these promotions are now worthless. Who will ever pay £7 for them knowing they could have obtained them for free?

Unfortunately, unless the industry unites behind an intelligent strategy, there are going to be a lot more covermount promotions, as there is no doubt that other newspapers will follow suit. Who can blame them? It is a great way to attract new readers.

Let us look at it from the *The Mail on Sunday*'s perspective. It normally sells around 2 million copies per issue and its three largest circulation figures, ever, have been:

- 2.9 million with the free Prince CD;
- 2.6 million at the time of the death of Princess Diana; and
- 2.3 million with a free CD of Mike Oldfield's *Tubular Bells* (a promotion objected to by Mike Oldfield himself).

With the paper retailing at £1.50, the Prince promotion generated a one-off revenue hike of £1.35 million, and the probability that a percentage of those new readers would be converted into buying the news-paper on a more regular basis. It is this conversion into a regular readership that *The Mail on Sunday* relies on.

The cost to the newspaper was a fee of around £250,000 to Prince and a further £750,000 on manufacturing, advertising and promotion.

Looked at from Prince's point of view, his career had been in decline for a long time and here was an opportunity to reach nearly 3 million people. No doubt a proportion of them would enjoy it and check out his back cata-logue. On top of that he was paid £250,000 – a sum far in excess of what he would have earned had the album been released in the orthodox way through UK retailers. During the 21-night run of Prince shows at the O2 Arena, in Greenwich, London, a copy of the album was 'given away' with each ticket (priced at £31.21) for the show. That is something like 420,000 copies shifted!

There is no longer the same core demand for items of recorded music that there used to be – in whatever format or whomever is selling it. Prince can sell 420,000 concert tickets in one month in the UK, but he'd be lucky to sell 35,000 copies of his new album, period. Fans, and people in general, will pay vast sums of money for a unique concert experience – especially by an act of his standing, but they will not pay even modest sums for another of his recordings.

Artists often say that they just want to get their music out to as many people as possible – and actually it seems that this is true. Of course they would like people to pay for it, but now that the fans have called their bluff, it seems that Prince has proven as good as his word.

My thoughts are that if newspapers did covermounts that featured a couple of tracks off the new album plus a collection of previously released material, then this would encourage the public to buy the new CD. It is when the whole album is given away that problems are created. None of my customers have been as badly affected by covermounts as Brian, as he still has hundreds of Danielle Steele DVDs so, if you are a fan of her, pop into Trowbridge, as I am sure Brian will offer you a great deal to take some off his hands.

One customer whom Brian will never forget is the Vicky Pollard look-alike who left him holding the baby. This is their conversation:

Customer: "Do you stock The Beatles?"
Brian takes her to the section and shows her the titles.
Customer: "Are these bootlegs?"
Brian: "No, they are legitimate CDs."
Customer: "Aren't The Beatles all dead? They must be bootlegs, because they died before CDs were invented."

For five minutes Brian tried to explain to the lady that thousands of CDs featured dead artists, but to no avail. The lady exited the shop, still denying the legality of Brian's CDs.

Ten minutes later she popped back and asked, "Did I leave my baby in here?" She had, and Brian had spent the time playing with the baby, waiting for the mad mother to return and collect her.

Another customer who was confused over bootlegs came in and asked whether Brian had any CDs by Irish old-timers The Fureys. Brian brought over the three CDs he had in stock.

"These are bootlegs aren't they?"

An exasperated Brian tried to reassure her that they were bona-fide, but the lady was convinced she was right. "Why do you think they are bootlegs?" Brian asked.

"Well, I went to see The Fureys last night and they were much older than that band on the album cover." Brian gently explained that the CDs have been recorded over a period of 20 years and that everybody ages.

A customer came up to the counter and whispered to Brian did he have any bachelor DVDs. Brian explained that he didn't have any DVDs, but he did have some CDs. The gentleman looked puzzled and somewhat disappointed. Brian offered to show him the selection. Off they ambled to the easy listening section, where Brian picked up the *The Very Best of The Bachelors* CD and proceeded to read the track listing. The gentleman started laughing and gave Brian a gentle dig in the ribs. "I am not after DVDs by The Bachelors. I am after bachelor DVDs – you know – the titles you normally keep on the top shelf." Brian explained that the only DVDs on his top shelf played music.

A sweet old lady came into the shop and told Brian that she was a huge Buddy Holly fan and had been searching everywhere for a CD, but nobody had a copy. She had heard about Sounds Interesting's reputation for tracking down those hard-to-find releases. Brian smiled and told her not to worry, as he would do his utmost to track down her request. Unfortunately, when the lady informed him of the title even Brian realised this task was impossible – the CD she was after was 'Buddy Holly sings The Beatles'. Despite Buddy dying before The Beatles were formed, the lady was adamant that the CD existed.

His shop takes great pride in the customer service it delivers. Assisted by his team of John, Alex and Rochelle, no matter how obscure the item requested, the team leaves no stone unturned in its determination to find it. There is a sign in the shop which declares, "We specialise in – 'I bet you haven't got it'". This sign acts like a red rag to a bull to many customers as, throughout the day, many of them will offer challenges. Mind you, if they do have the requisite item in stock, customers often then feel obliged to purchase it.

Their greatest challenge was when a man came in and said he had heard a song with the word 'balistine' in it, and he could not get the song out of his head, although that was the only word he knew. Brian found a website that published lyrics and eventually tracked down the song to a CD by Barclay James Harvest, which was available only in America. Thankfully, the customer was overjoyed when Brian presented him with a copy of the CD. I asked Brian if he would be one of the 'Last Shops Standing'.

"Of course," was his reply, "only it's likely to be in Cornwall". (Brian would like to end his music retail career there).

As I only deal with two record stores in the whole of Cornwall there is certainly an opportunity there – I still find it hard to fathom how Newquay, the surfing town, no longer has an independent record shop.

I do think Sounds Interesting will still be around in five years, as they learned a long time ago that you cannot survive on record sales alone and now they have a diverse range of stock).

*   *   *

From Trowbridge I move on to the historic city of Bath. Due to the problems in finding a place to park in the summer, I always call into Bath first thing in the morning or as my last call of the day. The shop I visit there should be a tourist attraction in itself, as it looks as if it has hardly changed in a hundred years. Opened in 1848, and arguably the oldest record shop in the world, Duck, Son & Pinker is as a record shop would have looked in the 90s – the 1890s. If *Are You Being Served*'s Grace Brothers was a record store, then this would be it. At any moment you expect to hear the cry of "I'm free!" or hear a joke about Mrs Slocomb's pussy. The shop is in desperate need of a lick of paint and some of the racking is so old that it is obvious that it was designed to hold 78s.

What it does have, however, is massive character, old-fashioned charm and quality customer service. William Duck founded the shop originally to sell musical instruments. Then, in 1878, he took his son Edward Duck and friend Thomas Pinker into partnership and thereafter the shop was known as Duck, Son & Pinker.

The company expanded over the next 50 years and incorporated a further nine West Country music businesses, including the famous Milson & Son. By 1944 it had six branches across Bath, Hereford, Clifton, Swindon, Swansea and Bedminster. It is a sign of the times that the Bath branch is the last Milson & Son standing. To gauge how large a company they once were, here are some fascinating facts:

- In its first 60 years of trading it sold 62,500 pianos.
- During the 1930s it averaged 65,000 piano tunings per year (and to this day it is still a piano tuner).
- During the First World War 44 of its employees fought for their country and in the Second World War it was 45 – astonishingly only one member of staff, a Mr G H Ryall, was killed in action.

The company name is famous throughout the West Country and it certainly inspires loyalty amongst its staff. The music department is divided into two sections – Classical and Popular. When I called on them, the three M's – Mary, Maureen and Martine, ran the popular department. I used to think it sounded like a 60s cartoon series featuring a young girl, a dog and a mouse. I imagined that the main criterion for obtaining employment there was that you had to be female with a name beginning with 'M'.

Both Maureen and Mary have been there for more than 30 years whilst Joe, the gentleman who ran the classical department, has been at the shop for 40 years – so four members of staff, past and present, had more than 110 years of service between them. In recent years the 'M' theory has been disproved, as Sabrina and Lucy have joined the staff.

My memories of the store include the time I was with my son Ben, who was five years old at the time. I introduced him to the staff by telling him that this was my favourite record shop. My son then announced to everybody that in every record shop that I had ever taken him into I had said that it was my favourite shop.

One day I was selling my albums to Maureen and had brought in samples of around 25 CDs that I placed by my feet in order to bring them up to the counter one at a time. I then noticed a man slowly moving closer to me. Perhaps he was just trying to be friendly, I thought, until, to my astonishment, he took off his coat, placed it over my CDs and slowly bent down, picked up the coat and CDs in one bundle and started to walk out of the shop. I tapped him on the shoulder and said, "Excuse me, but I think you'll find that those CDs are mine". He handed them back to me and apologised, saying, "Sorry, I thought somebody had just left them there". I could not believe his cheek.

The shop has had its fair share of unusual customers including the man who was looking for vegan CDs. Mary told the gentleman that she did not think that any CDs were edible. (I do recall an album a while ago by Arrah and the Ferns called *Evan is a Vegan*, but I guess it was not that he was after). I presume he was after CDs that had no animal by-product used in their manufacture, and I cannot really see the day when record companies print the ingredients of their CDs on the sleeves.

Another unusual customer is the 'Bird Woman of Bath'. This lady has been shopping at Duck, Son & Pinker for years, but purchases only CDs and DVDs with pictures of birds on the sleeves. It does not matter whether they are classical, pop, folk or country – if it has a bird on the cover, she has to have it.

I am confident that Duck, Son & Pinker will be one of the 'Last Shops Standing', as, after all, they've been getting it right for more than 160 years.

* * *

The following day I travelled down the M5 to visit my customers in Devon, starting with Martian Records in Exeter. If any of you makes this journey make sure that you check out Humphrey, the life-size fibreglass camel positioned in a field near the Bridgewater turn-off. He has been there for more than 25 years. At Christmas he is festooned in decorations, and during the rest of the year he is dressed up in a variety of different outfits. He makes me smile whenever I pass, as he looks over the hedge staring down the M5. On this particular day I noticed that he had a baby camel with him – apparently something had been going on in fibreglass-camel land.

Having been school friends in Broadclyst near Exeter, Ian McCord and Martin Alford started Martian Records – both had found jobs working in offices, but one night they were talking together and thinking that there must be something more that they could do with their lives. As they were both huge music fans, they came up with the idea of starting a market stall selling second-hand CDs. Both boys packed in their jobs and went on a tour of record shops and car-boot sales, buying music bargains and collectables. For the first few months of 1989 they had a pitch at a variety of one-day markets across Devon. After six months they were offered a regular pitch at Exmouth Market and that is still one of their outlets twenty years later.

They also foolishly took up the offer of a pitch at St Nicholas Market in Bristol – a mere 160-mile round trip. Soon realising that this stall was not cost-effective, the boys relocated to a site in Weston-super-Mare, which is now in its fifteenth year of trading. Weston and Exmouth have proven to be completely different markets – Exmouth is strong on rock music, but the clientele in Weston is older and gentler, with artists such as Foster & Allen and Daniel O'Donnell amongst the big sellers.

In 1994 the boys opened their flagship store in Exeter and, soon, their fourth shop in Taunton. Working really hard, the Martian boys also opened stores in Yeovil, Honiton and Cheltenham but, unfortunately, none of these stores achieved the volume of sales necessary to survive. They were especially unlucky in Cheltenham, as it is a town with a large student population, but their shop opened just as the students were beginning to download music en masse.

The Exeter shop is a real rock shop, managed by long-serving staff member Marcus. Ian highlighted to me how well it does with limited-edition rock titles, whilst being frustrated by the lack of support from the record companies. He cites the Slipknot album *All Hope is Gone* as a classic example. Martian ordered plenty, but still sold out within a week and then could not obtain any more supply.

For independent shops to survive they need to be able to sell physical product, which has something that is 'extra' not obtainable on download.

In the 80s record companies would release products on different formats, for example 7"; 12"; CD singles; double packs; some with free posters etc. These became collectable by fans. I do recall Frankie Goes to Hollywood putting out thirteen different re-mixes of one of their singles and hard-core fans would buy all thirteen. Gallup clamped down by making re-mixes ineligible for the chart, which ended a lot of the interest in collectable product.

If the record companies care about independent shops then they need to produce more special editions and more releases with bonus DVDs. They also need to do it in a manner unlike what happened during the 90s, when the record companies produced bonus discs, but in so doing shafted their own customers.

This exploitation happened principally to the fans of boy bands – a CD would be released, followed a few months later by the same CD but with a few bonus tracks. Consequently, record shops would be inundated with teenagers seeking to change their CD. Not content with this, the record companies would then release the CD for a third time, but with a bonus disc included, so fans got ripped off again. Of course, their target audience were those people who would buy all three versions uncritically. However, this short-term tactic soon backfired badly as the public wised up, and lots of people stopped buying CDs on their first week of release – in favour of waiting to see in what enhanced state it would later be released.

Exeter was once a great town for record shops, but in 2008 the last of the other independent shops in the city, Solo Music, closed, so now Martian's competition comes from HMV and from an unexpected source. There is now a retailer on the high street that stocks music in nearly 700 stores across the country – its name is Oxfam.

Revenue turnover on music alone has impressed Oxfam's management to the extent that they have now opened six specialist music stores – in Exeter, Glasgow, Edinburgh, London, Reading and Southampton. It is impossible to fault Oxfam – a superb organisation doing a fabulous job, and the more people who visit the stores the better, but what I did find unusual was that their prices are comparable with other record shops. I had expected its shops to be full of bargains, but this was not the case.

Another aspect of retail that has changed for the independent is the loss of the Christmas market. Ten years ago December would be one long rush, as people purchased their Christmas presents. Now, however, the rush starts two shopping days before Christmas when people realise they are too late to buy presents online.

I asked Ian about the future and he pointed out that diversity is what it is all about, and that Martian is practising this, as it has recently added clothing to the lines it stocks.

Ian also mentioned to me that one customer referred to Martian as a novelty shop and that, "That's what we will all become – novelty shops".

I have no doubt that Martian will be amongst the 'Last Shops Standing'. The boys have been shrewd in that all their sites are in locations just off the main drag. Therefore their rent and rates are well below the average.

Like nearly all independent record shops, Martian's sales were badly affected by the chaotic release of the Metallica *Death Magnetic* album in September 2008.

It is fair to say that, for independent shops, the Metallica album was the most anticipated release of the year so far – the typical Metallica fan is just the sort of music collector who shops in record stores in preference to going into supermarkets and buying his CD with his weekly shop. But, whilst the album was shipped out to major stores – supermarkets, HMV, Zavvi, etc – on time, the independent shops did not receive their stock until a day, and in some cases two days, later.

I received so many e-mails from disgruntled shop owners. Below is just one of them, from Sandra, who has a little rock-specialist shop called Aardvark Music, in Paignton in Devon. It illustrates the frustrations of that day well.

Hi Graham,

Being an independent retailer, to survive these days, you simply cannot afford to stock mainstream music. You have to stock more diverse tastes and more obscure genres and, in our case, being situated in a small town with both Woolworths and Tesco within a five-minute walking distance, this generally means classic rock, punk, hip-hop and heavy metal. As a result one of the biggest releases of the year for us, and probably quite a few other small independents, is the new Metallica album, *Death Magnetic*.

As promised, here are the events of today (Wednesday 10 September 2008) as more evidence of how hard/almost impossible it is to survive as an independent music retailer:

We opened up the shop this morning with one priority in mind...

to chase up our suppliers and make sure that our order for Metallica's new album *Death Magnetic* would be with us in time for its worldwide release on Friday 12 September 2008. Being one of the biggest releases of the year for us and, like many of the remaining independents, having some loyal return customers, we wanted to make sure it would be with us by the end of the next day. We e-mailed our particular supplier who informed us that they did not have any copies of the album left in stock, as they had already sent out their first lot (being a single store we didn't expect to be high up the list!) but that more would be coming in at some point during the day. Reassured, we then went about our usual routines of the day-to-day running of the shop.

At about midday, a customer of ours came in and asked us if we had the new Metallica album. We told him that we would definitely be stocking it but that it wasn't released until Friday, so imagine our shock/horror when he replied, "Well, Woolworths have got it." "You must be confused," we told him, "what, actually out for sale? You can actually go into Woolworths right now and purchase a copy and walk out with it today?"

"Yes," he replied.

Still not 100 per cent convinced, I went to my local Woolworths. When I got there, there was no big display promoting this new release, as there nearly always is, and there were none of those display cases on the shelves everywhere that Woolworths usually use to advertise something new so I started to think this may have been a wind-up, but just as I was about to leave, I spotted it. There it was, one solitary display case, sat at number ten on the Woolworths chart wall! I went to the counter and asked if the new Metallica album was out yet and was told that it was. I said that I thought that it wasn't due to be released until Friday but the clueless assistant simply said, "I don't know about that, but we got them last night and were told to put them out today."

Enraged, I went back to my shop where I decided to telephone a few other shops. I contacted the local Zavvi store in the next town about three miles from me and they too had it for sale. I asked about its early release and was told by the counter staff that they had received an e-mail that morning from their head office telling them to put it out today. She wasn't sure but she thought it was something to do with one of the supermarkets starting to sell it early.

Next I rang the nearest HMV, which is about 30 miles away. Once again, to my dismay, I was told the CD was for sale. Once again I asked about the release date and once again I was told that they had received a message telling them to start selling it today, though this assistant told me that no one had told him why.

I could not believe what was happening. I had not received my stock let alone any message telling me to start selling it! I started to ring the small independents in my area, first, a friend of mine with a shop in a town about ten miles away, then the ones in the nearest city. The more I talked to them, the worse the picture got from the independents' point of view. It was the same for them as it was for me. None of them had received their stock and only one of them had been informed by a rep to start selling them today ... even though he didn't have any!!! It was just another kick in the teeth for the independent retailers. They were all absolutely livid and talking to them I learned that they had all been offered different stories as to why the release date had changed; from supermarkets selling them early to the album being leaked on the Internet. What was also quite interesting was that they had all said where these CDs were being sold, they weren't being heavily promoted or advertised like they usually are. Was this some kind of secret? Were these businesses meant to be selling them yet? I decided to try and find out.

I started by telephoning ERA, the Entertainment Retailers Association and 'champion' of the independent retailer. I knew I'd probably be late to the party and that they'd have the situation under control, but I just wanted to know why. When I got through I asked about the situation concerning the new Metallica album release date and to my surprise (I'm being sarcastic now!) was informed by the person on the other end of the phone that they didn't know what I was talking about. I was put on hold whilst they went to find out, and when they took me off hold they told me that they had just received an e-mail of a similar nature and that they would telephone Universal Music, the European distributor for the album, and get back to me with an answer.

I decided to phone Universal myself. I was put through to the team leader of the information centre, a man called John, and I asked him what was going on. As far as he knew, someone, and he didn't know who, had started selling the album online so somebody from Mercury, Metallica's label, had told Universal to ship out as much stock as they had and to tell retailers to start selling it as soon as they got it. I asked what percentage of that stock went to independent retailers and he told me that he did not have that information. When I told him that none of the independents in my area had got any stock, but that all the major stores had, he said that he would try and find out that information and get back to me, but it wouldn't be until tomorrow. When I asked why the independents had not been given the message to start selling as soon as they got the stock, he said that Universal did not have the contact information for all the independents.

Now, I don't know if this is representative of what happened around the country, but for it to have even happened in one town is not right. Why isn't there an exact reason for the change of release date? Why, if there has been a legitimate change of release date, is it still listed as 12/09/2008 on all of the Internet sites, both retailers and information sites? Why, if everyone is meant to be selling it today, isn't it being heavily promoted in a lot of stores? Why wasn't everyone informed of this decision to change the release and not only the big nationals? Why haven't a lot of the independents received their stock of the new album but the nationals have plenty? I have since read on the Internet that a shop in France started selling the new album two weeks ago! Metallica know about this but don't seem overly concerned, which is strange for them. People are asking why hasn't anything been done about this as it's not released until the 12th? I'm not asking that. I'm asking where did they get their stock two weeks in advance of the release date?

With no answers, and no stock, it shows what you have to face on a nearly daily basis as an independent music retailer. It also demonstrates perfectly why there will soon be none left.

Speak with you soon,
Sandra

I forwarded this e-mail to various people in the music press. A couple of weeks later Aardvark Music received an apology by phone from Universal and the next day a large box of free stock arrived. Maybe it was a genuine mistake. I will leave you to make up your own mind.

Many shops questioned whether Universal were trying to close them down. I do not believe that for one second – every business knows that it is crucial to look after their big customers and the sad truth is that independent record shops are not big customers any longer.

One shop owner told me that, when he questioned his sales rep about the Metallica release, he was informed – off the record – that independent shops are not at the bottom of the priority pile – they are no longer even in the pile. And that observation just about sums up why your local record shop is fighting to survive.

In August 2008, Universal announced some good news and some bad news for independent shops. In the run up to Christmas, the good news was that it would be releasing some of their key CD releases in a deluxe version as well as normal versions, with a different price for each. The deluxe editions would include bonus tracks, lyrics, photographs and exclusive packaging. Universal compared this policy with the book industry, in which customers are offered both hardback and paperback versions of individual titles. If record companies had vision they would have done the deluxe packaging as a simultaneous release ten years ago.

Instead they went down the road of releasing normal versions and three months later releasing a further version with a bonus track and calling it a limited edition.

The bad news for independents was that Universal also announced its plan to release 500 albums containing overlooked classics, rarities and exclusive tracks – a brilliant idea, and one that would, in normal circumstances, be guaranteed to get thousands of fans rushing down to the record shops. However, the albums will be available only through Lost Tunes – which is what Universal describe as their online take on the local record store. If these albums had been released through record shops instead of online it would have showed the shops that Universal do care about them.

* * *

Until 2008 Exeter was also the home of Solo Music, at that point the largest independently owned chain of record shops in the South West. It started off in Truro in 1989, with other shops subsequently opening in Exeter, Barnstaple and Salisbury. Today, because of the difficult trading conditions facing independent record shops, when shop leases have expired they have not been renewed, and so Solo now trades solely from its Barnstaple outlet.

Owners Maggie Garratt and Penny Keen first met at university in London. Maggie's early career had been at Virgin Records, starting in her home city of Birmingham back in 1977.

She recalled that on her first day a man called in and asked if he could listen to the album *Dark Side of the Moon* by Pink Floyd. Maggie fetched the album from the racks and proceeded to put it on the turntable, but failed to notice that she had put the record on at 45rpm instead of 33rpm. As the shop was so busy, Maggie did not notice that Pink Floyd was sounding like Pinky & Perky on helium. Luckily for her neither did the customer who told her the album was far out and he would take it. Only after he left did one of her assistants ask why Pink Floyd had been played at that speed.

Maggie enjoyed working for Virgin and quickly rose through the ranks from area manager to commercial director, which involved her relocating to London. Like everybody who worked at Virgin during that period, she remembers it with great fondness and has happy memories of Richard Branson's parties at The Manor.

After a few years Maggie found herself working seven days a week and it was then that she had the idea to become self-employed. She resigned from Virgin; teamed up with her university friend Penny; found a suitable site in Truro; and raised the necessary funds (which was not too difficult, having walked into the bank armed with a glowing reference from Richard Branson) to start Solo Music.

Solo recognised the importance of supporting local talent and started promoting gigs at Exeter University. One day a shy young band asked if they might be allowed to be a support act at one of these events. Maggie explained that they already had three bands playing, but that she was happy to accommodate them providing they went on early.

The event started late as the band got lost and could not find Exeter University – despite the fact that it came from Teignmouth, just a few miles away. The young band blew the crowd away and it was difficult for the bands that had to follow them. From that night Maggie knew that the shy young men would go far – Muse was the band's name.

Over the next couple of years Muse released three singles independently and Solo sold hundreds of copies. The shop never took a penny from the band for selling their records, as they were just keen to help out local talent. Later, when the band signed to Maverick they did two more gigs for Solo – the last one at a time when it was filling stadiums.

Surprisingly though, Muse does not hold the record for the biggest-ever crowd at a Solo gig. That honour goes to The Wurzels. The band's record company, EMI, asked if they could play a gig in the shop to promote their new CD *Best of the Wurzels*. Maggie admits that she is no great fan and completely underestimated the popularity of the band, so much so that when they turned up early to do a sound-check, she asked them what their day jobs were. The Wurzels were unimpressed, remarking that they were usually paid thousands for a gig.

My favourite personal appearance story from Solo was the time The Levellers agreed to do a gig. Hundreds of people had gathered in the store before Maggie received a call from the band informing her that they were going to be seriously late. The crowd were becoming restless, and Maggie was worried about how they could placate the impatient mass. There was only one thing for it – five minutes later she came down from the Solo kitchen carrying a tray full of tea.

The Levellers eventually turned up – two hours late. By then the Solo team had despatched gallons of tea. I cannot get the vision out of my head of all the crusties sitting around with a 'nice cuppa', waiting for The Levellers to arrive.

The last few years have been very tough for Maggie and Penny and it has been especially difficult downsizing from four shops to one. However, despite numerous setbacks they are still going and their enthusiasm for music remains undiminished. They have decided to concentrate on selling folk, blues, jazz, world and classical and to leave the supermarkets to cater for the pop/rock fans of Barnstaple.

Another shop in Exeter I can recommend is Rooster Records in Fore Street owned by Jamie Fennell and his partner Sheryl. He gave up a career as a lawyer, having been in a practice for ten years, just to follow his dream of running his own record shop and hasn't looked back since. He gave his old pin-stripe work suit to his Brother-In-Law, who runs a gardening shop in Bath, to put on his scarecrow!

Jamie has some great tales amongst my favourites is the day he was playing a CD by the Byrds in the shop when who should walk though the door ... none other than Gene Parsons from the band. !!! In truth Jamie was going to see him in concert that evening so was getting in the mood, but had absolutely no idea he was going to come into his shop! And the bizarre thing was that one of his songs was playing as he walked in!!! Gene shook his head in disbelief and then shook Jamie's hand to introduce himself.

The shop has an excellent selection of second hand vinyl and CDs and

Jamie often visits people's homes to purchase record collections. On one occasion he went to see a collection and coming across a whole pile of CD cases with Rooster Records stickers on them. However, they were all empty. It was only then that the titles jogged his memory as having been stolen from the shop about a year earlier and here he was in the perpetrator's house having a cup of tea with him! Instead of confronting him … well, he was twice his size … he conveniently placed them in his bag while he was making a cuppa and later returned them to the racks in the shop. He was none the wiser.

When visiting Martian in Exeter I sometimes make time for a quick visit to see Julian at the Crediton Record Shop. It is a typical little record shop in a market town. Julian will never be one of our biggest customers, but we appreciate his business.

His stories include the occasion when a customer requested Gladys Knight and The Pimps. Another odd request was for a CD by a large Greek singer called Dennis Rissole.

It never ceases to amaze me what people ask for in record shops. My favourite tale came from David Williams who owned a shop called Tudor Tunes in Lichfield. A man came in one day and asked, "Do you by any chance have any bullets for a sawn-off shot gun?" Dave was tempted to say that he had "Rubber Bullets" by 10cc, but felt it wise just to decline the enquiry.

Two days later the local Post Office was held up by a man with a sawn-off shotgun – it looked like he had found some bullets somewhere.

Over the years I have had some funny titles to sell, but none more so than the release from the eccentric traditional Irish musician Derek Bell. He was a member of The Chieftains and was affectionately known as 'Ding Dong'. He was known for always wearing a red jumper (try finding a picture of the band without him in one). He also had a wicked sense of humour, no more evident than when he released his solo album *Derek Bell Plays With Himself*. As you can imagine I had a lot of fun selling that album.

* * *

From Exeter it is a short journey down the M5 to Newton Abbot, which is home to Phoenix Sounds. Will Webster took over ownership of Phoenix Sounds back in 2003 after buying out his business partner Dave Jones. It is an impressive looking store – very modern in design with a fantastic range of DVDs, far more than the average independent store. The reason it is named Phoenix Stores is that Dave had owned a previous record shop in Newton Abbott, which failed, so the idea of the Phoenix rising from the ashes appealed.

Like myself, Will found his way into the music industry via the job centre. In Will's case it was in Bristol and he started off working in Virgin Records as a singles buyer. In the 80s nearly every record shop had a singles buyer. The sales rep from Island records mentioned to Will one day that they had a young Liverpool band of whom they were expecting great things, and asked if the store would be happy to do a PA. The band in question was Frankie Goes To Hollywood. Its debut single was a little ditty called 'Relax'. By the time of the PA, 'Relax' was number one in the chart and Frankie Goes to Hollywood was the hottest band in the land. When the band arrived, a massive crowd greeted them. Nothing was too much trouble for the band and they signed hundreds of autographs and posed for everybody who requested a photograph.

After a while one of the band, who cannot be named for obvious reasons, sat down looking exhausted. Will had asked his friend Roger to help with security and he asked the tired-looking member if he could get him anything. The aforementioned band member replied, "I just feel like some coke." Eager to please, Roger rushed out to the newsagents across the road and purchased a bottle of Coca Cola. Arriving back at the shop, Roger handed the coke over to the band member, who rolled his eyes and replied in a thick Scouse drawl: "Thanks mate, but this wasn't the type of coke I was after."

Towards the end of the band's stay at the store Will asked them if they would pose for some pictures holding a poster saying "Frankie Supports The Bastille" – a Bristol nightclub, owned by Will's mate Dave Darling. The band was happy to oblige and Shane, a staff member who had persuaded Will that he was a quality photographer, snapped away. Will was eager to see the photos, and the next day he asked Shane if he had had them developed. "Sorry, Will. I forgot to put any film in the camera."

After Will's impressive performance in Bristol, he was soon given the chance to manage his own store. The only problem was that the store in question was in Torquay. But the chance to have his own shop in a seaside town appealed to Will, so he packed his swimming trunks, bucket and spade. However, by the time Will had moved to the coast, the smaller Virgin Records Stores had been bought by music retailer Our Price. Will was then asked to manage its branch at Newton Abbott, which was known as a manager's graveyard. This was the store you were moved to when Our Price wanted rid of you, and Will was no exception.

Disillusioned at working for Our Price, Will turned his back on the music industry and took up teaching. He remained a teacher for ten years and found it challenging and rewarding. However, once music is in your blood it never goes away, and when Dave offered him the chance to go into partnership, Will resigned and went to work at Phoenix Sounds. Unfortunately, Will returned to the CD retailing business at a time of major downturn. Dave himself became disillusioned, believing that there was no future in music, and offered Will the chance to buy his share in the store. So, suddenly, Will had his own business.

Swimming against the tide, Will invested heavily in a new site, which was more than twice the size of the original, with new racking and increased stock levels. It seemed to have worked – Will had no substantial competition as Our Price had long since closed down.

Will spoke to me about some of his most awkward customers. The first came into the store and asked for the new Frank Gillis album. Will searched high and low on his computer, but could find no sign of it, so he phoned up the import companies, who have databases covering every CD that has ever been released. Still no joy. Will tried other variations: Frank Gilles, Frank Gillas etc, but nothing pertinent existed. Will presumed the CD had not yet been released and asked the customer to come back the following week, when he might have more information. Week after week the customer called in for news on Frank. Exasperated, Will asked the customer to do more research. The next week, the customer came back and said Frank did the music for *Chariots of Fire*. It was then that Will realised that Frank Gillis was Vangelis.

At least Will was able to laugh at this customer, unlike the chap who brought ten 12" reggae singles to the counter and asked if he could listen to them all. As it was a busy Saturday afternoon, Will told him he could play only three of them. On hearing this the man leapt over the counter, pulled a knife out and bellowed his protest at poor Will. Luckily, the man's friends jumped over and restrained their infuriated companion. It is always great to see customers who are passionate about listening to music, but maybe this customer's enthusiasm over-stepped the mark.

Will and I had a conversation on how he felt the record companies had let the shops down and the one thing we agreed on was how many sales had been lost through radio stations playing tracks on the radio so far ahead of release dates. This problem is a consequence of the music industry scoring the most blatant own goal.

This is how it happens – a DJ on the radio plays, say, a new Oasis track and enthuses about what a fantastic new song it is. Unfortunately, the track is not to be released for another two months. A large number of listeners then visit the local record store and ask for the new Oasis song.

Shop assistant: "The new Oasis track has not been released yet."

Oasis fan: "But it must be – I have just heard it on the radio!"

Shop assistant: "Sorry, but we won't have it in for another two months."

Oasis fan leaves the store thinking the record shop has its facts wrong. As a fan he wants the track badly but, as the record shop does not yet stock it and he cannot legally download it, the only way he can obtain it is by illegal download. The music industry seems to be the only business that encourages its customers to break the law.

In the 70s, when I was growing up, if any of my favourite bands released a new record, I would get down to the record shop immediately after school on the day of release. Often I would not yet have even heard the record, as radio stations could play new material only from the day of release. The simultaneous release of records for radio stations to play and for the public to purchase created a buzz, which is now absent. Today it is common to hear a brilliant new song on the radio, yet by the time the song is available in the record stores – often two to three months later – it has been heard so many times that the appetite to buy has gone.

This has also led to the destruction of the chart. Playing songs up to two months before their release ensures that when a song eventually becomes available, people know the song so well that they either want it or they don't. Even worse are those DJs who play a song that is not scheduled for release for a while, but they do not announce the release date at all – allowing people to waste their time asking for titles not yet available. It upsets everybody.

One radical decision the industry should take is for product to be in store before radio play. This would create an environment in which people would go into shops regularly on a Monday morning to buy releases, which they know are going to be available. It would give records a longer selling life, as people would not lose interest in a song before its release. The net result would be that record shops would sell more products and everybody would be satisfied.

In the 60s and 70s it was very rare for songs to debut at number one – most songs would take four to five weeks to peak. Current practice has allowed a different pattern to develop – songs now often enter at the top of the chart on their first week of release, but on the subsequent week suffer a rapid decline. Some facts bear this out:

- During 1962 there were twelve different number ones.
- During 2004 there were thirty different number ones – of which sixteen entered at number one.

In the 60s Frank Sinatra's 'My Way' spent 49 weeks in the charts. In the 70s Judy Collins's 'Amazing Grace' hung around for 42 weeks, as did Frankie Goes to Hollywood's 'Relax' in the 80s. Nowadays, however, it is a momentous achievement for any song to occupy the charts for more than a month. Some number one's even struggle to stay in the charts after their debut week – McFly's double A-sided single 'Baby's Coming Back/Transylvania', released in May 2007, entered the chart at number one. By week two it was down to twenty, and in week three it had vanished completely.

In 2006 Orson debuted at number one with its song 'No Tomorrow', selling a measly 17,694 in its first week. Compare that with Wham, who in December 1984 sold more than 500,000 copies of 'Last Christmas' – and still did not top the charts. These figures show how fragile the singles market has become, and why so many independent record stores can no longer justify stocking them.

If the music industry does care, then one way forward would be to follow the example of supergroup The Raconteurs. They did something truly radical in the way they released their second album *Consolers of the Lonely*.

The band, formed by Jack White of The White Stripes and Brendan Benson, were unhappy with the marketing and hype that had surrounded the release of their debut album – the highly successful *Broken Boy Soldiers*, which spawned the worldwide hit 'Steady As She Goes'.

Consequently, the group announced on 18 March, via a press release, that their new album would be available one week later, on 25 March – to everyone and in every format – CD, vinyl, on the band's website and through iTunes. This is the press statement they released:

'The Raconteurs are happy to announce that in one week's time their second album, entitled *Consolers of the Lonely*, will be available everywhere. With this release, The Raconteurs are forgoing the usual months of lead time for press and radio set up, as well as forgoing the all-important 'first week sales'. We wanted to explore the idea of releasing an album everywhere at once and then marketing and promoting it thereafter. The Raconteurs would rather this release not be defined by its first week's sales, pre-release promotion, or by someone defining it for you before you get to hear it. The earliest date to have it available in every format at once became 25 March.'

The band went on to explain that they would not be doing any advance interviews or promotion on the album. I believe The Raconteurs should be applauded for the way in which they approached this project, as they have given fans the chance to hear an album at the same time as journalists and radio stations.

The normal method of releasing an album from a major company requires the spending of a fortune: advertisements in the music press; the hiring of pluggers to make sure the CD is played in advance on radio stations; and the release of copies to the media so that reviews coincide with the release date.

The Raconteurs release meant that nobody had been prejudiced by advanced reviews, something that has become almost impossible in the current climate of e-mail and blogs.

The standard method of promoting a new album can also have a downside – it needs only one influential journalist to review the album badly and suddenly the world will agree. Think of all those bands that produced superb first albums, yet whose second albums received poor reviews and their careers were finished. The lesson is don't believe the hype.

To illustrate this, I recall the press hailing the third Oasis album – *Be Here Now* – as a work of genius. *Q* magazine gave the album five stars and compared it with The Beatles' *Revolver*. Then, a couple of years later the magazine described it as a "disastrous, overblown folly" and as "the moment when Oasis, their judgement clouded by drugs and blanket adulation, ran aground on their own sky-high self-belief".

The album is now infamous for being the one most frequently offered to second-hand stores and charity shops. If you have a copy, try this experiment – find a record shop selling second-hand CDs and try to get it to purchase your copy of *Be Here Now* from you. I will be surprised if they don't burst out laughing. The album sold 420,000 copies on its first day of release, but if you require a copy now, simply go to any car boot sale and you will find lots of them. When it was released everybody loved it – now most people regard it as disappointing. My view – well, I quite like it, but then I never believe the hype. I asked Will if he still sold *Be Here Now* and he just laughed dismissively.

Since he moved from teaching Will admits to making lots of mistakes with his venture, but he is still glad that he made the switch into retailing. Newton Abbot is lucky to have such a fine record store, and if Will can keep making improvements Phoenix Sounds can be one of the 'Last Shops Standing'.

* * *

From Newton Abbott I drive to the town of Totnes, which has become a bit of a curiosity lately through gaining the attention of the national press as, reputedly, the UK's most hip place to live. I am calling on The Drift Record Shop. The town centre is a quirky mixture of shops selling New Age merchandise, ethnic clothes and vegetarian cafés and The Drift Record Shop sits quite well within the laid-back atmosphere that prevails. It is a unique shop specialising in world, folk and blues music and also has a cult film-rental library.

Jenny Morrison and her son, Rupert, run the operation, and I can confirm from having visited hundreds of record shops during my career that none are as tiny as The Drift Record Shop. Jenny is always keen to remind me that small is beautiful. It amazes me how much stock they hold – they have a real skill in utilising every inch of space.

Jenny found herself running a record shop by default. In 2003 her partner had been made redundant and, with his redundancy money, they decided that it was time to change the direction of their lives. A shop called World Music and Video was for sale, and Jenny and her family knew the business well because, as well as being regular customers, her son and daughter had both worked there. They made the owner an offer and were delighted when it was accepted. They all looked forward to their new exciting adventure.

They had just shaken hands on the deal when her partner's old company decided that they could not do without him after all and offered him a deal to return, which was too good to turn down. Jenny was left to run the new business having never worked in a shop before and having just qualified as a holistic therapist. It was a steep learning curve, as the video rental was dropping off at an alarming rate whilst everybody was switching to DVD. Jenny invested in stocking cult film DVDs and this turned out to be a shrewd move. Many other independent shops invested heavily in mainstream DVDs and had their fingers badly burnt. The invention of the DVD should have been the saviour of independent record stores, but instead it proved to be a major disappointment.

DVD was a fantastic format that appealed to anyone who was prepared to pay a premium for the chance to watch a quality film at home. Many stores enthusiastically embraced the format and devoted large areas of their shop space to it. Sadly, as soon as the format was established, a price war broke out – and again supermarkets led the way.

The format had no pricing structure and often there would be huge price discrepancies between stores. The record companies did huge deals with the supermarkets to promote blockbusters, leaving the independents at a disadvantage again as they were unable to match supermarket pricing. Budget CD companies also flooded the market with obscure films from the 40s which often sold for only £1.99. Confusion reigned, with the result that many stores that had embraced the format needed to pull out of the market, and many suffered heavy losses. These days most independent record stores stock only music DVDs and leave the film market to the supermarkets and online retailers.

Many stores lamented DVDs as a lost opportunity, but Drift had stayed ahead of the game by switching all their cult and art-house videos over to DVD. They also managed a more concentrated focus on the music side of the business following the release of the wonderful *Ry Cooder Presents Buena Vista Social Club* album.

Jenny and Rupert do not mind admitting that this one individual release changed their perspective on selling CDs. Previously they had been buying one or two copies of a title to see how it would sell. With the Buena Vista album they found that they were buying in boxes of the album to meet the demand. They realised that if you cared enough to listen to what your customers wanted, and to seek it out for them, people would come back time and again, and they would listen when you suggested new directions for them. This has enabled them to move away from the mainstream and take a gamble on stocking music and film which few others do. Jenny found herself confident enough to take the decision to extend the range of CDs.

Meanwhile Rupert, her son, decided to start recording and releasing the work of local folk musicians on his own label – Drift Records. The decision to start the record label came about as organically as the movement into greater emphasis on music sales had done.

The story goes that a couple of years ago in a small, dingy apartment with unpolished wooden floors and a tuneless upright piano, two young men were sitting on a bed – one played guitar, whilst the other beat a broken snare drum with one hand and plucked a bouzouki with the other. When the music finished and they had listened to the playback, they were comfortable with the quality of what they had just made; but would anyone agree to release it? Would anyone actually get to hear it?

Such was the beginning of the Drift Collective — an idea sparked between two friends in a house in Brighton. RG Morrison and Johnny Lamb became co-creators and now run the Drift Records label. It has expanded to become one of the most genuinely collaborative and respected small independent labels in the UK.

Having formed the Drift Collective, they began recording and releasing their own work, and that of fellow artists drawn from a large imaginary triangle between Devon, Brighton and London, who soon began to drift to the label, appreciating its collective ethos. Common ideals brought the shop and the label together, so World Video became The Drift Record Shop. The label is now highly respected, garnering considerable peer and industry support.

Of all the shops I visit, Drift is also one of the biggest supporters of ethnic music. One day, having priced some new music stock and placed it prominently on their 'new arrivals' stand, the staff were puzzled to receive an angry haranguing from a customer, who expressed how incensed he was by the bigotry and racial insensitivity of their display, before exiting the shop in a cloud of anger. In astonishment, and still standing open-mouthed at the outburst, Jenny's eyes strayed to the display stand. On a recent world music title, *The Best of Nigeria*, the price label had been placed in the top right-hand corner, accidentally obscuring the final 'ia' of Nigeria. The penny dropped and the staff burst out laughing. They re-positioned the label and, fortunately, the customer returned to the shop (probably to complain further), but even he found the incident amusing.

Jenny gauges her improvement in music knowledge by the sweet, dotty lady who called in five years ago and sang her a selection of songs that she was looking to buy. Jenny did not recognise any of the tunes, and the lady trundled out of the shop empty-handed. That lady is still a regular customer and these days Jenny recognises most of the songs she sings. Either Jenny's knowledge or the sweet old lady's singing has improved.

Times are tough for shops like Drift. It is very easy to get worried, hearing talk of recession and the rate at which independent stores are disappearing. This is down, in large part, to the music industry machine working to a profitable formula — producing recording artists to a perfect pattern, along the lines of TV shows such as *The X Factor*. This year's Christmas number one will no doubt, as it has for several years now, be from one of those shows. The mega music outlets choose to stock little else outside these major profit-yielding lines, leaving the smaller dealers like Drift to generate a little profit wherever they can. Who is losing out here? Ultimately, it is the shopper, who has to search further and further afield for anything new and interesting.

Why would we be surprised then to find that unsigned artists are turning to producing and releasing their own work on 'DIY' labels? This is where an increasing amount of the new and exciting music is to be found. So if you are a music fan, check out the excellent artists such as Tandy Hard and Cottonmouth Rocks on The Drift Records label, and if you are ever in Devon make a detour to Totnes to visit the smallest record shop I know. I am sure it will be standing for a long time to come.

*   *   *

My last call of the week means travelling over the Tamar Bridge into Cornwall. There is no charge to enter Cornwall – though they do charge you £1 to escape. I visit Upbeat Records, which was a chain of three shops at one stage, but like many others, is now down to just the one.

Keith Shepherd gave up a career in farming to pursue his dream of opening a record shop. The first shop he opened was in Bude and he soon added shops in Bideford and Padstow. Like most chains, Keith has downsized, moving out of Bideford first, followed by the closure of his Padstow branch in 2008. The lease of his shop in Padstow had expired and, because of 'the Rick Stein effect', Padstow has become a bit hip and trendy. Consequently, the downside for small businesses is that rates and rents have shot up, which made it impossible for him to make a reasonable profit.

Cornwall's record shops have been hit hard by the downturn in business. In 2001 I had 21 accounts in the county, but now it is down to five. Keith has recently moved into a smaller unit in Bude to help cut costs further and now employs only his daughter, Haddy, to help out.

Over the years I have noticed Keith becoming more cynical about the industry, and even becoming cynical about my contribution. I had recently informed him of a new CD deal I had for him, describing it as the best deal I had ever had. Keith congratulated me, and wryly observed that, since I had begun visiting him twelve years previously, this was about the 50th 'best deal' I had offered him.

2008 saw a major change at Upbeat – Keith finally bought a computer and is learning how to use it. Record companies which no longer send out reps on the road, and are also no longer prepared to fax or post information to him, have forced his hand. The only way stores are now able to obtain new release information is via e-mail.

One small phenomenon which has helped to keep Upbeat going over the years is the vibrant surf scene – surfers can latch on to artists years before they become mainstream. I recall, five years ago, importing twenty-five copies of Jack Johnson CDs each month for Upbeat, though nowadays Keith hardly sells a copy, as Jack Johnson has been abandoned by the surf crowd. (It now deems him as having sold out to the mainstream and becoming a supermarket artist). Other bands, such as Blink182 and Sublime, were all selling large quantities on import long before people had heard of them in the UK.

Whilst I was talking with Keith a lady came to the counter and asked for a record token. Keith informed her that, unfortunately, record tokens had been scrapped. We discussed this as another great gaffe by the industry. Unlike the National Book Token scheme, which, more or less, still works for book stores, the record industry shot itself in the foot on the day it scrapped the National Record Token scheme.

Can you remember when you were a child and your Gran or Auntie would be stuck for ideas on what to buy for your birthday or for Christmas? A record token was always a perfect answer. Each year thousands were sold, redeemable at any record store across the country. As well as providing a steady source of income for shops, they also enticed people into record stores who may not have otherwise considered entering. Many a child's first experience of buying a CD was redeeming a record token at their local shop.

The record token scheme was administered by EMI and was a consistent success. Then, in 1995, WHSmith broke rank and decided to no longer accept universally redeemable record tokens and, instead, introduced its own token scheme. It sold tokens which were redeemable only in WHSmith stores, 'locking-in' the customer transaction and taking advantage of its network of stores in most towns across the country. Soon HMV followed suit and, without the support of two of the biggest retailers in the country, EMI decided to abandon the National Record Token.

At this point, independents needed to join together and start a new scheme selling tokens, which could be redeemed at any independent record shop in the country. Nobody took the initiative, which has cost them millions of pounds in lost revenue.

Whilst many stores have started to sell record tokens that can be redeemed at their own store, the great thing about the old record tokens was that, if you lived in Inverness you could buy a record token for somebody living in Bude, confident that the recipient could spend it locally. During the last few years I have been in record stores dozens of times when people have come in to purchase record tokens, only to see them leave empty-handed after finding that a single-shop scheme did not offer what they needed.

I tried to lighten the mood by asking Keith if there had been any anecdotal incidents in his shop, and he recalled the day when he sold hundreds of T-shirts emblazoned on their fronts with the 'I'm Too Sexy For My Shirt' slogan, from the Right Said Fred song. Keith noticed a bloke looking intently at them. Suddenly the man exploded in anger, accusing Keith of encouraging paedophilia and declaring that he had seen children walking in the town wearing these T-shirts. Desperately, Keith tried to calm him down by telling him about the song and explaining that they came in three sizes and were not aimed specifically at young girls. The outraged man – who turned out to be a judge – was having none of it. He picked up all of the T-shirts, walked out of the shop and threw them in the road. He informed Keith that he was going to report him to the police.

The police did not pay Keith a visit, so he presumed they were using a little common sense. He assumed that he had heard the last of the nutty judge until, a few weeks later, he opened his local newspaper and, on the letters page, the irrational judge had written to declaim how a record shop peddling filth and corruption of young people had spoiled his holiday in Bude.

Keith was furious and wrote to the newspaper to, in turn, register his own outrage along the lines of "no wonder the country is in a mess when nutters can get to such positions of responsibility as judges". Honour satisfied – his letter was published in a heavily edited form.

Keith is now 62 and is relatively sanguine about the prospects for Upbeat. He hopes his Haddy will keep the shop going and leave Keith to concentrate on his other two great interests – football and walking, as Keith starts every day with a walk on the golden sands of Bude.

Chapter 8

Mr Dunlop and the Blow-up Doll

I start the second week of my odyssey in the south of England at one of the most famous names in record-retailing – Adrian's of Wickford.

Anyone who bought the NME throughout the 70s and 80s will be aware of Adrian's. For twenty years it had an eye-catching advert highlighting the latest releases in each edition.

When he left school Adrian wanted a career in the theatre and soon found work as a jobbing actor. To supplement his income he also helped out his mum, who sold wool on a local market stall. Then Adrian noticed that the adjacent stall that sold ladies tights and suspender-seconds (conjuring up some bizarre images) was not utilising all its counter space. Adrian rented the spare space and thus began his career in music – running the world's first 'Suspender-seconds and record stall'.

Soon however, with his mum's wool stall doing exceptionally well, she took the decision to rent a shop. Adrian also felt this was an opportune time to move his business forward, so he asked his mum if he could transfer his little business from the suspender stall to her new wool shop. This was progress indeed; the lucky people of Wickford were soon to have the world's first 'wool and record shop'.

Inevitably, problems arose from the beginning – Adrian's customers were teenagers, whilst his mum's customers were mainly pensioners. The wool customers complained that the music was too loud and this caused tension between Adrian and his mum. To solve the problem Adrian installed a partition between the two parts of the shop and also knocked through a wall to give his music store a separate entrance. The good people of Wickford struggled to come to terms with all this change. They no longer had the world's only 'wool and record shop', but, in its place, they now had the world's smallest wool shop and the world's smallest record shop.

Fortunately, his acting career soon took off when he landed a role in *Godspell*. The cast in this production included David Essex, Jeremy Irons, Marti Webb, Julie Covington and Robert Lindsay, and it was a huge success. Adrian was required to employ staff to run his store in Wickford.

Jeremy Irons became one of his first regular customers. Adrian remembers him as a big fan of 8-track cartridges, but he also always wanted a discount on every purchase.

Unless you have a long memory, you may wonder what 8-tracks were. They were launched in the mid-60s as a method of listening to recorded music, rather like a large version of the cassette. The Ford Motor Company offered them as an option on all their new cars. The format was successful for ten years before the advent of the compact cassette, which was smaller, cheaper and had a faster rewind capacity. Subsequently, there was a concerted effort by the record companies to reduce the number of different formats offered and 8-tracks bit the dust.

At this point in his life Adrian was earning good money and his agent advised him to invest it in bricks and mortar. Showing his entrepreneurial tendencies he bought a four-bedroom house in London, redeveloped it into four bed-sits, and let them out to his fellow actors whilst he slept on the lounge floor. Unfortunately, actors do not stay in one place for very long and soon Adrian had a steady stream of changing tenants, which was very hard work.

More dramatically, one of his tenants was psychotic. Her behaviour became so outrageous and aggressive that all of the other tenants moved out. She now had the house to herself and spent her time wreaking havoc and covering it in graffiti. Eventually, the unfortunate girl was sectioned under the Mental Health Act, so, accompanied by police, a social worker and a doctor, Adrian had to enter the house to have her removed. As he made his way into the hall the girl lunged at him with a knife, but, luckily for Adrian, the police were able to disarm her and remove her from the property.

After this experience Adrian had no further appetite for the letting business, and was left to ponder what to do with his large house with the large mortgage that accompanied it.

Adrian decided his next move should be to start a mail-order operation. He and his partner, Richard Burke, took over the upstairs bedrooms of the London house for stock and dispatch, and their first advertisement appeared in NME in 1975. They were astonished by the reaction, and within a short time were employing eight people and turning over £18,000 per week – a lot of money in the 70s for a business originally run from home.

By now Adrian had outgrown the wool shop, and indeed its successor – an upstairs floor of the new Wickford Indoor Market building – and had opened a new vinyl store with a rear warehouse for the mail-order operation in Wickford's High Street. Recognising the changes in the retail arena, he added a CD shop next door to the vinyl. This needed to be more modern and hi-tech than its vinyl counterpart next door, because, as Adrian remembers clearly, CD customers felt themselves to be far superior to mere vinyl buyers!

Next came a shop a few doors down the street for the selling and renting of videos. The video selling became so successful that it was necessary to separate the operation from rental, so a new store was opened for rental, whilst the original became the UK's first-ever stand-alone video retail outlet. The new rental store – immediately opposite – not only rented videos, but dispensed confectionery and soft drinks. The tally of Adrian's stores – all within 50 metres of each other – now stood at four.

This was during the days when chart manipulation was rife, and the record charts were compiled by writing sales of catalogue numbers down in a white book in a selection of record retailers. Adrian would leave his book on the counter whilst he made coffee for the sales reps, and on his return the book would suddenly be full of numbers. For being so hospitably careless he was often rewarded with boxes of free stock.

Also around that time a record-buying team was in operation. Funded by the record companies, this team would traverse the area buying the records its own label had on release. Each week the same gang of housewives would call in and buy several copies of targeted records to manipulate their chart position. They obviously had a set route, as you could set your clock by their weekly visit, before they swept on across the rest of the record stores in Essex.

By this time Adrian had reached a crossroads in his life. He had just finished a major tour playing the narrator in *Joseph and the Amazing Technicolour Dreamcoat* alongside Paul Jones, of Manfred Mann fame, who played the lead. Adrian felt that he had to make the choice between music and theatre and, fortunately for the people of Wickford, he abandoned his acting career to manage his shops.

Over the following years there were several examples of Adrian's shrewdness as a businessman.

His was the first CD store to install a National Lottery machine. It took him years of lobbying to Camelot before they relented and granted him one. Unfortunately, his sales of only £2,000 a week were unacceptably low to Camelot, who threatened to remove his machine unless sales improved dramatically. Adrian responded with a terrific ruse. He advertised that everybody who won a £10 prize in his shop would, instead, be paid out £11, with the extra £1 being in the form of a record voucher to spend in his shop. During the first week of the promotion they sold £10,000 worth of lottery tickets and, to this day, lottery tickets do a buoyant trade in store.

For ten years Adrian's had the contract to supply the British Council with all its CDs and videos, which brought in sales in excess of £200,000 per year. In its own words, The British Council's remit is "To build mutually beneficial cultural and educational relationships between the United Kingdom and other countries, and to increase overall appreciation of the UK's creative ideas and achievements".

They have offices in 240 countries and receive a yearly grant of around £200 million from the government ... and you can sure buy a lot of CDs and videos with that much money!

Unfortunately, Adrian's contract ended when his contact at the Council was replaced by a committee of eight people who introduced layer after layer of procurement red tape, to the point where Adrian decided not to bid for the new contract due to the undue effort required to service all 240 offices.

Another successful promotion was his launch of the video *Titanic*. Adrian announced that his store would open at midnight to enable the people of Wickford to be the first in the UK to own a copy and that all purchasers would receive a signed certificate confirming this fact. It was not even as if these certificates were signed by Leonardo DiCaprio or Kate Winslet – they were printed and signed by Adrian himself. Nevertheless, when the store opened, the queue extended halfway down the High Street. More than 500 videos were sold that night and Adrian had to spend the whole time photocopying and signing more and more home-made certificates.

It is rare for a shrewd businessman like Adrian to have a failure, but his initiative to open an outlet in a nightclub will not go down as his brightest moment. In the winter of 1976, one of his regular DJ customers was host at the infamous Zero 6 club in Southend (a sort of Essex Studio 54).

He persuaded Adrian that it would be a good idea to open a dance-record shop in the foyer of his club. So that is exactly what he did.

Every Friday and Saturday night they were open from 10pm until 2am. It was a tough assignment, particularly on the Friday night, as he had a market stall to set up at 6am each Saturday morning.

How could they possibly fail at the Zero 6? Easy.

On their arrival, clubbers were so keen to get inside and have a drink that the majority did not notice Adrian or his stall. Once inside, the majority forgot about him. And, on their way out, they were too pissed to give a toss about him and who wants to be carrying 12" singles around on a night out?

It was a total disaster. The upside was that he soon got his Friday evenings back to sort out stock for Saturday's Pitsea Market and his Saturday evenings were free to sleep.

In 1994 Adrian started an annual talent contest – a sort of *X Factor* for Essex. Adrian played the Simon Cowell role, whilst, amazingly the virtual Sharon Osborne of the panel was role-played by Theresa Gorman, the local Conservative MP.

As this was happening years before *The X Factor* began on television, Adrian regrets not taking his idea to TV stations. He called it "Stars on the Rise", which was a rather poor piece of wordplay based on *Stars in Your Eyes*, a TV show of that time. He doubted that enough local amateur talent would turn up, but the offer of prizes of up to £100-worth of CDs and videos proved irresistible.

Contestants included a pair of chaps who modelled themselves on Robson and Jerome, a comedian and three lots of majorettes – can you imagine the look on the faces in the audience when the third batch of grinning baton-twirling girls hit the stage?

In front of a packed audience, a Cher impersonator, who performed with great flair, won the contest. She became quite a local celebrity – fondly known as Billericay Cher.

The following year they decided to hold an Elvis impersonator contest and even attracted a contestant from Leeds. The trouble was that he turned out to be a professional and even brought his own three-piece band. Although he was musically the best Elvis impersonator he was passed over, as the event was designed to showcase local amateur talent, for a Wickford lad who, whilst not the finest singer, looked much more like the King. He, in his turn, also became quite a local celebrity, known fondly as The Wickford Elvis.

One niche specialist area of Adrian's is Christmas records. He informed me that he had an ambition to have the greatest collection of Christmas CDs in the world. This meant that, no matter who it was released by, he would purchase every CD with the word Christmas in the title. Consequently, over the years, he has accumulated hundreds of Christmas CD singles and albums.

By the late 90s CD singles had stopped selling, so he decided that the best way to rid himself of his extraordinary stock was to build a Christmas grotto inside the shop – employing a Santa, complete with a Santa's little-helper. Santa gave each child a 'lucky bag', each of which contained a little toy, sweets and, of course, one of Adrian's specially selected Christmas CDs. The CDs were self-selecting, as none of them had sold for years (these sound more like 'unlucky bags' to me).

It was a terrific effort by Adrian and deserved to succeed but, sadly, it proved to be a costly one – Santa's little-helper tripped over a toy in the grotto; landed on a pile of fluffy toys; damaged her spine; and, totally bereft of Christmas spirit, sued Adrian and won. Bizarrely, Santa's little-helper was none other than Adrian's mum! I suppose if you are going to be sued by an employee you might as well keep it in the family – there is always the chance that he will get his money back one day by inheriting it!

When interviewing shop owners I always enquire about awkward customers. When I mentioned this to Adrian his eyes lit up – and he proved to have had the mother of all awkward customers.

A woman brought a video back to Adrian's a video that she had purchased as a present for her mother's birthday. Apparently, on her birthday, her mother had tried to play the video and what came up on-screen was something other than the film listed on either the box or on the tape itself. The daughter claimed that her mother had burst into tears with disappointment, and was absolutely furious with Adrian for ruining her present and, thereby the entire birthday celebration. "My mother still hasn't gotten over it," she screamed.

His outraged customer demanded not only a replacement video, but also an additional free video of her own choice as an extra present for her mother; recompense for her not-inconsiderable taxi fares to and from the store, and compensation for the mental trauma she had endured.

In fact, she had been creating so much furore that Adrian had omitted to inspect the offending tape. He loaded it into the video machine and, sure enough, a totally different film came up onto the screen. It was, of course, the first in the usual series of trailers for other movies. The correct film – the one that mother was so distraught at missing – soon followed. The customer had jumped the gun too early.

The customer, however, did not receive this news graciously and was in no mood to apologise. Rather, she continued to rail at Adrian and vowed histrionically never to enter his shop again, which, in retrospect, Adrian decided was an opportunity lost ... because, had she re-appeared, he planned to seek compensation from her for the extreme trauma and upset she had caused to him, his seven staff members and the dozen or so customers who had endured her relentless outburst!

For Adrian, one of the enjoyable spin-offs from running his shop has been his regular appearances on BBC Radio Essex. Shortly after the launch of the radio station, he was invited to do a regular twenty-minute spot about the music scene. This ran for a couple of years until 1995, when he was asked to appear once a month on an hour-long *Sound Advice* programme hosted by Steve Scruton. The purpose of this segment is to discuss interesting records and music topics of the moment, and also to take calls from listeners who want their rare records valued. This has been quite challenging because of the unpredictable nature of the calls – but has also always been great fun.

One caller, whom Adrian will never forget, insisted that he had bought all of his 78s from Adrian during World War Two. Adrian calmly explained that his business had not opened until 1969, and that anyway he was too young to have been around during the War. The caller's self-confident retort completely stumped him – "I can assure you, Adrian, you've been around a lot longer than you think you have!"

Adrian loves doing the show and still appears each month. The most enjoyable aspect for him is that he can mix his deep love and knowledge of records with his showman instincts.

I asked Adrian where he would be in five years. Hopefully alive, was his reply. Over the last few years he has battled cancer yet his enthusiasm and cheerfulness are undiminished. Adrian was lucky to have made his money when ownership of a record shop offered the chance to make a good living. These days, in semi-retirement, and like many other shop owners, he has downsized by slimming his business down to just a single shop, although it still holds 30,000 CDs and 5,000 DVDs.

I feel he will be one of the 'Last Shop Standing' even if his involvement is just to call in one day a week. If he stopped, I am sure he would miss the cut and thrust of the music industry too much. Now, with the last of

Adrian's shop standing, he has come up with a new slogan: 'We nearly got too big for our roots'.

* * *

It is only a few miles to another of Essex's 'Last Shops Standing' – Fives Records in Leigh-on-Sea. I sometimes feel that this must be the most difficult shop in England in which to browse, especially if you are more than fourteen stone.

Somehow, they have managed to cram 40,000 units into a very narrow shop. There is not an inch of unused space –the racks are jammed full; boxes of top-selling artists like the Beatles, Pink Floyd, etc rest on top; and the floor is covered with yet more CDs. On entering the shop, I find myself instinctively tip-toeing between the racks in trepidation – scared that I will stand on something valuable. Above eye-level, and stretching up to the ceiling, are racks full of an extensive selection of box sets.

Pete Driscoll started off as a heating engineer, in partnership with a friend. When that business dissolved, Pete changed direction completely and opened his first record store in 1977.

Fives truly is a family business. It has been known for all three generations of the Driscoll family to be working there simultaneously – as well as Pete, pick any combination of helpers from daughters Sandra, Julie, Cheryl and Tracy, and grandchildren Dannielle, Kyle and Sarah.

Things went well for the first few years, until Pete had a major run-in with the VAT authorities, who were deeply confused by the consequences of some of the industry tactics within chart-hyping. Customs and Excise could not understand why there was obviously more product in-store than was shown in his purchasing records. They could not get their heads around a situation in which, ostensibly, Pete was cheating himself by under-claiming VAT relief – so they harried him for ages, simply borne of the suspicion created by their lack of understanding of covert industry habits.

During the next year he kept note of all of the free stock he received from his suppliers. Each Saturday he would receive a parcel containing up to a hundred 12" singles – all free-of-charge – from Warner. They were not the only company sending free stock, as the most effective retailer's ploy is to let slip to each record company rep how much free stock their competitors were offering to see what counter-offers resulted. The entire free product 'scheme' was an incentive for Fives to key extra catalogue numbers into the shop's Gallup machine.

There was a further complication that year as Warner were offering a promotion – buy 1,000 albums but pay for only 800. Pete bought 3,000 so, along with hundreds of free 12" singles, he also had an additional 600 free albums in store. It was a wearying two-year nightmare for Pete until the VAT Authorities reconciled themselves to the realisation that Pete was telling the truth.

Pete opened a second shop in Rayleigh in 1984, which lasted until 2007. The main reason why the Leigh shop had so much stock was because all of the leftovers had been transferred there from Rayleigh.

Fives are always keen to have bands do personal appearances and during the last few years Billy Bragg and Donny Osmond have both appeared at the shop. But nothing could prepare them for the day McFly appeared and 6,000 fans turned up, with the result that the police had to shut the high street.

One small tip Pete gave me for all other small shops is this: pay all suppliers by cash direct into their bank accounts – his bank charges are only £69 per quarter. This tip alone could save other shops hundreds of pounds a year in bank charges.

Pete told me that he intends to go into semi-retirement in 2010, when he will be 70, but hopes his daughters will keep the business going. Before he retires I hope that Pete has a huge – and successful – sale so that I will feel less guilty about selling him lots of CDs – when he already has 40,000 to choose from.

* * *

From Essex I make my way around the country's favourite car park – the M25 – to join the M2, and head on to the fishing and harbour town of Whitstable to call on Mike Winch at Gatefield Sounds.

Mike and Jan started their Kent-based chain of stores in 1972, which was when they opened their first store in Faversham. They did not expand too quickly – in fact, they seemed to have a seven-year step-plan, as their second store, in Whitstable, opened in 1979 and the third, in Herne Bay, in 1986. Those were the golden days of retailing and so they did not wait seven years to open their fourth – they rushed and opened in Deal six years later in 1992. The chain was completed with the final two openings – Broadstairs in 1995 and Sheerness in 1997.

The Deal and Broadstairs shops were opened in partnership with Paul Savage and trade under the name Soundhouse. Like the towns in which they are located, I would describe the Gatefield stores as slightly old fashioned, but they do retain a definite charm. They rely a lot on their friendly service and they do seem to have a loyal following, with many customers travelling great distances to visit some of Kent's last record stores.

Visitors to the Whitstable shop are more likely to know the name of its resident dog than of the proprietor – Buffy, a thirteen-year-old Basset, sits on her blanket from the moment the shop opens to closing time, hardly raising her eyes. Her idea of exercise is once – just once – around the CD racks.

Mike tries his hardest to compete with his local competition – always trying to match supermarkets on price, which often results in his making hardly any profit on some titles. The shop is a keen advocate of the multi-purchase and entices its customers with offers such as CDs and DVDs for £5.99 each or 2 for £10.

I asked Mike what record company incentives he had been able to capitalise on and he related how he had won a holiday to Kenya. EMI Record Tokens ran a competition with a prize for the shop that showed the highest percentage increase on turnover. On the very day the competition began Mike's only competitor in Whitstable took the decision to stop selling CDs. The timing was perfect and six months later Mike and Jan were sunning themselves on a Kenyan beach.

I asked about his daftest customer, who turned out to be a man who came in asking for a Sibelius CD. Mike picked out his best-selling CD by the world-famous Finnish classical composer. "Oh great", the man exclaimed, "Can you tell me what type of songs he sings?"

In 2008 Gatefield Sounds took advantage of Morrisons' supermarkets offer of all chart CDs for £6, which was £3.50 cheaper than the UK record company price (it is understandable that many record shops feel that the record companies are trying to drive them out of business). In Morrisons, Mike filled his trolley with CDs and the checkout girl enquired if he was a DJ. After clearing out Morrisons in Whitstable, Mike hit the road and did the same to the stores in Canterbury and Thanet. It is hard to believe that, when Morrisons struck its deal with the record companies, the result would be independent record-shop owners touring the supermarkets simply in an attempt to compete and to survive.

In addition to the supermarket phenomenon, Mike informed me that another development that has hit his shops hard is the death of the singles market. Ten years ago a high percentage of his business turnover was singles, but sales are now down to a trickle.

The majority of independent record stores no longer stock singles. Do you remember when you could walk into a store and the top 30 singles would all be displayed on the wall? These days it is not possible to do that, as many songs in the chart are only available via download. The physical single, which used to count for a fair percentage of a shop's business, has been in decline since the 80s because of gross mismanagement by the major record companies. The lack of a proper pricing structure; an expensive dealer price; a low margin; and the withdrawal of the sale-or-return deal for shops turned a once-profitable system into an unviable business.

Since December 2004 single downloads have outstripped physical CDs. If record companies had only created a sensible pricing structure in which all CD singles were £1.99, the format would still have a future. Consumers are not daft. They understand value-for-money and will not pay £3.99 for a single when a download costs 79p and you can pay as little as £7.99 for a whole album.

The record companies' policy of ignoring the CD single buyer has resulted in music fans abandoning the format in droves. People who only require a single track now seek it out via the Internet – mainly through illegal means.

In May 2008 Woolworths, the UK's largest seller of CD singles, announced that it would no longer stock them, leaving HMV and a few independents to carry on. It is only a matter of time before the physical CD single becomes extinct.

Because of deteriorating market conditions, Gatefield Sounds has found it necessary to close two of its stores. In 2007 Sheerness closed, followed in 2008 by Faversham. Mike still has five years to go on the lease in Whitstable and is in no doubt that he will see that through, but he feels that is likely to be enough. I hope that the good folks of Whitstable enjoy their last few years with a quality record shop in their high street.

* * *

My next shop is in Letchworth Garden City and trades under the name of David's. Originally opened as a bookshop in 1963, David's had soon established itself as one of the UK's leading independent record stores. As well as selling new books, David's advertised for used books and soon found people offering it second-hand records for purchase. It decided on an aggressive approach to purchasing stock, and soon had more product than it could cope with.

One day, in a moment of inspiration, it decided to hire a local warehouse and organised an auction to sell surplus stock. These auctions became legendary, with dealers travelling from all over Europe to attend. To cope with demand for the auctions, the store started purchasing new product.

In 1975 David's moved into a larger premises in a building that had previously been a branch of the NatWest Bank. But by 1984 the business was stagnating, and David's decided to inject some fresh blood into the staff.

The company appointed Andy Oaten to run the record shop. Andy had a rich musical heritage, originating from Knebworth, where his house backed on to the Knebworth Rock festival site. Some of his fondest memories are of sitting in his garden all weekend listening to the bands play next door. One particular memory is of Pink Floyd rehearsing their whole set the day before the festival started. It seemed eerie to hear all their classic songs being played to the sound of silence instead of applause.

After his appointment at David's, Andy quickly realised that the store desperately needed a revamp. Since the store opened its doors they had given over a section of the shop to 10p 7" singles, which took up too much space. Some of these records had been there for more than ten years and Andy took the decision to dump more than 1500 of them.

His shrewdest move was to convert the building's former bank vault. The original strong-room had walls 12-foot thick, but now it was being used simply to store hundreds of second-hand copies of the *National Geographic* magazine. The magazines were piled high on wooden tables and sold for only 10p each. They were the next batch to follow the 7" singles — into the bin.

Andy adorned the vault with posters and moved in all of the second-hand vinyl. It soon became the place to meet in Letchworth, with queues forming regularly on Saturdays. Back then, smoking was still allowed and, on a hot sunny day, it was a surreal site to see crowds of people sweating profusely and enveloped in a haze whilst flicking through the vinyl, a combination of the smoke and the heat coming off their bodies.

Andy was quick to realise that David's was missing out by not being a chart-return shop. He phoned all of the record companies and managed to get two reps to call on him regularly. Then, three years later, David's eventually succeeded in becoming a chart-return shop and during the next week the number of calls from sales reps increased from two to fifteen!

Andy could not believe how much free stock he was given. He summed up the madness of the period when he cited me the example of Virgin Records, who had two different reps on the road — both dishing out free records. Both called twice a week and one of them even popped in on a Saturday. All of the reps were vying to get their promotional displays on the walls of the shop. Often these would be displayed for a day before being ripped down and replaced by another company's promotional material. I get the feeling that whole forests have been chopped down to create all of the thousands of posters thrown away by record shops each year.

It is difficult to comprehend how record companies could employ fifteen people whose job was not to sell records, but to give them away. They did it because all of the other companies did the same and everybody copied each other's practices. No company had the bottle to say 'this is mad'. This continued for around fifteen years and it took a sharp decline in sales in the late 90s before record companies started re-examining their sales methods.

Can you imagine if this were to be discussed at, say, an EMI shareholders meeting? What would be the reaction if investors realised that EMI employed a team of people to drive around the country giving away free stock in return for persuading shop assistants to manipulate the singles chart?

Polygram offered an even stranger promotion. If certain records made the top 10 they would give record-shop staff £20-worth of wine vouchers for Victoria Wine — hardly responsible, considering how many record-shop assistants were school leavers. As with all of the stores, David's glory days are now over and, because of declining sales, it has now given over one-third of the shop to selling books.

Andy and I spent time discussing how the business has changed and he lamented the current lack of support from record companies. Throughout the early history of record sales, record companies were run by music people. However, during the 'corporate 90s' it became clear that record companies had lost any vision of the future. Executives would throw money at a group's first album and, instead of investing in bands for the long term and allowing them to develop as artists, if it did not take off immediately, they would be dumped pronto. The money lost using this approach during that period was scandalous.

This was the decade when every edition of the *NME* featured the 'next big thing'. Units shifted, market share and short-term profit suddenly became the only priorities. In the end, everybody from bands to record shops lost out in a complete absence of forward thinking.

Long-term investment in new artists dried up as budgets were cut. The music industry must be a very 'green' business as, during the last twenty years, most of its product has been recycled so many times. Hundreds of 'greatest hits' compilations have been re-done – in many cases simply by adding a couple of new tracks and changing the sleeve design.

Never has any artist been recycled more than Brian Ferry/Roxy Music. This is a listing of their 'greatest hits' compilations alone:

1977   *Roxy Music's Greatest Hits*
1983   *The Atlantic Years*
1986   *Streetlife*
1988   *The Ultimate Collection*
1995   *More Than This*
2000   *Slave to Love – Best of the Ballads*
2001   *The Best of Roxy Music*
2004   *The Platinum Collection* – a 3CD greatest hits box
2004   *Roxy Music – The Collection*

When you consider that they have also recorded three live albums – all containing hits – and that, during the last twenty years, Brian Ferry's major contribution to music has been to re-record classic old crooners, then it becomes apparent that Roxy Music have to be the greenest group in the history of music. Such compilations are then TV-advertised and heavily discounted in supermarkets.

In 2009 the CD everybody has been waiting for was released: *The Best of Brian Ferry*. Can you believe it? You can just imagine the record company executives discussing where they should invest their money. 'Should we get behind an exciting new band? No, why don't we put out a compilation of Brian Ferry's greatest hits?' Wow; what a brilliant idea. With his band Roxy Music there have already been 9 compilations and they all seem to have done well. I am sure a tenth will sell. As I sit here writing this I look the CD up on Amazon and despite a TV advertised campaign I note with interest it is 356 in their bestsellers list. Maybe the British public is sick to death of Brian Ferry and Roxy Music compilations. So through this book can I make an appeal?

BRIAN FERRY – YOU ARE A TALENTED MAN. PUT SOME NEW STUFF OUT PLEASE!

Endless various artists' compilations have also been released, recycling the tracks all over again. Every type of compilation has been released, such as:

'Songs for Mum'
'Songs for Dad'
'Songs for Driving'
'Songs for Cleaning the House'

These sorts of albums have no long-term sales. They sell quickly during their promotional period but, as soon as TV advertising ends and supermarkets remove them from their checkouts, sales quickly grind to a halt with, in many cases, the next stop at the local car boot sale. In the past, up-and-coming or established artists would use TV advertisements to promote new albums. Many of these albums turned into classic back catalogue, and still sell strongly today. Not many people have been into their local record shop recently asking for 'Songs to Clean the House to'.

There have been many opportunities for record companies to help the independents, especially in trying to break new artists. Simple ideas could include offers to independent stores of CDs with exclusive bonus tracks, or samplers of the label's artists to give away with other releases – anything that could give them a chance to compete on a level playing field.

I recall a few years ago, when Universal hosted an independent record shop conference where they told the stores how important they were to Universal and how much they appreciated their support. The dealers were delighted and told me how brilliant it all was. Such was the success of this conference that Universal announced it would become an annual event. The shops are still waiting for the second Universal independent store conference.

Andy, for one, would be delighted to attend a second conference and air his views. He is still as enthusiastic as ever and told me a couple of his whimsical tales.

The first story concerned the day he damaged Anglo-American relations. The shop had just taken delivery of the new Jeff Buckley DVD and, being a keen fan, Andy immediately put it on the player. The DVD started with Jeff Buckley thanking his sponsors – Bacardi – for helping finance the DVD. Andy was disgusted and thought only the Americans could do something so crass. He shouted across the shop floor to his assistant, Tom, that only dumb Americans could do such a thing. Immediately a voice piped up: 'Gee buddy, what's wrong with us?' The

Americans are incredibly patriotic and don't take kindly to people criticising their country. This angry guy was no exception. A red-faced Andy tried desperately to placate his customer by telling him all the things he liked about America: cheesecake, The Harlem Globetrotters, the Grand Canyon, etc. Luckily, Andy charmed himself out of a potentially embarrassing confrontation.

Then there was the day the lady came in and asked if they had any 'bread'. In response, Andy handed her a copy of *The Best of Bread and David Gates*. He told her that it contained all of their hits and was on offer. The woman looked at him bemused and replied, "But I was after a medium-sliced loaf". It never ceases to amaze me what people ask for in record shops. Staff in David's informed me of the customers who had requested semi-skimmed milk, bootlaces and even a car battery.

Another product area in which sales have declined in David's is the second-hand market. In the 90s, the way to sell unwanted music was through a second-hand record shop or through an advert in *Record Collector* magazine. Now, however, both eBay and car-boot sales have taken the majority of this trade.

Put simply, eBay is now the biggest second-hand record shop in the world. The roots of eBay lie in San Jose, California. It was created in 1995, when Pierre Omidayer set it up under its initial trading name, Auction Web. This was changed to eBay in October 1997. The website was launched in the UK in October 1999 and its importance in accelerating the closure of second-hand record stores is easy to underestimate.

There is one great tale about eBay – the first item ever sold on the site was a broken printer, which fetched the impressive sum of $14.53. So concerned was eBay founder Pierre Omidayer about the integrity of the transaction that he sent an email to the purchaser confirming that the printer was damaged. "No problem", was the reply, "I collect broken printers". This sums up the ubiquitous nature of eBay – somebody, somewhere will be looking for that obscure single, which they have heard only once. They can painstakingly search the record shops of this land, but the likelihood is that if they search eBay, they will discover their long-lost gem much more quickly.

I speak from experience – one of the bands that I managed in the 80s was Exhibit B. I had ten copies of their debut LP in my spare room, which had laid there for fifteen years in the hope that one day there would somehow be an Exhibit B revival. Eventually, I decided to put them on eBay, expecting to get a few pounds for my trouble. To my astonishment the albums fetched around £30 each, with the majority of them going to Japanese collectors.

eBay is customer friendly and easy to use. People list CDs they wish to sell and fix a price. This is called 'buy it now', and providing the purchaser meets the asking price, the CD is theirs. Alternatively the CD can be auctioned – it is listed for a specified number of days, and when the auction closes, the highest bidder obtains the CD. On receipt of payment the seller dispatches the goods to the purchaser who pays the postage.

Second-hand record sections were once prevalent in many record stores, but nowadays they no longer give up shelf space for second-hand – after all, in 2007 eBay turned over $7.67 billion, a percentage of which will have been made from sales of CDs, DVDs, and LPs, many of which would have previously been traded by record shops such as David's. My advice to record collectors is that, if you want to purchase, buy now, as prices will never be this cheap again. If you are a seller, keep hold of your collection for the time being, as it will be worth more in years to come.

My reasoning for this is that, as more than 400 record shops have closed in the last five years, where will a lot of their unsold stock go? On to eBay, of course. The market is currently flooded with stock from closed-down record shops. Whilst I know that record shops will continue to close in the future, they will do so at a much slower rate, because the people who have survived this far are doing something right.

I asked Andy if he was going to be one of the 'Last Shops Standing'. He responded by saying that, when he bumps into former customers walking in Letchworth town centre, listening to their i-pods, he recalls how many of them used to spend £50 a week with him, but now source their music in other ways and he often wonders how David's still survives.

I am confident that it will be one of the "Last Shops Standing'. Andy is a real asset and, with Hannah and Tom, the young staff members who support him so well, he has created an effervescent and vibrant atmosphere. Tom is also a member of There Were Bears, a superb band with a large following in the Letchworth area. David's also owns its own premises, which is crucial to the survival of any record shop these days. If it does survive, the main reason will be that the store has a huge and loyal customer base – with many people often travelling a long way to pay the store a visit.

Although David's has downsized from its peak of three stores in 1994 to just two, with one being solely a bookshop, I am confident that it will still be trading in years to come – even though, after all these years, it is still not sure which version of the 'Best of' Roxy Music it should be stocking. It is the last record shop standing in Letchworth, having already seen off competition from Ripple Records, Startime Records, Our Price, Sanity and Virgin. In the words of the Sparks' song 'This town ain't big enough for the both of us'. Letchworth can only sustain one record shop and that one is David's.

Although the decline of second-hand sales has caused damage to stores like David's, it has actually closed down nearly all of the specialist second-hand record shops. The biggest casualty was the shop which was once the biggest second-hand record shop in the world, Beanos in Croydon. I made contact with David Lashmar, its owner, who raised some valid points, the most interesting of which was that he believes that record companies had fuelled illegal downloading by being too greedy and by charging customers too much for legal downloads.

Here is the statement Beanos released to the world announcing its closure:

BEANOS FINALLY TO CLOSE – a message from David Lashmar, the owner

A severe and, I believe, permanent downturn in music retail has forced me to realise that I can no longer continue to finance this business as I have done for the last two years. Since, in fact, when we announced that we would have to close back in 2006.

Only ten years ago we were the leading second-hand record dealer in the world. Our three floors were absolutely crammed with every type of record you could imagine in every speed and size, CDs by the thousand, videos and memorabilia. This was the time when you were a 'collector' and you really had to search hard to find that elusive item and were damned glad to get it when you did. We had 24 dedicated staff who really knew their stuff and the whole place buzzed.

Then along came eBay. Then along came Amazon. Then along came 'downloading'. Then along came the time when it was no longer necessary to actually possess anything musical. Nothing tangible, like an LP cover, or even a CD-insert with some possibly interesting information. Nothing to file. Nothing to show off to friends. No, now your life can be on an iPod or a phone. Your music, your photos, your contacts. "Imagine no possessions," as John Winston Lennon once said.

Of course, we tried to embrace the new trend and at one time had ten enthusiastic typists working at our Sun House warehouse entering data as we started to sell 'online', but, in the end, the administration sapped the profits and we had to admit defeat in this field. (In fact, most professional dealers who spent their time selling online have also given up).

By this time, eBay had made a 'dealer' out of every enthusiastic collector and it was no longer necessary to go to a record shop to sell — they simply put it on eBay themselves. This was another nail in our coffin as we were rarely offered anything remotely interesting to resell, so the quality of our stock diminished.

Oh yes, Amazon. Well, we all use them don't we? At least I do! They are truly superb and have such a vast selection of second-hand CDs and DVDs that no shop could ever hope to compete unless it chose to add all of its stock to the Amazon database and, if it did, it would be a shop no longer. Roll on Amazon, I say. You are the new god of online retail therapy — search it; want it; click it; get it. Suits me, but it sounds the death-knell for many a small business, mine included.

Which brings me to the all pervasive, ethereal intangibility of downloading music. What a fantastic opportunity for the record companies to continue without ever having to actually make anything (except for huge profits). No factories, no reps out on the road, no faulty returned product and no warehouses full of unsold stuff. So, why have they all messed it up so badly? Greed. They tried to charge too much for their legitimate downloads and the punters simply would not cough up. So, the iPod world searched and loaded from the 'unauthorised' sites and embraced file sharing. How the devil were we ever going to persuade people that it was a really good idea to come into Beanos and buy an album when they could get it for nothing?

Five years ago the signs were there for me to read but I chose to ignore them, thinking there would always be a place for Beanos. Two years ago my accountants pointed out to me that we were losing a lot of money every month and, if the shop continued as it was, I would soon be bankrupt. That was back in August 2006 and I accepted the inevitable and started a closing down sale. The reaction to this news was fantastic with hundreds of emails and letters giving us great support — so much so, that I decided to close just the top two floors and continue to trade on the ground floor

But, I am sure you must realise how much I am going to miss the shop. It has been my life since it first opened in 1975. It has given me great rewards and been a major part in the musical lives of thousands of our loyal customers, many of whom I know personally and will miss greatly.

We will still have our doors open well into 2009 as we sell off stock.

This is both a sad time and an exciting time for me. Although I might be of a retiring age, I am not of a retiring nature so, please take note, David Lashmar has *not* left the building!

* * *

The next day I visit one of the UK's most expensive places in which to live – Cobham in Surrey, home to a shop with a real history. Threshold Records is owned by rock legends The Moody Blues, is frequented by a very up-market clientele and is, without doubt, the most highbrow record shop I know.

Its customers are a veritable who's-who of the entertainment industry and include Matt Lucas, Patti Boyd, Colin Montgomery, Phil Redmond, Frank Finlay, Diane Keen, Kenny Jones, actor Anthony Valentine who, according to staff, is charm personified, Max Clifford who, contrary to common perception, is described as one of the most affable and charming music fans you ever could meet, and ex-radio presenter Mary Costello, who has been one of their favourite customers for the past twenty years.

It is a proper record shop, which stocks a vast selection of rock, blues, country, world, folk, jazz and classical music, but which refuses to stock boy bands or reality TV stars.

Phil Pavling, the store manager, is proud to have created a Simon Cowell-free zone. Whilst it is unfair to blame Simon for declining sales across the whole industry, it is undeniable that his company has been responsible for changing people's music-buying habits. Nobody understands the global music industry and how to market CDs better than Simon. The man is a genius but, for independent music stores, he is a disaster.

Finalists in the *The X Factor* are all contracted to Simon's company, Syco, as are all of the writers and producers, and the resultant CDs are all released and distributed through Sony BMG. The *X Factor* is, effectively, an hour-long television advert for Sony BMG – its artists dominate the choice of guests and, if you listen to the songs covered by those guests, you will find that a very high percentage of the material used in the show is from original recordings by Sony BMG artists.

To reach the widest audience, Sony BMG market *X Factor* contestants through the supermarkets rather than through more traditional outlets. Its CDs will always be in a prominent position in store, often next to the till. To secure these key positions Sony BMG will have offered the stores substantial discounts, which are not made available to independent stores who, therefore, cannot match the price offered in supermarkets.

Even more damaging is the impact this has on the reputation of independent stores. If CDs are £4 more expensive in independent stores, customers are likely to perceive that they are being ripped off and so, in the future, their first port of call for buying music is increasingly likely to be the supermarket instead of the independent shop.

One example: supermarkets have been selling the Leona Lewis release *Spirit* for £7.99, whereas the distributor's price to independents is £9.14. What has the industry come to when lots of independent stores that I know of need to nip down to Tesco to buy their CDs? This way they pay only £7.99; can claim back the VAT; get points on their Tesco Clubcard; get a month's credit paying by credit card; and the shrewd ones even get 1 per cent cash back!

This situation is madness and is completely unfair to independent stores. Consequently, many independent stores now refuse to stock this type of CD, as they feel it does them more harm than good. The expression, "We are an *X Factor*-free zone" is often now bandied about by independent record-shop owners.

Leona's album has now sold more than 2 million copies, with only a tiny percentage going through traditional record stores. Imagine if they had been able to match the supermarkets on price – that would have given hundreds of thousands of extra sales, and a welcome lifeline to struggling independent shops.

However, even if Threshold were able to compete with supermarkets on the pricing of *X Factor*-related music, I still get the impression that Phil would not stock them on point of principle. Throughout the shop there are little signs declaring 'Threshold – Serious about music'. I have noted with interest that the magazine *Record Collector* has adopted the 'serious about music' phrase. I wonder if its editor has ever been shopping in Cobham.

Back in the 1970s record shops were thriving and Threshold quickly expanded by opening stores in Andover, Chichester, Birmingham and Swindon. By the mid-80s, however, these shops were no longer economically viable and the decision was made to close down all-but-one of them. John Lodge, a key member of The Moody Blues, was keen to keep open the store in Cobham as, by then, it had become his home town.

That the shop is still trading is down to the fact that the building itself is owned by The Moody Blues, who had based their administrative operation and fan club there. They also have an enormously passionate music fan in Phil, who manages the shop and plays a huge part in the continued existence of Threshold Records.

Phil told me the story of how he got involved in music. He was an ex-Our Price manager who was after a new challenge, so he lined up a couple of interviews for jobs at local record shops.

The first was at a shop called CD Vids, whose owner, interviewing Phil, asked his opinion of the shop's name. Phil commented that it was the first thing he would get rid of, as it read like they were selling pornographic videos! "I thought of that name," the owner replied. He next asked Phil what he thought of the coffee bar installed inside the shop. Phil told him that it was tacky and whoever thought that it would work was potty. "That was my idea," the owner replied. At this point Phil just said, "I'll get my coat", and walked out, hoping the interview that he had lined up at Threshold would go better.

Fortunately the owners of Threshold appreciated Phil's forthright views and, in 1988, he was taken on to turn around their struggling business. One thing that he introduced was Threshold's 'Recommended Wall', where Phil writes his own reviews of CDs that he seriously recommends. The work that is put into these reviews is impressive and his humorous writing style has convinced me that Phil could have had an alternative career as a rock journalist.

As an example of his writing, below is a letter which he had printed in the magazine *Music Week*, in response to Chris De Burgh's announcement that his new album would be available only from Woolworths stores.

"So then, Chris De Burgh, that colossus of crimes against music, has decided to make his new album exclusively available through the Woolworths chain. Unfortunately for him, our local high street has no Woolies to cater to the needs of his long-suffering fans. Fortunately for me, as Chris no longer wishes to sell his music via independents, I now have the perfect excuse to dead-stock everything in my store by this mawkishly sentimental, whimpering, simpering bag o' banal shite!"

I nearly choked on my cornflakes when I read this, and I would have loved to have seen the look on Chris De Burgh's face when he opened his copy of *Music Week*. Amongst the independent shops of the country Chris De Burgh is often referred to as 'Chris De Bastard'.

Mind you, I would also have loved to have seen the look on Phil's face on the day he opened his copy of *In Tune International*, to find that the magazine had printed a letter from a certain George Hulme, complaining about his being grumpy. Here is the letter, followed by Phil's published reply.

"I was alerted to the existence of a specialist CD retailer in Cobham, Surrey, and paid it a visit. The stock is large and covers classical (instrumental and vocal), jazz (all styles), blues and easy listening. They charge full price for the CDs and the manager is noted for being rather grumpy. The address is 53 High Street, Cobham, Surrey KT11 3DP (tel: 01932 865678). The shop is at the end of the High Street and I recommend a visit."

Phil's reply:

"Resisting the impulse to begin this letter "Nnnnnyeeeeeeah", I'm somewhat perplexed at being labeled (by George Hulme in your April letters page) as some kind of retail Victor Meldrew. I really feel I should query this curious and rather unwarranted slur on my generally upbeat and, even though I say so myself, 'perky' nature. At the end of a long day spent trying to identify the most obscure customer enquiries ("It was on the radio last week and it's got 'love' in the title") my general conviviality still shines through. Despite endless complaints as to why we (a small local independent store) can't match the prices at Tesco, my joyful exuberance remains undiminished. Even after seeing yet another ex-customer in the high street and being greeted with the words "I've got an i-Pod now and I just download everything", my joie de vivre continues unabated. Truth be told, it's only being so cheerful that keeps me going!"

Phil also wrote a splendid article for the local Cobham newspaper when The Moody Blues performed an official re-opening after a major shop refit in 2004. The shop had been transformed, and it confirmed to me that Threshold was committed to being one of the 'Last Shops Standing'.

On a sunny October afternoon in Surrey, the quaint old-English custom of queuing suddenly became the main topic of conversation amongst the Cobham locals. Stretching from the shop doorway of the recently extended and refurbished Threshold Music & DVD, right down to The Old Bear public house, around 175 excited Moody Blues fans eagerly awaited the arrival of John Lodge, Justin Hayward and Graeme Edge. Large sections of the queue were from outside of the UK. Americans, Dutch – even a chap from Bulgaria – all stood unbelievably patiently whilst yours truly buzzed up and down (not unlike the proverbial blue-arsed fly) handing out promotional CDs and apologising profusely for the delay in proceedings.

An in-store signing session had been scheduled from 2–3pm. John was already at the store chatting amiably with photographers and reporters but traffic jams had delayed Justin and Graeme's arrival. Considering that it was now approaching 2.30pm, and that the first person in the queue had arrived at 8.20 that morning, I was beginning to picture the headlines ..."Riot in Cobham High Street – Fans rampage through town!" I needn't have worried, however, as everyone behaved impeccably, waiting patiently as first Graeme, then Justin, finally drove into the car park.

A brief ribbon-cutting ceremony declaring the store officially open was followed by the moment everyone had been waiting for. The three 'Moodies' stood behind the counter being photographed and chatting with fans. They happily signed all manner of CDs, LPs, posters, books, photos, T-shirts, promos, and even artificial limbs! (Actually, I made that last one up).

The previous night had seen them play the last of three consecutive nights at London's Royal Albert Hall and the following days would see the band visit Ipswich, Brighton and many more venues as their tour resumed. On this, their 'day off', they had graciously offered me an hour of their time, but did have other appointments to attend to that afternoon. As more and more fans were joining the ever-increasing queue, I was really worried that we'd never make it to the end within the time available. Drastic action was called for and, at the risk of being labelled 'public enemy number one', I decided I'd have to try and hurry everyone through as quickly as possible.

In an ideal world, each fan could have spent as much time as they wished chatting to the band, but I desperately wanted to make sure that everyone at least got to meet them (even if it was only for a few moments). Amazingly, thanks to the band staying twice as long as they'd agreed and me constantly badgering everyone to speed it up, somehow we made it to the end of a v-e-r-y long queue. Far from being pelted with all manner of rotten fruit, I was quite taken aback by the amount of thanks and praise coming from all those who spoke to me afterwards.

So, in the event, a grand day was enjoyed by one and all. Many thanks to John, Justin and Graeme for taking the time to come down and wish us well, and a very special thanks to everyone who made the trip to Cobham and waited with truly infinite patience and good humour one sunny October afternoon.

I am also always impressed by Phil's honesty. I have been in Threshold on several occasions when customers have brought CDs to the counter and asked his opinion. I feel that Phil is sometimes too honest, as he declares some CDs "abysmal" or "absolute drivel". Needless to say, as that CD is put back on the shelf, Phil automatically moves into overdrive raving about the CDs on his 'Recommended Wall'. I smile with admiration, as it is rare for a customer to walk out without making a purchase – he even tries to sell me CDs. When I enthuse about the latest releases from Proper, Phil insists on playing for me CDs he has bought from other companies. He is rarely wrong, as he has an ear for discovering hidden gems.

My job is to try and get as many of my company's releases onto his 'Recommended Wall', as the subsequent sales are remarkable. For instance, he placed up there one CD which Proper distributes, by the Holmes Brothers, and, to date, he has sold more than 60 copies purely because of his sheer passion and enthusiasm for its quality. His sales are more than the whole HMV chain has managed during the same period.

As the store is close to the Chelsea FC training ground the players often frequent the store. Phil takes perverse pride in making sure that his beloved West Ham United mug is always prominently placed on the counter.

The shop is also close to a care-in-the-community centre, and one of Phil's favourite customers was a man called Graham who used to reside there. Although he did not purchase much, Graham did spend hours in the store, quietly browsing through the racks and chatting to Phil. Unfortunately he suffered from Tourette's syndrome and, as Pete from *Big Brother* has shown, sufferers can provide inadvertently humorous moments, usually caused by their repetitive behaviour or by sudden out-bursts of foul language.

Every time he visited the shop Graham would ask to listen on head-phones and he always requested the same song – 'Raining in My Heart' by

Buddy Holly. Graham would nod his head in appreciation of the music, but when it came to the chorus he would sing one particular line out loud, "Well it's raining, raining in my heart". Unfortunately he would always squeeze in an extra word in his version, "Well it's raining, raining in my f****** heart". Of course, other customers would be taken aback by this sudden outburst, especially as they could not hear the rest of the song and could not put it into context. Phil would continually remove Graham's headphones and explain the lyrics to him, but it was no use – every time he listened to the song the same thing happened.

Mind you, if customers were shocked by Graham's innocent outbursts it was nothing compared to the reaction to a visit from Threshold's most notorious CD buyer – Mr Dunlop. He was a builder by trade and was working on a large mansion in the Cobham area. It was a big job, and Mr Dunlop lived on-site in a small caravan. He was a massive man, looking not unlike the wrestler Giant Haystacks, with long, straggly hair and a bushy beard. Phil found it amusing to picture this giant of a man living in such a tiny caravan.

Then, one day, Mr Dunlop turned up, having decided on a new image for himself. He had completely shaved off all of his hair. Sadly, it looked as if the job had been done for him by Sweeney Todd, as his newly bald head was covered in dried blood.

On the very top of his head was a big grey cross. He had slashed himself badly and, no matter how many elastoplasts he put on the wound, the blood still seeped through. He eventually decided to stem the flow by covering the wound with a cross made from duck tape. This did not quite do the job, as blood still trickled out from under the cross. Mr Dunlop did not think it was important to wipe the blood off his head, so he walked the streets of Cobham looking like an extra from *Dawn of the Dead*.

As he did not have a TV in his caravan Mr Dunlop had to find alternative ways of entertaining himself. One of these was listening to music, which was why he was spending some of his hard-earned cash in Threshold. However, when he entered the shop on this day Phil suddenly saw how else he entertained himself on those lonely nights in his caravan in Cobham as, tucked under his arm, was a fully inflated blow-up doll.

Phil could not decide if he was more shocked by the sight of Mr Dunlop's slashed head or by the inflatable doll. Mr Dunlop nonchalantly propped the doll up on the counter and asked Phil to look after it (as if somebody was likely to steal it) whilst he flicked through the rock 'n' roll

CDs. Phil and the remaining customers stood there – as open-mouthed as the doll! For the next twenty minutes Mr Dunlop picked out a selection of CDs, before coming to the counter; paying for them in cash; wishing Phil good-day; tucking the doll under his arm; and strolling off down Cobham High Street.

Another of Phil's customers who made an impression was the lady who asked for an album for her grandson. She told Phil it was by 'Charley Marley and his Rego Orchestra' and, after a few seconds thought, Phil worked out that it must be Bob Marley and the Wailers.

The saddest day in the history of Threshold occurred in July 2002 when Phil's two favourite customers, Gus and Shelia Dudgeon, were tragically killed in a car crash. Gus was one of the world's most famous record producers and was renowned for the work he did in producing seventeen of Elton John's albums. He also produced for artists such as David Bowie, Fairport Convention, Chris Rea, Joan Armatrading, XTC, Lindisfarne, Jennifer Rush, The Strawbs, Elkie Brooks, Ralph McTell and The Bonzo Dog Doo-Dah Band.

Gus was also credited as being the first person ever to use a 'sample' on a recorded song – the African drum loop on the John Kongos single 'He's Gonna Step On You Again'. The song was a top-5 hit in 1971, and some of the best music of the subsequent thirty years owes its existence to the creative use of sampling.

Gus always bought his CDs from Threshold as he and Sheila lived in the house immediately opposite the store. He was always flamboyantly dressed, with a natty line in waistcoats.

Gus was actually far from your usual 'Music Biz' caricature. He was, first and foremost, a music fan, and he possessed an encyclopaedic knowledge of music. Needless to say Phil and Gus got on famously, and Gus would spend hours in the store, enthusing about music and recalling his musical anecdotes. For Phil it was a special pleasure to have as a regular customer the man who had produced the first record he had ever bought – David Bowie's 'Space Oddity'.

They became firm friends, and Phil would often go to their home, Mole Cottage, for dinner. One night Gus and Shelia were showing Phil some photos and an old black and white picture showed Gus with his arm around Muddy Waters. As a huge blues fan, Phil immediately recognised the other three people in the photo as Little Willie John, Sonny Terry and Brownie McGhee! Another photo had a faded signature. It read "To Shelia, with love John Lennon". Lennon's final live performance had been with Elton

John at Madison Square Garden in New York and Gus had been the producer of the resulting album.

The day before the accident Gus was in Threshold, steadily working his way through an huge pile of new CDs. I could see that Phil was enormously proud to have known them and it was confirmed when he described Shelia as a 'Top Bird' and Gus as a 'Diamond Geezer'. Since his death, the Gus Dudgeon Foundation has been set up in his memory. Based at Thames Valley University, it is a facility that teaches students from all walks of life the art of production and recording techniques.

As for the future, I feel Threshold will be one of the 'Last Shops Standing' as they have adapted well to a changing market. Phil reminds me of the day nearly twenty years ago when a company phoned him up to pre-sell the new Kylie Minogue album. Phil ordered 100 copies. He was phoned up recently and asked how many copies of her new album he would like. "None," was his reply "I will leave Kylie to Tesco". How times change.

* * *

It is only sixteen miles to my next call, which is at Record Corner in Godalming. If the BBC ever produces a series titled 'Record Shops with Talent', then Record Corner in Godalming would be the certain winner. The husband and wife team of Tom and Sue, who co-own the business, are both accomplished singers and Sue also does ballet. Danny plays guitar in a band and the shop's fourth member, Nicki, plays in an orchestra.

The shop is in a most unusual location, tucked away down a cul-de-sac off the High Street. This means that they don't get any passing trade, instead relying on a small portable sign that stands on the High Street pointing in the direction of the store. It is to the store's credit that they are still trading, as they have to count on their regulars for business.

As you enter the store you notice it is divided into a jazz/classical room run by Tom, which is a haven of tranquility and, in contrast, another room in which Dan rocks the shop by playing the latest releases.

One of the shop's claims to fame is that it influenced the career of Genesis. Back in the 70s, when the band were schoolboys at Charterhouse, the well-known public school, Peter Gabriel, Tony Banks and Anthony Philips would meet up at the store most Saturdays.

One celebrity that Sue has asked me to mention in the hope that he reads the book is Alvin Stardust. He ordered an Adam F 12" single six years ago and he has still not been in to collect it.

The shop's other claim to fame is that Tom is so respected in the classical world that Buckingham Palace asked him to suggest suitable music for Prince Charles and Camilla to walk down the aisle to on their wedding day. This followed their earlier request for him to recommend a suitable piece of music for a memorial service held for Princess Diana. Another wedding Record Corner provided music for was Chris Evans's who popped in and said he was buying CDs for a wedding in Portugal. It was only later that they realised it was for his, to Billie Piper.

Sue gave me a great tale to illustrate why shops like Record Corner are dying out. A customer comes into the shop and opens with the line: "I don't know what it's called and I don't know who sings it, but I heard it on the radio last week".

"Which programme was it on?"

"I don't know, I was driving."

Sue then mentions radio stations to jog the customer's memory – if they can remember the station and the time of day, Record Corner will then contact the radio station direct to find the song. No joy, so Sue asks if they can sing it. The customer doesn't know the words, but is able to hum a little of the tune. Sue doesn't recognise it, so she gathers the rest of the team to have a listen. At last they've got it. Everybody is happy. Sue asks the customer if they would like the CD.

"No, it's OK, I will order it off the INTERNET!"

If Sue gets stressed out she goes out to rip cardboard in the back room. That day she was still ripping cardboard in frustration, long after the shop had closed. It's not only the person who calls in to obtain information about CDs before ordering off the Internet that drives shops mad, it's also the customer referred to by record-shop staff as 'Last Chance Larry'.

In the past, customers known as Last Chance Larry's used to purchase their CDs from record shops. These days they buy them anywhere but. They call in as a last resort. How often I have heard the cry, 'I tried to get it in Asda, but they didn't have it, so I tried Woolworths and WHSmith, but they didn't stock it either so I thought I would try you'. I can see the shop owner gnashing his teeth in frustration, before saying, "You should have come here first, then". Last Chance Larry will laugh and say 'you're right', but next time he needs a CD he will purchase it with his grocery shop. Then you get the Last Chance Larry who calls in and says, "I was going to buy it off the Internet, but I've left it too late so I thought I would get it off you". At that point Larry expects the shop owner to be grateful. Every day this scenario is played out at record shops up and down the land.

Record Corner told me about some of its unusual requests. One customer wanted a CD for horses to dance to. (How about 'Crazy Horses' by The Osmonds.) The local cinema wanted a suitable record to alert the staff to evacuate if there was a fire. The choice is endless:

Anything by Arcade Fire or The Alarm
The Move – 'Fire Brigade'
Arthur Brown – 'Fire'
Talking Heads – 'Burning Down the House'

Amazingly, they rejected all of these and settled on David Rose's 'The Stripper'; maybe they wanted the staff to signal there was a fire by taking their clothes off.

Its most awkward customer was the punter they christened the 'mouldy old lady.' She bought a CD from Tom then returned it a few months later, saying it had gone mouldy. Tom had a look at it and explained that the mould was just a green pattern. The lady insisted it was mould, so Tom showed her another copy of the CD that had exactly the same pattern. "See," the lady said, "that's mouldy too". Tom, attempting to be scientific, tried to explain that the chance of mould growing in exactly the same pattern was an impossibility, but before he could finish his Einstein theory the lady had stormed out.

Record Corner's most awkward moment occurred when one of its regular customers came in and showed them a squashed berry inside a plastic bag, insisting it was the image of the Holy Spirit. What on earth are you meant to say to that?

Record Corner was the victim of the worst case of overcharging I have ever seen. They ordered a 40 CD Maria Callas box set from EMI. Instead of the box set, they were sent a Dave Gahan 12" single and charged a whopping £250, which was the price for the box set. Luckily, they spotted the error before paying. I do hope it will be one of the 'Last Shops Standing', not only because it is the only store I have ever visited that always offers me a selection of herbal teas, but because to see the team in action is to witness true customer service.

* * *

After the stores of Surrey I drive down to visit my accounts in Sussex, starting off in Lewes at Octave Music. Andy Howe began his record-shop career in Music Lovers in Horsham. It was a fantastic job for as passionate a music fan as him, although he did have his eyes opened to some of the seedier sides of the industry. As I have previously mentioned, in those days the chart was compiled by shops writing the catalogue number of every record sold in a little white book, which would then be posted at the end of each week to the British Market Research Bureau (BMRB), who compiled the charts before losing the contract to Gallup. A new book would be dispatched in time to ensure sales were not lost. In return for free stock the owner would allow the sales reps to borrow the book overnight, as long he had it back next day. One day, one rep took things a bit too far. He was under intense pressure to get the new single by a band called The Pinkies to enter the chart as high as possible. The rep had arranged for a PA by the band in the Music Lovers store. Everything went really well – a big crowd attended, and the shop sold 80 copies of the record. The rep was pleased; according to the record companies' research, the record would enter the charts at around number five. Sadly the rep over-egged the pudding. He filled in over 500 ticks in the book. Smelling a rat, BMRB withdrew the single out of the chart and, due to excessive hyping, it didn't even make the top 75.

Music Lovers had ambitious plans. Not being content with just a shop, they decided to start their own record label. Not for them putting out a single by a local band – they decided to sign international singer/actor Murray Head, famous for his top 10 hit 'One Night in Bangkok', and drafting in Richard Thompson and Jeff Beck to play guitar on the album and ex-Yardbird Paul Samwell-Smith to produce. Samwell-Smith is famous for producing artists such as Cat Stevens, Jethro Tull and Carly Simon. Money soon became a big issue. Having spent all of it on recording the album, they had none left for promotion. Sadly the music lovers of Horsham would soon lose their local record shop, as the business collapsed.

To tide him over Andy took on work as a portrait photographer, which kept food on the table and a roof over his head. After five years of photography Andy was keen to get back into music full time. He had kept his hand in by buying and selling at record fairs and working as a mobile DJ. One day at a record fair in Crawley he started talking with a dealer, who left him with the impression that he no longer had the enthusiasm for the industry. By sheer coincidence, Andy was working in Lewes the next day and popped into the local record shop, only to be greeted by the man he had spoken to at the record fair the day before: 'Mr Unenthusiastic record shop owner'. After a brief chat he asked Andy if he would like to buy the business. They went upstairs and by the time they had finished a cup of tea the deal was struck.

At the time, Andy was living in Horsham and phoned his wife Wendy just to confirm that it was OK to buy a record shop (the way you do). It turned out to be an eventful day, as their house went up for sale that day, helped by the fact that Wendy worked in an estate agents.

That was 1988 and twenty years on the Howe family still live above the shop. It has its advantages, travelling ten metres into work each day. When he bought the shop it was called The Lewes Record Centre. Back in the 80s you found that a lot of shops used their name to describe what they did and where they were based – The Lewes Record Centre was no different. Andy kept the name for a year before changing it to Octave, which was the name of his mobile disco. Andy has an encyclopaedic knowledge of music, which has certainly come in handy over the years when deciphering the cryptic clues given to him by the people of Lewes when requesting records.

"Have you got the new album by the Jammy Rocker?" one lady asked? Think she meant Jamiroquai. Another lady asked for the new 'Greg Orian' album. Andy asked her for more information, as he had never heard of the artist, and she replied that the album was called *Chants*. "Greg Orian Chants," he said out loud and the penny dropped – she was after an album of Gregorian Chants.

His favourite, though, was the old lady who asked for a copulation album. Resisting the temptation to say "How about *Songs For Swinging Lovers?*" he asked her did she mean compilation album?

Octave is another of the stores who have won prizes for their window displays – no doubt Andy's photographic background has been an advantage. He did excel himself when he won a holiday in New York for his display for the Lenny Kravitz single 'I Built this Garden for Us'.

Andy filled the window with a glorious floral display and had to laugh when men came in requesting bouquets or flowers for their wife. He also won a trip to Berlin for his display for the Scorpions' track 'Wind of Change'. The point of focus was a giant live scorpion, displayed in a large tank in the window. I do feel Octave will be one of the 'Last Shops Standing'; it's a big advantage to own the property, as Andy and Wendy do. Combining Andy's excellent music knowledge and great customer service, they have built up a large loyal following within the town.

* * *

From Lewes I move on to the city where I have three independent accounts, virtually unheard of these days. When I started this book I vowed to write about only one shop per town or city, so that if you were in that area and wished to visit the best independent shop, you would know where to go. In Brighton it has to be Borderline Records.

Situated in Brighton's North Laine, and surrounded by trendy coffee bars, a vegetarian shoe shop, a vegetarian burger takeaway and immediately next door to the Komedia music and comedy venue, Borderline Records is the sort of shop you would expect to see in Haight Ashbury in San Francisco. Owned by Dave Minns and Sian Davies, partners in business and partners in life, it first opened its doors in 1983.

Original framed posters by artists such as Martin Sharp, Australia's foremost pop artist; Rick Griffin, who designed sleeves for the Grateful Dead and Man amongst many others; the recently departed Alton Kelly, also famous for his Grateful Dead album sleeves, and concert posters for the likes of Jimi Hendrix and Janis Joplin hang on the wall. Sian has a vast collection of these posters, which she rotates and a visit to the shop is worth it alone to marvel at them. The music they play also reflects those times, and the shop has a wonderful relaxed atmosphere.

I defy anybody to find a better plastic carrier bag than the one Borderline supplies with your purchases. They feature two cartoons by one of the world's greatest cartoonists, Robert Crumb. As I watched people purchase from the shop I couldn't help thinking that they might be best-advised to throw the CD away and keep the bag. Crumb's work is much sought after and highly collectable; he is famed for swapping six of his sketchbooks for a house in Southern France. My favourite Robert Crumb story is this; he did the sleeve for the Janis Joplin and Big Brother and the Holding Company classic album *Cheap Thrills*. So impressed were the Rolling Stones, that they asked him to illustrate their next album. Crumb turned down the offer, as he thought their music was rubbish.

I always feel that Borderline are missing out on marketing by not having a big poster in the window saying 'Free Robert Crumb bag' with each purchase. I asked Dave what was the biggest challenge to his business; it wasn't the supermarkets or the Internet, but the lack of support from the local council combined with the high street rents.

Although the turnover for independent record stores is dropping every year, high street rents continue to rise. Margins are being squeezed and inevitably there comes a time when having a record shop on the high street is no longer a profitable business. A few of my stores have relocated to cheaper parts of their respective towns. As shop leases expire, store owners are reluctant to commit to a new lease. In most cases the leases tie them into five or ten-year deals, and such has been the drastic transformation in record retailing over the last ten years that nobody can be confident of committing to a lease that far into the future. Moreover, the new leases are nearly always accompanied by a price rise; usually well above the rate of inflation. Landlords have lost touch with reality: they seem unable or unwilling to accept that their greed is gradually killing the high street.

Out-of-town shopping centres with free parking increasingly appeal to the consumer. However, like the supermarkets, their stereotype stagnates choice, as every centre has virtually the same shops. Meanwhile, the independent traders struggle on. The high street is not only losing record shops, but also travel agents and bookshops, all closing down as they struggle to compete with the Internet. In addition, thousands of bakers, butchers and greengrocers have moved out, unable to compete with the supermarkets. Go down any high street and there are more charity shops than any other type of business. Last time I visited Brighton, to sell to Dave at Borderline and my other two customers, it cost me £12 to park my car in the centre for the day. If I were a potential visiting shopper I think even I would save my money and go the shopping centre.

Nevertheless, despite all the problems with high street rates and expensive city-centre parking in Brighton, I am sure Borderline will continue to trade for a long time to come. It has a superb range of stock with a great selection of reggae, world, folk and vinyl, and they keep their prices low.

After an overnight stay in Brighton at my all-time favourite guest house in the country, Paskins, (quite an accolade from me, considering I have stayed in over 500 different places over the years – maybe I will send them my own award), I decided to get the train in to London, as I thought it would be cheaper and less hassle. No congestion charge or exorbitant parking charges. The shop I was visiting was the Rough Trade store. I had thought long and hard about whether I should include more than one London shop in my top 50, but I decided to stay true to my original idea of 50 shops in 50 different locations. It was a shame to leave out such great record shops as Pure Groove, If Music, Honest Jon's and Sister Ray.

The choice of Rough Trade as London's best independent was an easy one to make, as Rough Trade is the future of independent record shops and is one of the most famous names in the music industry. Its story commenced in 1976 at 202 Kensington Park Road, Notting Hill, when Geoff Travis started the Rough Trade record label. The first release was 'Paris Marquis' by Métal Urbain, soon to be followed with releases by Stiff Little Fingers, Swell Maps, The Raincoats and Cabaret Voltaire.

Mark (The Jinx) Southall of Newport based vinyl specialist Diverse\

The excellent Rough Trade East store

Antiques 78's Records in Cardiff - Photo by Llinus Griffiths - griffiths_llinos@hotmail.com

Dave Wedgbury of Congleton based A&A Music

Two of the most popular people in music retailing Chris Lowe and 81-year-old Mavis Slater of Yeovil based Acorn Records

CD Sid of rock specialist Muse Music in Hebden Bridge

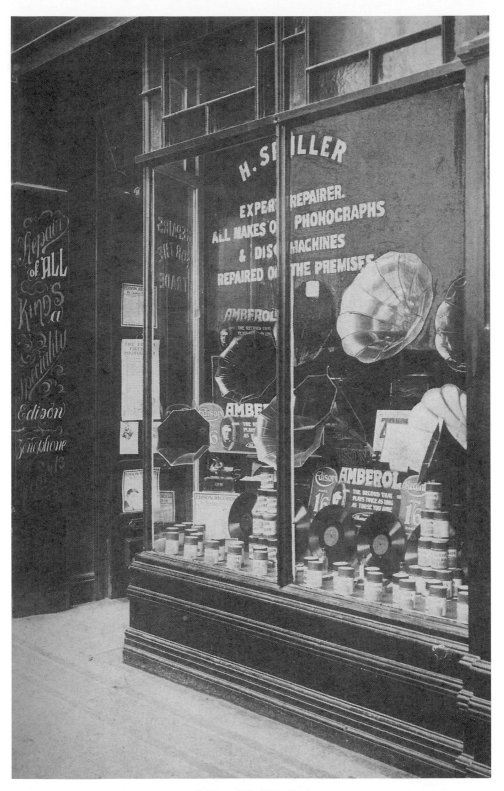

Spillers of Cardiff in 1929

Elliott Smaje of Wall of Sound in Hudderfield

Diane and Tony the mother and son combination of the delightful Musical Box in Liverpool

Keith Shepherd of Bude's Upbeat Records looking surprisingly Upbeat for a change

Phil Pavling the manager of Threshold Records in Cobham a shop owned by the Moody Blues

Another of my customers bites the dust - Round Sound, Burgess Hill

Geoff has had an amazing career in the industry, and has been involved in the signing and developing of such acts as Babyshambles, Belle & Sebastian, The Fall, James, The Libertines, The Strokes and, most famously of all, The Smiths. The tale of how they were signed is now famous. Johnny Marr ambled into the Rough Trade warehouse and collared Geoff who was making a cup of tea. He handed him a cassette of *Hand in Glove*, with the words, "This isn't just another tape – go and listen to it". So impressed was Geoff that he called Johnny back on the Monday, and the next day the band were in the studio recording their debut single for the label.

Rough Trade's first shop opened in 1978 and originally specialised in US and Jamaican imports. It soon became one of the leading outlets for the burgeoning punk scene, and subsequently a pilgrimage point for anyone buying or selling DIY New Wave music and fanzines.

After a period of rapid growth, the shop and label businesses separated in 1982. Nigel House and his partners Pete Donne and Judith Crighton, who were all Rough Trade employees, bought the shop. As a result, they moved around the corner to 130 Talbot Road.

In 1988 they opened a second store, together with Slam City Skates, at 16 Neal's Yard, Covent Garden. In the early 90s the bold decision to go international was taken. It was an exciting venture and they opened branches in San Francisco, Tokyo and Paris. Although the stores flourished, it was difficult for a chain spread so far around the globe to be profitable, and they decided to go back to their London roots and close the international shops.

In 2001 Rough Trade celebrated its 25th anniversary with a series of gigs and the release of a commemorative CD compilation. The same year, they also received an award from *Music Week* in recognition of their unique contribution to the British Music Industry.

In 2004 they launched The Album Club, a premium music recommendation service, aimed at those people without the time or opportunity to visit a store and therefore in need of honest and exciting new music recommendations. The club came about after a gig by the Gotan Project at London's Festival Hall. Rough Trade had a stall there, and before the gig had even started they had sold out of all of their Gotan Project CDs. It inspired Nigel to the thought that there must be thousands of people who loved this type of music, but could no longer purchase it. Many would be ex-customers who had moved away from London and no longer had time to flick through the racks of record shops. As people marry and have children, they find they have less time, but it doesn't mean that they have lost their taste in music. So, with the help of Steve Godfroy, the club was born. Each month members receive a parcel through the post with the shops recommendations. The criteria for being chosen is simple. The team at Rough Trade has to love the CD, no other reason. The idea is to give exciting new music the chance to be enjoyed by people who appreciate something more stimulating than chart music. Customers choose what genres they like and how many CDs they wish to receive each month – anything from one to ten. The club now has 2000 members, who I am sure look forward to their monthly package. Members also receive exclusive goodies, such as rare bonus recordings, as well as invites to members-only gigs.

One such gig was for Radiohead, who agreed to play at the shop on 16 January 2008. After 1500 fans queued outside the shop, the police forced Rough Trade to move the gig from the shop to a club called 93 Feet East. It was a credit to everybody involved with this gig that it went ahead. Nigel remembers the day fondly, with fans travelling from as far away as Los Angeles to attend.

I have no doubt that the Radiohead gig at 93 Feet East will go down in rock folklore. People will talk about it in years to come in the same way as they talk about attending the first Sex Pistols gig now. I seem to have met a thousand people who attended that gig, even though the venue only holds 200. No doubt in the future thousands will claim to have attended the Rough Trade Radiohead gig.

Not every independent record shop is as big a fan of Radiohead as the team at Rough Trade. At a time when record shops needed the support of artists they have promoted and championed over the years, they got the ultimate kick in the teeth when Radiohead, arguably the UK's top band, released their album *In Rainbows*, not only as a download, but they gave the consumer the chance to pay whatever they wanted for it. Although this was revolutionary and the band deserves credit for being innovative, they were not the first major band to release their album online.

In 2005 Cleveland industrial rock band Nine Inch Nails released *With Teeth*. The band embraced the Internet, and after previewing the first single off the album *The Hand That Feeds* as a video on the band's website rather than on MTV, they then released the source files in Garage Band format, which allowed the band's fans to remix the song themselves. This started an unofficial remix competition in which hundreds of fans submitted their efforts. I feel Trent Reznor, who is, effectively, Nine Inch Nails, has embraced digital distribution more so than any other artist. He has been heavily critical of the Universal Music Group and openly encouraged the band's fans to steal the music illegally online rather than purchase it legally.

I feel Radiohead noted the success of Nine Inch Nails, but took the concept one stage further by aggressively promoting the idea behind the project: that idea made them appear radical and ground-breaking.

Gigwise.com reported that 1.2 million people downloaded the album and one-third were rumoured to have paid under 10p for the privilege. The average price paid was around £4. Just to knock the stores as they were down, the band offered a box set of the album containing the CD and two 12" vinyl albums, a CD containing enhanced new songs, photos and a lyric book for £40, exclusive to the band's website. Normally, a new Radiohead CD would be one of the retail highlights of the year for an independent store, as Radiohead are the type of artist whose fans don't normally purchase their new CDs from supermarkets.

The loss of sales on this CD for independent stores was vast. Dealing direct with your fanbase is the future, but sadly it is the local record store that is hit hardest. When Radiohead were trying to break through, the local record stores were the only place you could purchase their product – supermarkets and Woolworths didn't want to know. It is only when all the hard work has been done that supermarkets step in and take their slice of the action. It will be interesting to see how many bands follow Radiohead's example – if it is a blueprint for the future, then things are really black for the local record shop.

Things would be even worse if bands followed the idea of Nantwich band The Charlatans. Their last album, *You Cross My Path*, was given away free as a download via XFM radio station. Thirty thousand people downloaded it. The fans were happy, as they received a free album and the band must have been pleased that 30,000 fans were interested in their album. The only person not happy was the band's accountant who saw them get zero pounds in sales for an album that cost thousands to record. It is hard to believe that other bands will follow suit. Many artists can achieve 30,000 downloads if the music is free.

One innovation that impressed me at Rough Trade was their 'Counter Culture'. Piled high on the sales counter are a selection of CDs recommended by the staff. When a customer purchases a CD, the staff will often recommend a similar title that they feel they would appreciate.

One customer who didn't appreciate this service was Van Morrison. He called in one day and asked for the new Dion CD. Sadly, the shop had sold

out, but Pete took this opportunity to engage Van in conversation and recommended a title he felt he would enjoy. Instead, Van barked back at him:
"Young man, if I wanted your opinion I would ask for it", and with that he
turned on his heels and left the shop. I admire Van Morrison; he is no doubt
a true music fan, but I do sometimes wonder if he has a secret hobby where
he travels the length and breadth of the country upsetting record-shop staff.

Nigel pointed out to me that when bands like The White Stripes and
Scissor Sisters first came on to the scene Rough Trade would sell hundreds
of copies of their records. As soon as the bands crossed over to the mainstream and were stocked by Woolworths and Tesco, sales would drop to a
trickle. It can't upset you, as it's a sad fact of the industry – that's the way
it happens. It means that to make a profit Rough Trade is constantly
looking for the 'next big thing'. I liken them to talent scouts.

The year 2006 was a big one for Rough Trade, as they celebrated their
30th anniversary, commemorated with the release of the double album *The
Record Shop – 30 Years of Rough Trade Shops*. This was also the year that they
launched their digital store. Nigel has an excellent team backing him up,
with the shop being managed by Spencer Hickman.

Any music fan visiting London should make the effort to visit the shop,
a remark that applies to all record-shop owners looking for inspiration.

Chapter 9

Clashing with Joe Strummer

The third week of my tour I visit the shops in the Midlands. When I think of customers in the Midlands there is only one name that springs to my mind. His name was Dave Evison, and still today I have nightmares over what was my worst customer ever.

Dave Evison was a character I will never forget. He had a business selling Northern Soul Records and music from the 60s to shops from the back of a little white van. He was quite famous on the Northern Soul circuit and supplemented his income by working as a DJ. He bought a lot of product off me, but he was very high maintenance. He would phone me at all hours asking what CDs he should stock and often, when he was in the area, he would pop to our house for advice. It wasn't just music advice he was after; he seemed to have lots of problems in his private life and seemed to think I was some sort of amateur psychiatrist. My then wife Rachael began to lose patience with these visits, but one day Dave overstepped the mark.

He had called around the previous day to buy stock; as usual we had made him a cup of tea. Later that day he fell ill and had managed to convince himself that we had poisoned him. We would never claim to be the best tea makers in the world, but this was the first time we had been accused of poisoning somebody. Days later he turned up at the door telling us he had been to the doctor and dentist and it was imperative that we told him what poison we had used so that the hospital could find the antidote. If we weren't prepared to tell him, he was going to the police. Rachael told him if he ever came to our door again she would more than poison him. We never met him again and a few months later we heard his business had folded.

One thing that strikes me about the Midlands is that places like Derby, Leicester, Loughborough, Coventry and Wolverhampton all had numerous independent record shops. These days, none of the aforementioned places have a single shop that we sell to. One city that still has some independent retail outlets is Nottingham. As well as the excellent jazz specialist Music Inn and the easy listening specialist Pendulum, based in the Victoria market, Nottingham is home to one of the most famous record shops in the country – Selectadisc.

Brian Selby originally opened the shop in 1966 and for 43 years it has been one of the UK's top record shops. In 1991 they opened a second branch in the heart of London.

The Nottingham store's manager is a Notts County fanatic called Jim Cooke, whose knowledge of indie music is second to none. I always enjoyed calling on Jim and over the years he has told me some great tales. He has always been a huge fan of The Clash and he is also passionate about politics – his views are certainly left of centre. One evening he visited The Garage, a club in Nottingham, and noticed that The Clash was drinking at the bar. Jim engaged Joe Strummer in a conversation on music, where they had plenty of common ground. Soon the chat turned to politics and Jim informed Joe of how disappointed he was that The Clash did not better-support the miners in their battle against Margaret Thatcher's Government back in 1984. Unlike bands such as The Redskins, The Housemartins and The Three Johns, The Clash did not do any benefit gigs in support of the miners. Joe Strummer was taken aback and slightly embarrassed by Jim's onslaught. By the end of the conversation Joe suggested that the band call into Jim's shop the next day and do a gig. The following day, with Joe Strummer standing on the counter, The Clash rewarded Selectadisc punters with a magnificent performance.

One young man also enjoyed the show, but clearly did not realise he had just witnessed a performance by one of rock's greatest-ever bands. When the gig had finished, he approached Joe Strummer and introduced himself as the social secretary of Clarendon College. He told Joe that he was most impressed with the band's performance, especially some of the cover versions of Clash songs. He told Joe that he was looking for a good group to play The Colleges ball and was willing to give him £100 if they were prepared to play. Jim can't recall Joe's exact answer but remembers it did contain the words f*** and off.

Another tale that made me smile was when a lady said to Jim that she was after an album by her son's favourite singer, 'Reg Zeppelin'.

The last few years have seen many changes at Selectadisc. Most notably, the shops have been bought by Phil Barton, who is also involved in Brighton's Rounder Records and London's Sister Ray.

They have recently opened an online store, so I hope Selectadisc will be around for a long time to come.

The Midlands is home to one of the largest independent chains in the country – Pendulum Records. Completely independent of the shop in Nottingham with the same name, they have four stores spread across the East Midlands. The chain is based in Melton Mowbray with the other shops being in Market Harborough, Stamford and Retford.

Here is their bizarre tale of how Pendulum obtained their stock of one of the biggest CD releases of 2008 – Coldplay's *Viva La Vida*, which I wrote about in a feature for the *Independent* newspaper, titled 'Slipped Discs'.

In better days, say ten years ago, they would have ordered about 1200 copies of such a major release for their shops. These days, however, business is not so good, so they limited the initial order to EMI to just 50 copies. EMI's dealer price for the album was £8.95.

When the CD was released, it generated much excitement. It was put out for sale at £10.99 – a fair price. But regular customers soon flocked into the shops telling them that Morrisons were selling the Coldplay CD for £6.99 each.

The owner had no wish to upset his customers, so he took the decision to reduce his CDs to £9.99. Despite being £3 more expensive than the supermarkets, the shops still sold out. What was he to do now for additional supply? Should he order from EMI at £8.95 or should he pop down to Morrisons and buy for £6.99?

No contest – so off he popped to the supermarkets. Unfortunately, he was limited to five copies per visit, and after two visits Morrisons made it clear to him that he had become an unwelcome customer. There was only one thing for it – each of the staff took it in turns to pop out to the supermarkets during their lunch hour to buy five copies apiece.

It became an exercise in espionage – in order not to arouse suspicion, they staked out each supermarket and learned when the staff changed shift. Now they could each buy up to fifteen copies a day – five from each shift. The chain has now obtained more than 250 copies of the album from Morrisons and Asda, who also sold the CD at £6.99.

The shop owner has also been helped out by relatives and friends who have organised themselves into little buying teams, raiding both supermarkets for the CDs.

This is no way to earn a livelihood – instead of selling CDs, staff are touring supermarkets. An important point is that, with so many record shops doing this, the figures for album CD charts become false – the Coldplay CD has first been registered for the chart when purchased at Morrisons and has then been registered again when sold at the independent record shop, therefore counting as two sales for chart purposes.

Just when it appeared that things could get no worse for independent record shops, in June 2008 Morrisons decided to sell all chart CDs for £6 – more than £3 less than independent shops can purchase them for from record companies.

During June 2008, the biggest suppliers to Pendulum were:

Morrisons supermarkets
Universal Music
Asda supermarkets
EMI Music
Proper Music

During that month I was inundated with shops calling to tell me about the Morrisons promotion. One dealer informed me of how he was beating the system. It had become clear to him that some Morrisons outlets were not bothered how many CDs were purchased, so he would turn up on a Friday evening to find out how many copies they had in stock of the CDs he was interested in purchasing. If the quantity was small, he would buy the lot. This ensured that Morrisons would have no chance to re-stock and that, for the busy weekend period, it would be sold out of some of its top titles. Therefore, the only way people could buy those titles during that weekend would be to visit his shop.

It is good to see one customer fighting back – but how long can it last? When you mention this tale to the general public they just cannot believe the madness that is the UK record industry.

Dave Gibbs, the chain's owner, has a fascinating background, as he has seen record shops from the other side – previously he had been a sales rep for Impulse. The roll of Impulse was to hype records. They employed a team of sales reps who drove around the country with cars full of CDs and singles to simply give away to chart-return shops. The Zomba Group owned the company, now famous for artists such as Britney Spears and Justin Timberlake. Dave's salary was mainly commission, which he received for obtaining top 20 hits for the titles he was promoting. To earn money, therefore, he needed to encourage shops to enter numbers in the chart-return machine by fair means or foul. He was allowed a fair amount of freedom and could offer up to ten full-price CDs a week to each shop in return for numbers entered into the machine. One shop in Rotherham called K&D was known amongst the sales reps of the time as 'Hypers Delight', as in return for free stock they allowed the reps to type in as many numbers as they liked.

Dave remembers fondly the day, after two years of giving away free stock, he was given a new release that had to 'sell' to shops – it was Kylie Minogue's new album.

In 1997 Impulse were merged with Pinnacle distribution and Dave was made redundant. He was approached by one of his customers, Mike Eden, who had two record stores trading as Pendulum in Melton Mowbray and Market Harborough. Mike was keen to expand and suggested to Dave that they go into partnership together, as he had noticed that Retford was a town in need of a record shop. They opened Retford in 1997 and two years later the boys opened a fourth store in Stamford. In 2005 Mike retired from the business and Dave purchased his share in Pendulum.

Dave's favourite customer is the man known as 'Trolley Man'. In all the years he has been coming into the shop, Dave has never seen him wearing anything else other than his beloved Eddie Stobart T-shirt. He is always accompanied by his shopping trolley, which he calls his 'shopping lorry'. He only ever purchases CDs with lorry songs or with pictures of trucks on the front. His favourite band was Leeds' 80s rockers Red Lorry Yellow Lorry. Dave scours the record and DVD companies to find anything truck-related knowing he has a guaranteed sale.

With Pendulum, like lots of other record shops, finding it more profitable to obtain its CDs of Coldplay *Viva La Vida* from Morrisons rather than from the record company, Dave struggles to understand the logic of this, as he has been particularly hard hit, because all of his shops have supermarkets on their doorstep. The supermarkets are the main reason why record shops are vanishing on the high street.

I'm not certain that the record companies really supported getting the supermarkets involved, but certainly they had no choice. Supermarkets are expert in seizing on products that have a high-perceived value by the public and offering them at much lower prices, so as to encourage the consumer to believe that all products are of such value.

The overvalued CD was perfect for this: a top 40-chart rack would take up very little space, and a £10 chart album was a real bargain. The UK record companies had no choice. If they chose not to supply the supermarkets then the stores would have simply used the new EU single market to source the same product elsewhere.

During the 90s CDs where cheaper to buy in Germany than they were to purchase from UK record companies. This enabled supermarkets to source their product at a rock bottom price, due to their huge buying power. The record companies operated as little fiefdoms – certainly the sales director of EMI Germany wouldn't be unhappy if one of his wholesale customers suddenly placed an order for 20,000 Robbie Williams CDs – he may even have given a nice bit of discount, and not been too choosy where they ended up, as long as it wasn't on his patch. The likelihood was that the German wholesaler who had bought the CDs from EMI Germany would sell those Robbie Williams' CDs to a UK customer for a lower price than that which they could purchase off EMI in the UK.

Where the record companies slipped up was that neither they nor the specialist retailers could agree on how to move forward. The retailers still wanted the generous support, but the record companies refused to offer them the terms to do so, partly, I'm sure, because they felt that the indie retailers had gotten too powerful. The supermarkets took advantage of this situation and turned the pressure up on the independent record shops by selling some CDs at cost (or even less), as it perfectly suited their purpose. It didn't matter that they were not making money on music – what cheap CDs did was entice people into the store. How many people go in to a Supermarket just to purchase a CD? The answer is hardly anybody, most people come out with a basket full of goods and it is on those goods that the supermarket makes their profit.

The next ten years saw increases in the number of units sold, but decreases in overall revenue. In other words, more CDs were being sold for less. As the gates opened on price reductions, the consumer flooded in, but the retailer's margins kept getting squeezed. Take into account the following situations: to send a box out to 400 independent record shops, three times a week equates to dispatching 57,600 boxes a year. Imagine the amount of cardboard used, not to mention the staff and time involved; bare in mind the 57,600 invoices that have to be printed.

Alternatively, is it better to deliver to five supermarkets and a couple of online retailers who purchase more anyway? Only seven deliveries need to be dispatched a day – that's 420 per year. Think of the economic differences – which situation is more viable?

This is only half the story. Have you ever heard of a supermarket breaking an unknown artist? By throwing their hat in with the supermarkets, the record companies have allowed music to stagnate. Endless compilations, greatest hit packages, and Reality TV stars have produced a dull market devoid of excitement. The supermarkets are not the sole reason why music has stagnated. It is also about the decline of musical culture. In times gone by, if there was a new Beatles or Led Zeppelin record, people would be queuing outside the record shop on the day of release. A release from a major artist would create such a buzz. These days, such excitement is now created for the release of the new Grand Theft Auto video game, and purchasing music is a much lower priority in people's lives.

With the record companies selling their musical souls, it was not long before the supermarkets were calling the shots. Prices were driven down; release dates were influenced by whether a supermarket could promote the CD. The knock-on effect of this was to force record stores out of business. Previously the biggest percentage of independent shop sales came from chart CDs – this was their core business. By undercutting record stores by £3 to £4, not only were the independents losing business, customers were leaving in droves due to the record stores being perceived as expensive. Record shops never stood a chance. If the record companies had considered the interests of record shops at heart, they would not have supplied the supermarkets on sale or return.

Every week tens of thousands of CDs are shipped out to supermarkets and thousands of unsold CDs are then shipped back. The most galling thing for independents is that often this returned stock is then sold on to them. Nearly every shop I go to can tell me a tale of purchasing stock and receiving it with a Woolworths/Asda/Tesco etc sticker still on the CD. Although record shops do get offered certain titles on sale or return, if they could return all unsold stock, they would be in a far healthier position. If record shops make a mistake with their buying they have to retain the stock and will usually have to reduce the price of their overstocks to sell them, often at a loss.

My own experiences at Proper show how powerful the high street's biggest seller of CDs has become, and that company is not a CD retailer – it is Tesco.

We were putting out what was our biggest album of the year. It was to have a £50k week-one TV advertising spend. The label were very keen that the album was available everywhere. All the supermarkets, except Tesco, signed up at a fair rate of discount from dealer price. Tesco asked for an astonishing 50 per cent discount, which equated to Proper selling the album to them for £4. We went to the label and told them. They said that this was too much. Could we try to get 50p more? So we went back to Tesco and asked if they could increase their offer to £4.50. They said no. We asked them at least to consider it. They did, and we rang them the next day. They said they had considered it and their offer was now £3.50. The point behind all of this is that Tesco is the biggest seller of CDs on the high street. That CD had to be in Tesco and they knew it. We decided to give them a miss.

They got that power by undercutting everyone else and if the British record companies wouldn't supply them, they simply bought from Europe.

Once they got to be the biggest they put the squeeze on and there was nothing the major record companies could do except to play ball in the hope of a few favours now and again. In 2007 Tesco's exclusive supplier told us that we would have to pay them £10,000 per year just for the right to present product to them. No guarantee of any sales, just the right to speak with them. The *Sun* picked up this story. Tesco immediately denied it. Ten days later (when the fuss had died down) they wrote saying the price was indeed £10,000. Although our company sells 1 per cent of all CDs sold in the UK, we have never sold to Tesco, and I am sure you can understand why.

If supermarkets had to retain overstocks they would stock far less. It is possible that record companies' resultant profits would be higher, as they would have no need to employ the people who man their returns departments. The biggest problem has been that supermarkets have been allowed to have separate companies based in the Channel Islands. They have then been able to import any audio product without having to pay VAT, providing it is not being sold for more than £17. This legal loophole costs the taxpayer a fortune. Record shops, in a rare show of unity, organised a petition – signed by the owners of most record stores in the country – demanding this practice be stopped. The petition was delivered to the House of Commons, but had no effect.

My thoughts on the subject are that the independent shops should have launched their own campaign of awareness and let the general public know how the supermarkets are avoiding paying tax. They needed to point out that, by doing this, they are indirectly depriving hospitals and schools of investment.

Most worrying for independents is the recent trend for supermarket exclusivity on a CD release. The Katie Melua and Eva Cassidy cover version of the Louis Armstrong classic 'What a Wonderful World' was available on CD exclusively from Tesco. At least 100,000 customers went to Tesco instead of to their local record shops. In America Garth Brooks' CDs are available exclusively through Wal Mart stores. Chris De Burgh released his last album through Woolworths. There was an angry backlash from many independents, as several stores scrapped their Chris De Burgh sections. I would be surprised if you could find any of his CDs in your local record shop; that is if you have a local record shop! The danger is that more easy-listening artists will follow his example.

It is time for independent record shops to take a long, hard look at their business. Those stores that have embraced the changing markets have survived, whilst those who have refused to adapt and have relied on chart sales have gone.

* * *

From Melton Mowbray it's a long way to Dereham to visit a delightful shop called Sounds, a little oasis in an area that is a desert for record shops. East Anglia has been decimated by record-shop closures, with only a handful of independent shops in the whole of the counties of Norfolk, Suffolk and Lincolnshire.

John Lawson's passion for record collecting started in the months leading up to Christmas 1964. He knew that he was getting a Dansette Senator Record Player for Christmas so, being a sharp-minded teenager, he figured that it would be an astute move to purchase at least one record, so that the Dansette could be fired into action on Christmas morning. So, one damp, dark November evening after school, with a few half-crowns in his pocket and sixpence for the bus fare, it was off into town to make a purchase. This significant event can be summarised thus: the first record he bought was the Dave Clark Five EP, with its shiny, laminated sleeve depicting an aerial view of the group in glorious black and white. A record that to this day is treasured. From that day on there was no stopping him and every week his collection grew, as he spent all of his spare cash on his hobby.

John's collection grew so big that along with his partner, Sally King, he decided to sell some of his LPs off at a local record fair. This soon became a regular event, and they took the decision to have their own stall. John and Sally plied their trade at record fairs in Cambridge, Norwich, Ipswich, Brighton etc, meeting like-minded people and being able to indulge in a hobby that was both sociable and slightly profitable (well, most of the takings were spent buying more records, but there was usually enough left for a curry on the way home!)

During this time John's day job was as an Art teacher at a comprehensive school, but after sixteen years it was time for a change. He had wanted to start his own second-hand record shop but, at the time, he felt that the smaller towns were not big enough to sustain such a venture and all the larger towns and cities had more than their fair share. One day he noticed that Sounds Music & Entertainment Centre in the small Norfolk town of Dereham was up for sale as a going concern and, after negotiations with solicitors, bank managers, business advisers etc, he opened for business on 1 September 1993.

He abbreviated the name to Sounds and set about transforming its slightly 'pipe and slippers' vibe into something a little more rock 'n' roll. This was done by not taking on any of the electric organ stock and replacing it with electric guitars. Within a few months he had installed a couple of Lift CD systems to almost triple the CD display facility. This was at a time when vinyl was being phased out, so very few new releases were arriving on LP format.

John reminisced to me that if he hadn't have been behind the counter for the past fifteen years, he wouldn't have been in the bands he had played with during that time, he wouldn't own original copies of The Beatles' 'She Loves You' and The Small Faces' 'Here Comes the Nice' in his sheet music collection, he wouldn't be the proud owner of a 1976 Fender Jazz bass, and he wouldn't have obtained a second Dave Clark Five EP to go with the first that started his record collection way back in 1964.

Through musicians coming into the shop John was asked to form a band, which they called Souled Out. Thinking it would be a laugh, he decided to give it a go. They made their debut performance with a line-up of guitar, bass, drums, keyboards, alto sax and three female vocalists. In true Commitments style, there were sackings, punch-ups, affairs, back stabbings, pregnancies, divorce and loads of brilliant gigs. After six years they agreed to disband and go out with a bang at a big gig on Millennium Eve and, from that first gathering in the Norwich rehearsal studio back in 1994, John was the only original member left!

A month or two into the new millennium he was offered the bass role in another soul band, The Soul Traders, who he is still with to this day.

The second-hand record side of the business (the department titled 'low-profit obsessive hobby dept') came about following a bit of customer interaction. A punter who led a successful folk-rock band was having a clear-out of his record collection and asked John if he could leave a box of albums in the corner of the shop to see if anyone was interested. Well, people were interested, and as the box emptied he topped it up with stock left over from his record fair days. This got him back into buying, selling and trading once again, the by-product being that this activity was also providing him with an opportunity to expand his own collection. A similar thing happened with his sheet music collection; it's probably hard for a non-obsessive to comprehend the thrill of sifting through the unwanted contents of a piano stool in the hope of finding 'Subterranean Homesick Blues' by Bob Dylan on sheet music.

Although business has been tough for John over the last few years, he always has a smile on his face and is so passionate about what he does. I asked him if he thought of what he did as a job or a hobby. After a little deliberation he said that he thought of it as neither a job nor a hobby; 'It's what I do, I just turn up every day'.

Long may he continue just turning up every day.

*   *   *

It is a 155-mile drive from Dereham to the city of Birmingham to visit my customer there. Not so long ago it would take me two days to call on all of the record shops in the area. Now we only have one independent shop that makes it worthwhile for me to visit, and what an amazing store it is. If *Dr Who* ever wished to locate an episode in a typical 60s record shop, then The Diskery would be their natural choice. The shop has hardly changed in 40 years. In fact, the store has gained itself a reputation as the shop location for TV. It has featured in *The Doctors*; *Dalziel and Pascoe*; and *Where Are They Now* and has been used as a backdrop for interviews with Bill Oddie and Jim Bowen.

Posters from a bygone era adorn the walls, including original Beatles, Elvis Presley and Eddie Cochran material, whilst the shop is filled with vinyl and music memorabilia – my favourite is a newspaper article pinned to the wall informing you that, in 1969, Delia Smith baked the cake which featured on the front cover of the Rolling Stones album *Let It Bleed*.

The Diskery stocks an amazing collection of old wind-up gramophones; copies of *Melody Maker* (from as far back as 1947); matchbox cars; and a selection of photographs from the *Carry On* movies. Personally, I think that Maurice Hunting, the owner, is missing a trick – he should turn the shop into a music museum that stocks records and charge visitors an admittance fee.

Jimmy Shannon and Liam Scully run the shop. They obviously enjoy the work, as they have been there for 81 years between them. Jimmy could have had an alternative career as a comedian, because whenever I visit he has a whole new batch of jokes to tell me before we discuss business. Inevitably, customers are also treated – or, should I say, subjected – to Jimmy's latest jokes. If anybody hears that Frank Carson is running out of gags, then pass them the telephone number of The Diskery. Jimmy would be delighted to help.

The shop has an incredible history. It is the only shop I know which was started as an act of revenge. Maurice, the owner, was a huge fan of music and regularly purchased his 78s from a Birmingham record store, called Mansell's, until one day, in front of a crowd of customers, the shop owner challenged him to open his coat. "Why?" asked Maurice.

"So that I can see how many records you are trying to steal," responded the owner. A perfectly innocent Maurice was really embarrassed and angry, and he vowed never to set foot in the store again.

Soon after, Maurice was the innocent party in a road accident, for which he received compensation. He used this money to set up The Diskery – just along the road from Mansell's in Hurst Street. He was determined to show them how a record store should treat its customers. Today, Mansell's is long gone and The Diskery is the most famous independent shop in the Midlands.

At first, Maurice leased a room above a second-hand store but, thanks to record company snobbery, he did not stay there long. When he first applied to EMI for a credit account, he was told that his first order would need to be £500 (which was a lot of money in 1951). So, he looked through their catalogue, selected £500 worth of records, and sent off his order. Next, he received a letter from EMI informing him that they would send a company representative to inspect his premises to see if they were worthy of stocking EMI product. To Maurice's horror, EMI duly rejected The Diskery, as it did not have a glass-fronted window.

The store quickly relocated to a ground-floor building with a glass front, and finally EMI agreed to supply it. Its big break came when Gerry Mulligan broke into the charts. He was on the Vogue record label and The Diskery was the only shop in Birmingham to have an account with them. It sold thousands of copies of his albums, whilst rival shops were struggling to open accounts with Vogue.

The shop has many famous customers, amongst them all of the members of Black Sabbath, Robert Plant, Steve Winwood, Joe Cocker and the

American superstar Chaka Khan, who calls in whenever she visits Birmingham.

One star who made the wrong impression was legendary jazz artist Roland Kirk. One Tuesday he popped in to browse the shelves. Jimmy had seen him perform the previous evening at Birmingham Town Hall and also had tickets for another performance that evening. Jimmy put a record by blues artist Son House on the turntable. Immediately, Roland barked at him, "What the f*** is that?" Jimmy replied Son House. "What the f*** do you know about the blues?" was Roland's curt reply. That night Jimmy attended the gig. Roland performed brilliantly, but was no longer one of his heroes.

Another famous person to disappoint was Frank Sinatra Jnr, who called in and bought a considerable number of LP's. He asked what the record was that they were playing, and Maurice replied that it was a new LP by Art Tatum. "Never heard of him," Frank replied and strode out. The staff were shocked that a famous artist such as Frank had never heard of Art Tatum, one of the greatest jazz musicians of his generation.

One of the nicer tales Jimmy told me was when he played Santa Claus to Ozzy Osborne. Ozzy's first wife, Thelma, had ordered a Christmas present for him – the album *I Feel Like I'm Fixin' to Die* by Country Joe and the Fish. Then Jimmy received a phone call on Christmas Eve, from Thelma, explaining that she would not be able to get down to the shop to collect the album. "No problem," said Jimmy, and, after the shop had closed, he dropped it off at the Osborne house to ensure that it would be under Ozzy's tree on Christmas morning.

One artist who will always be grateful for support from The Diskery is blues artist Sherman Robertson. Sherman can be described as a journeyman blues artist in the sense that he has been around a long time and has never really received the recognition he deserves.

In 2007 he released an album called *Guitar Man* (which Proper Records distributed). I recall The Diskery ordering a copy. Six weeks later I visited to be greeted by Jimmy enthusing about Sherman. He had been to see him live and told me he was one of the greatest guitarists he had ever seen. Even more amazing was that the shop had sold over 30 copies of the CD. I was astonished, and when I got back to the office I checked the national sales. We had sold a total of 61 copies – of which 32 had gone to one shop – The Diskery.

At Proper Records we release about 60 CDs each month, so every now and again a release slips under the radar – meaning that it does not get promoted as well as it should do. Mortified, I e-mailed the record shops of the UK recommending the CD to any shop that stocked blues. The album then started selling, and by the end of the year it was one of our top 10 best-selling blues CDs, with The Diskery having sold more than 100 copies – all down to Jimmy's enthusiasm.

Will The Diskery be one of the 'Last Shops Standing'? You bet. They are immune to changes in the music industry and I am sure that, like Ole Man River, they will just keep rolling along.

One shop I used to really enjoy calling on in Birmingham was The Record Centre. The proprietor, Ray Purslow, is a great character and he is not only a jazz collector; but he is also a prominent member of The Sinatra Music Society and known for his expertise on the great entertainer. Because he was over retirement age, and as he was retailing in a poor location, Ray decided to close his shop in May 2007 and has continued with his well-respected and very reliable mail order service ever since. He has a wealth of musical knowledge on the swing bands and about vocalists who sing the Great American Songbook. He has, in fact, assisted with over 100 CD releases in conjunction with several of the majors, as well as independent labels too, particularly with the two-on-one releases where he has often had to loan original sleeves and sometimes even the records themselves!

He is an avid Sinatra collector and has dozens of related anecdotes, my favourite being the tale about a gentleman who called in and asked for a vinyl copy of *Sinatra Sings Great Songs from Great Britain*. Ray explained that he did have a copy and it was a Japanese pressing. The man enquired if Sinatra was singing in Japanese. Ray reassured him Sinatra was, indeed, singing in English and the quality of recordings on Japanese vinyl was superior to any other issue. The gentleman bought the LP and then to Ray's surprise called in the next day with the album and demanded his money back. He told Ray that Sinatra was singing in Japanese. Ray mentioned he had sold over 100 copies of this album and nobody had ever complained before. Ray put the record on the turntable, and both agreed that it was Sinatra singing on the record and that was definitely singing in English. The gentleman was flummoxed – how come he sang in English on Ray's turntable but sang in Japanese on his?

Ray suggested he took the LP home to try again. Later that day, Ray received a phone call from the embarrassed gentleman, explaining his son had changed the speed on his record player from 33 to 45 and the sound of the sped up Sinatra had made him believe it was Frank singing in Japanese.

Chapter 10

What Sound Does Bread Make?

The following day I head to the roundabout capital of the world, Milton Keynes, a town I am never sure of whether it is in the Midlands or is the beginning of the south. One thing I am sure of is that it must have more roundabouts per square mile than anywhere on the planet. I recall the first time I visited the town, as it took me an hour to find my customer, as I seemed to be touring all of their 400 roundabouts. There are few places to stop to check your map and if you ask a local well you have no chance. I recall stopping at a BP garage and asking a man if he knew where the Stables theatre was? I followed him up to the 7th roundabout but I gave up when his instructions included take the third exit at the 8th.

I am glad I made the effort to find The Stables – it was worth it in the end. The record shop there is housed within the theatre, and is one of my favourite shops. The theatre was originally owned by jazz legends Johnny Dankworth and Cleo Laine.

A charming couple – Vic and June Chamberlain, runs the shop. None of my customers is so fanatically supportive of a single artist as Vic – he is the world's number-one fan of Paul Rodgers and Free. It does not matter who or what is playing the theatre, from jazz to Shakespeare, the foyer will still be rocking to 'All Right Now', 'Wishing Well', 'My Brother Jake' or some other Free classic. I sell to Vic every month and cannot recall ever having received an order from him without it containing a Free album.

He has done everything within his power to persuade the theatre to book Paul Rodgers but, so far, he has not been able to afford him. So, let me make a direct appeal through this book – if any reader knows Paul Rodgers, will you please ask him to do a gig at The Stables for an affordable fee so that one committed fan can die happy, in the knowledge that his dreams have been fulfilled?

I enjoy selling to The Stables. Often I can visit Vic in the late afternoon and then stay to watch a gig. There have been some great shows there, but The Waterboys were my own favourite.

Vic is a good customer, as he uses his imagination and so can often buy CDs that interest nobody else. For example, at one time we had quantities of a 1998 World Cup CD sitting on our shelves, which we could not sell at any price. Then, out of the blue, Vic offered to buy 50 copies! I was flummoxed – how on earth was he going to sell them?

But Vic had a plan – it turned out that Jimmy Greaves, the famous ex-footballer, was appearing at the theatre to perform an evening of his reminiscences and amusing anecdotes. Vic persuaded Jimmy to sign the CDs and then sold them as signed World Cup albums.

Now, that's real enterprise.

The Stables' opening hours are irregular, as it stays open during the evenings whenever concerts are on, which are frequent. The theatre's opening performance was in February 1970 and its Grand Opening Gala featured Johnny and Cleo, along with John Williams, Julie Felix, Marion Montgomery and Andre Previn. It is astonishing to think that at that time you could see the top jazz artists of the day for as little as 50p.

For nearly 30 years the venue offered the best in entertainment, until, towards the end of the nineties, when it became obvious that a bigger, waterproof building was needed. With support from the National Lottery, a new building was built between April and October 1999. Today The Stables is a registered charity, which is funded by, amongst others, the Arts Council, which helps it to further the cause of music.

The Stables was re-launched with a Gala Concert, featuring Rod Argent and Colin Blunstone, along with nearly all of the artists who had performed at the opening of the original theatre. The new building was built on land donated by Johnny and Cleo and had room for a café and CD store when, previously, artists had had to sell their own CDs after each gig. Although The Stables has its own record shop, many artists prefer to sell their CDs themselves. This frustrates Vic and highlights a much bigger problem.

Whether it is via the artist's own website or at their gigs, vast quantities of CDs are sold direct to the public, therefore cutting out the record store. It is easy to understand the artists view; why give part of the profit to the distributor and the record shop when they can keep it for themselves? This is short-term thinking, however, as both the distributor and the record shop brings the artist to a wider audience. What is more disturbing is the new trend for artists to sell direct to the public via their own website, then months later give the lucky record shops the chance to sell their product. Again, stores should stick together and refuse to stock artists who do this.

Nobody should begrudge an artist selling their wares, as long as they are not selling it before it is available to the general public. At Proper, we used to distribute a fabulous folk singer called Kate Rusby. Although we loved selling her music, it could be a frustrating experience. We handled her CD *Little Lights*, which just scraped into the top 75. Kate had been selling the CD at her gigs a full month before release. This created a short-term profit, but if people had purchased her CD at traditional outlets instead of at the concerts, I have no doubt that Kate would have been a top 40 artist many years ago.

Despite problems with artists selling their own product, The Stables will be one of the 'Last Shops Standing'. I thoroughly recommend you turn up late afternoon; browse through the excellent selection of CDs in the shop (keep moving or Vic will flog you a Free album); enjoy a bite to eat in the café; and stay on to watch a performance. It is a lovely place, and I am sure you will have a memorable day.

* * *

Once I manage to escape the confusion of Milton Keynes roundabouts, I head across country to a great shop in the heart of Oxfordshire, Rapture Records.

Owned by Gary Smith and Mark Sharman, Witney-based Rapture is typical of the independents that have survived the drastic changes in the industry over the last five years. The shop is like a community centre, with many customers calling in several times a week, often just to chat.

Gary's first job in the music industry was at the appallingly named R.E.Cords in Burton-on-Trent. He noticed an advert for shop staff and instinctively knew that it was the job for him. The advert stated that you had to include your five favourite artists on your application. Gary's were Theatre Of Hate, The Jam, Japan, Bruce Springsteen and Orange Juice. Although Springsteen wasn't actually one of his favourite five, he said he was because he had seen the guy behind the counter wearing Springsteen badges. It was a shrewd move. The interview went well, with Gary taking every opportunity to tell the owner how magnificent Bruce Springsteen was. The tactic worked and Gary was given the job. For a school leaver in 1982, this was a dream job.

The shop sold tickets for Rock City in Nottingham and in return Gary was on the guest list for any band he wanted. He found himself with many new friends and attended gigs several times a week. In 1985 he saw an advert for Our Price. It was opening a store in town and was recruiting.

In its early days it kept chart prices cheap and had a customer service policy that extended beyond pointing and grunting (the traditional response from many independent stores at that time). This led to rapid expansion in London and the South East. Our Price floated on the stock market, which showed its approval by providing lots of capital for expansion.

It has been intriguing observing many of the independent shop owners who worked at HMV, Virgin or Our Price on this tour. Record-shop staff who had previously worked in a music chain seemed to have fond memories of HMV and Virgin, but they do not remember Our Price with such affection. It was good to talk with Gary and Mark, who did their best to redress the balance, pointing out that Our Price employed a huge number of people in its time. A lot of these people are still scattered around the industry today. There are band members, record company executives, TV executives, music programmers, festival organisers, music journalists, record label managers, DJ's, and, of course, retailers.

Gary told me of Our Price's commitment to customer service. Once a year new managers would meet up with Our Price founders Gary Nesbit, Barry Hartog and Mike Isaacs. Gary Nesbit would tell the tale of how he was in an independent shop one day when a man came up to the counter and asked where the Van Morrison albums were. The assistant didn't even look up from reading his copy of *NME*. He grunted at the customer, "Over there," pointing in a general direction. The man walked out. A couple of hours later he spotted the man again. Another record shop in the town had their logo on clear, see-through bags, and as he passed the man, he noticed some Van Morrison albums in his bag. That is why Our Price drummed it into staff that if a customer asked for something, they had to take them to the section.

Gary joined Our Price the week before Live Aid, and it was an exciting time for the industry. The new Midlands' stores represented the first time Our Price had ventured north of Watford, and there were lots of job opportunities. Within a short time Gary was managing Our Price stores around the Midlands.

The mid-80s was not a difficult time to sell music. Most market towns had an independent store and an Our Price – and most customers would frequent both. WHSmith bought Our Price for £46 m in 1986. At its peak there were 330 Our Price stores.

The Oxford Our Price, on Cornmarket Street, was a who's who of the exciting Oxford music scene, with members of Radiohead (Colin Greenwood), Ride (Steve Queralt), The Egg (Dave Gaydon), Tallula Gosh (Amelia Fletcher), and The Jennifers (Nic Goffey, who became a video director and who's brother Danny formed Supergrass) all working there at some time. Mark has fond memories of working with Amelia Fletcher, who worked at the shop by day and sang with Tallulah Gosh in the evening. Whilst working at Virgin, he had bought all of her records and was now overawed to be working with her. Michael Eavis called in one day and asked who they thought he should book for Glastonbury. Gary still cringes when he remembers all of the fantastic bands around the Oxford scene, and yet the shop suggested Jesus Jones.

During this period a man called Mike McGinley was the operations manager for Our Price. It is fair to say that he terrified most of the staff. He was a perfectionist for cleanliness. If they knew he was coming, they often spent the whole day cleaning the shop, as Mike was the type of guy who would wet his finger and run it down the racks – if he found dust, he would explode with anger.

On the day of one of his visits the Our Price manager was confident the shop was spick and span and the shop looked good, as it was full of customers. He noticed one toddler being admonished by his mum, who then dragged the youngster out of the shop. At that moment, Mike marched in. The manager noticed a little pile where the toddler had been. Sure enough, the toddler had deposited something on the carpet. There was only one thing for it. The manager rushed to the pile of poo, and with a kick Gary Lineker himself would have been proud of, he deposited the deposition under the rack. After greeting Mike, the manager rushed to the toilet to clean the poo from his shoe.

After working for an independent and Our Price in its many guises and in many roles, Gary hooked up with friend and previous colleague Mark Sharman. Mark and Gary first met whilst running rival Our Price stores in Oxford in the early 90s. For a while there were four Our Price stores in the city.

Mark's journey in the music industry started when he was given a temporary job over Christmas at Virgin in Peterborough. His sister had just left on the first leg of a world tour starting in Holland, and the idea was for Mark to earn some money over the next couple of months and then fly out to join her in some exotic location. When Christmas ended the management at Virgin had been really impressed with his enthusiasm and asked him to stay on. It was a tough decision, as he loved working there, but he was also determined to see the world. In those days there were no mobile phones, so he had to delay his decision until his sister contacted him to let him know what exotic location she was at. When his sister called and told him she was still in Holland picking tomatoes, it made Mark's choice easy.

Mark lived in Spalding and commuted into Peterborough each day. He felt like the coolest kid in town. Whenever he went out in Spalding he kept his Virgin uniform on, as it was a great talking point with his friends. In fact, working at Virgin was like being one step down from being a pop star. After a fantastic year at Virgin, what happened next seemed like a calamity. In 1987 the Virgin shops were taken over by Our Price.

Mark had some friends in Oxford and he made it known that if there where any jobs going in that area, he would be keen to move there. Our Price immediately transferred him to one of their Oxford branches. He will never forget his first day, because when he arrived the manager, a girl called Jackie Baker, informed him that he would be in charge of hoovering, so he spent his first morning vacuuming the carpets. Mark really felt he was on the way down, as Virgin had their own professional cleaner.

He will never forget an incident when a large, but tired-looking, Labrador lobbed into the store. Mark found it amusing that, after looking around the store, the dog took residence under the CD racking, where he promptly fell asleep. The shop was busy and nobody could be bothered to wake the dog from its slumber. Come closing time, Jackie gave the dog a shake to wake him up before letting out a shriek: "The dogs dead!" As she was manager and Mark was new, he felt it best that she handle the situation. Jackie phoned the council to ask them to collect the dog, who was now residing in a black plastic bin liner in the stockroom. The council told her that they would not be able to collect the dead dog for a couple of days. Jackie felt that they couldn't wait that long, so the poor Labrador was thrown out with the rubbish.

At Virgin, Mark's role was rock CD buyer. Now, when his friends enquired what his role was at Our Price, he was reluctant to admit he was chief hooverer. Mark pestered Jackie for more responsibility and eventually he was given the job of ordering Pinnacle product.

At this time Mark was a huge rock and metal fan and was the first to admit that he had not latched on to the emerging Madchester scene. When Pinnacle called for his first order, he played it safe and ordered just one copy of the debut Stone Roses album. On the day of release the shop opened at 9am. By 30 seconds past 9am the shop had sold out of all Stone Roses product. Mark worked on the counter with Jackie that day and it seemed as if every minute somebody wanted to buy a Stone Roses album. Mark just wished the ground would swallow him up.

After that episode Mark knew that he was never going to make a name for himself in Oxford, and when the chance of a transfer to High Wycombe came up, he jumped at the opportunity. He did a great job there and was offered the chance to manage his own shop. Mark was delighted, but disaster soon struck. Mark had been living in Oxford and commuting to High Wycombe by bus. One week into his job as manager the bus service was scrapped. There was only one thing for it – Mark stuck out his thumb and hitch-hiked to work and back every day. This went on for months before a member of staff took pity on him and informed the area manager, who transferred him to the Reading branch. There was a train service to Reading, and it was a bigger shop and, therefore, more exciting.

1990 was World Cup year and Our Price entered into the spirit of things by offering World Cup tickets as prizes in some of their larger stores. To qualify for the competition customers needed to purchase a World Cup video. On the run-up to the prize draw the shop sold hundreds of videos.

On the day of the draw one of England's greatest footballers, Gary Lineker, was to do a personal appearance and draw out the winning ticket. Mark described it as one of the most disappointing days of his life, as Gary Lineker made it clear he would rather be doing anything else than signing videos. When the big moment arrived, hundreds of people with their draw tickets where in the shop. Gary drew the winning number and the lad who won was overwhelmed with joy when he came to the counter to collect his prize. The feeling of euphoria didn't last long when he was informed of his prize. The poor lad was probably expecting a ticket for an England match, if not maybe Scotland or even Ireland. Would it be the quarter-final the semi-final or even the World Cup final itself? Unfortunately not. The prize was a single ticket, without transport, to Italy for a first-round match between Austria and the United States.

By the mid-90s Our Price was struggling and Richard Handover was brought in as managing director to turn things around. He made some good moves, such as cutting costs and introducing computer systems, but he also made the disastrous decision to open a chain of Our Price video-only stores, just as the video was going out of fashion.

Both Mark and Gary found themselves working for Sanity after a decision was taken to offload Our Price stores. Sanity was (and still is) a successful Australian retailer with over 230 shops in its native country. With unique ideas and a brash entrepreneurial ethic, the fortunes of the unloved Our Price stores were quickly turned around.

In September 2003 an opportunity for a profitable sale arose and £5 million was too good to resist for the business that cost nothing. The Australians made the sale and returned as heroes. The new owner, Lee Skinner of Primemist, wasn't a hero to the ex-Our Price staff, as the business soon floundered.

It was clear to those in head office that something fishy was going on. Primemist introduced a new scheme whereby any customer purchasing items worth £20 would receive a voucher for £20-worth of free stock that could only be redeemed after the New Year. They informed all of the managers that the one who sold most vouchers would receive a Mercedes car. Gary and Mark truly believe that there was never any intention to give a manager a car, and that the issuing of the vouchers was just a scam to increase cash flow before winding up the company. Sure enough, a couple of weeks into the New Year the chain folded. It had been a desperate time for the staff. Throughout December the chain had purchased nothing, and therefore by Christmas there was hardly any stock.

Worse was to follow. As soon as January arrived, hundreds of customers came in brandishing their £20 vouchers, but there was hardly anything for them to take. Needless to say they took their frustration out on the staff. The lucky voucher holders received £20 worth of crap stock. Thousands got nothing, and the Mercedes never left the showroom.

The administrators were quickly called in. This was the absolute end of the line for the chain that had opened way back in 1971.

By now Gary had been working at the Sanity head office and he decided to start his own business. He was in a fortunate position, as he was able to access head office records, which showed that the most profitable Sanity shop was Witney. It had also been one of the best shops when it operated as an Our Price. Gary also knew the store, as he had been its regional manager in the past.

The Game chain took over quite a few of the Sanity stores, and Witney was one of them. Therefore Gary located a unit as near as possible to the old store. He befriended the Game shopfitters who were very helpful – a lot of the racking that was skip-bound became Rapture racking.

The two boys did a quick tour of other record shops nicking lots of ideas, with Fopp being a major influence. Gary was even more buoyant about future trade when he received a phone call from a man asking if it was true that the unit was going to be a record shop. When Gary confirmed that it was, the man on the end of the phone whooped and cheered and told Gary he would call into the shop every day. True to his word, the un-named customer does call in every day – sadly for Rapture, it is just for a chat. They can count his purchases on one hand.

Gary and Mark opened Rapture in June 2004. They will never forget their first day. The first customer called in and asked for the new Peter Andre single 'Insania'. They told her that she was the very first customer. She asked if there was a prize. Gary offered a free Peter Andre single. The next customer came in and they, too, asked for 'Insania'. Suddenly there was a huge panic at Rapture. It was their first day of trading, the shop had only been open five minutes, and they had already sold out of Peter Andre's 'Insania'. Mark got on the phone straight away and asked how quickly the record company could get twenty copies to them. The good news was that they would have the CD delivered the next day. Mark told Gary not to panic and to promise the customers it would be back in stock the next day. They need not have worried, because they never got asked for 'Insania' ever again, and six months later twenty copies still sat on the shelves of Rapture, before they took the decision to clear them out for 10p each (rumour has it they still have nineteen left).

Within two years there were three Rapture stores, the other two in Evesham and Carterton. They have since closed Carterton to concentrate on the growing Internet business. The Carterton store started off well but, thanks to George Bush, takings soon dropped off. The whole town is geared towards catering for RAF Brize Norton. Due to various international conflicts, they found that their customer base had moved to Iraq and Afghanistan.

Whenever they walked the streets of Witney, the boys were always proud to see people carrying Rapture bags. However, although they spent most of their social life in Oxford, the shop had been open for months and they had yet to see anybody carrying one of their bags. Gary commented that he would feel they had 'arrived' when they noticed somebody carrying one. Not long after, Gary was driving in Oxford when he noticed a lady carrying a Rapture bag. He was ecstatic and couldn't wait to tell Mark. Just then, the lady reached into the Rapture bag, picked out her pooper scooper and scooped up the mess her dog had just made.

The day I arrived to interview the boys they had just received the least cost-effective order ever. They had ordered twenty units from Sony. However, each unit had arrived in a separate jiffy bag with its own invoice, making twenty packages in all. Hard to believe it wouldn't have been easier to send them all in one box. Who am I to give advice to a corporate giant like Sony?

Gary and Mark had some great anecdotes. One day a guy with a thick Northern accent came to the counter and asked for turps. Despite the customer walking past 3000 CDs, here he was expecting a record shop to have turps. Gary politely explained that the customer needed a hardware store and pointed him in the right direction. The customer looked puzzled before replying with, "No, I want turps to play on my turp recorder".

On another occasion a customer had asked for *The Sound of Bread*, the popular compilation album from the band fronted by David Gates. They lost the sale, because despite searching through all of the 'B's, the sleeve was nowhere to be found. During a routine sleeve check days later it was found – in the Sound Effects section, sitting alongside *Sounds of Horror*, *Sounds of Nature* and *Sounds of Sci-fi*. This was not a careless customer, but a new colleague who genuinely thought he was doing the right thing! What sound does bread make?

Rapture has one lady who suffers from 'multiple purchase syndrome' – everything she buys is in sixes, no matter how many times the staff ask her if she really needs six copies. The lady still gets upset if they suggest she just takes one.

One day Gary was behind the lady in the local supermarket and she was clearly buying her breakfast. Standing on the conveyor belt by the till was six packets of cornflakes, six jars of coffee and six jars of jam.

Another eccentric customer they have is 'double bagman'. He insists that every CD he buys is put into two bags. Now when he comes in they automatically place his purchases in two bags without him asking. I asked Mark for the reason behind this strange behaviour. It turns out the customer collects Rapture bags.

One connection the boys are proud of is their association with Radiohead. On the day of the release of the album *Pablo Honey* the band launched it with a personal appearance at Our Price in Oxford. It was through Colin Greenwood, the bass player, that the PA was arranged.

Colin had worked with both Gary and Mark at Our Price, and they still regard him as a friend. When working there, Colin pestered Gary and Mark to come and see his band play at the Jericho Tavern in town. Working at Our Price, Gary and Mark had seen lots of bands that featured store members, so they went along not expecting much. To say the boys were blown away was an understatement. The band, who at the time where called On A Friday, played many of the tracks that later became *Pablo Honey*. From that day on the boys spread the word about this exciting new band.

It was through working at Our Price that the band was signed. The EMI rep at the time, a guy called Keith Wozencroft, told the staff that he had a new job at EMI working in A&R (artist and repertoire). This role involved him signing up new bands. On hearing this news, Colin gave Keith a tape of the bands songs, and the rest, as they say, is history. Keith had the Midas touch, as he also signed Supergrass.

Gary was standing next to Colin when Thom Yorke phoned up to say that EMI had offered Radiohead a deal. He remembers the bear hug that Colin gave him upon hearing the news. To this day, one of Gary and Mark's most valued possessions is a cassette of the band's first demo tape with the artwork drawn by Thom Yorke. Both Colin and Thom have since shopped at Rapture.

Another connection Rapture is proud of is their involvement with The Cornbury Festival. The festival is held at the home of Lord and Lady Rotherwick in the grounds of their stately home, Cornbury House. The house is near the village of Charbury in Oxfordshire. The festival is set in 6,500 acres of beautiful English countryside where deer graze and blue peacocks strut amongst the gardens. On the estate is a large lake, and each year the festival hires a lifeguard just in case a drunken reveller decides on a midnight swim.

I am lucky to attend many festivals and I can say that Cornbury is my own personal favourite. I feel that it is a hidden gem, as it has such a relaxed vibe and attracts artists of the calibre of Amy Winehouse, Joe Cocker, Robert Plant and Paul Simon. The festival is aimed at families with a fabulous children's fairground. My own favourite memories are of Postman Pat dancing to the music, but not very well. Mind you, he was moving a lot better than two smartly dressed gentlemen who were swaying next to me at the Echo and the Bunnymen gig in the big top. I thought they looked familiar and then realised it was David Cameron, leader of the Conservative party, with all-round good guy Richard Curtis.

Not long after the boys opened the shop the festival organiser, Hugh Phillimore, called in and took Mark and Gary down to the pub. He asked if they would sell tickets for the festival in the shop and hire a stall to sell merchandise. He also asked if there were any artists they could recommend to play there. At the time the boys were unaware of Hugh's background and they suggested Hayseed Dixie. Hugh's day job was as an organiser of corporate events. These are no ordinary events – if you want Elton John or Whitney Houston to play your private party, and if money is no object, then Hugh is your man. I think he was hoping Gary and Mark would come up with something grander than Hayseed Dixie. If you only go to one festival this year, make it Cornbury, where you will come across the Rapture record stall, as the boys market their wares there.

Talking with Gary, it is clear that they love the job they do and are proud to be in Witney. They feel they are an important part of the community.

Rapture will be one of the 'Last Shops Standing' as their customer service is second to none. To emphasise this point Gary told me of a lovely customer they have called Helen.

Times had been tough for Helen and she was talking to Mark about how she would like to go to a gig at The Academy in Oxford. She did not own a credit card and, with the cost of the fare into town, she probably wouldn't go. Mark explained that he went into Oxford every week and he would be happy to pick up some tickets for her. Mark now regularly collects tickets for Helen and her boyfriend. Other customers have heard of this free service, so each week Mark is at The Academy saving his customers a few precious pounds personally collecting tickets for them. All part of the service at Rapture.

Mark and Gary would like me to thank their customers, many of whom have become friends. They would also like to say a massive thank you to their wives, as the girls both earn more than they do, which allows them to indulge in their time-consuming hobby, Rapture.

It is amazing that I do not call on a single independent rock record shop in a city the size of Oxford. I do call on Blackwell's Books who despite being a bookshop do carry an excellent range of classical, folk, jazz and world music. I mentioned to the manager Mike Summers that I was writing a book and he proceeded to tell me enough funny tales to have a chapter of his own. Here are a few of my favourites.

Customer (over the phone): "Hello, do you have 'Hark the Herald Angels Sing'?"
Blackwell's "Ah yes, is it a CD or sheet music you're looking for?"
Customer: "It's a Christmas Carol – I'd have expected you to know that!"

Customer: "Hello, I'm looking for a CD for my mother for Christmas – it's 'Carry-On Fidelio'. Do you stock Carry-On CDs here?"
It was established that it was Karajan's Fidelio that was required.

Customer: "Do you have Eugene Onegin on DVD?"
Blackwell's "Yes, this production has a great cast and…."
Customer (interrupting emphatically): "No, no. This won't do at all; the woman on the front is fat."

Customer (thickly-accented Scandinavian): "Can you help? I am looking for whores!"
Blackwell's: "Erm…"
Customer (animatedly): "Good whores, Oxford whores!"
Blackwell's: "Erm, sir we are just a Music Shop…"
Customer: "Oxford whores are famous, yes? Whores in Churches?"

Blackwell's (with a flash of realisation): "Ah! Choirs!"

Customer: "Yes, whores. I am particularly interested in boy whores."

Blackwell's "Sir, it is pronounced 'Choir', and it is quite important that you say it like that."

After examining a member of staff's recommended recording of Bach's 1st Prelude & Fugue.

Customer: "It isn't a remix, is it?"

Whilst standing in the middle of the CD department, surrounded by 1000s of CDs

Customer: "Where do you keep your CDs? Are they tucked away in a corner somewhere?"

Customer: "Will they have this CD at HMV?"

Blackwell's: "Possibly, yes."

Customer: "Well can't you check for me?"

Blackwell's: "Erm… I'm afraid not, no."

Customer: "Why?"

Blackwell's: "Well they're a different shop."

Customer: "But you sell the same things!"

Young, attractive, American woman: "Excuse me, can you check me out?"

Blackwell's: "How do you mean, madam?"

YAAW: "Well, you know, like check me out!"

"Do you have *Donkey Oaty* by Strauss? (Don Quixote)

It goes to show that classical shops too have their fair share of unusual requests and wacky customers. Blackwell's have bookshops all over the UK with the Oxford, Cambridge and Edinburgh branches all having excellent music departments.

* * *

From Oxfordshire I continue west into Gloucestershire to the town of Stroud to visit Kane Jones, owner of Kanes Records.

It is fair to say that amongst the record shops of the Home Counties, mention the name Kane Jones and the proprietor will break out into a broad smile. This is not just because Kane is an engaging personality – it's more likely because of the events of Christmas '93. Kane was working as a sales rep for Virgin records. For most of the year, reps spent the majority of their time giving away free stock, but during December they would fill their car with product and call on their shops to sell them titles they were short of. Being the salesman he is, Kane had a fantastic month and was expecting a big bonus for the amount of sales he had achieved. The bonus he wasn't expecting was the sack. Although he was a fantastic salesman, he wasn't great on paperwork. To his horror, when he took a pile of paper to be recycled, he realised that in amongst it was an envelope containing tens of thousands of pounds worth of invoices for his December sales.

Virgin didn't take kindly to this, and Kane's Christmas present from them was a P45. As Virgin had no record of the sales achieved by Kane they wrote the money off. Many shops had spent thousands of pounds with Virgin, so to them it was a massive Christmas bonus. Kane turned out to be the record shop's own version of Santa.

To be fair to Virgin, it was not the first time that Kane had caused them problems. A few months earlier, Virgin held a sales conference at a hotel near Heathrow Airport. The company had booked all of the staff who did not live in the London area into the hotel for one night's accommodation. Following the day's speeches and discussions the staff had dinner. Throughout the meal the complementary drink flowed, courtesy of Virgin. After finishing the meal, everybody retired to the bar where more drink flowed. By the time the barman called time, those Virgin staff remaining were in various states – anywhere between inebriated and paralytic. Kane was nearer the latter and decided to re-open the bar, which had not been locked properly. The shutters went up and Kane was happy to take on the role of barman, and he started pouring out drinks, much to the delight of his colleagues. After twenty minutes of revelry the hotel manager came down to see what all the noise was. The appearance of the manager took Kane by surprise, and he dropped the bottle of wine he was holding, which smashed on the floor. The hotel manager did not recognise his new barman and decided that he had stumbled upon a thief. The police were called and Kane was taken away to spend the night in the cells. Luckily, the next day the police decided not to press charges, but Kane's career as a barman was certainly over (fortunately, he still had a job as a sales rep ... well, not for long).

Kane remembers his Virgin days with great affection, probably more so than his family. On days off, most families visited the zoo or went to the pictures. Kane's family weekends were spent touring the local record shops, buying singles from his own company, Virgin. Each week, Kane's boss would phone him up and tell him which of their records were just outside the top 40. All record companies had access to a mid-week chart, so they could see their own records' chart position. Now most wives would love to spend their Saturdays shopping – not so Mrs Jones. Kane would spend the morning driving around the local record shops and would send his family in to buy the records. He would then keep the receipts and forward them to Virgin, who would reimburse him. The Saturday morning hyping-trips did have their financial reward. Not only was Kane paid overtime, but he would also receive a £75 bonus if one of the records he was 'working' (the record companies' term for 'hyping') entered the top 40 that week. The problem with this system was that nearly all of the record companies were doing the same, so nobody really gained an advantage. The losers were the independent record companies, whose records sold solely on merit. The smaller companies didn't have the money to get involved in the game of hype.

One incident that Kane will never forget was the Friday night he was relaxing at home watching TV, when he received a phone call from none other than Donny Osmond.

Kane was stunned that Donny was just phoning to thank him for helping him get back into the charts. Donny was one of the biggest stars of the 70s, but throughout the 80s and early 90s his releases had failed to have any impact on the chart. It was only when he signed with Virgin that his music career got on to an upward curve again. Kane thought Donny was a top bloke, and enjoyed his conversation with him, although he laughed when he recalled Donny's parting words: "Keep promoting my record now". If Donny is reading this, Kane did.

After being released by Virgin there was a lot of sympathy for Kane and he was offered a job with his former employer Longplayer. Back in 1977 Kane had started work as a Saturday boy in their Margate branch. After leaving school, he worked there full-time.

Things had now come full circle and Kane was back working at Longplayer, this time at their Cheltenham branch. During Kane's employment with Virgin there had been a lot of changes at Longplayer. When he had left them to take up his post with Virgin they had eight shops. They sold off six to the rapidly expanding Our Price chain, keeping just two stores in Cheltenham and Tunbridge Wells. As well as being a record shop, Longplayer had a business supplying insurance companies with CDs.

If people had their house burgled often their CD collection would be stolen. Rather than give them cash, some insurance companies preferred to replace their clients' CD collections by obtaining them from companies such as Longplayer.

With rents rising in its locations Longplayer decided to sell the shops and concentrate on the insurance business. This now involved Kane working in an office all day, which was not what he wanted. He resigned and spent three years working at the Bruce Springsteen specialist record shop, Badlands, based in Cheltenham. Kane noticed that a lot of customers travelled up from Stroud, indicating that they didn't have a record shop there. Why should he make money for somebody else, when he could do it for himself? He paid a visit to Stroud and was immediately struck at what a vibrant place it was. He instantaneously decided that Stroud was his future and he would open a shop there. When he looks back on that decision, he thinks that on that first visit the carnival was in town and that had probably made the place seem more vibrant than it really is. He found a great location next to the Halifax bank – perfect for people to draw their money out and pop next door to purchase some CDs at Kane's Records.

One of his memories of the early days was chatting to a customer outside the shop, when a brick fell from a roof and hit the customer on the head. The blood poured from his head and Kane took him inside to bandage him up. Kane did his best, but the man left the shop to go to hospital, looking like he had a red turban.

One thing Kane does is to put on as many free gigs as possible in his shop. These gigs always attract a vast crowd; Kane can never work out if it is because he gives everybody who attends a glass of wine or a beer (soft drinks for the under 18's) or if they are genuine fans of the band.

The most memorable personal appearance was made by EMI artist Seth Lakeman. Seth is a fabulous fiddle player, but he turned up without his chin rest – an essential part of a violinist's kit. Often the cry "Is there a doctor in the house?" goes out to the crowd. Kane had to appeal to the assembled crowd: "Is there a chin rest in the house?" Incredibly, a young ten-year-old boy was on his way home from violin lessons. He was a big fan of Seth's and, as a treat, his mum had brought him down to Kane's to see Seth play. So, a young boy with a chin rest saved Seth's gig at Kane's. As a reward, Seth invited the family to be his guests at his concert in Cheltenham.

One thing I do notice about Kane is that he does try to encourage the teenagers to shop in Kane's Records. His willingness for any local band to play there has helped establish a rapport with the youngsters of Stroud. The average age of the customer is certainly lower than other shops I visit. I do feel he will be one of the 'Last Shops Standing' – even my next-door neighbour thinks so. On being introduced to him, he asked me what I did for a living. I told him that I sold CDs. He told me that I should check out what he felt was the best record shop he had ever visited – it is in Stroud, and its called Kanes. I thanked him for the tip.

Chapter 11

Flat Caps and Massage Parlours

Week four of my tour starts with me heading north up the M6, a motorway on which I must have spent months of my life waiting in traffic jams. My first shop of the week is A&A Music in the Cheshire town of Congleton.

As A&A are always on the first page in any record shop directory, I felt it was apt to start with them. When I congratulated Alan Farrar on his shrewdness in getting his shop name at the front of every listing, he admitted that the company name was simply a coincidence. His business partner at the time was Alan Slater and it had seemed sensible to use the first letter of each of their names when they started A&A Music.

The partnership had evolved from A&A Enterprises, which had sold records, clothes and jewellery on a local market stall. A&A realised that they were making far more money from sales of records than of clothes or jewellery, so they came to the conclusion that music was the direction they should be taking. It was also a great time to open a shop, as punk had just taken off and the indie record shop had become the place to hang out.

After opening in Macclesfield market, they heard that the owner of Congleton-based record shop Sounds Around was looking to sell his business. The duo raised the money to buy his shop, and on 17 August 1977 had an incredible first day's trading in their new shop. The sales were, of course, boosted by the sad and untimely death of Elvis Presley. Elvis had died the previous day and, although it was a depressing day for music, the boys had had a roaring first day.

I have never understood the British public. Why, when a rock star dies, does everybody want to rush out and buy their music? Why not appreciate it when they are alive, and give them the chance to spend their royalties? The money is no good to them when they are dead.

During these early days, A&A were unable to open accounts with any of the major record companies, because they each required a deposit of £2,000 before they would commence trading with any retail outlet. Consequently A&A were forced to purchase their stock from wholesalers, of which two became legends: Oldies Unlimited and Terry Blood.

Oldies Unlimited was a unique operation, as it had the contract to buy up all of the used 7" singles from jukebox suppliers across the country. They then sold them on, both to shops and through a mail order operation. Everybody who bought the music papers, like *NME*, *Melody Maker* or *Sounds*, during the 70s and 80s may be able to remember their advert, which featured in the classified section each week. The Oldies Unlimited advert always attracted my attention, because it looked as if a four year old had drawn it.

The company's proprietor, Anthony Lewis, was quite cunning. He had access to the electoral roll, and so, each year, he chose to mail his catalogue to all of the 18 year olds in the country to establish a customer base from scratch.

Another of Anthony's features was that he always wore his cap. It was his trademark – no matter how hot the weather, the cap was firmly stuck on his head. To this day I have no idea if he was bald, or even what colour his hair was.

We got on well. When I worked in van sales I would sell to Anthony. He would purchase any 7" single that I had on the van, which earned me a lot of commission, which helped me to like him. Eventually I visited him to be told that it was the last time he would see me, as he was moving on to work on other projects. I heard nothing of Anthony for several years until, one night, whilst flicking through the TV channels, I noticed something familiar on a Channel 5 programme entitled *Massage Parlours – The Real McCoy*. The programme showed a well-endowed blonde lady, who had seen better days, massaging a gentleman's legs. She gradually worked her way up to his buttocks; then up his back; and started work on his shoulders. It was at this point that I recognised something familiar – IT WAS THAT BLOODY CAP! Sure enough – lying on that massage table, completely naked apart from his cap, was my old customer, Anthony Lewis.

It turned out that, writing under the name George McCoy, Anthony had become the most prominent commentator on British massage parlours. He has a best-seller called *McCoy's British Massage Parlour Guide*; although he has also written four regional guides. This book is currently competing with his new release – *Massage Parlours of the South West* – for the book-buying public's hard-earned cash.

Alan bought all A&A's singles from Oldies Unlimited, whilst they bought their CDs and cassettes from Terry Blood.

Terry Blood was a wholesaler who stocked product from all of the major record companies. Music retailers would visit his company and buy records by the trolley-load – it was a music cash and carry.

A&A's Alan became quite friendly with Terry himself, and so he was very surprised to receive a letter informing him that in future Terry Blood would only take orders by telephone. Alan dismissed the letter, thinking it was just a circular sent to all customers, whereas he was a friend of Terry. Accordingly, as he had for the previous two years, Alan set off on his Friday evening, 30-mile journey to Terry's warehouse where he was met at the door by Terry himself.

"What are you doing here?"

"I have come to buy records, like I always do".

"Didn't you get my letter? From now on we take orders only by phone".

"But I've got a list of stuff that I need. Can I give it to you?"

"No – phone it in".

"OK. Can I come in and use your phone to call you?"

"No – there's a public phone box a mile down the road".

So, with no other options open, Alan drove away, found the phone box, dialled the number, and Terry answered and took his order. Bizarre. Amazingly, Terry Blood sold his business to Total Home Entertainment a few years later for a considerable sum.

A regular customer at A&A's Macclesfield branch was the late Ian Curtis, lead singer of Joy Division. The staff liked Ian, so were disappointed to see that the film of his life story – *Control* (2007) – implied that he stole his records from their Macclesfield store. Alan says that it isn't true, and remembers him as a regular guy with a passion for music.

After Ian sadly hung himself in 1980, the store became an unofficial Joy Division tourist information centre. Fans from as far away as Japan and the USA would pose for photographs in front of the shop.

Another famous A&A regular is Noddy Holder of Slade, who is slightly old-fashioned, in that he still pays by cheque and never forgets to ask for a discount.

Alan recalled the day a lady came to the counter and asked if he could sell her a joint. After he explained that the shop did not sell drugs, she looked perplexed and told Alan that it was a joint of meat she was looking to buy. Alan reasoned that, although A&A stock Meatloaf, Lambchop and The Meat Puppets, they were definitely not a butcher's shop, so he pointed her in the right direction.

In 2004, due to declining market conditions, they closed the Macclesfield branch. A&A is now down to just three people – Alan, his wife Judy and local legend Dave Wedgbury. Dave is a big name around Congleton, as he is a gig promoter and a player in two local bands, one of which is a Pixies tribute band known as T Nimrods Massif Monkeys (the other band is Sugarlust).

Alan is confident he will be one of the 'Last Shops Standing' thanks to his heavy investment in musical instruments. As I have previously mentioned, many musical instrument suppliers offer the record shops their stock on a consignment basis. This means that shops only pay for what they sell, which is the main reason that so many record shops have started selling instruments – it helps their cash flow. If record companies had been bold enough to offer record shops this kind of incentive, many would still be standing. Without revenue from instrument sales, Alan feels that it is likely that A&A would have become just another statistic on the list of record shop closures.

* * *

From Congleton I venture into the Peak District to visit the Bakewell Bookshop. It is unusual for a shop with 'bookshop' in their title to be featured in a book about the best record shops in the UK. The Bakewell Bookshop is no ordinary shop, and Keith How, the owner, is no ordinary owner.

Keith originally bought the shop to sell books, but his passion for music and desire to play his customers the music he liked resulted in him stocking CDs. Each month, he would buy more and more CDs, and eventually the shop stocked an eclectic selection.

Keith's passion for music started at an early age, when his parents bought him a little transistor radio. Each night he would go to bed with the radio under his pillow and listen to Radio Luxembourg until he fell asleep. Often Keith would be woken by a whistling in his ear, informing him that the batteries were running flat.

Keith was brought up in the tiny Derbyshire village of Castleton. Every Sunday, Keith and his friends would walk to the top of Winnats Pass, where if they pointed their radio in the right direction, they could pick up John Peel broadcasting *The Perfumed Garden* radio show. This became a ritual. Every weekend, rain or shine, the boys would be found on top of the hill, each taking turns to hold the radio until their arms tired.

Upon leaving school Keith obtained work as a labourer, and with his first pay packet decided to make the 40-mile trip to Sheffield to buy his first records. He chose Jimi Hendrix's *Are You Experienced* and *Sgt. Pepper's Lonely Hearts Club Band* by The Beatles. He could not wait to get back to Castleton. A few months earlier his uncle had given him an old second-hand mono record player, but Keith never had the money to buy a record. Keith recalled the excitement of that day – he invited his three friends over to his house, none of whom owned a record or a record player; and Keith was the coolest cat in Castleton.

The friends turned the lights out as they rocked to the sounds – this was far out, this was rock 'n' roll and this was the future. Well, it was until Keith's mum came in, turned on the lights, sent Keith's friends home and told him it was time for bed.

Some time after this, Keith's cousin's boyfriend started taking him to beatnik poetry readings and folk gigs at a coffee shop in Sheffield. He recalls trying coffee for the first time as an amazing experience. Coffee seemed to have passed Castleton by, and this was exciting stuff; a night out with a coffee and a poetry reading.

For years Keith did a series of dead-end jobs, and his last job before he took over the bookshop was as a gravedigger. The local cemetery was over-looked by the infant school, where his wife Susie worked. He would spend his time doing as little digging as possible whilst waving at his wife, much to the amusement of the children. Lunchtimes were spent leaning on his spade chatting to his wife and the schoolchildren over the wall that divided the school from the graveyard.

The local bookshop advertised for somebody to work there one day a week. Keith jumped at the chance, and will never forget the first customer who came in. The lady asked him if they had any George Eliot books. Keith told the lady that George had 'his' own section. Keith still cringes when he recalls the incident, as any fan of literature would know that George Eliot was the pen name of Mary Anne Evans, author of novels such as *Middlemarch*, amongst many others.

One day the owner of Bakewell Books fell ill and Keith was asked if he could run the shop for a while. Keith packed in the grave digging, and from that day has spent six days a week working in the shop. In 1986 Keith and Susie were given the opportunity to buy the business, and they did not need to be asked twice.

Following his decision to start stocking CDs, Keith needed to work out how to market his small selection of music. Any music fan driving through the Peak District should make a diversion to the Bakewell Bookshop to have a laugh at Keith's different music sections.

CDs are filed under sections such as:

- Shock, old geezers make excellent albums (Tom Waits, Neil Young, Van Morrison)
- More old 'uns proving they can still cut it (Robert Wyatt, Donovan, Leonard Cohen)
- Strange stuff we like
- Prog rock freakout (Syd Barret, Gentle Giant, Yes)
- Really good stuff by people nobody knows (Panda Bear, The Notwist, Efterklang)
- Bits of Bob (Bob Dylan)
- Alternative folk goings on (Incredible String Band, Wicker Man, Mellowcandle)
- Scorching minimalist blues
- New folk/Americana possibly? (Speck Mountain)
- Icelandic demi-gods who make brilliant music
- The great purchasing error section (this holds all of the CDs Keith wished he had never bought).

One day Duran Duran called in, along with Yasmin Le Bon. It was 5.15pm and the band started picking out lots of CDs and books. The band asked if Keith would stay up late, as they loved the shop's selection. At 6.30pm the band brought a massive pile of CDs and books to the counter. After they had paid, Simon Le Bon turned to Keith and thanked him for staying open late just for them. As a gesture of thanks, Simon offered Keith two tickets for their gig in Sheffield and a pass for the back-stage after-party.

Keith thanked them for their kind gesture, but said he had other things to do (he has always had a great taste in music).

I asked Keith about the future. He loves what he is doing and is going to carry on for as long as possible. He is a very youthful looking 59, but he does admit that age is catching up with him. He realises this, as quite a few customers have left the shop with empty cases due to him forgetting to put the CDs into them.

One recent visitor to the shop told Keith his shop was just weird. Keith agreed that they are 'just weird', then informed me that when my book comes out it will go into his weird book section.

* * *

From Bakewell I drive to the city of my birth; Liverpool. I was born there in 1960 and spent my childhood in Anfield. I remember so many record shops in the city and am amazed that they have all gone. Outside the city centre, in an area called West Derby, stands a wonderful old-fashioned record shop called The Musical Box, who have some great tales to tell.

The Musical Box started off in 1947 as a shop selling toys, model railways, 78rpm records and music boxes. It has always been in the Cain family. Current owner, Diane, started helping her parents out in the early 1950s. They had bought the business from their Uncle Jack for the astonishing sum of £500.

These days Diane works in tandem with her son, Tony, and they are a great combination, with Diane being an expert on country music and nostalgia, whilst Tony's field is rock and pop. The shop reminds me of the corner shops of my childhood in which people shopped for their groceries and a chat. Whenever I have visited, a steady stream of regulars pop in for a cup of tea and a gossip. Nobody seems to buy anything much, but the result is that the shop has a warm and friendly atmosphere.

Diane also works on Radio Merseyside as a DJ and broadcasts her country show once a week. She has a wealth of stories about the history of the shop. She fondly recalls how, in the 50s, the store would stay open until midnight on Christmas Eve to capture all the men who staggered out of the pubs at closing time needing a last-minute present. At about that time, records gradually started taking up more space in the shop and fancy goods were phased out.

The shop established a reputation for being the best country shop in the North West. Many of their customers were American GI's based at RAF Burtonwood Airfield near Warrington. One week a number of airmen came in and asked for material by a new vocalist, Elvis Presley. Diane and her mother, Dorothy, had never heard of him and presumed he was a country and western singer. The next week they noticed on their new release sheet a single by Elvis called 'Heartbreak Hotel', and so decided to purchase a boxful, as there was such a buzz on this record. On a sunny Wednesday afternoon their new releases arrived and Diane could not wait to hear this hot new singer. They put the single on the turntable and could not believe what they were hearing. "This is rubbish!" exclaimed Dorothy. Diane agreed, and couldn't understand what the fuss was all about. Both firmly agreed that this Elvis chap had no future.

In 1959 The Musical Box opened a second shop, which Diane managed in Liverpool's Old Swan district, whilst her parents continued to run the West Derby branch. Whilst the 50s were exciting times, running a record shop in the 60s in Liverpool was really something else.

Even so, Diane had some intriguing views of those times, citing that the A&R departments of record companies had lost the plot. Her view was that, whilst Liverpool had a few great bands, such as The Beatles and The Searchers, most of the rest were rubbish. But nonetheless, if you spoke with a Scouse accent and could play the guitar or sing a bit, you were inevitably given a record deal. Diane felt annoyed that some great American music of the time did not make the charts, because they were full of average music from the Mersey bands.

For Diane, though, the 70s were a golden period for the shop, as she loved the disco music of the day.

One day Fred, one of her regular customers, popped in and explained he had £2,000 on him, as he had been left some money by his uncle. Whilst Fred bought a few LPs, Diane asked him why he was carrying such a large sum on his person. Fred carefully explained that, as he used the Royal Bank of Scotland, it took ages to withdraw his money, because it had to come all the way from Glasgow.

After he left, Diane noticed an envelope on top of the record racks. She peeked inside and was astonished to find it contained £1,000. "It has to be Fred's," she thought. The next day Fred called in and Diane assumed it was to ask about his lost money. But no, he just picked out more records. Eventually Diane asked him if he had lost anything? "No, I don't think so," replied Fred. Diane reminded him that he had brought £2,000 into the shop the previous day and she asked how much of it remained. Fred checked his pockets and found that he had only £300. He had not noticed that the money was missing. Diane gave him the £1,000 and told him to put it in the bank – it would be safe in there, no matter how long it took to withdraw.

Another regular customer was a Scottish gentleman who had lived in Liverpool for a long time. It was clear that he missed Scotland, as all that he bought was bagpipe or other traditional Scottish music. The man was Bill Shankly, the man who managed the transformation of Liverpool Football Club.

A more recent visitor to the shop was David Guest, whom they found to be a charming man. Tony, ever the salesman, tried to flog him all of the

Liza Minelli CDs which had been gathering dust on their shelves for years. David declared that the lady had made only one decent CD – the one he had produced for her. Word soon got round that David was in the shop, and several locals called in to have their picture taken with him. David was most amenable, posing for photographs and signing autographs. Before he left he spent £90 and told Diane and Tony that they had a great little shop.

Then there was the day when Diane took a phone call from an American enquiring about a Ringo Starr album and wanting directions to the shop. Diane informed him that she had the album in stock, would reserve it for him and that, if he was in the city centre, he should catch a number 12 bus, which passed their door. "That's OK," said the American gentleman, "I'll catch a cab".

"Don't be silly," scolded Diane, "That will cost about four quid, and the bus fare is only 30 pence!"

"No matter," said the American, "I'll still catch a cab". When Diane put down the phone Tony asked who the caller had been. Diane replied, "Some American called Tarantino with more money than sense".

"Not Quentin Tarantino?"

"Yes, that's him," said Diane, "Do you know him?" And sure enough, it turned out to be Quentin Tarantino.

A few years ago the shop was used as a backdrop for the mystery guest section of *A Question of Sport*, with Mel C (of the Spice Girls) playing the part of a shop assistant serving Sander Westervelt, the Liverpool goalkeeper. (But Diane and Tony's favourite goalkeeper was David James, who during his Liverpool days was a regular, and who always had time to chat to customers.)

The shop has also been featured on an edition of *Songs of Praise*, during which presenter Sally Magnuson played a copy of 'Amazing Grace' in the store.

On my last visit to the shop I noticed they were running a video sale. Tony explained that the videos were taking up too much space and that they just wanted to get rid of them. I was mildly surprised at the price – 'All videos free'. As each customer was leaving, they were urged to help themselves to the videos, but most declined. Perhaps they simply could not believe the offer, but it just goes to show that these days you cannot even give videos away.

The shop has an unusual bestseller – Vicki Brown's album *Forever*. Vicki was a much underrated singer, who sadly died of cancer in 1991. She was married to Joe Brown, of The Bruvers fame, and is mother to singer Sam, who still often belts out the tunes in Jools Holland's band. Although famous throughout the continent as a singer in her own right, she was better-known in the UK as a backing singer. *Forever* sells well, as the track 'Look For Me in Rainbows' is often played on local radio. Vicki wrote the song during her illness and, although it is a sad song, it also inspires people to appreciate life.

When I asked Diane if The Musical Box would be one of the 'Last Shops Standing', she reassured me, saying, "We are a quirky shop and all of our customers are quirky people. So, as long as there are quirky people out there, The Musical Box will be here for them". At that moment, as if to illustrate her point, a man rushed in shouting, "Guess what? I've just won £400 at the bookies, so I'm going to treat myself to some CDs". A minute later he had picked out £40-worth and had dashed off again. Tony tried to remind him that he still had £360 to spend, but the man was off – no doubt back to the bookies. Another typical day in Liverpool's oldest record shop: The Musical Box – a national treasure.

* * *

From Liverpool I join the M62 and then on to the M6 for my journey to Preston to a rendezvous with Gordon Gibson, owner of Action Records.

The shop was established in 1979, starting off as a second-hand record stall in South Market in Blackpool, just as the independent music scene was emerging. Gordon was a native of Stranraer, not exactly known for its music scene. He spent his weekends hitching his way around the country going to gigs, and he remembers those days fondly. He would make his way to the nearest road services, where he would join the queue of hitchhikers waiting for a lift. He recalled how civil it was; no one pushed in and he enjoyed the camaraderie of his fellow travellers.

He ended up in Preston thanks to an appeal on Radio 1 on the Bob Harris radio show. In 1971 he hitched from Stranraer to The Lincoln Festival to see The Byrds, James Taylor and Tim Hardin amongst others. On the way down, fellow festival travellers Alan and Shelia Cookson picked him up. The three of them got on famously and had a fabulous weekend. After being dropped off they vowed to stay in touch, but in 1971, of course, e-mail and mobile phones did not exist. One evening whilst listening to Bob Harris on the radio Gordon heard his name mentioned and that Alan and Shelia were trying to get in touch. Bob gave their phone number over the air, something you could never imagine happening these days, and Gordon immediately got in touch. After visiting Alan and Sheila a couple of times, he decided to move down to Preston, the hometown of his friends.

To earn money to pay for his festival travels, Gordon took on numerous dead-end jobs, citing being a banana-sorter as his least enjoyable. To earn a little extra cash, he started buying and selling LPs at record fairs. Gordon vowed to get out of bananas and into music full-time. On a trip to Blackpool he noticed a sign outside the South Market advertising stalls for £20 a week. He gave the banana business the slip and started working for himself instead.

Gordon missed the first wave of punk, but quickly established Action as the place to go for the second wave of punk. Bands such as Discharge, Anti-Nowhere League and The Exploited were his best-selling artists.

Travelling from Preston to Blackpool each day was beginning to become tiresome so, in 1981, he relocated to Preston, meaning he could have an extra hour in bed each morning. Like many independent shops in the early 80s, Action established its own record label, releasing records by bands such as The Boo Radleys, Dandelion Adventure, Big Red Bus, Genocides, Tompaulin, Fi-Lo Radio, and Monkey Steals The Drum, amongst others. Thanks to support from John Peel, The Boo Radleys album *Ichabod and I* took off and attracted the attention of Rough Trade who, to Gordon's frustration, signed them up.

Action's biggest project so far has been recording The Fall and Mark E. Smith as a solo performer. After meeting at the band's gig at Ronnie Brown's bar in Blackpool, Gordon asked Mark whether Action could release some of The Fall's product. The partnership has been most fruitful, with three of their releases on the Action label: Mark E. Smith's spoken word album called *Pander Panda Panzer*: and two albums by The Fall – *2G Plus 2* and an album that has sold over 15,000 units, *Country on the Click*.

Action is always keen to promote up-and-coming bands. One young band from Devon that, at that point, had just released a couple of singles approached the shop to ask if they could play in store. The band gave a magnificent performance and the crowd of 30 people enjoyed it enormously. Over the years, Gordon has met so many people who claimed to have been at that gig – it seems like 3,000 witnessed Muse, not the 30 who were really there. Every generation seems to have a gig like that. For me it was the Sex Pistols at Manchester's Free Trade Hall in June 1976.

During my travels to record shops in the North West I must have met around 40 people who attended this legendary event. Apparently Morrissey, members of Joy Division, The Buzzcocks, and The Fall were also in attendance, along with music journalist Paul Morley. It is also possible that some normal people attended the gig – the sort of people who don't work in record shops, are not in a band, are not about to start a band or who are not about to write about a band. Music journalist Dave Nolan has written a witty book called *I Swear I Was There*, which documents the events of the gig, and he reckoned just 40 people were there.

I asked Gordon what the future had in store for him. His reply was that he still had years to go on his mortgage and is determined that Action will still be trading. He believes his biggest problem is generational changes – he hardly sees a customer below the age of thirty visit his shop.

This is a massive problem for all independent record shops, as the demographics of the record-buying public have dramatically changed. Whereas, as late as the end of the 80s, music was the undoubted force fuelling each generation (the Teddy Boys, the Mods, the Rockers, the Hippies, the Glam Rockers, the Punks, Indie kids and then the Dance generation), the combination of the Internet, computer games, satellite TV and DVDs has created many more options on which to spend your disposable income. Radio, the primary source for new music, became less popular, and TV splintered into 200 different channels meaning long-running programmes, such as *Top of the Pops*, were doomed. Worst of all, the new generation, if they were into music, were those most able to find it for free.

To understand how far we've fallen, think on this: recent pressure has forced the record companies to stop encoding digital music so that it can only be played via approved devices, and therefore cannot be swapped or shared. The Digital Rights Management (DRM) free music was a campaign that resulted in the record companies retreating and adopting policy that is probably counter to their longer term interests. The prevailing view was that a track downloaded for 79p should be able to be played anywhere the consumer wants. Contrast this with computer games: you pay £35 for a new game for your PlayStation. Six months later you upgrade your console to an Xbox. Can you play your PlayStation game on your Xbox, or your PC, or your Wii? No – you have to purchase the game again.

As the bigger stores move their CD racks to the back and present DVDs and computer games at the front of store, music has become their poor relation. As Gordon pointed out to me, his biggest problem with the new generation is that they do not expect to pay for music – it's often something they don't do unless they are buying a CD as a present for their parents.

Action was once one of the top independent dance shops in the north, but no more. They have recognised that, to survive, they need to look after their regular customers, the over-30s. So instead of dance they have now invested in increasing their selection of blues, country and folk. Despite this, the shop has lost none of its cutting edge atmosphere, and a visit there is like calling on the record shops of my youth. These are tough times for record shops and only the strongest will survive. Gordon is a tough cookie and I have no doubt he will be one of the 'Last Shops Standing'.

* * *

Another Gordon I usually visit when in the area is Gordon Oakes, owner of the excellent Vibes Records in Bury. Sadly our paths did not cross on this tour, but I do have a couple of memories of the store. The first involved a furry grey creature that they christened 'psycho squirrel'. To picture the scene you have to imagine the location of Vibes, stuck in a shopping precinct without a tree in the vicinity. One day 'psycho squirrel' ambled into the store before climbing up the back of one of the customers and settling on his head. As the customer tried to knock him off, 'psycho squirrel' leapt on to the top shelf, which was where Vibes displayed all of their quality box sets. The shelf was 10 feet off the ground and ran around the entire perimeter of the shop. Soon 'psycho squirrel' started darting along the shelf, knocking the box sets everywhere. These box sets retailed between £30 and £200 and, as they fell, the staff desperately tried to catch them. After a few minutes there wasn't a single box set left on the shelf. For a few seconds there was silence, as if 'psycho squirrel' was taking time out to survey the damage he had caused. Unexpectedly, he leapt off the shelf and went into hiding behind the CD racks. The staff started moving the racks to encourage 'psycho squirrel' to leave. He darted out, then leapt on to the back of Lee, one of the staff members, digging his claws into his T-shirt. As Lee shouted to get the squirrel off, 'psycho squirrel' fell to the floor and darted out of the shop, heading off in the direction of the bus station.

Gordon surveyed the damage; there was squirrel poo everywhere. He started to inspect the box sets for damage and contemplated how much he would have to reduce them by to sell them.

It was at Vibes that I met the worst sales rep I have ever met – even worse, I employed him. At the time I was working for Panther and was offered the chance of promotion. The role was for a sales manager, supervising six van salesmen. For a while I continued on with van sales combining it with my new role. It soon became clear that the two were incompatible. I therefore decided to employ a new rep and I had a good idea who I wanted. Whenever I visited Vibes in Bury, a Robert Plant look-alike, called John Brent, would always express his desire to work for us. He showed his enthusiasm by doing an impression from an Alan Bleasdale play called *Boys from the Blackstuff*. The play became a TV show and featured an unemployed Scouser called Yozzer Hughes. His catchphrase "Gizza job, I can do that" became engrained in the nations psyche. Whenever I called, John would do his impression and ask me for a job. I was impressed by his enthusiasm and personality, and so I decided to offer him the chance to take over from me selling CDs off the van. After spending a few days training in London, I invited him around to my house on his way back so that I could give him advice on his customers. It was around 5pm when John called in, and I offered him a cup of tea. As I was bringing the tea in I heard the sound of the key in the door. It was Rachael, my then-wife. I immediately introduced her to our new sales rep. "This is John, I announced. I was slightly taken aback by her reply: "Would you like me to get my tits out now?" I looked at John, who had gone crimson. Ten minutes earlier she had been walking home when a Robert Plant look-alike driving a big blue van popped his head out of the window and shouted, "Hey darlin, show us your tits". John had not got off to the best start, and over the next few months things did not improve.

The next day I went out with John on the van to offer him my words of wisdom and experience. I had booked his appointments, including some big accounts that would be likely to give him a good order. This would give him confidence. What I wasn't prepared for was John's driving – it was like he was driving a go-cart, as opposed to a large Mercedes van. He would have his foot hard down on the accelerator. It was a big vehicle and, with a heavy load, it would just about reach 70mph on a downhill stretch with a following wind. Whatever speed it managed, it wasn't fast enough for John and he would shake the wheel in frustration. His habit of cursing every driver who dared overtake us with the phrase "C'mon you bastard!" hardly endeared him to me. I did point out to John that Mercedes vans don't have ears, but it seemed that the van was not the only thing that was deaf, as John didn't change his way of driving.

Every time he took a corner I could here the CDs falling off the racks. I wondered what was going to last longer, John's job or the van's engine. I was constantly asking him to slow down. At traffic lights he would eyeball the driver of any vehicle who drew alongside and then try to burn them off. He nearly always failed – Mercedes vans are not known for their acceleration.

I soon discovered that John's music knowledge started at rock and ended at rock; he was great at selling rock albums, but as soon as he had to sell another genre, he was like a fish out of water. At the end of the day we had a review – it had been a disaster. I explained to John that if you are at a rock 'n' roll shop, it is pointless trying to sell Journey or Boston CDs, and if you are at a jazz shop, it is not a great sales technique to start enthusing about Led Zeppelin. I also gave him a few phrases to use when recommending a CD, as describing an album as 'f***** shit hot' was unacceptable. In my heart, I knew then I had a made a big mistake.

The next day John was on his own, and I had left him to book his appointments himself. I suggested that five appointments a day was the norm. I called him late in the afternoon to see how he was doing. An extremely stressed John answered the phone. "How's it going?" I enquired. "Not very well," John replied, "I have just cancelled my last two accounts, as I am not going to have time to call on them".

"Why not?" I asked. John went on to explain that he had only done two shops – one in Manchester, the second in Leeds, and now he was driving like a maniac trying to get to Sheffield before the third shop closed. I pointed out to John that we had around five shops in each of those cities and asked why he had not just concentrated on staying in one city. John offered the excuse that some of the shops had staff off or they were ill and that some couldn't see him in the morning, others in the afternoon. Over the next few weeks it became clear that John could just not plan his route. He continued zigzagging his way across the North West averaging only three calls a day because of bad planning. Sometimes he was doing more mileage in a week then I had been doing in a month.

I decided to spend another couple of days out on the road with him. I noticed an Esso mug in his van and John informed me that he was collecting them and that you received one every time you filled your tank. He reckoned they would be worth something in years to come. Based on his mileage, I thought to myself "I bet you can't move in his kitchen for Esso mugs". In fact, it crossed my mind that John was doing all of the mileage just to collect Esso mugs. Even when I took over the booking of his appointments, it was clear that it was just not working.

Luckily for me I had only taken John on for a three-month trial. I was relieved when the time was up and I could let him go. I often wonder what became of John – perhaps he is now making a living in a Led Zeppelin tribute band?

* * *

That evening I stayed overnight in a cheap hotel. After twenty years on the road I still resent paying through the nose for accommodation. As long as a place is clean, has a shower, a TV and a good breakfast, what more do you require? I did always laugh when I stayed in Blackpool, as many of the B&Bs advertised that they had hot and cold water (fantastic). Over the years I have stayed in hundreds of different hotels and B&Bs and did think I could write a businessman's guide to bargain places to stay, but maybe that can be my next project.

The first call of the day is in the heart of Lancashire, to meet up with the owner of one of the country's few independent record-shop chains, Townsend Records, who have branches in Leyland, Clitheroe and a head office based in Great Harwood.

Steve Bamber had been selling luxury cars for five years when he felt an entrepreneurial urge to go into business for himself, and so began looking for a retail opportunity. He discovered Jerry's Records, an old-fashioned, enigmatic music shop in Great Harwood, which opened only three days a week. Steve did some research and learned that Jerry's was owned by a wealthy couple for whom the shop was merely a side-line for the wife, who felt that three days work a week was quite enough for her.

Steve knew that the shop had tremendous potential and realised immediately that it was for him. His brother already owned a musical instrument shop locally and Steve reckoned that the two businesses could complement and promote each other.

Steve borrowed £500 and paid this princely sum for Jerry's Records, leaving the previous owners even more leisure time to recover from their hard graft.

Great Harwood could not believe its luck – it now had a record shop that was open six days a week. Steve revolutionised the business immediately, simply by installing cassette racks. The previous owners had not stocked cassettes, as they had believed that the format had no future. Fortunately for Steve the format still had twenty years of sales before its eventual rapid decline.

Steve adopted a shrewd policy of expansion by acquisition. He targeted shops similar to Jerry's, whose owners were either elderly or disillusioned and were looking to move on. It proved to be easier to buy established businesses and improve upon them than to open new record shops from scratch. This was the punk era, and many shops would not embrace this exciting change in the industry and were therefore finding themselves out of synch with the times.

Steve's second acquisition was a shop in Chorley, quickly followed by a third in Leyland. Business was booming, and four years later another opportunity presented itself. Reidy's, a well-established record shop in Blackburn, owned a second shop in Clitheroe. However, owner Chris Nuttall had recently started work with EMI Records putting together compilation albums, and so was struggling to manage both shops. He offered the Clitheroe store to Steve and so the Townsend chain expanded to four shops.

A significant bonus for Steve was that all of his shops were 'chart return' stores, and, of course, this ensured that he received plenty of free stock from the sales reps hoping to manipulate chart positions.

One rep took advantage of this opportunity, to the point where even British Market Research (who compiled the chart at that point) picked up on it. Chris Rea had released a new single on Magnet Records, and the rep had taken it upon himself to fill in pages of bogus sales in one of Steve's shops. BMR realised something was wrong when, according to the books, the Leyland store had sold more than 100 copies, whilst the other three stores had sold five copies between them. (Maybe Chris Rea had a lot of relatives in Leyland or the Chris Rea fan club was based there). Steve was furious with the rep, as he employed a young girl in Leyland and he felt that the rep had taken advantage of her naivety.

The reason why Townsend is still thriving is down to Steve's recognition that he needed to diversify. Bruce McKenzie joined from HMV Bolton to work on ways to do this. Two projects he initiated bore fruit.

The first was to establish Townsend's own label, offering many exclusive-to-Townsend releases and all others being distributed by Universal. Artists it is associated with include Mike Harding, Ian McNabb, Puressence, David Sylvian, Thunder and Black.

Secondly, Townsend is also into a successful partnership with a company called Concert Live, which obtains the licence from record companies to record live concerts and to produce the resultant CD for purchase on the night. The licence allows the manufacture of 1,000 CDs per gig and concert-goers can pre-order before the gig, purchase after the gig, and have the CD delivered to their door. It's a great concept, as it gives everybody the opportunity to buy a souvenir of the gig.

Steve and Bruce are shrewd businessmen, always on the look-out for other money-making opportunities. Other than Concert Live and its record label, its retail outlets do more than simply sell CDs – they also have a thriving trade in the sale of musical instruments and i-pods.

I believe that Townsend will be one of the 'Last Shops Standing' thanks to their recognition that the industry was changing rapidly and that shops needed to diversify to survive.

* * *

From Townsend I travel into Yorkshire and call in on a shop that has not changed in years. Muse Music in Hebdon Bridge is not the easiest shop to communicate with – they have no website, no fax and no e-mail, but it is rumoured that you can contact Sid Jones, the owner, via carrier pigeon.

Known throughout Hebdon Bridge as CD Sid, in 1997 he realised his childhood dream and opened a unique record shop in his hometown. The shop is stocked full of psychedelic and progressive rock and Sid's policy is if he likes it, he stocks it. To visit Muse Music is like being transported back to the hippy era. The shop is adorned with psychedelic posters, and Sid looks as if he should be playing with Hawkwind instead of running a shop.

After leaving school Sid drifted between jobs before getting a job with Groove Records in Halifax. After ten years with Groove Sid sensed that the shop was going downhill and decided to branch out on his own. He opened in Hebdon Bridge in a small shop and filled it with all his favourite records.

On his second day of trading a man walked in and Sid could see he was impressed with the collection. The man started saying complimentary things about the shop, and couldn't believe that a record shop like this had opened in Hebdon Bridge. Suddenly the man opened his arms and looked up to the ceiling then screamed "I am in heaven!" and with that he left the shop and Sid has never seen him again. Another customer who Sid will never forget was 'Ginger Jim'. He was not called 'Ginger Jim' due to the colour of his hair, it was down to the fact he carried a pack of ginger biscuits around with him.

One Wednesday morning 'Ginger Jim' called in carrying a four-pack of lager and, although it was only 10.30am, he was clearly drunk. He came up to the counter and dealt out his ginger biscuits as if they were playing cards. Sid looked astonished to see his counter covered in ginger biscuits. For the next twenty minutes 'Ginger Jim' shouted abuse at Sid for no reason at all. Sid is a pretty easy-going guy and just let him shout his frustrations. 'Ginger Jim' then asked Sid if he could use the toilet, and Sid suggested the alleyway behind the shop. When he tried to re-enter the shop, no doubt to carry on his abuse, Sid barred his way. He handed him his four-pack, which was now a two-pack, along with his ginger nuts and sent him packing. 'Ginger Jim' never came back to Muse as the next week he set fire to his house and suffered serious burns. Following his recovery he moved away from the area, and Sid never had to deal with that particular ginger nut again.

I asked Sid what his biggest selling CD was and also whether he had an unusual regular seller that he thought other shops didn't stock. He gave me the same answer to both questions: the album was *Into the Electric Castle* by Ayreon. Since its release in 1998 Muse have sold over 500 copies. I was staggered by this figure, but, as Sid was telling me this, the customer in the shop joined in the conversation telling me Sid had persuaded him to purchase a copy and it was now his all-time favourite CD. The album is a 'space opera' on two CDs. It tells the story of eight characters that find themselves in a different dimension and then take part in an alien experiment. Amongst the vocalists are Fish (ex-Marillion) and Damion Wilson formerly of Threshold. If Muse can sell 500 copies, then every CD shop in the country should be stocking this album.

I am sure Muse will be one of the 'Last Shops Standing'. Sid is a great character and his knowledge of progressive rock is second to none. If you are a fan of this genre, and you're in Yorkshire, take a trip out to Hebdon Bridge and check out Muse (don't forget to ask to listen to the Ayreon CD).

*   *   *

From Hebdon Bridge to my next call in Huddersfield is only a few short miles, but the disparity between the shops is enormous. Elliot Smaje started Wall of Sound Records in 1987 as a one-man market stall around West Yorkshire. At a loss after returning from studying in Northern Ireland, and in need of some instant cash, he hired a table in Leeds market to sell his unwanted books and records. His parents came from a market background, and Elliot found he was a natural salesman. Delighted with his first day's takings, he decided to go back the next week. People came in and offered him their unwanted books and records and he soon realised that there might be a future in it. He decided on a positive approach, and each record he sold he purchased three. Within months he was plying his trade at four different markets in West Yorkshire.

After four years of selling at markets and record fairs, he took the plunge and opened his first shop in the historic Piece Hall in Halifax. At the time this was quite a gamble, as the premises was previously occupied by an unsuccessful retailer, Vinyl Tap, and Halifax also had a vast collection of record shops.

However, after ten years the stock expanded so much that he also moved into next door. After seventeen years there, it is time to move on again, as ever since he has been in Halifax, he has been in a battle with the council, who seem determined to stop him improving the shop.

The Piece Hall is one of the most impressive buildings in Britain. It was built in 1779 as a place for the weavers of Yorkshire to trade cloth. These days it houses over 50 shops, yet in all the time I have visited it there are always plenty of empty shops. In his time there Elliot has tried so hard to move to a larger unit in the Piece Hall, and he has tried to expand his current unit, but he has been thwarted every time by the bureaucrats of the council. Two points illustrate this. When Elliott acquired his second unit, he applied to have a wall knocked down to join both units together. After years of indecision the council eventually refused permission. This resulted in him having to stock all of the rock product in one unit and all of the jazz, country and folk in the other. If a customer came to the counter with a rock CD and asked for a jazz CD, Elliot would tell them to go next door and he would meet them there to show them the jazz section. Elliot had a door between the two units, so he would walk through, whilst the customer had to leave the shop and go next door.

Each year the Piece Hall holds a concert by a Pink Floyd tribute band called Off The Wall. The concert starts at 7.30pm and attracts a crowd of around 4,000. Elliott applied to the council to see if it was OK to open in the evening, as it was a great opportunity to sell. After a series of letters the council turned him down on health and safety grounds, citing that they felt it was unsafe for people to be walking around at night. Despite Elliot pointing out that people have been walking around at night since dinosaurs walked the earth, the council wouldn't relent. (Elliot has a motto for Calderdale Council: 'Too incompetent to be corrupt'.)

By 2007 Elliot threw the towel in with his battle with the council, and Halifax lost a fabulous record shop. The Piece Hall, despite its size, is easy to miss, as it only has a small entrance. The week Elliot opened in Halifax, he attended a meeting with other traders from the hall requesting that they put signs up to direct people to the building. The day he was moving out of the Piece Hall he noticed the council putting up signs with directions to the building. For Elliott it was nice to see that the meeting had brought results, just eighteen years too late.

Halifax's loss was Huddersfield's gain. Wall of Sound has moved to a new, much larger premises in nearby and more vibrant Huddersfield, where they are based today. It is ironic that five years ago I felt that Halifax was the most overstocked town for record shops and now they have no independent record stores left.

Wall Of Sound will be one of the 'Last Shops Standing', mainly due to Elliot being one of the dealers to recognise the importance of the Internet. His collection of vinyl is one of the best in the country, and he has a number of albums valued at over £500, including the very first Elvis album in mint condition. Whist many dealers were saying vinyl was dead, Elliot was buying more. It has turned out to be a shrewd move, as vinyl is now back in vogue, and many shops that scrapped their vinyl section have now re-instated it.

The majority of shops featured in this book now embrace the Internet, instead of fighting it, and the way forward for shops where possible is to have a page on the website that has revolutionised how music is sold – Amazon. No organisation has changed the way the public purchase CDs more than Amazon. It is hard to believe that Jeff Bezos formed the company as recently as 1994, initially specialising as an online bookseller.

Back then, when the Internet was in its infancy, Bezos had the vision to realise that shopping online would become the future of retail. Amazon expanded at an astonishing rate and transformed from being simply an online retailer into a channel that opens up into a broad customer community. Music customers are encouraged to post their own CD reviews and Amazon profiles customer tastes so that they can recommend further titles that customers might also enjoy. Such was its rapid growth that Amazon was launched on the American stock market in October 1997, raising an amazing £54 million.

However, things did not always go to plan and, in 2001, the company posted a staggering $1.4 billion loss, because of problems generated by over-rapid growth.

Many people predicted its demise but, essentially, Amazon was a company, which had the potential to dominate Cyber commerce. It had already established strong customer loyalty by offering product at an extremely low price and with a reliable delivery service.

Amazon first started selling CDs in 1995 and, despite competition from Play.com and HMV Online, it is far and away the seller of the largest number of CDs online in the UK. There is no doubt that Amazon's sales have hit independent stores hard but, on the plus side, independents can see at a glance on the web what price the largest online CD retailer is charging, so they have the opportunity to undercut them. Unfortunately, this is often difficult, because of the additional costs independent stores carry for being on the high street.

Amazon is also proactive when it comes to selling. Whenever you purchase a CD off Amazon, they will recommend you titles purchased by other consumers who have bought the same title as you. This method of cross-selling is hugely successful, and the more titles you purchase, the more titles Amazon will recommend.

Where Amazon has really hit the independent shops is that they have attracted the rarity buyers. These are the customers who would go to independent shops to search for the unusual or collectable titles. These people no longer visit. Why should they when the world's biggest choice of music is available through the click of a mouse?

Since I started researching this book I have been struck by the variety of attitudes record shops have towards Amazon. Many stores see them solely as their major competitor, but many others embrace them as a supplier, spending thousands of pounds with them. Previously, just about every record shop dealt with a wholesaler called Total Home Entertainment (THE), a company whose aim it was to stock every single CD, DVD and computer game available. This was a fantastic service for independent retailers, as ordering from the major record companies required a minimum spend of £100 per order. Although it was more expensive to buy from THE than the record companies themselves, shops could purchase stock from a broad selection from all of the major companies and also smaller distributors, such as Proper, Vital and Pinnacle. Record companies would supply stock to THE at a discount, and so the arrangement worked well for everybody within that retail 'model'. For the record companies, it meant that their stock was in store and that they were not spending their time dispatching small non-profit making orders direct to stores. For the record shops it meant that if they sold out of just a few titles, they could replenish them promptly, as THE offered next-day delivery – unlike the major record companies. This was especially useful if a store sold out on a Friday – it meant that they could get the title in for Saturday, the shop's busiest day.

In September 2006 THE was acquired by Entertainment UK (EUK). Unfortunately, Woolworths owned EUK. Many record shops regarded Woolworths as their main competitor, so things looked ominous for their future. As well as being the sole supplier to Woolworths, EUK were also sole supplier to Tesco, WHSmith, Morrisons, Sainsbury's and Somerfield. EUK accounted for nearly one in three CDs sold in the UK. It didn't take long for service to independent record shops to decline, as it was not in EUK's interest to service shops that are in direct competition with the supermarkets.

In November 2008, after trading for 99 years, landmark high street retailer Woolworths, a company with 30,000 employees, finally went into receivership. As a music retailer, the company had long been a mess, but had also been a constant thorn in the side of independent record shops.

I think that Woolworths' main problem was that it never had a unique selling point. Its only strength was the number and location of its outlets. It was full of toys, which could usually be found cheaper in Toys R Us and in supermarkets. It stocked cheap bric-a-brac, which, again, could often be found cheaper in Poundland and Wilkinsons. The supermarkets almost always beat them on price for CDs and DVDs. The range was extremely limited and, as such, was incomparable to what was available from independent record shops.

My first experience of Woolworths was as a youth. I had heard this great new song called 'Hocus Pocus' by the band Focus, so I called into Woolworths and asked if they stocked it. The assistant asked me, "Is it in the chart?"

"Well," I replied, "it is a new record, so I don't think it will be in the chart yet". With that she handed me a list of the top 50, grunting, "there you go – check for yourself".

Even as a thirteen year old I was less than impressed with this customer service. I looked through the chart listing and told the assistant that it was not listed in the top 50, to which she barked, "If it's not in the chart, we don't stock it". I then asked her, "If Woolworths only stock CDs in the top 50 how does a record ever enter the chart?" By now I could see she was losing patience with me. "Look," she said, "This isn't my normal department, I normally work in confectionery".

That about summed Woolworths up for me: poor stock, poor customer service and a record department staffed by people more at home in the Pic 'n' Mix section.

I do not know if Woolworths ever improved over the years as that assistant ensured that, despite purchasing hundreds of records and CDs over the years, I never made a single purchase from Woolworths – although I do recall buying a Toblerone once (they were half price).

Woolworths' wholesale arm – EUK – also went into receivership. Whilst EUK's core business was to supply to Woolworths, Borders, Zavvi and many of the supermarkets, it did also supply to independent shops.

Its failure led to serious supply problems during the Christmas 2008 sales period and was decisively inopportune for Zavvi who, unable to secure alternative sources of supply, were forced into receivership on Christmas Eve 2008.

This brought to an end the retail record business first started by Richard Branson in 1971, under the brand-name of Virgin. The chain had expanded rapidly from its inception and, in 1979, had opened the first record mega-store, on London's Oxford Street.

I feel that Richard Branson was ahead of the game in realising that music retailing was facing difficult times ahead. In September 2007 a management buyout, led by Simon Douglas, resulted in Virgin Megastores breaking away from the rest of the Virgin group of compa-nies. The new company started trading under the name of Zavvi, but retained most of the buying team from Virgin. It was always going to be difficult for it to survive as it started off at a time when many other music retailers were closing down.

My personal view is that Zavvi lacked an identity, in contrast to Virgin, which was a great brand with a famous name and a terrific history, with the public always seemingly able to associate it closely with Richard Branson.

Zavvi's name sounded more suitable to an ice cream parlour than to an entertainment retailer. Still, its demise was terrible news for the industry as a whole and, in particular, for all the staff who lost jobs.

So, with Zavvi's 125 stores across the UK and Ireland added to Woolworths' 815, the total impact is that there are now another 940 shops which will no longer stock music.

Then, during what was possibly the worst few weeks ever for music retailing, Pinnacle Distribution also went into receivership.

This company was responsible for the distribution of more than 400 record labels, which included artists of the calibre of Katie Melua, Morrissey, Moloko, The Strokes, The Libertines, Feeder, Black Sabbath, Gary Numan, The Kinks, The Pretenders, Frank Zappa, Echo and the Bunnymen, The Small Faces, Tom Waits and Fleet Foxes, amongst many others.

According to the British Phonographic Industry (BPI), Pinnacle had been responsible for 4.3 per cent of total UK music sales during 2007. It was certainly the largest supplier to many independent record shops and its failure was a disaster for them as it ensured that, for many, 2008 would be their last Christmas. The 94 staff that Pinnacle laid off also endured a miserable festive season.

The fact that EUK had collapsed owing it a lot of money was the final straw for Pinnacle. The company had not kept pace with a shrinking market. It was responsible for the distribution of hundreds of bands, but insufficient numbers of them became successful. It was saddled with too much quantity and not enough quality. When the market downturn occurred it was badly positioned to cope with it.

Consequently, many record labels were left with huge losses and hundreds of bands with nobody to distribute their records to the shops during the busiest trading period of the year.

It has been left to Amazon and my own company Proper Music to pick up the business of supplying those obscure and difficult-to-get CDs, which the independents need to survive.

It is ironic that many independents now embrace an organisation that was initially thought to be detrimental to independent stores. For a small commission lots of shops have their own page on the Amazon website.

* * *

After calling on Wall Of Sound I travel down the A629 to meet up with a man who I met on my first day of selling music as a sales rep, over twenty years ago. It's off to Sheffield to visit Barry Everard, owner of Record Collector, a shop that has had a real impact on the UK music industry over its thirty-year history.

Barry was brought up in Kettering, in a particularly flat part of England, and on leaving school chose to study at Sheffield University, primarily because it was a city surrounded by hills. An avid hill walker, he felt it would be the perfect place to study and hike. Barry's other great passion was music. As well as listening to music he took every opportunity to read about it, purchasing all of the music magazines of the day. An opening arose for Barry to join the University Entertainments Committee. His role was to publicise their gigs. His first four gigs were the stuff of legend:

1 Free supported by Uriah Heep – admittance was five shillings (25p)
2 Deep Purple – admittance ten shillings
3 Colosseum also charged ten shillings. However, according to Barry, due to their dire performance this was nine shillings too much.
4 The Who charged £1 for tickets in advance, 25 shillings on the night. This led to mass protests around the campus. Many students who had never paid over a £1 for a gig boycotted the band's performance.

The most memorable gig was when Roy Harper played Sheffield University's Christmas ball. Roy thought it would be a great idea to smash up all of the Christmas decorations that the students had lovingly put up earlier in the day. As the axe wielder smashed down his guitar on to the polystyrene snowmen, the students looked on in horror. Some students were so incensed that all of their hard work was being treated with such contempt that they attempted to storm the stage, only to be held back by the burly security – probably a blessing in disguise, with a guitar brandishing maniac on stage.

I had my own experience with Roy a few years back. Not only was he capable of destroying polystyrene snowmen, he managed to destroy the first ever Proper Music conference. We were a young company and we had decided to hold our first conference. Roy was one of the biggest artists on our roster, and our job was to ensure that the record shops stocked Roy Harper's CDs. The idea was to invite all of our artists and records labels and tell them about all of the plans that we had to raise their profile and what we were planning to do for them in the coming year. Steve Kersley, our managing director, had shown me his planned speech. It was full of self-deprecating humour, and I knew he would have the audience in stitches. All was going well until the question and answer session before Steve's closing address. Roy Harper stood up and started off by upsetting all of our Irish labels, saying that we spent too much time and effort promoting the Celtic fringe (our Irish labels didn't consider themselves fringe, and neither did we). He then launched into a tirade shouting to the room that Proper was rubbish. He told the crowd that we didn't sell enough of his CDs, and he then started to list record shops that he had visited who didn't stock any of his CDs. Whatever we did, we couldn't shut him up to give somebody else a chance to ask a question. Eventually, Roy did sit down, but not before he told the audience that he was taking his business elsewhere. Steve's speech didn't seem so funny after that.

My favourite Roy Harper tale comes from the respected *Independent* newspaper journalist Andy Gill. In 1994 Roy released the album *Descendants of Smith*. Andy reviewed it and, to put it kindly, he expressed the view that it was not one of Mr Harper's "finest pieces of work". Andy thought nothing else of it until a couple of weeks later when a package came through the post. It contained a closely typed 30-page letter from Roy explaining why Andy was wrong and why his album was magnificent.

I told this tale to the music journalist, David Sinclair, who then informed me of his Roy Harper experience. In his 1985 review of Harper's show at the Fairfield Hall, Croydon for *The Times*, David Sinclair described a performance "of startling ineptitude" and complained of "the spirit of drugged torpor, which pervaded the entire show." Sinclair was rewarded with a six-page, handwritten letter from Harper in which the ageing folk singer lambasted the hapless critic for his "blend of minimal mental equipment and an over-inflated sense of self." The letter concluded ominously: "Unfortunately for you moonshine, I am not going to go away." Unfortunately for everyone, Harper was as good as his word.

I must admit I am already having sleepless nights myself anticipating Roy's forthcoming letter to me.

One thing I would say about Roy is that you have to admire a musician who cares so passionately about his work. Andy Gill, Barry Everard, David Sinclair and myself will never forget our experiences with the legend that is Roy Harper.

At the end of the road in which Barry lived stood a farmhouse which housed a collective, who performed as a group under the name of 'Principal Edwards Magic Theatre'. The band had fourteen members — all living under one roof. They had met up at Exeter University and were signed to John Peel's Dandelion label. John once told his radio listeners that he would play the band's track 'The Kettering Song' to drive away visitors who had overstayed their welcome at his home, Peel Acres.

Many people in Barry's road resented Principal Edwards Magic Theatre. They did not enjoy having a bunch of hippies live amongst them. Barry, however, was not one of them, and was delighted to have these regulars from the John Peel Show on his doorstep. He took every opportunity to see the band play and to call down to the farmhouse. Because Kettering is in the middle of England, the farmhouse became an unofficial B&B for bands returning from or travelling down to London.

Another artist who left a huge impression on Barry Everard was Richard Thompson. They met when Sheffield University booked The Sandy Denny Band to perform, with Richard on guitar and an old friend of Barry's, Dave Richards, on bass. On the day of the gig, and following the band's soundcheck Barry called into the dressing room with the intention of just saying hello to Dave Richards but, after a while, Sandy Denny started singing and her fellow musicians joined in. Soon everybody in the room became involved in this spontaneous jam. Barry was amazed to find himself singing along in such illustrious company. Before long Sandy stopped and left the changing-room, taking her entourage with her. Slowly the changing-room emptied until eventually there were just Richard Thompson, playing his guitar, and an overawed Barry.

As Richard continued to play, Barry was asking himself if he should leave. He constantly looked into Richard's eyes to see if he could gauge whether he wanted him to leave or was happy for him to stay, but his eyes gave nothing away. On the one hand Barry was honoured to be accidentally sitting-in on this elemental tour de force by one of the greatest guitar players of all time, but, on the other hand he felt that he might be intruding on something that was intensely private and definitely not a performance intended for public consumption. It felt inappropriate, and he likened it to standing in the same cubicle as somebody having a crap. For the twenty minutes Barry stood there watching; he truly was 'The last fan standing'. Eventually the rest of the band filed back in and neither Richard nor Barry had exchanged a word.

One contact who delighted Barry was someone who came to have a colossal impact on his life, his favourite DJ, John Peel. To this day he can still remember the first record he heard on his show. It was Captain Beefheart's *Electricity*. Barry did his utmost to listen to every programme, and then at the weekend he would be down to Virgin to buy what he had heard on John's show. Not only did the music that John played shape Barry's life, but he also adopted his ethos. Barry would leave no stone unturned in his pursuit to find new music.

Like John, he would give every artist a chance and, if he considered it was good, he would promote it in his shop. He was a champion supporter of Sheffield bands. This is highlighted by the fact that if any local band released a self-financed single, Barry would sell it in the shop for free. Furthermore, all of the money (minus the VAT) would be given to the bands, often with the words, "Go and buy yourself a new guitar with the proceeds" ringing in their ears. Little did Barry know that John Peel was soon to become a life-long friend.

Through his weekly column in *Sounds* music paper, John told the story of when he had fled Dallas in the 60s, where he had been working as a DJ, leaving all of his records behind. He had started going out with a young lady who didn't tell him the truth about her age. Her father was not impressed with his daughter having a relationship with the local DJ and came gunning (literally) after John. He got out of town quickly, leaving his possessions behind in the process.

In the intervening years he had managed to replace almost all of his record collection. However, he hadn't managed to replace Annette

Funicello, of whom he was a big fan, as all of her records had been deleted in the UK. So John appealed to the readers of *Sounds*, the music paper, that if they had any of her records he would be delighted to purchase them.

Annette Funicello was a 50s teen idol that graduated from appearing in Disney productions to starring in the beach surf movies of the 60s. When she signed her contract to do the first beach movie, Walt Disney himself insisted that the film not be allowed to show her navel, as it was too provocative. Annette became a cult star and had some success singing – her biggest hit 'Tall Paul' reaching number seven in the Billboard chart of 1959.

Whilst flicking through the racks of a local record shop, Barry came across three of her records. He bought them and wrote to John asking him if he wanted them. John phoned Barry up. It was a great surprise, and Barry said that John had given him so much pleasure that he would be happy to send them to him for nothing as a sign of his appreciation. John insisted on sending Barry some LPs in return.

As a result, these two true music fans, Barry and John, became friends. Barry would send John records that he felt he would appreciate; in return, whenever Barry paid a visit to London he would meet up with John, go for a drink and often sit in on his radio show.

In August 1974 a package arrived for Barry. When he opened it up he found an A–Z of London, and tucked into one of the pages was an invite to John and Sheila's wedding. On 31 August he travelled down to London to John's marriage ceremony. It was a lovely warm, sunny day, and the ceremony was held near the Kennington Oval. Barry found the whole day surreal, as he recognised everybody there, but knew nobody. Finding himself adjacent to him in the queue for the reception, Barry decided to ask fellow Yorkshire resident, Bill Nelson, a singer and guitarist with the band Be Bop Deluxe, if he could hang around with him. Thus throughout the day he was introduced to many people he had only previously listened to including Nick Mason of Pink Floyd, Robert Wyatt, Alan Freeman, Ivor Cutler and Roger Chapman of Family.

Barry remembers fondly that John and Sheila had invited their local youth football team to the wedding, who then found themselves playing keepy-up with Rod Stewart and The Faces in the gardens at the reception (despite the alcohol consumption, Rod Stewart was pretty good). He also recalled John Peel spending a good deal of time talking with Terry Wogan. It is fascinating to think that two great stalwarts of radio, from opposite ends of the musical spectrum, would be firm friends.

I have the utmost respect for Barry, as he had never revealed to anybody that he was a friend of John's until after his untimely death in 2004. During the time I had known Barry I had told him about my own acquaintances with John, yet Barry never let on, as he regarded John as a true friend and didn't want to be seen as trading on his name.

What is most astonishing is that, throughout their friendship, Barry never revealed to John that he was the owner of a record shop. It was not until 2003 that his secret was discovered. John's son Tom was studying at Sheffield University and had informed his dad that he had discovered this fabulous record shop that he must visit. So one day, whilst Barry was standing at the counter, John and his wife Sheila walked in. John was delighted to meet his friend and asked him what he was doing there. Barry informed him that he was the owner. John was stunned and touched that Barry had kept this from him. Barry was then able to fill John in on his own career in music. Barry remembers this meeting with great fondness, as it was the last time he met John. Barry did attend his funeral and cites John Peel as the greatest influence on his life.

Barry's career in music came about thanks to his photographic memory and ability to absorb and recall music facts, which landed him his first music job at the Virgin Record shop in Sheffield. Whilst standing in the queue to purchase some LPs, the customer in front asked the assistant if he knew anything about a forthcoming Gentle Giant album. The assistant knew nothing about it. Not wishing to disappoint a fan, Barry piped up with, "If it helps, it's called *Octopus*, it's on the Vertigo label and it will be released two weeks on Monday". At the next till another customer was after a song that they had heard on the radio and a couple of assistants were trying without success to identify it. The customer told them the lyrics, Barry recognised the song and so Virgin gained a sale. Unbeknownst to Barry, one of the assistants was the shop's manager and, as Barry went to leave the shop, he buttonholed him and asked him if he would be interested in working for Virgin. Although Barry was keen to pursue a career in music journalism, he was willing to work in any aspect of the music industry. His encyclopaedic knowledge of music impressed the Virgin hierarchy and he was soon promoted to manager.

At this time, Virgin shops were encouraged to support artists on the Virgin Record label. The shop rocked to the sounds of Gong, Tangerine Dream and Mike Oldfield. Often artists would call in and make personal appearances. Barry recalled taking Tangerine Dream for a Chinese meal. He was also invited to the Albert Hall to witness the first performance of David Bedford's *Orchestral Tubular Bells*, in which Mike Oldfield played guitar.

During this period Mike was notorious for not showing up because of his stage fright. If this happened, Steve Hillage was there as a stand in. Barry was hanging around with Steve and found himself acting as his unofficial minder. Needless to say Mike Oldfield didn't turn up to the Albert Hall and Steve was informed that he would be performing. Steve Hillage and Gong had played a free concert outside Virgin Records only a few weeks before. Barry and Steve recognised one another from this, and somehow Barry found himself delegated to get Steve, complete with Fender Stratocaster, to the stage door. Barry will never forget arguing with an over-zealous Royal Albert Hall commissionaire, who was attempting to eject this long-bearded rock star with the tea cosy hat and rainbow striped jumper. Barry was trying to explain that Steve was to be the star of the show, but the commissionaire was insisting that Mike Oldfield would be performing and was doing his utmost to get the pair thrown out. Luckily, common sense prevailed and Steve Hillage, with Barry's help, saved the day.

Barry also had trouble at another gig, when the German Krautrock band, Faust, played City Hall in Sheffield. The performance was punctuated by Faust drilling a huge concrete block with a pneumatic drill. This was truly art. After an hour of music and drilling, the majority of the band left the stage, leaving just the bass player and drummer to carry on playing on a stage now littered with lumps of concrete. After another ten minutes the bass player left, leaving the drummer on his own. After a ten-minute drum solo the drummer stopped. He didn't leave the stage. There were several TV sets strategically placed around the stage and he sat on his stool watching them whilst the crowd, who were wondering what the hell was going on, sat there patient, but confused. This was art, and they wanted to enjoy it somehow. After a while the manager of City Hall put the lights on and took to the stage. A portly man in his sixties, he clearly felt that Faust was taking advantage of its audience and told everybody to go home. The crowd was incensed by his requests to leave, and the louder he bellowed at them to evacuate, the louder the crowd booed and jeered.

Eventually he gave up and, as some gesture of respect to its audience, Faust came back on and played a few more numbers amongst the rubble, with all of the charisma and enthusiasm of disinterested workers returning from a long tea break.

To this day Barry is still a big attendee of gigs, going to at least two a week. Barry had experienced a gig even more memorable than the Faust performance, when he was the only David Bowie fan at a David Bowie show. In March 1972 Sheffield University held their Union ball. Throughout the course of the day over twenty bands were to play at ten different venues.

David Bowie, whose career was then in a bit of a lull, even though he had achieved a number one single with 'Space Oddity' was due to go on at 1.30am. As a fan, Barry expected the venue to be full, but when he entered the room he found that the only people in attendance were the barman and four male lecturers who were very loudly chatting up four young female students. Barry couldn't understand why nobody was there. Perhaps other acts were appearing at the same time or more likely, after a day of drinking, most students had crashed out. So David Bowie and his brand new band The Spiders from Mars took to the stage to play to just ten people. Throughout the first few numbers the lecturers carried on chatting up the students much to the annoyance of Bowie. Eventually he stopped the gig, glared at the lecturers and told them if they didn't shut up he was going home.

David carried on as more people started ambling in and, by the end, the crowd must have doubled to all of twenty people. I guess those lecturers and students now tell the tale of how they attended a David Bowie concert with only twenty people in attendance – probably forgetting to add that they spent the whole performance chatting.

One unusual feature that Virgin had in its stores was aircraft seats in which you could sit and request records to be played through the headphones. Barry recalls one enthusiastic rock fan that spent hours in the seats. Little did he know that a few years later the enthusiastic rock fan would be spending a great part of his time travelling the world sitting in aircraft seats, as the young man was Bruce Dickinson, who later joined Iron Maiden. Bruce became a successful pilot and in 2008 he flew a Monarch plane full of passengers from the Egyptian resort of Sharm El Sheikh following the collapse of the holiday company XL. He then brought back a second batch of stranded tourists from the Greek island of Kos. Dickinson has flown commercial 747 aircraft for many years. When touring the world, Iron Maiden use their own 747 piloted by Dickinson, which is brilliantly named 'Ed Force One' after the band's mascot Eddie. All of those stranded passengers can be grateful for the time Bruce Dickinson spent in the aircraft seats back in Virgin Sheffield, as it may have encouraged his interest in flying.

Barry took the life-changing decision to leave Virgin and start his own record shop. In July 1978 he rented a property on Fulwood Road in the

Broomhill area of Sheffield, in which he was ideally placed to capture the student market. He called it Record Collector, as that's what he was. He decided to start off by dealing only in second-hand records, and his original stock consisted mainly of his own huge record collection. Barry will never forget his first customer, Clare Fellows, a girl who has since become a good friend. She was to become a regular customer and also went on to marry the chef, Ainsley Harriott. Barry purchased a signed copy of Lindisfarne's 'Fog on the Tyne' from Clare. Little was he to know that his first transaction would cause so many problems. Clare is also the sister of Graham Fellows, the comedian who had had a hit single under the name of Jilted John. These days he is known for his comic character John Shuttleworth. The first LP Barry had bought had been sold without the owner's permission – Graham claims to this day that his sister had no right to sell his beloved LP.

Another of Barry's early customers was Martin Fry, who was soon to achieve fame with ABC. In those days he didn't come into the shop in his gold lamé suit. His habitual sartorial choice was usually an ex-army greatcoat. Martin had produced a fanzine that covered punk and new wave and he asked Barry if he would stock it in the shop.

One customer Barry will never forget is the young man who regularly came in and hung around the shop. He was the singer in a local band and always asked Barry for advice on how he could bring his band to a wider audience. One day he turned up and asked Barry if he would be able to recommend record companies that he should send a tape to. Barry spent two hours going through the *Music Week Yearbook*, advising him on which companies would be worth contacting and which would be a waste of time. The young man thanked Barry for his time, but as he was about to leave, Barry suggested that instead of sending a cassette maybe the band should record a single, which Record Collector would sell allowing the band to sell the rest at gigs.

A few weeks later the young man turned up with a box full of records and asked if it was OK for Barry to sell them. He left him 150 copies, which at the time Barry thought was far too many. However, to his surprise, within two weeks it had become his best-selling single ever by a local band. The young man returned to the shop to collect his money and was gobsmacked when Barry told him he could keep the lot. Barry only took the VAT money from the transactions. "Barry, you're a brick," the young man said (I presume this is a Sheffield term of affection). The young man, whose name was Joe Elliott, then gave Barry £5 and told him to get himself a drink. So that is how Barry helped Def Leppard on the road to stardom.

As I write this, I note that on eBay the Def Leppard EP, with the same red label that was on the 150 that Barry originally sold, is currently selling for £300. By my calculations, Barry must have had the worst deal in music industry. He received £5 for records that ended up being worth £45,000. Talking to Barry, I felt the sadness in his voice when he told me about how he eagerly purchased a copy of the band's biography, only to discover that his efforts promoting them were not even mentioned. However, he still talks about them with great fondness and remembers them as a great bunch of lads.

These days, many American tourists call in to the shop and ask about Def Leppard. Barry is always happy to take them on a tour of the group's old haunts, which include visits to the local working men's club that now has a plaque proudly proclaiming 'Def Leppard played here'. It's now more likely that you will catch The Krankies or some artist knocked out in the early rounds of *The X Factor* playing at this venue. The tour always concluded at the band's local, The South Sea.

The shop was visited one day by an American vinyl collector. Barry and he got on famously and amused each other with their anecdotes about the industry. Barry told him the Def Leppard tale, and the American replied that he had a story to match it.

One day, an elderly gentleman had called in and handed the vinyl collector some albums, asking if they were worth anything. The dealer got quite excited by one album, telling the elderly man that it was a much sought after cult album and worth a few hundred dollars. The elderly man then dropped a bombshell, revealing that back in the 60s he had been in that band. The collector asked if he had any more copies of the album. It turned out he had kept over 500 in his house for over 35 years, until his grandchildren had destroyed all of them. The collector was puzzled and the old man explained that one hot summer day he built a slide to entertain the children. His garden had quite a slope, and he decided to cover it with some of his shrink-wrapped albums. He then turned on the hosepipe to wet them, and his grandchildren slid down the records to the bottom.

The grandchildren had a fabulous time, screaming with joy. When the albums were wrecked, they were disappointed that the fun was over. "Not to worry," said the grandad (member of much sought after 60s cult band) "I have hundreds of them in the cellar". That summer the grandchildren took every opportunity to visit their grandad and slide down his albums, oblivious to the thousands of pounds worth of damage they were causing. When told of the value, the grandad didn't seem to be worried. He was content that the records he had recorded forty years ago had given his grandchildren so much pleasure.

Another band whose story is connected with Record Collector is Gomez. Two of the band members were students at Sheffield University. Ian Ball, Gomez guitarist, singer and songwriter became a regular customer. His interest in 1960s psychedelia, folk-rock and blues caught the attention of Steve Fellows of Sheffield band the Comsat Angels, who was working in the store. Steve was intrigued and impressed by Ian's musical tastes and the pair took to conversing on Ian's visits to Record Collector. Then came the fateful conversation.

Steve: Are you a student?
Ian: Yes.
Steve: Do you play?
Ian: Yes.
Steve: Are you in a band?
Ian: Yes.
Steve: Do you play gigs?
Ian: No, but we've got this tape…

When Steve received the tape from Ian it contained most of the songs that would eventually make up the first Gomez album *Bring it On*. Steve Fellows was convinced that the band and their songs were extraordinary. He played the tape to Barry, who was similarly impressed. Steve and Gomez then embarked on a campaign plan. Steve Fellows was writing, rehearsing and recording with his fellow Comsat Angels alongside his day-job at Record Collector. Gomez knew Steve had experience of the record industry. Between them they selected the band's songs and sent them out to record companies. They secured legal representation, and the band asked Steve if he would manage them. He agreed and they successfully persuaded their parents that leaving university to pursue a career in music was a sensible option. What followed was a record-company bidding war for this Sheffield-based band – a band who had not yet recorded a single, nor played a gig, and who's only product was a cassette tape recorded in a garage.

Steve Fellows was working in Record Collector, because Barry had offered him a job both as a friendly gesture and because the Comsats were Barry's favourite Sheffield band. The Comsat Angels was one of those groups that deserved more success than it actually achieved. For years the band hovered on the edge of the mainstream. The breakthrough nearly came with their album *Chasing Shadows*, which was co-produced by the late

Robert Palmer. Today, BBC film critic Mark Kermode is a big fan, whilst bands such as Interpol and Editors cite the Comsat Angels as an influence on their sound.

Around this time, Barry recalls that each day they seemed to have more record companies and music publishers phoning the shop to speak with Steve than members of the public phoning up with CD enquiries. The band then embarked on a campaign of two showcases a day to two executives at a time for two weeks at a Sheffield rehearsal studio. When it concluded, Steve informed all of the record companies that the band would do one final open-rehearsal, following which they would accept the best offer on the table. The best offer came from Virgin subsidiary Hut Records. Gomez went on to considerable success, including winning the prestigious Mercury Music Prize in September 1998.

The band never forgot the help that Record Collector gave them and agreed to play their fourth ever gig at a private party at the Boardwalk in Sheffield to celebrate Record Collector's 25th anniversary. This was March 1998, the week before their first single '78 Stone Wobble' was released. The band played free of charge, and Barry simply bought every band member and everybody in the audience a drink. Barry recalls the club being full of friends and relations, who had mostly never seen Gomez play live before, yet singing along to songs they knew only from that demo tape.

One musician that Barry was delighted to meet was Nick Lowe, who at the time was signed to Stiff Records. Stiff had issued badges with the phrase 'Nick Lowe bought me a drink' (rumour has it that Nick wasn't famous for getting his round in). Barry found the complete opposite. He was wearing his badge on his lapel when he introduced himself to Nick, who bought Barry a drink. Barry found him charming company.

Looking through the 7" single section one day Barry noticed the young man picking out a large selection was none other than Kurt Wagner, lead singer of Nashville-based alternative country band Lambchop. When Barry counted Kurt's selection there were over 50 singles and he was delighted to sell them to such an illustrious customer. Kurt was overjoyed to find such an interesting record store, telling the staff how, "You don't come across shops like this in the States!" That evening, at the band's gig in Sheffield, Kurt made an impassioned plea to the audience between numbers to support their local record stores. He told of his youth which he had spent in record shops. "Now there are hardly any independent record shops in the States. Don't let the same happen in the UK," he pleaded.

Following his speech the crowd cheered, and he then brought his big pile of singles bought from Record Collector earlier in the day on to the stage. He then distributed the singles amongst the audience.

The shop is frequented by a number of BBC DJs including Steve Lamacq, Mark Radcliffe, Andy and Liz Kershaw and Marc Riley (otherwise known as 'Lard'). One day on Radio 1 Lard told a five-minute tale of how he had been after a particularly rare David Bowie album and of how he had contacted Barry at Record Collector, as he knew that his was the one shop that would have it. So Lard set off from Manchester at great speed and drove over the Pennines only to find that Record Collector was shut because of half-day closing. I asked Barry about this tale, and he informed me it was a shaggy dog tale. None of the events had ever happened, and Lard was making it up as he went along.

Barry told me the most tragic of all music tales, which involved one of his customers, the Radio Trent DJ Graham Neale. Graham presented the Castle Rock show on Radio Trent in the mid-80s. It was a very popular show, winning many awards, and, as Graham was a customer, Barry listened to the show as often as he could.

Graham's partner was the Radio Trent receptionist Lynne Goldingay. For a while they were the golden couple of Midlands radio, but a lot of relationships problems occurred, resulting in Lynne moving out of their home and back to her parents' house. It turned out that Lynne had started a relationship with a young man called Duncan McCracken.

A couple of months after the split Graham asked if she would like to accompany him to a concert in Nottingham by Lynne's favourite artist, Paul Young. Lynne checked with Duncan if he was comfortable with this. Duncan was fine and Graham (who was completely unaware of her new partner) attended the gig with Lynne.

After the gig the couple returned to Graham's house where he had high hopes of rekindling their relationship. Lynne made it clear that the relationship was over and told him that the only reason she went out with him was to see Paul Young. She then told Graham that the only man for her was Duncan McCracken. Picking up a hammer, he battered his ex partner about the head until she was dead. It was March 26th 1985 and Lynne Goldingay was just twenty-four. Graham buried her in a shallow grave near Ratcliffe-on-Soar power station.

Graham continued broadcasting and Barry recalled his show at that time, as he started appealing over the air for people to look out for his girlfriend who he said had gone missing. This strange behaviour aroused suspicion and the police were called. Graham confessed and led police to where she was buried.

Tortured by guilt for allowing her to go to the gig, on May 28th Duncan McCracken gassed himself in a private garage near his workplace. In the car with him was a notebook, on which he had written a message saying he could not live without Lynne.

Just over a week later on 6th June whilst awaiting trial in Lincoln prison Graham Neale hung himself. In just ten weeks three young people met their death in a tragic manner.

Record Collector certainly had the furthest travelling customer. Barry recognised one customer as somebody he hadn't seen for a while. The reason became clear; the man had emigrated to Australia. He then explained to Barry that he was a great collector of West Coast vinyl and he used to purchase his LPs there. Since he had moved to Australia he had not been able to get hold of any LPs so he had based a holiday in England around a visit to Sheffield to call on Record Collector. He went back to Australia with over £400 worth of vinyl in his suitcase.

As well as having an impact on the Sheffield music scene, Record Collector has also had an influence on the Sheffield film industry following a visit from a prop guy after some music for a local film he was involved in. The film was called *The Full Monty* and the prop guy was after 'You Sexy Thing' by Hot Chocolate. After digging it out, Barry also supplied them with some brass band music. There is a scene in *The Full Monty* where two of the characters are flicking through a record collection, and Barry proudly informs me that they changed the script to incorporate the titles of the brass band records he had supplied. The film company sent him a letter to thank him for his contribution to one of the most successful British films of the last twenty years.

I also asked Barry about his experiences with reps. He recalled the day when a Warner's rep was over-enthusiastic about an album titled *Black Gold*, a soul compilation, and promised Barry that whatever he didn't sell he could send back to the record company. He told every customer in his area the same tale. Unbeknownst to the record shops of Yorkshire, Warner's were giving a weekend in New York to the rep who sold the most copies. Hours before the appointed flight, Warner's head office received a phone call from a rock and metal specialist shop less than happy at the arrival of 100 unsolicited disco albums. Following further enquiries, the rep's trip was re-routed to Warner's London HQ to explain himself. Somehow he kept his job, but Barry recalls him as somewhat chastened by this experience.

As well as losing out on making any money from the success of Def Leppard, Barry invented a game that was enjoyed every day by millions of people, yet he never received a penny or even any recognition for this inspirational idea. One evening he went out for a drink in Sheffield with the renowned journalist and broadcaster, Martin Kelner. During the evening, Martin informed Barry that he was going to stand in for veteran DJ Ray Moore on his Radio 2 show for the next few weekends. As the drink flowed, Barry came up with a suggestion; "Why don't you have a quiz where the listener phones in and then you read a list of older celebrities and sportsmen who are no longer in the limelight or have faded into obscurity? The caller then has to guess if the person has died or is still alive". He then reeled off some examples:

Reg Varney from *On the Buses*, etc
Blakey from *On the Buses*
Arthur from *On the Buses*
Olive from *On the Buses*
Terry Scott
Hugh Lloyd
George from *George and Mildred*
Charlie Drake
Derek Nimmo
Wendy Craig
Richard O'Sullivan
The little one from *Last of the Summer Wine*
Tommy Steele
Gene Vincent
Eartha Kitt
Marty Wilde
Tom Finney
Tommy Lawton
Dennis Compton
Lee Trevino
John Conteh
Michael Foot

Martin was impressed and told Barry he would use it on the Radio 2 show. How about calling it 'Dead or Alive?' said Barry. Martin phoned him to say he was going ahead with the quiz under the title 'Brown Bread'.

A few weeks later Barry received a phone call from Martin after his Radio 2 stint had concluded. Martin told him that Simon Mayo had taken on the quiz and was now featuring it on the Breakfast Show under its original title of 'Dead or Alive'.

'Dead or Alive' became one of the most popular features on Simon's show. I used to listen to it myself every weekday, not knowing that it was one of my own customers who had come up with the idea. Every time I listened, I half expected Simon to say Pete Burns – Dead or Alive? So Simon Mayo, should you ever be in Sheffield, call into Record Collector – you owe Barry a drink!

Of all the shops I have visited nobody has given me more material than Barry. At times I felt I could write a book on Record Collector. He told me some great anecdotes about his friends. He first met the Transatlantic Records van sales rep, Tony Michaelides in 1972. His head of sales was Sheffield-based Ray Cooper, who later went on to become head of Virgin America. Their core material at the time were comedy folk albums by Billy Connolly and Mike Harding, the latter of whom invited Tony to visit his cottage in the Yorkshire Dales. Mike was later to become president of the Rambler's Association and today he is known for his passion and support of folk music through his excellent Radio 2 show. Guests were invited to partake in a country walk. To forestall excuses about not having suitable footwear, Wellington boots in every shoe size were available by the door.

Tony went on to be a van rep and then did promotions for Island and was responsible for accompanying artists on radio and TV studio tours around the country. Amongst others, he worked with U2 from back when they were doing their earliest small club tours. Barry remembers seeing them first with Tony, Radio 2 DJ Martin Kelner and about 100 others at the Limit Club in Sheffield.

Tony once showed Barry photographs of U2 attending a barbecue at his home in Cheadle Hulme. This event encouraged him to name his house 'The Edge', after David Evans, the U2 guitarist known as 'The Edge'. He added that one of his friends who lived nearby to him had, as a result of this, named his own house 'Close To The Edge'.

When the 'Madchester' scene took off, Tony had an influential alternative rock show on Piccadilly Radio and had opened the biggest independent promotions company in the north of England. He was working virtually every happening band in Manchester – all of the Factory bands, and everyone from the Stone Roses to Simply Red. Most Fridays Barry was in Manchester visiting shops like Robinsons, where he found a single called

'Paralysed' by the Legendary Stardust Cowboy. As a collector of the bizarre and curious, he was attracted to the name and picked up several copies of this 60s American deletion. Having played it, he sent a copy to John Peel, who listened to it and phoned him to say he was passing it to Kenny Everett, as he thought Kenny would like it. He did and, as a result of heavy play on Kenny's radio show it was re-issued as a single and made number fifteen on John Peel's *Festive 50* of 1976 and number three on Kenny Everett's *Worst Records in the World* ending up on the album of the same name.

Other Manchester shops Tony visited included Virgin on Lever Street, whose manager, Andy, later moved to Newcastle. He has a great anecdote about joining Lowell George and Little Feat on a shark fishing expedition from Newcastle on their day off from their UK tour. From what I can gather, they did not catch any Great Whites. He also checked out Tibb Street Records for collectable product. One of their assistants had a pet rat draped around his neck. While visiting, Barry once also encountered a cockroach crawling out of a 7" single sleeve as he was looking through the racks. He didn't know if it was related to the fact that Tibb Street had several pet shops, because the strangest customer 'attraction' in that small store was a cage in the corner, measuring about five-feet square. In it lived a monkey, which seemed far too large for the space in which it was confined. Quite understandably, every few minutes the monkey would explode in frustration, grabbing the bars and violently shaking its cage. This resulted in a cloud of dust particles being expelled across the shop, filling the air and settling on stock and customers alike.

Through Tony, Barry became friends with Marc Riley and Mark Radcliffe. Another good friend of Tony's was Roger Eagle, who set up the International Club in Manchester after running Eric's in Liverpool. In the 80s American and Australian bands would tour Europe extensively, but often have only two UK gigs, usually one in London and the other at the International. Barry spent many evenings there during REM's first tour watching the bands of the unfolding 'Paisley Underground'. Several times he talked to Craig Cash (pre-*Royle Family*) in the audience, at the time when he was a DJ on Stockport's commercial radio station.

In Sheffield's Leadmill he bumped into Craig (at a gig by American rock band Green on Red) and the evening ended with them returning to Craig's house to play some records and Barry then sleeping over on the sofa.

Tony is now living in the USA lecturing on his life in the music business, working with everyone from Tony Wilson to David Bowie.

Barry also used to visit shops and warehouses in London in the 80s and catch the odd gig whilst there. It was at the Clarendon Ballroom in Hammersmith that he saw the first UK performance of the Rain Parade. Jeffrey Lee Pierce of the Gun Club and Dick Taylor of the Pretty Things were at the bar. Andy Kershaw introduced him to Robyn Hitchcock and Nigel Cross, who used to write for Sounds. Nigel has since become one of his best friends. It seemed appropriate that Robyn Hitchcock should be there, as Nigel has since told Barry that his previous band, The Soft Boys' were pretty much Nigel's favourite, having seen them in excess of a hundred times! A real music fan, Nigel started the influential fanzine *A Bucketful of Brains* to promote the bands of the Paisley Underground (Long Ryders, Green on Red, Dream Syndicate, etc). In so doing he became the first person to publish interviews with REM and Robyn Hitchcock in this country, amongst many others he championed.

Nigel is a self-deprecating guy and seems uncomfortable with the following story, but nevertheless it is true. On their early tours, REM would phone Nigel to meet for a drink upon their arrival in London. REM and Robyn Hitchcock soon found themselves sharing a record label in IRS. Peter Buck from REM was recording side projects with Robyn Hitchcock and, whilst searching for a name, both fell to talking about the fact that Nigel had done much to champion their careers. Therefore, they named their band Nigel and the Crosses in his honour. They played a few gigs under this name.

One day Barry was in Steve's Sounds near Leicester Square. He caught sight of someone wearing a black leather jacket, hand-painted in white with the names of his favourite bands. Central to the design was a white cross, surrounded by the names REM, Robyn Hitchcock and, in the largest letters under the cross, Nigel and the Crosses. Few of us have our own tribute band, but you know you've made it when your name is on someone's jacket. How embarrassed Nigel is every time Barry reminds him.

Sheffield's oldest established second-hand record store in the 60s and 70s was Violet May's. Violet and her two female assistants had a collective age of around 200. Violet was often unaware of current trends. Barry was in the shop when a customer asked if Violet had anything by The Eagles. He had in mind the million-selling *Hotel California*. "Yes, love. I believe I've got something somewhere," said Violet, and proceeded to delve into a large cardboard box in the window. After a couple of minutes she extracted a copy of 'The Eagles Versus The Kestrels' EP on PYE Records from the early 60s. Unfortunately, the wrong Eagles.

Barry has been a friend of Richard Hawley since he was in his early teens. When he was in the Longpigs, he phoned Barry. MTV were doing a series that called for one band from each of the larger cities to choose their favourite places in their hometown. MTV had chosen the Longpigs from Sheffield and they had picked Record Collector as their favourite place. A camera crew and the band duly arrived, filmed and left. Amazingly, Barry has never seen the programme, but for several years people would tell him they'd spotted him in the repeats, particularly those shown in Australia.

I asked Barry about his future and he explained that, although he had been selling music for forty years, he was not yet over the hill, but was looking forward to retiring in a few years to spend more time walking on his beloved hills. When listening to the Record Collector story you realise how much his life was influenced by John Peel. The way he has supported local music, he could be aptly described as Sheffield's mini John Peel. That's just what independent record shops do – they support local talent. When all of the independent record shops have gone, who is going to help the next Def Leppard or the next Gomez get their foot on the ladder? Certainly not the checkout girl at Asda.

My view is that if ever a dealer deserved recognition for services to music, then it's Barry Everard. It would be nice to think that the music industry, Sheffield Council, or even the honours list would recognise this champion of Sheffield's culture and music over the last forty years. If you are ever in Sheffield, call in and say hello to Barry. You will recognise him – he will be the one wearing the loud Hawaiian shirt. The same style of shirt he's been wearing for forty years.

* * *

After leaving Barry, I have arranged to meet up with another of my customers who I visited in my first ever week of selling music. By the time I arrive the shop is closed, so the owner, Hunter Smith, and I go for a meal at a local Italian restaurant, where he gives me the story of Jumbo Records.

Hunter established Jumbo Records in September 1971, the name and logo deriving from the successful disco and DJ business he was involved in called Jumbo Mobile Discotheque. The shop was started because an acquaintance had wanted someone to sell records at the back of his tape equipment store. Hunter, who was still DJ-ing in the evenings around the clubs and dance halls of the area, and not being one of the most early of risers, decided, after a lot of deliberation, to take up the offer. Loans, shop fittings and stock were organised, and he tried to learn as much as possible about the business and keep abreast of all new releases each week (the Tams' 'Hey Girl Don't Bother Me' was at number one in the charts, followed by Rod Stewart's 'Maggie May'. Isaac Hayes' *Black Moses* was their first good-selling album).

Within two months the 'acquaintance' got greedy; he wanted Hunter and his kit out so that he could utilise the space for himself. Needless to say, Christmas and New Year 1971 was a worrying time for Hunter. Deep in debt and with all his stock in a lock-up garage, Hunter trudged around Leeds to find somewhere to trade from so that he could pay the bills. Eventually he rented a small room for £5 per week, on the balcony of the Queen's Arcade. The fixtures and fittings were squeezed in, some having to be left in the lock-up garage due to lack of space. A large part of the existing stock was sold to 'a man in the trade' for less than cost, in order to release some cash to help reduce the ever-increasing pile of bills.

Hunter then stuck to selling mainly singles (hits of the day plus imports and all of the latest soul and reggae releases). People would call by to ask for the 'tunes' they had heard at one of his club evenings, and DJs were encouraged to purchase their records in the store. By late 1973 a full-time member of staff was required to help serve the ever-increasing flow of customers coming through the door. Enter Trevor Senior. Hunter asked him to help him out until Christmas. What he failed to mention was which Christmas, as 30 years on, Trevor is still working there.

Soon after, Hunter's partner, Lornette, joined the business to help out at weekends. During the week she was taking a degree at Birmingham University. She has since become the driving force behind Jumbo, and without her contribution the shop wouldn't be going today. As with many record shops, Jumbo Records has some loyal long-serving staff. As well as Trevor, both Adam and Sally have been there for over twenty years. By 1974 they were running out of space and the property was due for redevelopment, so a move to 102, Merrion Centre was completed in the September of that year. Trading was good in the Merrion Centre to start with, but then they seemed to lose their way a little and the sales stagnated (good job the evening DJ-ing was still going).

Then in 1977 – BANG! – along came punk rock. Jumbo was in the right place at the right time. They broadened their range became the hip place in Leeds for music. In 1988 they required more space and a modern shop unit to sell their ever-expanding range of stock, so they moved to their current site in the St John's Centre, Leeds.

Jumbo is in a poor location, tucked away on the top floor of the St John's Centre, and therefore doesn't get any passing trade. It relies on word of mouth, but the personal appearances helped attract publicity and bring people into the store.

Most PAs involve the artists doing an acoustic set. One exception was when Asian Dub Foundation came to town. Hunter was uncomfortable from the moment the security guard in the loading bay phoned up to tell them a huge truck had pulled up full of musical equipment. Soon, a steady stream of amplifiers was brought up to the shop. Eventually, there was so much equipment in the store that there was no room for customers to browse through the racks. When the crowd turned up, there was no space to accommodate them and most had to watch the show from outside the shop. Then the band started – BOOM! The music was so loud that the floor vibrated. Within seconds the café next door to Jumbo had cleared out as people fled, leaving the crockery shaking on the table.

Various people from the Centre came in to try and stop the concert, but Hunter felt that their might be trouble if the gig was halted abruptly. He did ask the mixing desk to turn the volume down. They kindly obliged, but the sound went down by around one decibel and the Centre still felt as though it was in the middle of a minor earthquake.

One area the shop excels in is ticket sales, which now accounts for over 50 per cent of their turnover. Even that area is becoming difficult for independent record shops to make sales, as Internet ticket sellers muscle in on the market. Over the last couple of years Jumbo have had to fight tooth and nail to maintain their allocation of tickets.

Like most shops, Jumbo gets its fair share of awkward customers, and none more so than a Scottish gentleman they have christened 'Jock Mctwat'. He complains about everything, has only ever bought stock from the bargain bin and is never happy with the service he receives. Whenever he is unhappy he will scream at the staff 'I hope you get the flu!' I am sure many record staff have had worse things said to them, but despite threatening the staff with a contagious virus, he still calls in.

Like most stores, Hunter has a wealth of tales about smelly customers. Through this book, I would like to appeal to the CD buyers of the UK. Before you visit a record shop, please make sure you are clean. This applies especially if you are visiting Jumbo, as Lornette is known for marching smelly customers out and banning them until they have had a bath.

Jumbo sells a fabulous rock 'n' roll magazine called *Now Dig This*. The fans are very passionate about it, and if the magazine is late in hitting the shelves, Jumbo receives endless complaints from its readers. The staff calls this phenomenon 'Attack of the Killer Quiffs'. Some of the fans have the most amazing quiffs, and the staff have named them The Family Quiff. Here are the members of the family.

- Granddaddy Quiff – A pensioner with hardly any hair, but what he does have he uses to make the thinnest quiff possible.
- Granny Quiff – The greyest quiff you will ever see.
- Mummy Quiff – A middle-aged lady who has a fabulous female quiff. She comes in with her young son, Baby Quiff, who must be the youngest child with a quiff in the country.
- Curly Quiff – He somehow manages to style his hair in a quiff, although their is always a curly bit that refuses to be shaped.
- Moody Quiff – A handsome young man, who looks like a young Elvis as he snarls his requests through a curled-up lip.
- Sad Quiff – Imagine Bobby Charlton trying to get his hair into a quiff and you will get the idea.

However, the shop's favourite is the man who is obsessed with collecting all of Cliff Richard's re-issues – none other than Quiff Richard.

How I would love to be in the shop when The Quiff Family call.

I noted that the staff in Jumbo seem to talk in their own code. It is not only the Killer Quiffs who have nicknames – every regular customer is tagged. There is Teacher Dave, Bus Driver Dave, Postie Steve, John the Dentist, Doctor Ian, Mr T, Mr P, Mr B (collectively known as The Zion Guys) and Damned David, who has been coming since his punk days and will buy any re-issue by The Damned. In the 70s Damned David used to be very cheeky. After being very lippy in a competitor's record store, the staff bound him with parcel tape and left him outside on the precinct to be unravelled by a few passers by that took pity on him. Jumbo reckons they must have two of the most difficult and mistrustful customers ever to tread the streets of Leeds. They are both unsmiling senior citizens and nothing Jumbo does for them seems to be right. There is always an invisible mark on the cover of a CD or a microscopic piece of dust that causes them to demand another copy. They are not related and they don't know each other, but they are known by the staff as Grumpy Grandad Mk1 and Grumpy Grandad Mk2.

Then there is the 'Saturday Lads Leeds' version of the TV comedy *Last of the Summer Wine*. They usually stay for about half an hour or so, but sadly, only one of them buys music, whilst the other two look on and discuss the merits of a distant Roger McGuinn re-issue that might be coming out sometime the following year, or a Byrds bootleg that is extremely difficult to get. The last ten minutes of their visit will be spent arguing about who is going to pay for the coffee in the café next door. These exchanges can sometimes get quite heated, as each one is convinced that he paid for the drinks the previous week.

I asked Hunter about the problems that affect shops like Jumbo. He told me that the problem is that they receive too much information, as stores are drowning in e-mail. With the demise of the sales rep, record shops now rely on e-mail to obtain the information on new releases. Many stores like Jumbo inform me that they receive over 100 e-mails a day. You could virtually employ somebody just to read all of them. I know from my experiences in my own company that if we e-mail 100 stores with a fabulous offer only a handful will take advantage. We then phone all of the shops that didn't reply to the offer, and nearly everyone will place an order. The result of all of these e-mails is that stores miss out on important information, due to the vast amount of SPAM they are sent. Due to this overload of information everybody loses. Hunter did make me smile by informing me that the way forward for shops like his was to stock only CDs that were not remotely popular.

One idea Jumbo has taken up is to produce cool Jumbo T-shirts with a unique design in ten different colours. Throughout my travels in the UK it always makes me smile when I see somebody wearing one. Every record shop should follow its example. I am confident that Jumbo will be one of the 'Last Shops Standing', as wherever I go in the country, if I meet somebody from Leeds and mention music, Jumbo Records is immediately brought into the conversation.

Chapter 12

Beatle Bricks and Betting Coups

The next day I am up early to travel over to the seaside and visit Scarborough, home of an unusual record store – half-shop, half-café – called Record Revivals.

Rod and Sue Emms opened Record Revivals in 1982 in Victoria Road, Scarborough, selling used LPs and singles from cardboard boxes. Rod was an insurance broker and a huge music fan. To supplement his income, Rod started selling LPs at record fairs in places as far afield as Leeds, Newcastle and York. He acquired his records by leaving cards offering to purchase record collections in the windows of newsagents and Post Offices. As records were beginning to occupy every room in the house, Rod and Sue decided to rent their first shop. The shop only opened for three days a week, as Rod still combined his insurance work with selling records. The best deal Rod ever made resulted from his insurance work. Through his company Royal Insurance, Rod learned that the famous Cavern Club in Liverpool was being demolished. He shrewdly contacted the demolition team and purchased some of the bricks.

One day a huge pile of rubble was delivered to the shop and Rod numbered them and started selling them in the shop as Beatle bricks for £5 each. You could argue that Beatle bricks laid the foundations of the business!

Maybe the deal wasn't as good as Rod first thought, as he has seen his bricks selling on the Internet for up to £100. How he wishes he had kept the odd wall or two back.

Sales in the shop took off and new CDs, LPs and videos were introduced. In 1986 the shop moved to Falsgrave Road. Although the rent was low, the shop was a mile outside the city centre and did not pick up much passing trade. Three years later they decided to return to the town centre at 7 Northway.

In 2000 yet another move took place, as Record Revivals crossed over the road to much larger premises at 18 Northway. The idea was to use half the building to sell music and the other half as a café. At the time, this was a revolutionary move. After visiting the Hard Rock Café in London, Rod was inspired to go into business with his daughter, Mel, and her partner, Steve who was a qualified chef. They called the cafe Mojo's and it has a distinctive retro feel. It created a unique music experience where customers could select CDs to listen to whilst they tuck into some quality food.

As a specialist rock 'n' roll store, Rod ordered ten copies of the 50-CD Elvis box set when it was released. The box was a limited edition, and when placed side-on the CDs spelt 'Elvis'. Rod retailed the box set for £399. The first few sold straight away, but the last few just trickled out. After two years, Rod still had one left so he put it in the window with a sign saying 'Special Offer £299'. The next day Rod turned up to open up and there was a man already waiting, who said that he had got there at 6am to secure the box set before anybody else. As Rod took it out of the window and started wrapping it for the gentleman, he smiled and thought what a great start to the day – two minutes past nine and already £300 made. When Rod held his hand out to collect the money he expected a credit card or a bundle of notes; instead, the man placed three gold coins in his palm. "What's this?" Rod said.

"£3," the man replied, "but don't worry about the change". Rod couldn't believe it – the man had thought that his 50-CD box set was £2.99. He then blamed Rod for not making the sign clear enough and off he went.

Another incident occurred when a customer asked whether Record Revivals stocked 'The Millennium Prayer' by Cliff Richard. Rod politely informed them that he did not and, when the person had exited the shop, he told his friend at the counter that he couldn't stand Cliff Richard and refused to stock any of his records on a point of taste. Unfortunately, somebody heard his comments, and later that day he received a call from the *Scarborough Evening News*. They asked if it was true that he refused to stock Cliff Richard records. Rod explained that it was, since Cliff had spoiled his viewing of Wimbledon by getting up and singing. The paper asked Rod if they could come down for an interview and whether it be OK for them to take a picture of him looking unhappy holding a Cliff Richard record. Rod explained that they would have to bring their own, as he did not stock any. So the paper popped into Woolworths and bought a copy of 'The Millennium Prayer' for Rod to hold. A full-page feature appeared in the paper, and Rod still feels the wrath of Cliff Richard fans in Scarborough. Nevertheless, Record Revivals remains proud to be a Cliff Richard-free zone.

Recently I tried to sell Rod the new Daniel O'Donnell CD. Rod recoiled in horror and explained that, as with Cliff, Record Revivals is a Daniel O'Donnell-free zone. He asked me not to tell anybody, lest all of the fanatical Daniel fans in case they start phoning the shop to complain. I agreed, as those Daniel O'Donnell fans are truly fanatical and worship their hero.

One local music fan would call in every week to purchase records. He was a young man, who told Rod he was an actor. It was clear that the young man was a big music fan and Rod always engaged him in conversation about his purchases. One week the young man stopped his weekly visits. Rod forgot about him until two years later, when he walked back into the shop. Rod greeted him like a long-lost friend, asking where the young man had been all this time. The man modestly explained that he had found a job in television and had been working away. Rod asked him if the TV show was any good and the young man replied it was OK. It was at this point that Rod noticed all of the customers had stopped looking through the racks and were looking at the young man. When he had left, Mel rushed over to him and asked him if he knew who the young man was. Rod replied that he was Martin, one of his regular customers from a couple of year's back, who went to work in the theatre. He then advised Mel to look out for him, as apparently he has a part in a TV show. Mel explained to Rod that the young man was Martin Freeman, one of the stars of *The Office*. Rod thought he had heard of the programme and asked if it was any good, much to the amusement of the listening customers. These days he never misses an episode, but deep down he still cringes with embarrassment when the staff fondly remind him of the day his long-lost customer returned.

Rod has a couple of unusual customers. One is nick-named 'Shrink-wrap Man'. He selects his CDs, brings them to the counter and then asks Rod to order in the same CDs, as he will only purchase a CD if it is shrink-wrapped. Like the majority of record shops, when Rod gets a delivery of CDs, he takes the shrink-wrap off, puts the case out and keeps the CD behind the counter for security reasons. Rod therefore has to re-order the CD for 'Shrink-wrap Man'.

Record Revivals' favourite customer is 'Duplicate Man'. This customer always purchases two copies of each CD, one to play and the other to store.

When I first visited Rod, he had stiff competition from four other record shops in town: Andy's, Our Price, Studio 1 and Bernard Dean. Rod has seen them all off and will no doubt be the last independent record shop standing in Scarborough. Because of Mojo's café, I feel the shop has a real future, even though Rod is looking to retire in five years' time, to spend more time on his beloved golf course. (Record Revivals is closed on a Monday, as that is Rod's golf day. This truly is a unique store).

* * *

The journey north from Scarborough to the fishing town of Whitby is spectacular. Whitby is famous for Count Dracula, notorious for sucking the blood of his victims. There I meet Dave Longmate from Folk Devils, who feels the music industry is akin to Dracula sucking the lifeblood out of his shop.

Dave had been working as a teacher in Further Education for over twenty years when the local authority announced that there would be serious job cuts. Dave survived the redundancy job cull, but it did make him think about his future. Armed only with his credit card, he hit on the idea of purchasing CDs and selling them at local gigs. He soon progressed to selling at folk festivals in Yorkshire. As well as thoroughly enjoying it, he was also supplementing his teaching income. In 2004 Dave felt it was worth opening a shop in Whitby specialising in leftfield music, world, reggae, folk, Americana and blues. He found a property on the east-side of town and opened in November, just in time to catch the Christmas market. He decided to teach part-time so he could concentrate on his new venture, although he kept his festival business going (these were busy times indeed).

As a Sociology teacher, Dave is well-versed in dealing with customer quirks. He told me of a couple of odd customers who came into his shop and never bought anything. This does seem to be a record shop phenomenon, as nearly every shop I have interviewed seems to have customers like this. Dave's oddities are 'Double CD Man', who comes in picks out a CD, brings it to the counter and asks whether he has got the two-CD set. Of course, there is no two-CD version of any of the releases he asks for, and Dave politely informs him. The man always looks disappointed at this fact and tells Dave he will leave it. He returns the CD to the rack and leaves the shop.

Then there is 'Cellophane Man'. He picks up a CD, and then walks around gently rubbing the cellophane between his fingers. It is clear he is getting off on this, but what should Dave do? Ask him to stop getting aroused by rubbing his CDs? A psychiatrist would probably have a field-day with this customer.

I asked Dave about his favourite sale and he told me it was when he sold his whole jazz section to one customer. I was really impressed, and asked how much he had taken. "£10," was the reply. I was puzzled, until Dave explained to me that he doesn't stock jazz, but will order CDs for people who call in. One customer asked for a CD by Alex Welsh, the jazz saxophonist. After Dave ordered it, the customer never returned to collect the CD, so he was stuck with it. He created a jazz section in his shop and thought it was quite amusing to have a section with only one CD in it. Later that day a man called in and spent some time looking through the racks before enquiring if the shop had a jazz section. Dave smiled and pointed to the Alex Welsh CD standing alone in the rack. The man spent a couple of minutes looking at the CD, before bringing it to the counter and announcing: 'I think I will take this Alex Welsh CD." In one stroke, Dave had disposed of his complete jazz section.

The British public are not really known for speaking clearly. Dave appreciated this point after a visit by a gentleman who was clearly of West Midlands heritage.

"Hoi might yowgorreny door stripes," he asked. Thinking he was either after something to decorate his furniture or maybe a type of draught excluder, Dave suggested he tried the hardware store B&Q. "Do they stock CDs then?" the man enquired. Dave realised that due to the customer's thick accent he may have misheard. The man repeated his request, and whist Dave was trying to work out what it was, the man stressed that door stripes were a band. At last, the penny dropped ... he was after Dire Straits. After Dave composed himself, he explained to the unfortunate man, with the thick accent and of West Midlands heritage, that he didn't stock rock music.

Dave's most eventful day of trading occurred in June 2007. He was selling his wares at The Big Session festival in Leicester. Dave travelled to Leicester the day before the festival to set up his stall in a brand new marquee on the site. Dave and his team had never set up a tent before, so they gave hours of amusement to onlookers as they struggled to pitch it in what was becoming quite a strong wind. Eventually, after a mammoth struggle, the tent was up. However, it wasn't for long ... a fierce thunderstorm erupted, and whilst Dave was inside the marquee, it was hit by a mini tornado. The marquee was blown down and Dave's stock was completely soaked, leaving many CDs in no fit state to sell. Being the entrepreneur he is, the next day Dave opened his stall with reduced prices, billing it as a 'tornado-damaged sale'. Needless to say, the Great British public appreciate a bargain and Dave had a storming day (forgive the pun).

Dave and his team have developed a game that keeps them amused at festivals, called Folk Bingo. They write the following on a card:

- Beard
- Tankard
- Woolly jumper with a hideous pattern
- World music trousers (ethnic weave in unflattering colours)
- Ethnic hat
- World music shoes (painted doc martens etc the sort of footwear you could never wear to the day job)

As you spot each one on the list, you tick them off and the first to complete the card wins. Dave will never forget the day he got a full house in one go. He spotted a man with a beard carrying a tankard, wearing an ethnic hat, a woolly jumper with a hideous pattern, ethnic trousers and painted Doc Martens. BINGO!

When Dave opened in Whitby there were already two record shops there – Fusion Records, which specialised in vinyl, and the worst-named record shop I have ever heard of, The Fruit Shop. I asked myself why a record shop would be given such a bad name, and it turned out that the premises were previously a fruit shop. Good to see a shop putting so much thought into their name. No wonder they didn't last long. Folk Devils is the 'Last Shop Standing' in Whitby, and I feel he will also be the 'Last Shop Standing' in North Yorkshire.

* * *

From Whitby I travel north through what has become another record shop wasteland. Both Sunderland and Middlesbrough were formerly great places to call on as they had multiple independent record shops, but no longer – all of them have closed. Newcastle was once a city that had so many record shops that it took me over two days to visit all of them. Unlike other cities, Newcastle still has three excellent independent shops: Roots, a folk specialist; JG Windows, which is the oldest established record shop in the North East; and Reflex, which has some of the lowest-priced CDs in the country.

JG Windows opened in 1908 and is situated in a beautiful 18th century arcade with a massive selection of classical music. Brian, Helen and Neil manage the shop, and I first visited them in 1988. Like most shops, they have had a customer ask for a song that they have heard on the radio with love in the title, but this particular customer was beyond belief. Here, word-for-word, is the conversation.

Customer: "Hi, I heard a song on the radio. I'm not sure who it's by or what it's called, but it's quite a sentimental song and it's got love in the title".

Staff member: "Hmmm ... that's a little vague. I need to narrow things down a bit – if you can let me know which radio station you heard it on and the time you heard it, I could check the Internet for the programme listings?"

Customer: "Fantastic ... it was on Radio 2 about nine years ago."

Although I would have liked to write in depth about all three shops in Newcastle, the shop that I chose to interview was Reflex.

Reflex work on the principle of high volume and low margin, constantly striving to offer the people of Newcastle the best value. Owner Alan Jordan has been working in the record shops of the North East for almost 30 years and has had a somewhat colourful career. After abandoning his university course to become a DJ, Alan was on the look out for a day-job. At that time, he bought his records at Volume, a Newcastle shop. Volume mentioned that it was looking for knowledgeable staff to work in a new project, the Volume/Virgin enterprise, and offered him a job, which Alan accepted.

In November 1982 Richard Branson approached the owners of Volume, both formerly Virgin employees, with an unusual proposal. The idea was for Volume and Virgin to go into partnership and open up new stores in Durham, and ultimately Sunderland, South Shields and Blyth. The Newcastle shop would remain independent, keeping the name Volume, with the others opening as Virgin shops. Alan was given the role of singles buyer for the Sunderland branch.

After a year, he moved to the Durham branch where he soon became manager. In 1988 Virgin was looking to sell its shops to the Our Price chain, with the intention that it would keep its Mega Stores and offload its smaller shops. The Virgin/Volume deal was a thorn in the side of the negotiations. It was clear Volume needed to buy Virgin out, or vice versa. As Richard Branson had a few more pounds than Volume's owner, Virgin became the sole owners, with Volume keeping their Newcastle shop.

1988 was, therefore, a turbulent year for Alan. He had started the year working for Virgin/Volume. After Virgin purchased Volume, he worked just for Virgin. Our Price then bought Virgin, and Alan found himself working under a different boss. Alan didn't enjoy working for Our Price, and he was on his fourth employer of 1988 when he returned to work for Volume, which had bought another shop in Sunderland called Chartz.

Alan was scathing about his experience with Our Price, regarding his manager's role as nothing more than a glorified shelf-stacker. Both Virgin and Volume had given him freedom to purchase what he wanted; however, Our Price had a different method. All stock was bought by head office and scaled out to the stores. The job consisted of opening boxes, stacking shelves and taking money at the till.

Personally, I could never understand the success of Our Price. All of the shops were exactly the same. They had a bargain section that attempted to give the public the impression that Our Price was cheap, but more often than not it were dearer on its chart and back catalogue CDs. I feel it survived because the public were comfortable with the brand. They were big on every high street, yet I felt that they were cold, soulless stores, completely lacking in atmosphere.

Alan told me the tale of when Virgin took over the shop in Blyth. The previous owner of the shop called in and told Alan how he had 'put one over' on Woolworths. Whatever price he sold his 7" singles at; Woolworths always undercut him. If he did them at 99p, they would reduce theirs to 89p. Similarly, if he charged 89p, Woolworths would price theirs at 79p. He decided to fight back and hatched a plan. Late Friday afternoon, he put a notice up in his window saying that all 7" singles would be sold at 59p. As it was late in the day, hardly anybody noticed his offer, but he left it in the window overnight. The next morning, Woolworths had a poster up saying all 7" singles would retail at 49p. He and his family immediately went to Woolworths and cleared them out of all good 7" singles. He then went back to his shop and sold the singles for £1.30. Meanwhile, Woolworths had no singles to sell on a busy Saturday.

Alan stayed at Volume until 1996. By then it had expanded and had opened shops in Sunderland, Washington and Durham. The chain over-stretched itself and got into financial difficulties. As part of his settlement with Volume, Alan acquired the Washington branch.

However, he did not enjoy life in Washington and decided to take his life in a different direction, taking out a stake in the Grapevine pub in Whitley Bay. Alan ran the pub and still worked in the shop in the day.

Eventually, the phenomenal workload took its toll and he disposed of his interests in both businesses. After a few months of boredom he offered to help out an old friend, Dave, who had a shop in Durham called Concepts. After helping turn the shop around, which involved replacing the existing staff, he decided it was time to open his own record shop. In 1998 Reflex of Newcastle opened its doors.

Alan was quick to recognise the importance of the Internet and established the business online. He was also determined to establish a reputation as the lowest-priced seller of CDs in Newcastle.

Over the years, Alan supplemented his salary at the bookmakers. His best coup was in 1993, thanks to Mr Blobby, who will always have a place in Alan's heart after making him £8,000 richer.

On December 11 1993 Mr Blobby reached number one in the charts. The following week, Take That knocked Mr Blobby off the top spot with their single 'Babe'. Bookmakers had Take That as a certainty to be number one on Christmas Day, when the next chart was released. The bookmakers had priced Mr Blobby at 12/1 to be Christmas number one, because it was unprecedented for a song to be knocked off the top spot then regain the position two weeks later. Alan was a shrewd cookie, and he noticed that the Take That single had only sold a few thousand more copies than Mr Blobby. He also took into account that Take That fans were a dedicated lot and were likely to have purchased the record on the release date. He became convinced that Mr Blobby would regain the number one spot, as lots of parents would be buying it for their children to play on Christmas day. Alan toured the bookmakers of the North East, backing Mr Blobby.

He then put into action part two of his plan. He phoned up every record shop he knew of and told him his theory that they could get Mr Blobby back to the top and that they should rush down to the bookmakers to put a bet on. He then instructed them to phone every shop they knew and do the same. Over the next few days the odds on Mr Blobby being Christmas number one were slashed, as more record-shop owners placed their bets. There were huge celebrations in record shops throughout the land when Mr Blobby was announced as the Christmas number one. Alan knows of many other shops that made small fortunes on this coup.

Nobody will ever know if Take That sold more singles that week than Mr Blobby, but one thing is clear: thousands of bogus numbers were entered for Mr Blobby in the Gallup machine that week, whilst the record shops involved in the betting coup were probably quite 'forgetful' when it came to entering the catalogue number for Take That. Needless to say, there was plenty to drink in the Jordan household that Christmas.

This was not the first time Alan had made money on the Christmas number one. In early November 1992 Whitney Houston hit the number one spot in the UK chart with the Dolly Parton classic 'I Will Always Love You'. Alan looked at the release schedule for December and came to the conclusion that there wasn't any exciting forthcoming releases. He began to think that, although Christmas was nearly two months away, Whitney's song was so strong that she might just be able to hang on. He made enquiries with bookmakers and was offered odds of 10/1. Alan felt the odds were too good to be true and placed a substantial bet. Sure enough, Whitney spent ten weeks at number one and managed to cling on to the spot, much to Alan's relief. For that reason, Christmas '92 is fondly remembered in the Jordan household.

Alan made his final coup when Michael Jackson's 'Earth Song' reached the number one spot in Christmas '95. Mr Jackson's career seemed to be in tatters after revelations about his private life. Alan was not so sure that this would hit his record sales as hard as the bookmakers thought and, when he found out that the odds were 8/1, it was time to take the plunge again. Michael Jackson did make Christmas number one, and it was another happy Christmas in the Jordan household. After 1995, bookmakers became more alert, as they had by then been stung too many times. Over the past few years the Christmas number one has been easy to predict as it has been pretty much a dead cert that whoever wins *The X Factor* will get the spot.

My own experience of betting on the Christmas number one was a disaster because I broke a golden rule: never trust a record company sales rep. Whilst in a record shop in Swinton, called Play Inn, I bumped into a rep who asked me if I wanted to make an easy £500. He told me that his company had a record that was certain to be the Christmas number one and that if I was quick, I could still get 25/1 with Ladbrokes. He told me that his company believed that its newly signed artist could be bigger than Madonna. Both the record-shop owner and myself were impressed. The rep told us that he had £100 on so, eyeing the Ladbrokes shop opposite, I said to the owner that I would go over to put £20 on and he gave me £20 to put on for himself.

I duly went into the betting shop and placed my bet. Before taking my money, the manager needed to check with head office whether he could accept this bet. I thought this was a good sign, as there was obviously a betting coup occurring, or so I thought. I was relieved when the manager informed me that 25/1 was OK. As I walked back to the record shop I was working out in my head what I was going to spend the money on.

When I got back into the shop, they were playing a dreadful pop song. "Who's this?" I enquired.

"It's Malandra Burrows, star of *Emmerdale*, and this is the song that's going to be Christmas number one," said the rep. The colour drained from my face. One thing was certain; this song was never going to be Christmas number one. The owner of the shop thought different, but I knew he was trying to convince himself that he had not wasted £20. I knew different – I was 100 per cent certain that I had lost £20. I couldn't believe I had been so stupid. How could I place a bet on a song I had never heard?

I asked Alan about hyping and he told me about the worst case he had come across. EMI had spent a lot of money on a band called, funnily enough, Reflex. They had produced an expensive lavish video for their single 'Politics of Dancing'. Despite the company's endeavours, the single entered the chart at number twenty-eight. In a desperate attempt to get the single higher, the EMI rep informed Alan that if the single progressed up next weeks' chart, he was authorised to give him ten free CD albums. Multiply this by the number of chart-return shops: if the single had climbed the charts, and this deal was offered to all independent shops, thousands of free albums would have been given away. The following week 'Politics Of Dancing' dropped out of the chart. Gallup got wind of what was going on and penalised the record. Sometimes companies would take the hyping too far, to the detriment of the artist.

My favourite tale from Reflex recalled the day a shoplifter fled with a pile of CDs. Alan chased him down the road, despite being the first to admit that he is not as fit as he used to be. The thief attempted to climb a wall and Alan dragged him down by his feet. As he fell to the floor, he knocked Alan over. The thief was first to his feet and, like the closing sequence on *The Benny Hill Show*, the chase was on again. As they ran down the road, the thief was gradually getting away from Alan. Suddenly, the Number 14 bus pulled up beside him. The driver opened the door and told Alan to hop on. The driver had seen what had happened and, with Alan hanging on to the silver pole and with the doors of the bus open, the chase was on again. The thief thought he had given Alan the slip and got the shock of his life when the bus pulled up beside him and a furious Alan leapt on top of him. So, the streets of Newcastle became a safer place, as another criminal was apprehended by the dynamic duo 'Reflex Alan and the Number 14 bus'.

I am sure Reflex will continue to do well, as Alan tries so hard. Recently, the American band Journey released a three-disc set called *Revelation*. Sadly for fans it was only available through one of the great names in rock retailing Wal-Mart. This was bad news for Journey fans in the UK, as the record company put an import ban on the set, meaning that no UK record company could import the box set. Ever resourceful, Alan phoned one of his mates in the States. He asked him to pay a visit to Wal-Mart and purchase twenty copies. His mate then posted them to Alan at Reflex, (in fact, his mate now does this on a regular basis). Therefore any Journey fan in the UK who requires a copy, get in touch with Reflex Records. It's this dedication that makes me confident that Reflex will be one of the 'Last Shops Standing'.

Chapter 13

DJ Ango and The Loneliest Monk

Week five of my journey is the one I had been looking forward to, as I would be interviewing my customers in Scotland. I lived in Glasgow in the early 90s and it would have been my favourite place to live if it wasn't for the weather. It was always raining, or about to rain, or had just finished raining. Back then I sold to all of the record stores in Scotland and it would take me a month to visit all of them. Now I would struggle to find a weeks' worth of work. There are still some great independents trying their best. One of them is Apollo Music, based in the town of Paisley, which is eight miles from Glasgow.

It is fair to say that Mike Dillon, the owner of Apollo Music, is a true larger-than-life character. Not only does he work in his shop six days a week, he is also a Liberal Party councillor and one of Paisley's top DJs. After working for other record shops, Mike decided he would be better off working for himself and in 1977 he found a premises in Dumbarton Road. He called his shop Sleeves, as he felt it sounded hip and trendy (how times change). Mike targeted the disco and DJ market, coming up with the idea to gather the DJs together to play them the new releases. Through word of mouth on the disco scene, Sleeves soon attracted a huge following. The shop had a major influence on how successful a disco record could be, which was highlighted by the sales of 'Groove Me' by Fern Kinney. She is regarded as a one-hit wonder, as 'Together We Are Beautiful' was a number one single, but Sleeves sold over 500 copies of 'Groove Me', her previous single, because of their relentless promotion of a song they believed in.

Mike's big break came when two young girls walked into his shop and asked if he was interested in stocking badges and posters promoting the new film *Saturday Night Fever*. Mike bought a few, and they quickly sold out. He decided to contact the distributor, a company called Factors Incorporated, and ask if he could have the licence to sell the products in Scotland. The company refused Mike's request, but did agree to give him the rights to sell the products in Glasgow. Mike also asked if he could have the rights to sell the products in Ireland and was told that, if he wished, he could have this licence. The company then told Mike about a new project called *Grease* that featured John Travolta and Olivia Newton John. The rest, as they say, is history. Mike sold tens of thousands of badges, whilst the iconic poster of Olivia Newton John with her arms around John Travolta's neck became one of the best-selling posters of all time.

To transport the posters and badges over to Ireland, Mike flew them via Aer Lingus. At the peak of *Grease*'s popularity, the suppliers informed Mike that they had a huge back-log and that it would take a week to deliver his pallet. That was no good to him, so he started making personal deliveries by driving his estate car over to Ireland, full of badges and posters. He would always zoom through the 'Nothing to Declare' channel, as he didn't think he would need to declare badges and posters. On one journey he was pulled over by the police, and later that day came before the judge for not declaring that he had a car full of *Grease* product. He was fined £100 – a small price to pay for the thousands he was making from each journey.

After four years, Mike realised he needed to move to larger premises. He moved out of Glasgow and found a much larger store to rent in Johnston Street, Paisley. As it was a new shop he gave it a new name, with Sleeves changing to The Record Factory. Mike knew how important personal appearances could be to the shop and he always tried to persuade disco artists to come in and meet fans. His favourite was Kenny Thomas, who had such a great time in the shop that he stayed all day and even served people when they came to the counter.

Mike told me of the worst personal appearance the shop had ever had. Ex Soul-II-Soul singer Caron Wheeler (famed for the song 'Back To Life') was doing a tour of record shops to promote her debut solo single. Mike had worked hard to promote her visit, contacting local press and radio for publicity. A substantial crowd had gathered for the 4pm visit. However all was not well, as by 4.30pm there was still no sign of Caron. Mike worked hard to keep the crowd interested, playing her record and giving out free-bies. At 5pm there was a knock on the back door. Standing with Caron was a rep from her record company. Mike told Caron how great it was to have her visit and that she had pulled a huge crowd. Caron replied that she had worked hard that day and was tired, so she wouldn't be posing for photos or signing autographs. Mike was shocked and explained that many people had been waiting a long time to see her. Caron said she would just pop in to say hello, then be off. Mike told her to get lost and to leave the store. He then went to the front of the shop and announced that Caron Wheeler couldn't be bothered to spend time with them and he was going outside to burn all of the posters and records that he had been given by the record company. Outside the shop, he did just that. The crowd cheered, and Record Factory never stocked a Caron Wheeler record again. It is probably no great surprise that her solo career never took off.

At the complete opposite end of the scale, Will Mellor, the star of *Hollyoaks* and *Two Pints of Lager and a Packet of Crisps*, made a personal appearance. Will had released a cover version of the Leo Sayer hit 'When I Need You'. Now, it wasn't exactly a pop classic, but Mike was impressed with Will's attitude. Over 200 people were queuing outside the shop, nearly all of them young girls. When Will arrived, one girl asked if she could have a kiss. Will told the crowd they could all have a kiss if they wanted. True to his word, he gave a kiss to every girl that wanted one. What Mike found amusing was that many of the girls, having been kissed, went to the back of the queue and waited for another. In some cases girls, rejoined the queue three times. Will took it in good spirit and never stopped smiling, laughing and kissing for nearly three hours. Like Caron, Will's singing career never took off, but a few hundred people in Paisley will never forget his appearance at the Record Factory for all of the right reasons.

The shop has also shaped Mike's life; one day a customer asked him if he would host a show on a pirate radio station. Mike jumped at the chance, and it wasn't long before Q96, Paisley's top radio station, offered him a job. These days, as well as having his own show, he helps compile the play list for the station. Mike's show is very popular, as he is somebody who tells it as it is. He often criticizes the local council over issues such as the roadworks that dominated the town centre for many years. He also offers suggestions on how to improve the quality of life for the people of Paisley. Being a shrewd businessman, Mike also takes every opportunity to promote his shop via the radio station, and it would be fair to say he is one of the most recognised figures in Paisley.

The Liberal Democrats acknowledged this and asked him to stand as a councillor and he now represents his local ward. This is no mean achievement in a political area dominated by Labour and the Scottish National Party.

Mike has been at the forefront of the campaign against offshore retailers on the Channel Islands avoiding the payment of VAT on CDs. This legal loophole is understood to deprive the treasury of around £60 million per year. He has led groups of record-shop owners to the House of Commons and has had meetings with the Treasury to discuss this problem and explain why it is the major reason that independent shops are closing down. Sadly, it has so far been to no avail.

Mike recalled some amazing tales about the days of chart hyping. One incentive he became aware of was that if he helped a record achieve a Top Ten entry, the record company would give him a returns note to send back unsold stock. He first became aware of this when the rep for Sony told him that if the Barbara Dickson single 'January February' made the Top Ten, Sony would give him an allowance of £100 to send back unsold stock. This soon became a regular occurrence with all of the record companies. Mike had no qualms about taking advantage of the situation and would often be given boxes of 25 free singles in return for putting numbers into the chart return machine.

Did the hyping work? When an unknown American artist called Phyllis Nelson released the self-penned ballad 'Move Closer', the label told Mike that they really believed in the song and were determined to make it a smash. They started off by giving Mike 25 free copies per week; and this went on for over two months! He recalls the day that his staff laughed when he was given his 200th free copy of the record. So many were donated that he was wholesaling the record to other dealers in Scotland. 'Move Closer' became a massive hit, reaching number one in the UK and staying in the chart for six months. Sadly, Phyllis Nelson was a one-hit wonder; and I am in no doubt that her royalty statement would have made interesting reading, record companies deduct the cost of promotional stock from the artist's royalties. So many copies of 'Move Closer' were given away that it wouldn't surprise me if Phyllis Nelson ended up owing her record company money.

There was a joke amongst dealers about the company they considered the one that best-played the chart hype game: WEA Records. Dealers referred to WEA as 'We Enter Anything', which was an indication to putting numbers in the chart return machine.

Before the days of the chart machine, the rep from Phonogram would call in and give Mike 25 free albums worth around £200, in return for borrowing his chart return book. He would sit in the backroom with a cup of coffee and add hundreds of bogus numbers into the diary. Alcohol was given to Mike on a weekly basis throughout the 70s, 80s and early 90s as an incentive for help in hyping. He never bought a bottle of alcohol for nearly thirty years. His storeroom looked more like a wine cellar. He counted up that he had over 100 bottles all given to him in return for his help in manipulating the chart.

These days with hardly any reps on the road Mike receives no free gifts from the record companies. He is sold records over the phone or via e-mail. Nearly every record he is told about is 'going to be a smash', needless to say most aren't. What other industry sells you a product that you can't hear, can't touch and you can't see? But that's how records are now sold to shops. Can you imagine that happening in the clothes industry? Imagine the manufacturer phoning up to sell his jackets … 'Oh, they are really nice with three buttons on and come in black or brown'. The result is that shops are reluctant to take a chance on new artists and prefer to spend their money on regular sellers, which leads music to stagnate. For many years Mike has held the controversial view that the record companies decided years ago to withdraw the support for record shops and left them to fall by the wayside whilst encouraging the growth of business with supermarkets and online retailers.

I asked Mike for tales about his customers. One lady came in and asked for a record that Mike had sold out of. The lady enquired if it would take them long to make another one. Mike was puzzled. It turned out that because the shop was called The Record Factory she assumed that they manufactured the records in the back.

One of the shops most memorable customers is a chap the staff refers to as 'Anorak Man'. This gentleman not only seems to know everything about every record ever made, but he also permanently wears a zipped-up anorak with the hood up. It doesn't matter if it's a boiling hot day or freezing cold, that hood never comes down. The staff speculate about whether he is bald or maybe has a tattoo on his head or he just has a permanently bad haircut, but if Mike ever closes down he vows to ask 'Anorak Man' to put his hood down.

The second memorable customer is 'Tape Man'. This gentleman owns a home studio and records himself murdering songs. He insists on Mike listening to his latest efforts whilst he looks through the shops racks. As he is a good customer Mike obliges, and then does his best to keep a straight face whilst listening to the warbling of 'Tape Man'. One day he brought in a batch of cassettes, on which he had recorded some of his songs. He asked Mike if he would hand them out to the record company reps. Mike duly did and, due to the comedy value, 'Tape Man' became a cult amongst the reps. Many a rep has driven up and down Britain's motorways laughing at 'Tape Man's' antics. Personally I feel Mike is missing a trick and should release 'Tape Man's' efforts on CD. The most popular part of *The X-Factor* is the first few episodes of the series, which feature misguided members of the public no doubt convinced by family members that they have a talent for singing, yet destroying classic pop songs. A few years ago The Record Factory had a refit and Mike decided to change the name to Apollo after the god of music. I have no doubt that Mike will keep going as long as he can make money from music.

*   *   *

From Paisley it's a 60-mile journey down the M8 to one of my favourite cities, Edinburgh, to visit the spectacularly located Coda Music. Owner Dougie Anderson is certainly one of the great music retailers to come out of Scotland. In all the years I have known him he has fought battles to keep offering the people of Edinburgh a quality record shop. He has done it with a wonderful sarcasm that always makes me laugh.

He started his career in 1970 at Bruce's Records, which was the place where rock fans hung out. He worked there for two-and-a-half years and found it an education in business! At the time, John Peel was incredibly influential on everyone's musical tastes. Dougie was a big fan, but his respect for John went downhill, however, when at a seminar he told Bruce's staff that if they really cared about the music, they should give it away for free to anyone who wanted it. Maybe John was years ahead of his time, and was foreseeing the future of downloads. On the other hand, maybe he was taking hippie ideals a bit too far. When quizzed about how the shops would pay the rent, rates, or even the staff, John commented that in an ideal world no one would need money!

Dougie left Bruce's to set up a chain of record shops for John Calder's Better Books, but this project never got off the ground. At a loose end, he took a job with Virgin Records at a tiny shop in Thistle Street and after a while became the manager. Virgin was great in those days. Richard Branson and Nik Powell were a joy to work for, with a huge sense of adventure, and the shops were innovative. He became good friends with people like Johnny Fewings, who went on to become one of the top people at Universal and Jon Webster, who was to become managing director at Virgin and is one of the most respected figures in the music industry. Dougie regards them both as good pals today, thirty-five plus years later.

For many years Virgin was successful, and it was the most fashionable chain of record shops in the country. When punk came along Virgin was hipper than ever as they grasped the punk ethos long before many of the other record companies. Richard Branson signed The Sex Pistols and the shops continued to do well. One day Dougie arrived to open the brand new Virgin shop in Frederick Street only to see the window covered with National Front stickers. The shop had received many phone calls warning them to stop selling 'nigger music', but Dougie never took them seriously. When he went to peel off the stickers one of his staff stopped him and said he should call the police. It was a good job he did. It turned out that each sticker had a razor blade behind it, so when you peeled it off you would slash your hand.

In those days Dougie was invited to meet many of the artists after gigs. Following a heavy night at an Alice Cooper gig Dougie crashed out on a hotel floor. He woke up at 6am in the morning only to see a giant boa constrictor heading towards him. It was a great hangover cure and Dougie leapt to his feet. It turned out that he was sleeping on Alice Cooper's hotel floor and, luckily, Alice came and picked the snake up. Fortunately both the snake and Alice were lovely.

Over the years Alice Cooper has certainly mellowed. These days he is a golf-playing Christian. Dougie didn't recall much evidence of Christian behavior back then! At one Virgin social occasion, during negotiations for an increased discount with A&M Records, it was agreed that for every item of clothing Richard Branson removed, the Virgin record shops would receive a half per cent discount. Always up for a challenge, Richard stood on top of a table and started removing his clothes. Virgin ended up with four-and-a-half per cent discount. Richard just wished he had worn more clothes that evening.

After impressing Virgin, Dougie was promoted to area manager for Scotland and the North of England. With the help of assistant area manager Rose Norton, and along with some fantastic managers and staff, they lowered overheads and increased sales dramatically. Everything was going swimmingly, but something didn't appear quite right. Dougie had been instructed to open as many shops as possible and as quickly as achievable. Believing in Virgin, this he did, not knowing that the plan was to sell them all off to Our Price once they had expanded the chain. Looking back, I can tell Dougie felt betrayed. He was somebody who loved Virgin and was proud to be part of the company. The fact that he worked so hard, motivated his team to work their bollocks off, and then was forced to tell them all that the rumours of a sell-off were completely false still hurts him today.

It was clear that Virgin was changing radically. It became frowned upon if managers didn't wear a suit (Dougie didn't) and people were brought in who had no feeling for the company, and no love of music. Bigwigs, such as Don Cruikshank, appeared. Dougie recalls being driven around Scotland by him and when they came to a pedestrian crossing he would stop, even though the lights were on green. He would wait for the pedestrians to start crossing, then zoom off whilst shouting at the poor pedestrians that the light was on green, much to his own personal amusement. Dougie found this behavior strange, but smiled – after all, he was his boss. Maybe Don was just looking for some early customers, as he later went on to run the National Health Service!

By now Nik Powell had left Virgin and Richard was more interested in airlines and suchlike. Nik was the voice of reason and used to prevent Richard from entertaining his more wacky ideas, such as Virgin Brides. Dougie regrets the day Richard Branson started taking a back seat with regard to music retailing. Johnny Fewings was running Virgin Retail, and in Dougie's opinion, doing a really good job in very trying circumstances. Because they were planning to float on the stock exchange, they needed to make a five per cent return on sales, which in the record business is very difficult indeed. This was a bad time for Dougie, as he was witnessing the vibrant and exciting company he loved going through major change. He remembers the back stabbers who wanted to employ what they considered to be better businessmen to run the company. And yes, they all wore suits.

At a training course that he attended run by Emerge Education, there was open talk of how to oust Johnny, from people who Dougie says he wouldn't trust as far as he could throw them. He recalls how Emerge encouraged all of this, and split people into factions, many agreeing that yes, indeed, Johnny was useless. Remember at this point that Virgin was still making a steady £1 million profit nearly every year. Dougie and many of the long-serving staff supported Johnny, as he knew how record shops worked and had a good business brain.

However within months Johnny was sacked and an Irish accountant named Simon Burke was brought in to replace him. On his opening speech Simon talked about Virgin's great history. Then, with a flourish, he slammed a big book shut declaring, "That chapter has closed!" Burke told Dougie and the other area managers that they didn't need to 'know' about music. He'd employ people at head office who did. Dougie raised the point; how did those who readily admitted to not 'knowing' about music, recognise that the people they employed did. Dougie's argument was that Burke and his besuited cronies didn't understand that one of the main strengths of any record shop was the knowledge of their staff in the store. Any record shop worth its salt has staff that can make recommendations to customers and suggest alternatives that might appeal to them. As the good staff with that knowledge left Virgin, the sales started falling. Time has proved him right, with the result that Richard Branson pulled out of music retailing and off-loaded the Virgin stores to the ill-fated Zavvi.

After a while Dougie and Rose became completely disillusioned and left to set up their own shop. Richard Branson was very fond of saying, "Anyone who works for me for a length of time will become a millionaire". After 17 years service, Dougie received £4,000. He is not bitter towards Richard and will always regard him as a decent bloke, but the people around him during that period were totally alien to what made Virgin great in the first place. There's no way that Virgin would have succeeded if these people had been there at the beginning.

The £4,000 enabled Dougie and Rose to get a bank loan to set up Coda Records in Edinburgh's Waverley Shopping Centre. Coda was pretty successful straight away, and they paid off the bank loan very quickly. They soon opened second shop at Glenrothes in Fife, and that also did well. By now Dougie and Rose had a vision to expand the Coda model throughout Scotland and soon opened a third shop in Livingston. Their vision was to have a chain where the public knew they would receive a quality service, from staff that knew about music. Strange idea, but it seemed to work! They then took a gamble and opened Coda Music On The Mound, a specialist folk music shop in Edinburgh.

At that time they were the biggest independent chain in Scotland and things were very enjoyable. They had some terrific staff that ran good shops and they made a profit that, whilst not huge, was acceptable. Dougie and Rose were delighted with how things were going, especially as they didn't have men in grey suits to answer to.

Over a period of fifteen years the supermarkets were gradually hitting the shops, and their profits started to slump. Things started to get difficult, and Dougie felt badly let down by the record companies, describing them as being unhelpful and actively hostile to him as soon as they found out everything wasn't rosy in the Coda garden. The result was that one of the most popular people in the industry was forced to close down the Coda chain. Here, in his own words, is Dougie's take on this and his warning to other independent record shops:

When we closed our three regular music shops we owed £4,000 to both EMI and Universal. This represents about £1,500 each to them at cost. Our turnover with each of them over the life of the shops was around £8 million each. Yet for the sake of £1,500 they tried to make me bankrupt, threatened to take my kids to court, and had sheriff's officers at my front door one evening. If you're a retailer, remember that your lovely, friendly rep works for these bastards. If you choose to go into liquidation, which we did to stop running up more debts, remember that liquidators have a thing called liquidator's booty. This means they steal your stock, basically. They also try to stop your remaining staff being paid for work they've done, which we utterly refused to be a part of. One thing we are proud of is that pretty much all of our staff still speak to us, because I think they realise we didn't shit on them!

Fortunately, we'd made the folk shop a separate company so that we could carry on trading. Though it wasn't doing great at that point, Rose and I have turned it around in the last five years and we're now doing OK. We love our little shop, love the customers who keep coming in, and love the musicians who have become good friends. It's funny ending up back behind the counter talking to people about music, turning them on to stuff they might never have heard; and we're really happy! Our hope is that at least our little shop will keep going for a few more years until we're even more senile and have to retire. Despite all of my bitter memories, it's been fantastic being involved in music all these years. I've loved 95 per cent of it, worked my bollocks off, but at least I didn't end up a fucking banker!"

A warning to record shops from a man who has had his fair share of knocks. As the saying goes, 'you can't keep a good man down'.

* * *

Coda is a record shop that specialises in folk and traditional Scottish music. If you are looking for rock or indie music in Edinburgh, it is worth checking out a couple of others shops. Record Shak, which specialises in classic rock back catalogue and second-hand and, Avalanche Records, which is a real cutting-edge store. In my years on the road they were both regular customers for me, and Avalanche also has an excellent franchise shop in Dundas Street, Glasgow. The Edinburgh shop has been trading for over 25 years and at one point they had three outlets in the city. These days it's just the one.

Their passionate owner, my fellow Liverpudlian Kevin Buckle, has told me a couple of great tales over the years. My favourite is the time Kylie Minogue called in to purchase the David Holmes CD *Bow Down to the Exit Sign*. When Kylie came up to the counter she handed in the CD and her credit card. However, the shop did not have a credit card machine at that point. Like our own Queen, the diminutive Queen of Pop also did not carry cash. The staff pointed out to her that there was a cash machine around the corner, but Kylie could not remember her pin. It all ended in disappointment. David Holmes lost a sale, Kylie didn't get her CD and the staff at Avalanche could not dine out on their tale of serving Kylie Minogue.

Another tale involves Dead Kennedys' vocalist Jello Biafra, who called into the shop and purchased some vinyl. The shop's manager, Andy, is a massive Dead Kennedys fan and was in his element chatting with Jello for a good 45 minutes. Just before he left, Jello asked if he could use the toilet. It was around ten minutes before he emerged, so it was clear that he had not been having a 'Jimmy Riddle'. As soon as Jello had departed the shop, Andy rushed to the toilet, shouting, "I have to sit on the seat used by Jello Biafra". It was an eternity before he emerged. My advice to anybody visiting Avalanche is do not ask to use the toilet. Rumour has it that that toilet seat has not been cleaned since the visit of Jello Biafra.

* * *

It's a long journey from Edinburgh to the granite city of Aberdeen, where my featured shop, One Up Records, is located.

Inspired by seeing Bob Dylan in concert at the ABC Lothian in Edinburgh in 1966, Ray Bird knew that he wanted to have a career in the music industry. After leaving school he attended Heriot-Watt University, where he studied civil engineering during the day and listened to John Peel most evenings. When friends informed him that they were opening a shop in Aberdeen selling jeans and Afghan coats, Ray asked if he could have a concession in the shop from which he could sell second-hand records. The shop was called Happy Trails, named after the album by psychedelic San Francisco band Quicksilver Messenger Service. In those early days Ray's big-selling albums were by artists such as Mike Oldfield and Peter Frampton.

Any listener to the John Peel Show in 1976 will remember how his playlist changed almost overnight, as out went hippy and progressive music and in came punk. Ray embraced this new exciting music and decided to become *the* punk shop in Aberdeen. He found a shop on the first floor above a department store in Union Street. As the shop was one floor up he decided to call it One Up. Unfortunately, the deal fell through at the last minute, but Ray quickly found new premises in Diamond Street. As he had told everybody that his new venture was called One Up, he decided to stick with the name, feeling it was catchy.

The shop quickly became *the* hip place in Aberdeen to hang out. As well as stocking all of the latest releases, the shop had a wide range of punk clothing and accessories. Ray encouraged bands to call in and play. Some of his most successful personal appearances included Bloc Party and the Stereophonics. His most memorable, however, was the Teenage Fanclub PA, at they pulled a crowd of nearly 200. Sadly, the band did not turn up, leaving Ray to inform the vast crowd that there would be no appearance (not one of his better days).

Being a cutting edge type of shop, the store has had its moments of controversy. One of these moments occurred when a junior member of staff came down to see Ray (who always worked in the basement) to tell him that there was a gang of pissed apprentices in the shop. This was an annual occurrence. Each year Aberdeen has Trades Fortnight, when the manufacturing industry shuts down for two weeks, and the employees pick up their holiday money. Apprentices receive their wages and celebrate by going into the town centre to get drunk. Many then hang out in the shop and spend nothing. Ray was sick of it and said to his staff member, "We should put up a poster saying 'If you are not going to buy anything, don't bother coming in, just fuck off!'" The staff member took Ray's words literally and went away, made a poster and stuck it in the window. Ray, being in the basement, was unaware of the controversy this poster was causing. It was not until the staff called him upstairs to help to calm down a woman who was calling the police to see if she could get Ray arrested that he realised what had happened.

Another fracas occurred thanks to the selling of a T-shirt. Back in 1981 San Francisco punk band Dead Kennedy's released the single 'Too Drunk to Fuck'. It became famous for being the first top 40 single to feature the word 'fuck' in it. My memory is of Tony Blackburn doing his top 40 countdown, and referring to it as 'that record by the Dead Kennedys'. Needless to say, the record wasn't played on Radio 1.

To coincide with the release, the band brought out T-shirts featuring the title of the song. Ray did a brisk trade selling them in-store. Unfortunately, one of his junior staff sold one to a fourteen-year-old schoolboy. His mother immediately went to the police and Ray received a visit from the boys in blue.

I asked Ray if he had any famous people call in to the shop and he informed me that one day Billy Connolly called in to the shop when he was looking for a dye for his beard. Ray suggested purple, and since then Billy has sported a purple beard.

The shop has received some unusual requests. One man asked for something by 'The Loneliest Monk', no doubt referring to the great jazz pianist Thelonious Monk.

The person who asked for DJ Ango left Ray perplexed. Thinking he was a dance DJ, he searched the hip hop and rap sections. He checked out the dance section and the Internet, but there was no sign of DJ Ango. Ray asked the man if he had any more information on the mystery artist and the customer explained that he was a blues DJ. This left Ray more puzzled than ever. Suddenly Ray had a brainwave and asked the customer if it was by any chance Django Reinhardt. "That's him," the excited customer replied, "DJ Ango Reinhardt".

Another satisfied customer.

I have no doubt that One Up will be one of the 'Last Shops Standing'. Ray believes that many more record shops will still close, but that the tide will turn, because there will always be a demand for his type of shop. The spirit of punk still shines brightly in a little corner of Aberdeen.

Chapter 14

Van Morrison Continues to Upset Record-Shop Staff

Week six and I am off over the Severn Bridge, paying £4.80 for the pleasure to see my Welsh customers. I have spent a four-figure sum on tolls over the years, but one toll that always made me smile was the one in North Wales that charged 5p to go over a tiny bridge. I always felt that surely it was not worth the man standing there all day to collect such a paltry sum. On one tour, I handed the gentleman my 5p. He was most apologetic and informed me that the price had increased to 10p. "Wow, a 100 per cent rise!" I sarcastically joked. The man failed to see the humour of the situation and went on to tell me how much trouble this price increase had created with the locals.

It is a mystery to me how Wales has not been as affected as the rest of the UK by all of the problems in record retail land. Plenty of shops have closed, although my best five Welsh accounts in 2003 are still trading today. One such account is Diverse Records of Newport, where I meet up with Mark Southall, one of the owners.

Mark's record shop journey started in 1976 when he landed a job in Soundwave Music Shop in Cwmbran. The first record he ever sold was the *Spiral Scratch* EP by Buzzcocks. Sadly, the Soundwave Music Shop has now closed.

Mark then found work in a dance/soul/new wave/indie orientated shop in Newport, called Flashback Records, selling all the latest UK/US funk/soul 12" singles and many 7" independent vinyl releases. It worked for a few years, but it ran out of steam in 1980. At the time Mark was also working as a DJ and has fond memories of being known locally as Elvis Costello, thanks to his black horn-rimmed glasses. Sadly Flashback Records has also now closed.

In 1980 he was lured back to Cwmbran to work in a shop called Tracks, the most popular name for an independent record shop. I can think of seven shops in the UK that traded under that name over the years. Tracks in Cwmbran was a shop that stocked probably the best vinyl back catalogue in Wales.

In 1983 the shop changed ownership and Mark was laid off about a year later, because the new owner changed the music policy. His ideas didn't work: a once successful shop brought in less business, and, for Mark, some of the harmony was missing. The search to find another job was on. Sadly Tracks has also now closed.

Mark worked part time (paid in vinyl and travelling expenses) between 1981 and 1985 for a soul/reggae radio show on Cardiff CBC radio (community radio) with some great people, including Phil Suarez, who used to spin the tunes at Cardiff City Football Club. This was Mark's dream job, taking a bag of his favourite records to a radio station, getting them played and talking about music. In 1985 Mark was back in a record shop called Hippo in Roath, but it didn't last long. Sadly, Hippo has now closed.

The next record shop to snap up Mark's talents was Roxcene in Newport. Mark will never forget the interview. All of the applicants had to take a music exam. It was like going back to school. Luckily, Mark was top of the class and he was given the job. Sadly, six months later, Roxscene closed.

Mark was then offered the chance to manage a shop in Pontypool called RPM, but once again it didn't last long. Sadly, RPM has now closed.

By this time Mark had worked at six record shops and they had all closed. I couldn't work out if he was the jinx or he was just unlucky. Eventually he found his spiritual home at Diverse in Newport.

In 1988 Diverse had three outlets in Newport and John Richards, whom Mark had worked with at Tracks, asked him to manage one of the shops. Mark remembers two different doom merchants who both said it wouldn't last six months. I do wonder if they knew that Mark had already worked at six shops that had closed. However, Mark was to prove the doom merchants wrong and for twenty years he has helped turn Diverse into one of the most famous record shops in Wales, as well as establishing it as one of the top vinyl dealers in the UK.

Two days after they opened, Mark felt a tap on his shoulder and a fellow with an Irish accent barked "Have you got this on tape Sonny?" He turned around to see none other than a grumpy Van Morrison (no doubt on another of his UK tours of being abrupt with people who work in record shops). Van was often seen in Newport and became a frequent guest at the local Kings Hotel, playing there on many occasions; I guess he felt comfortable, as he was never mobbed when spotted. The Kings Hotel hosted many nights of blues, soul, rock 'n' roll legends and occasional rock performers. Van constantly appeared there, usually cutting his teeth on new material.

One day the owner of the Kings Hotel invited Diverse to put a record bar together, which was a great way of selling CDs and of promoting the shop to an audience that may not have looked for them in the town centre. On one of these nights Georgie Fame appeared, and played a few numbers, joined by Van Morrison. Van stayed on stage with Georgie for over an hour. Seeing these two legends of music playing in the bar of a hotel is something the punters will no doubt always treasure. Needless to say, takings at the record bar were bigger than ever.

The first shop Diverse traded from was small, but very intimate and it didn't take too many customers to fill it up. However, they utilised the stock space very well, putting vinyl at waist level and CDs around neck level … perfect, unless you are a midget with no interest in vinyl.

After five years Diverse moved across the street into a much bigger unit. Business was on the up and up, and a bigger store it had to be. The new shop housed a specialist dance music section run by Andrew "Flid" Floyd, which brought in a different type of customer. One day the then-world number one snooker star, Steve 'Interesting' Davis, called in and was impressed with the huge range of vinyl that they had in stock. Steve and Mark spoke for ages about soul music, and he seemed to be grateful not to be talking about snooker for a change. Steve Davis is one of the biggest fans of French jazz-fusion band Magma. His dedication to the band is famous and he once arranged and promoted a concert for them in London. He was delighted to talk with Mark, as most people think that when he talks about Magma he is a fan of volcanoes.

Diverse are proud to have supported some of Newport's finest bands such as 60ft Dolls, Dub War, Goldie Lookin' Chain and the Redlands Palomino. In 1998 Mark and his fellow staff member, Paul Hawkins, bought the business from John Richards, the original owner, and moved to 10 Charles Street.

A major feature of Diverse is the vinyl label Diverse Records, set up by John Richards after he sold the shop business to Paul and Mark. The vinyl label has spawned some fine albums by the likes of Alison Krauss, Richard Thompson, Rickie Lee Jones, Frank Black and Dr John. In more recent times the shop has been used for a series of programmes on Newport past and present. The ever-popular Eggsy, from Goldie Lookin' Chain, presented the feature and talked to the camera about his affection for the shop and his love of vinyl. In 2006 the shop was invaded by the BBC crew for scenes filmed for an episode of *Doctor Who*. They hired the shop for three days, which was great, as the whole of Charles Street got an enormous lift from getting a visit from the best Doctor in recent memory, David Tennant, and his lovely assistant Martha, played by Freema Agyeman.

Today Diverse is down to just the one shop, which is virtually a window for Diverse's vinyl mail-order business. Nevertheless, the shop still sells CDs and remains passionate about supporting Newport bands.

Diverse will be one of the 'Last Shops Standing', as Mark and Paul's faith that vinyl would come back into fashion has been proved to be right. Whilst a lot of independent record shops and nearly all of the chains were abandoning the format, Diverse was living up to its name by stocking more vinyl. Most importantly, it also managed to establish a database of worldwide vinyl fans who feel like Diverse do about the format.

* * *

From Newport it is a short drive to the Welsh capital, Cardiff, where I visit the legendary Nick Todd, owner of Spillers Records. It is unusual to find a record shop that has had a two-part documentary about them broadcast on ITV. Then again, Spillers is no ordinary record shop.

The documentary *The Oldest Record Shop in Wales* told the history of Spillers and it's amazing battle to keep trading over the last few years. Opened in the Queens Arcade in 1894 by Henry Spiller and Joe Gregory, it was quick to recognise that there was money to be made in the recorded music business. Originally it sold wax phonograph cylinders and shellac phonograph discs. In the late 20s Henry's son took over the running of the business and, with the help of well-known band leader Joe Gregory, he added musical instruments to the stock range. The shop relocated in 1948 to its present site in The Hayes. It remained in the Spillers family until 1962, when they sold the business to a consortium of local businessmen. The current owner, Nick Todd, became involved in 1975 when he was asked to manage the store. In 1986 he bought the shop.

Nick and Spillers go back a long way. He bought his first record there in 1965, which was a copy of *The Chirping Crickets* by Buddy Holly. He had no idea at the time that 30 years later he would be the owner.

Nick took an unusual journey to the music industry. He has always had a great love of riding horses and keeping them is an expensive hobby and Nick took a job at Lloyd's Bank to fund it. He was offered the chance to help out a local DJ in some of Cardiff's nightclubs, and soon he was doing his own gigs. Lloyd's Bank was not impressed with Nick's nocturnal activities, and one day he was called into the manager's office. He was given an ultimatum – it was to be either banking or DJing. The bank gave him seven days to answer. He replied within seven seconds and there ended Nick Todd's career in banking.

The next few years were spent establishing himself as a top DJ, until that fateful day in 1975, which changed his life. He called into Spillers every week to buy his records and one day the manageress explained she was planning to leave and was on the look-out for a new manager. She told Nick that if he was interested, she would recommend him to her bosses. Nick jumped at the chance. After an interview, he was given the job in the store that he will forever be associated with. It is fair to say that Nick is probably the most well-known record-store owner in the UK now that Richard Branson has sold his Virgin record stores. There is hardly a person I've met in the industry who does not have a tale to tell about Nick.

I have dealt with him for many years and he has high standards, which can only be a good thing. We have hardly ever had a conversation without Nick giving me his words of wisdom on how my own company, Proper, can improve its service. His comments are always constructive and made with the best intention. Providing I agree with him, I have often implemented his advice.

The shop's famous customers read like a who's who of Wales. The Manic Street Preachers seemed to spend half their leisure time there. If they were not in the shop buying records, you would often find them outside busking.

Nick's passion for real music is infectious and the shop has a place in the hearts of the people of Cardiff, attracting a large following of loyal customers. The music in store is dominated by the latest blues and country releases. A very knowledgeable team back Nick up; his daughters Ashli and

Grace along with Liam, Steve and Sophie. One thing that always impresses me is the amount of gigs the staff go to. There is hardly a day when one of them isn't out watching a band.

Spillers is a true family business, with Ashli and Grace pushing the shop to a broader audience via the Internet and MySpace, whilst Nick makes sure their conviction and political ethos as an independent is maintained. One thing is clearly evident – the team's passion and enthusiasm for the music itself.

They informed me that their bestseller in 2008 came from a local promoter, who put together a compilation of music by the crème de la crème of local talent and called it *Twisted by Design*. So far, this one shop has sold nearly 300 copies. It is sales like this that make me feel that shops like Spillers have a fighting chance. After all, can you imagine trying to get that CD stocked in some of the other big music retailers in Cardiff, such as Tesco and Asda? It is only independent shops that support local music at grassroots level.

They pointed out that it is not worth their while stocking the latest release of Wales' biggest selling male singer, Tom Jones, as, "Nobody comes to Spillers for that kind of thing". Anyone who wants a new release by a commercial artist knows that they can buy it for much less in "those other places". If someone does ask for Tom Jones, however, a lengthy debate about the current state of the industry always ensues.

I asked Ashli what effect the major regeneration of Cardiff was having on the shop. She told me that everything seems to be getting homogenised in the city centre, just as it is in all the other major cities. How did we as a nation allow things to go this way? She continued: "You know how it's the same shops selling the same shit wherever you go? You don't get that in independent shops (music or otherwise) – each and every one is guaranteed to carry a unique stock which reflects not only the individuals who run the place, but also the patrons who frequent them. If you go to Bath or Brighton, you don't find yourself saying, 'Oh joy, another Starbucks and now I can have the same generic coffee as I could be having 100 miles away...'. You do, however, get excited when you see a bookshop or an independent deli where you can experience something new and unique".

That is what we are at risk of losing as all of our city centres build American-style, uniform malls. It has happened to our food industry as local producers and those with specialist knowledge of the product they were selling got priced off the high street by the superstores. As a nation we are now all heading for Obeseville, but how many people actually savour what they are consuming?

Nick told me a lovely story about a couple who fell in love whilst browsing through the racks of Track Records in York. Each year on their wedding anniversary the couple would make the trip back to York for a day out and spend an hour picking out some new CDs from the racks. Sadly in 2007 Track Records closed. After seeing Spillers on the BBC's *The One Show*, the couple thought that it was such a great shop that they continue their tradition and spend their wedding anniversary picking CDs out at Spillers and having a day out in Cardiff.

Spillers have produced a range of T-shirts advertising the shop. They have become cult items of clothing and you can always spot somebody wearing one if you look around the city centre. Nick recently noticed Henry Rollins wearing a Spillers T-shirt. Even more impressive, Jamie T was wearing one when he collected his NME award. A few months later Nick was watching highlights of the Reading Festival on TV and Jamie T was wearing his Spillers T-shirt again. It goes to show they are top quality, as it still looked good even after a few washes.

The last few years have been tough for Spillers. A major new development called St Davids 2 is dominating Cardiff's centre, with the result that many of the stores surrounding Spillers have been knocked down. Add this to the fact that the noise from the building site is impossible to get away from and it is easy to see why trade is suffering.

In 2006 the shop faced a review of its lease. With a brand-new shopping complex being built opposite, it was clear that there would be a substantial increase in rent. When presented with the figures, Nick made it clear that the business could not absorb such a raise. The outcome would have meant that Spillers would have had to move out, and Nick wasn't prepared for the shop to fold. With the help of Hywel Thomas, who as well as being a loyal customer happened to be Plaid Cymru press officer for the Welsh Assembly, they organised a petition to save Spillers.

The response from the public was amazing – over 20,000 people signed the petition including music stars such as Bob Dylan, Bruce Springsteen, Justin Timberlake, Beyoncé and long-standing customers The Manic Street Preachers. The petition attracted publicity from all over the world and was featured in the music and national press. Everybody's hard work paid off, as the landlords relented and agreed not to increase the rent. Is it only a temporary stay of execution, as Spillers faces another rate review in 2009.

I hope Nick is up for continuing the fight, as without Spillers, Cardiff just would not be the same.

*   *   *

From Cardiff I drive the 38 miles to the home of Swansea's Derrick's Records. A Swansea institution, Derricks is one of Wales's oldest record shops, the business is family owned. It originally opened in Port Talbot in 1956 as an electrical store, run by the current owner Chris's Uncle Derrick. They stocked a few LPs, and like other electrical shops at that time, they soon found that they were making more money selling records than electrical goods. The family therefore decided to open a new shop selling just records.

In 1968 Port Talbot was being redeveloped and the Derricks site was due to be demolished. The family decided to move the record shop to Swansea, and in October of that year they became the eighth outlet to sell records in the town.

Like a lot of stores that have survived the downturn, the major reason why Derricks is still standing is that Chris owns the building and is able to rent out the upstairs, bringing in much needed revenue. Branching out into supplying libraries and providing insurance companies means that Derricks has a strong base. Chris also has one long-serving member of staff with 25 years' service – Siân Jones. This helps to make the shop a part of the community.

One other advantage it has is that it was the first shop in Wales to embrace the selling of concert tickets. Today this accounts for nearly 50 per cent of its business. It's a shame that more record shops did not get involved in this trade – if they had have done, there would be a lot more of them left. I also find it strange that the ticket agencies have never tried to link up with the shops by offering discounts on the ticket if the customer also bought a CD or vice versa.

I have always enjoyed visiting Chris as he has some great anecdotes from his childhood. His Uncle Derrick was a friend of Richard Burton's brother and, one night, Richard Burton and Elizabeth Taylor looked after him whilst his parents had a night out. Not many children have had Elizabeth Taylor cook their chips for them. Chris told me of the day he came home from school and called into the shop to find his uncle, Richard Burton, Elizabeth Taylor, Harry Secombe and another of Port Talbot's famous sons, Anthony Hopkins, all seated in the shop's backroom drinking cups of tea.

In his youth Chris was the Welsh surfing champion and spent his time after school competing in various championships. Following the death of his father in 1984 Chris devoted his energies to Derricks. He shrewdly started selling tickets and contacted Gallup about becoming a chart-return shop. As soon as the machine arrived, reps from the major record companies arrived in Swansea. Chris was very shrewd and played each company off against each other. If one rep asked him to put a catalogue number in the Gallup machine to get a record into the chart, giving him five free albums to do so, Chris would inform the next rep that he needed to beat that number. Soon he had companies giving him ten free CDs in return for his help in promoting the record. One day he even took a phone call from Jonathan King asking for his help to promote a record that he was involved in by putting a few extra numbers in the Gallup machine.

Chris also says that the biggest mistake the music industry ever made was to tinker with the TV show *Top of the Pops*. Although there is more music on TV today than ever before, thanks to stations like MTV, the music is so fragmented that new songs lack the impact they had during *Top of the Pops*' heyday. It is hard to appreciate fully the impact this show had on the music-buying public between the 60s and 70s. It regularly generated audiences in excess of 15 million. If you speak to any music fan over 30 years old, nearly all of them will be able to identify the programme's first theme tune as the Led Zeppelin classic 'Whole Lotta Love'. However, they would have to be real anoraks to know that the theme between 1995 and 1998 was 'Red Hot Pop', composed by Vince Clarke of Erasure.

Top of the Pops created so many images that are ingrained forever in the memories of music fans. Who could forget these classics?

- The growling vocal performance of Nirvana's Kurt Cobain, singing 'Smells Like Teen Spirit'.
- Mud singing 'Lonely This Christmas', with the vocals shared by singer Les Gray and a ventriloquist's dummy (which appeared slightly less wooden than the band).
- David Bowie, with his arm draped around his lead guitarist Mick Ronson, doing a fabulous version of 'Starman'.
- Glam-rock stars The Sweet, looking like bricklayers in drag, camping their way through 'Blockbuster'.
- John Peel pretending to play the mandolin, as Rod Stewart performed 'Maggie May'.

- Oasis performing the track 'Roll With It'. The Gallagher brothers thought it would be great fun to swap roles, so Noel mimed the vocals whilst Liam pretended to play guitar.
- Dexy's Midnight Runners belting out 'Jackie Wilson Said' to a backdrop of beer-swilling darts player Jocky Wilson. Was this BBC incompetence or a wicked sense of humour?
- An unknown Jimi Hendrix descending out of nowhere like a cosmic voodoo god the week before Christmas 1966 and playing a white Stratocaster guitar with his teeth. His outrageous (for the time) performance of 'Hey Joe' prompted a whole raft of "Who is this wild man of rock?" stories in the Fleet Street press.

Most memorable for me was the plight of the unlucky All About Eve, who were supposed to perform their song 'Martha's Harbour'. Unfortunately, because of a technical error, the track started and the TV audience watched in horror whilst the band sat motionless, waiting for their cue to start singing. I felt so embarrassed for singer Julianne Regan that I am still cringing for her as I write this.

By the 1980s the audience had started to fall and various producers began tinkering with the show's format. Then, in June 1994, the BBC made a massive mistake when they changed the evening the show was broadcast from its traditional Thursday to Friday. This pitted *Top of the Pops* against ITV's biggest audience-drawing show – *Coronation Street*. Teenagers had to choose between *Top of the Pops* or watching one of their favourite soaps. Add to this the fact that, at the time the show was being broadcast, many people would have been getting ready for a night out and others would already have left for their Friday night frolics.

By the 90s viewing figures had dropped to around 3 million – only one-fifth of what they had once been. On 30 July 2006 the once great institution was put out of its misery when, after 2,206 episodes, its last show was broadcast. Even then, regular presenter Fearne Cotton, who was away filming ITV's *Love Island*, did not bother to come back for the last ever show, which was an indication of how much its status had declined.

Two other television shows that generated sales for record stores were *The Tube* and *The Old Grey Whistle Test*. Although *The Tube* ran only for five years, it introduced the public to new music and, as it was broadcast on a Friday evening, it had a major impact on Saturday sales. It became imperative for shops to find out who was performing each Friday, so that they had enough stock to cope with the weekend surge in sales for those artists that had appeared on the show.

Ironically, *The Tube* was also responsible for hastening the demise of *Top of the Pops*. As *The Tube* was a live show, you never knew what was going to happen next. Indeed, it often seemed the case that the presenters didn't know either, but, in Jools Holland and Paula Yates, the show had two charismatic presenters who revelled in the chaos of it all. In contrast, *Top of the Pops*, on which most bands mimed to backing tracks, suddenly looked old fashioned. *The Tube* became *the* show on which most credible bands wanted to appear, whilst *Top of the Pops* became home to boy bands and other artists aimed at the pre-teen market.

Like *Top of the Pops*, *The Tube* had many memorable moments, notably the first appearance of Frankie Goes to Hollywood and identical twins Charlie and Craig, known as The Proclaimers, belting out 'Letter From America'.

But my favourite memory of *The Tube* is of the band that wouldn't appear – fellow Tranmere Rovers fans Half Man Half Biscuit, who turned down the chance to appear on the show, as it clashed with a Rovers' home match. This created a lot of publicity for the band, much to the annoyance of *The Tube*. The problem for the production crew was that the nation wanted to see this mad band. So, they swallowed their pride and contacted the band to see if they would appear on the show. The band confirmed that they would be happy to play. *The Tube* press department released the news that the band would be appearing on the show in two weeks. What they failed to do was check the football fixtures, as Tranmere Rovers had a game on that day as well. Half Man Half Biscuit phoned *The Tube* to pull out of the show for a second time. This time *The Tube* threw in the towel and rock fans never got the chance to see what many believe to be the most under-rated band in the history of music appear on the show.

Sadly the programme is probably best-known for a moment of madness from presenter Jools Holland when, in January 1987, during a live trailer for the show, he used the phrase "groovy fucker". This was made worse by the fact it was broadcast at tea-time, when children would be watching. The furore this caused was astonishing, with the show being taken off the air for three weeks. Soon, both the show's producer and the Tyne-Tees Director of Programmes had resigned.

Whilst the show ran for 121 episodes, Tyne-Tees TV decided against commissioning a further series, leaving a hole in the schedules that has never been filled.

The Old Grey Whistle Test was the only other music show that had a serious impact on the record-buying public. It ran from 1971 to 1987 and gave an opportunity for non-chart artists to be heard. OGWT seemed to be shot on a shoestring, with no special effects and bands performing in a spartan studio. Its first host was Richard Williams, the editor of *Melody Maker*, who was replaced by 'Whispering' Bob Harris, who soon stamped his mark on the show. Bob is one of the great broadcasters, and still enthuses over new music. These days his home is at Radio 2, where he broadcasts Bob Harris Country.

My favourite tale about Bob Harris came from the music buyer for Tragomills, Peter Beall. Tragomills have three superstores in Newton Abbot, Falmouth and Liskeard. Before joining the company Peter was in the RAF. Whilst stationed in Gibraltar, Bob arrived on a tour and was booked to play a few records and host a pop quiz at the Royal Navy Fleet Pavilion. Earlier in the evening Peter and his friends had been making merry, and by the time Bob took to the stage for his quiz, Peter and his friends were well away.

As Bob read each question, Peter would shout the answer out, much to the amusement of his friends. Bob asked Peter to stop, but Peter was enjoying himself far too much to pay too much attention and a few minutes later he was back to shouting out the answers, to the continued amusement of his friends. Eventually Bob lost patience with Peter and marched to the front of the stage, looked Peter in the eye and hollered at the top of his voice: "Will you please SHUT UP!" Peter's reply of "I thought you were 'Whispering' Bob Harris" brought the house down … even Bob was laughing.

OGWT was broadcast last thing on Friday night on BBC2 during the days before 24-hour television, meaning that there was no problem when the show overran. Amazingly, the show could differ in length between 25 minutes and an hour-and-a-half, depending on how well it was going. However, OGWT made a huge mistake when it didn't acknowledge the punk movement – suddenly the show was seen as seen as catering solely for rock dinosaurs, and it fell out of fashion. In an attempt to move the show forwards, they employed Annie Nightingale and belatedly embraced punk, but it was too late. They tried out various presenters such as Andy Kershaw, Richard Skinner, David Hepworth and Mark Ellen. I recall all of them doing a fine job, but without Bob Harris, the show had lost its identity and did not seem to know which kind of music fan to appeal to.

Sadly, in 1987, the show came to an end, but, like *The Tube* and *Top of the Pops*, left us with some great memories. My own favourite was of John

Otway and Wild Willy Barrett performing 'I'm Really Free'. Soon afterwards they cancelled their British tour, because Wild Willy wanted to stay at home to watch World Cup football on TV. I have been in record shops a number of times over the years when people have come in and asked for *The Old Grey Whistle Test*'s distinctive theme music. For the record, it's called 'Stone Fox Chase' and was recorded by the American band Area Code 615.

Since the demise of these shows, only *Later*, hosted by Jools Holland, contributes to encouraging the public to visit record shops. Jools Holland first came to prominence as the charismatic keyboard player in Squeeze – the best group ever to have come out of Deptford. After his co-hosting of *The Tube*, it was a shrewd move by the BBC to offer him his own show. *Later* began life as a spin-off from BBC 2's *Late Show*, but soon became a programme in its own right. In addition to showcasing fresh talent, it became the first mainstream music programme to give an opportunity for folk, blues, country, jazz and world music to be heard. The list of people who have played on the show is a veritable who's who of the whole music industry. *Later* has a relaxed atmosphere, featuring a mixture of interviews, live performances and an opening jam session featuring Jools and his guests. It is hoped that Jools continues to broadcast – for the record shops of the UK, his is the 'Last Music Show Standing'.

Amazingly, there are some TV shows that actually damage sales for UK independent record stores. Reality TV shows, such as *The X Factor*, *Fame Academy*, *Pop Idol*, etc. create huge sales for their participants and, in particular, for the winners. Record shops should be delighted with this 'extra' business but, lamentably, only a small proportion of the successes of these shows is allowed to trickle down to independent record shops. Sony BMG, which owns the rights to release the winners of *The X Factor*, will deal with the major outlets provided by the supermarkets and high street chains, but offer poor discounts to independent stores. This arrangement allows supermarkets to sell these CDs at such a huge discount that they are often retailing them at a cheaper price than the independent store can purchase them direct from Sony BMG. The whole operation supports supermarkets at the expense of independent stores.

I agreed with Chris regarding his thoughts on *Top of the Pops*, although I felt that its producers lost touch with what was happening in the music scene and, by the end, the show looked jaded and old fashioned.

Derricks will be one of the 'Last Shops Standing' due to their recognition that you need to diversify to survive. Times have changed and it has been necessary for shops to evolve with the times. So many people came into the industry in the 80s and 90s, as they had become aware of all of the stories about record shops receiving free stock. However, these people opened their shops for the wrong reason: to run a successful record shop you need to have a passion for music. So many of those shops have now closed. Chris has a thoughtful phrase. Music is not life and death. It is here to make the bad times better and the good times even better. I feel the future for Derricks will be better.

*　*　*

I rejoin the M4 and head further west past the steelworks of Port Talbot until I come to the market town of Carmarthen, home to Slipped Discs.

In 1982 Oona Crawford decided that her collection of vinyl LPs had taken over the house and hired a table at the local market to sell those titles she no longer listened to. The idea was to spend a day selling – 25 years later she is still there and trading under the name Slipped Discs. On that first day of trading, people asked her to buy their own records and, although after her first day's trading she had more records than when she had started, she was shrewd enough to realise it might help her generate some much-needed income. Those early years were difficult for her, as she had three young children and could not afford a babysitter. In the school holidays her shop rocked to the sounds of Led Zeppelin, Deep Purple and children playing, as her only option was to bring the children in to the shop with her.

Whenever I think of Slipped Discs, the two Elvis's come to mind. The first is Elvis Presley. A life-size dummy of Elvis dominates the store. People are constantly calling in to be photographed with their arm around him. He is so life-like that one day a short-sighted old lady came in and started chatting to him about the weather, before asking him if he had any James Last records in stock. Oona constantly changes his outfit, and following Wales's Triple Crown win in 2008, she dressed him as a Welsh rugby supporter. One of her customers commented that she thought she knew everything about Elvis, but had never realised he was a Welsh rugby fan.

The second Elvis is their most loyal customer; a Declan McManus look-alike who, due to his horn-rimmed glasses, is known throughout Carmarthen as Elvis Costello. For the last ten years he has turned up every Saturday morning before Slipped Discs opens and has waited for Oona to arrive. If she dares to be late, he chastises her. Each Saturday he starts off with £20 to spend and, instead of making a multiple purchase, he brings up individual CDs and gets his change. It will often take over an hour to spend his £20. He has an encyclopaedic knowledge of music and insists on chatting to Oona about each purchase. The first few times he visited the store he drove her mad, as he just would not stop talking. Eventually Oona asked Elvis if she could have 'A Little Less Conversation'. When Elvis took no notice, Oona decided that she didn't really want him as a customer and, to discourage him, she started insulting him. Elvis thought this was a real hoot, and the more vicious Oona's insults became the more Elvis laughed. This really frustrated her and she was delighted whenever 'Elvis left the building'.

Over the years Oona has become accustomed to Elvis's quirks and now enjoys his visits. When you take into account that over the years he has spent around £10,000 in the shop, Oona wishes she had 100 customers like Elvis.

Oona's favourite customer in the history of Slipped Disc is a world music fan called Dave. Each week he would purchase a CD from Oona's tiny world music section. She immediately liked Dave, and to encourage his custom, she started expanding the section. Whenever Dave called in, Oona would enthuse over her latest world music purchases. The couple got on famously, and by the time Dave asked Oona out, she had probably the biggest world music section in south Wales. By the time he asked her to marry him, she definitely had the largest collection of world music in Wales. I am sure Oona will be trading for a long time to come. Thanks to Elvis (that's the mannequin, not the eccentric customer) Slipped Disc is a bit of a tourist attraction, and they come from all over to have their photo taken with him – Japanese tourists especially. It is worth a visit, especially if you are after rare 78s or 45s, as Oona stocks a great selection.

* * *

My next call is in one of my favourite towns in the UK, Tenby in Pembrokeshire. For more than 50 years Dales Music Store has been selling to locals and holidaymakers in the lovely west Wales seaside town.

The store opened as a piano retailer and was run by current owner Laurie Dale's father. As a teenager, Laurie was always spending his pocket money on 78s so he persuaded his father to start stocking them in the shop to complement the piano sales. No doubt his record collection soon expanded.

Laurie and his shop manager, Richie Westmacott, are real characters and are well-known to locals. Laurie is a singer and actor whilst Richie is guitarist in one of Wales's premier blues bands, Elephant Gerald. The band has quite a following and has played with Dr Feelgood and Albert Lee amongst others.

In fact, Richie always looks as if he is about to go on stage, as you never see him without his beloved bandana on his head. Richie started his music career in the record department of his local WHSmith. It was not really the job he had hoped for as, at that time, WHSmith had a policy of silence in the record department, not wishing to disturb the customers browsing through the book department. The resultant atmosphere was more akin to a library and Richie found it incredibly frustrating, as all he wanted to do was to blast out the current AC/DC album. Meanwhile, however, Laurie had an unfortunate accident, which rendered him unable to manage his shop for a long period, so he approached Richie and asked him to run Dales in his absence. Richie was delighted and, 25 years later, he is still there blasting out AC/DC.

A visit to the store is a must for anybody going to Tenby. Laurie and Richie are like a double act bouncing banter off each other, and their sheer enthusiasm for music creates a really happy atmosphere. When I sell a new blues album to Richie by an artist he likes, he reacts like I have just told him he has won the lottery.

In the summer Laurie can often be found sitting on a stool outside the store engaging holidaymakers in conversation and encouraging them to browse through this treasure trove of a store. The decor is old fashioned and the racks are jammed with too much stock, but this just adds to the shop's character. They keep a wide selection of LPs, CDs, DVDs, musical instruments, T-shirts, music memorabilia, belts and they have the biggest selection of button badges I have ever seen.

Dales is one of the last shops I visit that still sells quantities of videos and cassettes. There are thousands of them displayed above head-height and all the way up to the ceiling. They are stored so high that it is impossible to see individual titles at floor level, which results in Richie and his customers constantly climbing a stepladder to identify them. One day they all came crashing down after a Volkswagen, whose owner had left the handbrake off, ploughed through the shop window. Luckily no customers were hurt, but the sight of Laurie buried under hundreds of DVDs and cassettes is something Richie will never forget.

Today CDs only account for 25 per cent of sales, with musical instruments now responsible for the major portion of Dales turnover. Richie will ruefully never forget the man who asked if they stocked Yamayamahaha keyboards. Richie good-naturedly informed him that they didn't stock Yamayamahaha, but they did have Yamaha keyboards.

"C-C-Can I h-h-ave a look at them p-p-please?" the man replied. To Richie's embarrassment, the man had a stutter.

Another embarrassing keyboard tale occurred the day a woman called in and asked Richie 'if he could help her lay her hands on an organ', to which he burst out laughing.

One day a well-spoken lady called into the shop asking if he had any 'Jaws' CDs. Richie replied that he did have one, at which a look of disappointment spread across her face. Eager to please, Richie bounded over to the racks and found the original soundtrack to *Jaws*. As he got back to the counter, the lady mocked the shop's selection commenting that the shop had a low standard stocking only one 'Jaws' CD. Richie explained that there wasn't a great demand for them, then handed her the CD. The lady asked what it was, and Richie explained it was the *Jaws* soundtrack by John Williams. The lady burst out laughing, exclaiming that it wasn't *Jaws* she was after, but 'Jawzz.' It turned out that she was just a jazz music fan with an incredibly posh accent, and was after something by Duke Ellington.

Laurie takes great pride in having many customers who first visited the store as teenagers in the 60s and are now grandparents who call into the shop with their children and grandchildren. It is quite satisfying to see three generations of Dales customers all in the shop at the same time.

The shop has an interesting music policy. Six days a week they play Richie's choice, which tends to be rock and blues, whilst Sunday is 'Easy Listening Day' and there is a much more relaxed feel to the store as Laurie plays his favourite crooners. Dales really hasn't changed much over the years and, whilst holidaymakers still flock to Tenby, they will be there for a long time to come.

*   *   *

From Tenby I head north, hugging the beautiful Pembrokeshire coast to the university town of Aberystwyth to meet one of the Welsh music scene's most well-known characters, Andy Davis of Andy's Records.

Not to be confused with the defunct chain of record shops who were a feature of many high streets in the 80s and 90s, Andy's in Aberystwyth is 'The Last Andy's Standing'. Andy started his career in music as a Christmas temp in the Scottish record shop, Bruce's Records. Andy remembers his bizarre interview in which they asked him the following questions:

Bruce's: "What was the last record you bought?"

Andy: "'Runt' by Todd Rundgren."
Bruce's: "What label was it on?"
Andy: "Bearsville."
Bruce's: "What was the catalogue number?"

Sadly, Andy couldn't answer this question. The interview continued in this style, with the manager interjecting his questions to ask Andy to name three bands from a country, for example, Wales. Meanwhile Andy was worried that he wouldn't get the job as he didn't know that catalogue number. But he did get the job of course.

Bruce's Records' claim to fame was that it was owned by Bruce Findlay, who was managing a band called Johnny And The Self Abusers. They changed their name and had massive success as Simple Minds.

Christmas came and went and Scott, the manager, explained that he no longer had a role for Andy, who was made redundant. Andy soon found work in the record department of an upmarket department store called Graham and Morton's. In an ironic twist of fate he was given the task of interviewing for an assistant and who should be one of the interviewees? Scott, his old boss who had made him redundant at Bruce's Records. Of course, he didn't offer him the job.

After a short spell at Graham and Morton's and a period running the record department at Debenhams in Stirling, Andy packed it all in to become a professional hippy. He spent the next five years travelling and living the hippy lifestyle. Eventually Andy found a base in Aberystwyth.

One day the Job Centre called him in and explained that he had been a regular client of theirs for a long time and that it was about time he found a proper job. Whatever they offered him, Andy turned it down. Exasperated, they asked him what work he would do. Andy reminded them that he had worked in record shops and would be quite happy to go back to that. He heard nothing from them for a few months, until one day out of the blue they called him to say that they had arranged an interview with WHSmith for the role of record buyer. Andy felt that it was time to join the working world and went to great lengths to obtain the job. He visited his local Oxfam and purchased a suit for £2.50 and for another £2.50 he picked up a pair of leather shoes. His girlfriend gave him his first shave of the year, removing his long beard, and followed that up with his first haircut in two years. So, with his new £5 image, Andy set off for his interview.

When he arrived he could not believe his luck. The interviewer turned out to be his second cousin. Although they had not met for many years, they got on famously, and to the surprise of everybody at the Job Centre Andy landed the job. He was given free reign to improve the record department and soon made his mark. Andy remembers it as probably the only WHSmith in the country whose best-seller was the Cocteau Twins. Head office would send memorandums around citing which albums they were not allowed to stock. The Smiths self-titled first album was banned because of the track 'Suffer Little Children', which was about the Moors murders. They also banned the Van Halen album, *1984*, which featured an angel smoking a spliff on the cover. Andy ignored these orders and both titles became big sellers. Back then WHSmith did not use a computer system, and so nobody was aware of what he was selling – they just knew that the sales figures increased dramatically overall. Because Andy was doing so well, the manager allowed him to stock whatever he wanted and didn't object to Andy growing his hair long again.

A local musical instrument shop, called Cerdd Ystwyth, approached Andy to both manage the store and to start a record department. Aberystwyth University has a lot of English students who could not pronounce the shop's name and, as Andy was always there, the shop was referred to as 'Andy's'. After a couple of years the shops owners suggested to Andy that he buy the record side-of-the-business off them and they would carry on selling musical instruments. So, in 1986 he found a small premises and Andy's Records officially opened.

The shop soon came to the attention of the British public when Andy was featured on BBC News. Andy decided to make a stand against Phonographic Performance Ltd (PPL), an organisation that collects licence fees on behalf of record companies for allowing their music to be played at a variety of premises, for example pubs, clubs, shops etc. The PPL issued a writ in the High Court in London seeking an order to stop Andy playing music in his shop unless he paid his £70 fee. Andy was quoted in the press describing the PPL as vampires, adding that shops selling music should be exempt. His reasoning was that a record shop playing music was providing free advertising for record companies by playing their artist's music. Eventually Andy backed down, but his David versus Goliath battle brought him respect from his fellow dealers and lots of great publicity for the shop.

As his shop had the same name as Andy's, the largest independent record chain of the 80s and 90s, many people assumed that he was one of its shops. This did have its advantages. Often he would receive a parcel of stock destined for one of the Andy's stores. Andy would look through the paperwork to see what discounts the record companies had given them, then phone them up and demand parity.

I asked Andy if he ever came across chart hyping, to which he explained that, due to the shop's unique position, they did not get many record company reps calling. The nearest record shop north of him is over 50 miles away, as is the nearest record shop to the south. The nearest shop east is 30 miles away, whilst the nearest west is in Ireland.

The shop has an unusual bestseller, which came about after the Super Furry Animals, who at the time were an unsigned band, played a local gig and gave away a free EP to fans in attendance. The EP was called 'Llanfairpwllgwyngyllgogerychwyrndrobwllllantysiliogogogoch (In Space)'.

The man whose job it was to distribute it to the crowd only gave 85 away and called in to Andy's the next day with 115 copies of the EP. Andy offered him £100 for the lot and then sold them in his shop for £15 each – great business.

Andy has also had Van Morrison call in to his shop. Andy immediately recognised him and, bursting with enthusiasm, he rushed over to chat to him. Van made it clear that he wasn't as thrilled to meet Andy, as Andy was to meet him. Van bought a cassette of Negro spiritual songs titled *Songs From the Fields*. One track off the cassette, 'Sometimes I Feel Like a Motherless Child', featured on the album *Poetic Champions Compose*, which Van was recording at the time.

Before Van left, Andy told him about his favourite Van Morrison gig, which was when he played with The Chieftains at Ingliston Park in Edinburgh in 1979. Van nodded and left and the following year, 1998, the album *Irish Heartbeat* by Van Morrison and The Chieftains was released. Andy likes to think it was he who inspired Van to get back together with The Chieftains.

I asked him what the most unusual thing a customer has asked him for was. He informed me that one man came in and asked if he sold grass. Andy guessed he wasn't a gardener, but he still didn't stock grass.

As Andy's is near the university he has been hit by the download revolution harder than most. Andy is worried that downloading will become an even bigger challenge for shops like his in the future. My own view differs, as I see a parallel with that which happened in the 70s and 80s, when the music industry spent millions of pounds telling us that home taping was killing music. Full-page advertisements were placed in national newspapers to discourage people from recording songs from the radio or borrowing a mate's LP and taping it instead of buying their own copy. I believe that the industry got it completely wrong.

Like many kids, I would spend Sunday afternoon recording the songs that I liked from the top 40 countdown on to my cassette player. There was always a skill to ending the song before Kid Jenson or Tony Blackburn burst in with their enthusiastic chitchat. When the show finished, I would spend ages deleting their voices so I had a good recording. But was it a perfect recording? No! The sound quality could never match that of an LP or a CD, and did it stop me buying records? No, it had the opposite effect, as playing my tape during the week, the songs would grow on me and, by the weekend, I would go down to the local record shop to purchase the artist's CD. Soon I would lose interest in the tape and, if it didn't get mangled in my machine, then I would re-record on it or, more often than not, misplace it. A cassette never had a long-term value, whereas an LP or a CD was added to your collection, ready to play whenever you wanted.

The same applies to download. The quality is of major concern, as is the cost of downloading. On average a downloaded album is around £2 cheaper than that which you can expect to pay for the physical format from a record shop. Then you have all the hassle of downloading, and after all of that, you have paid for something you don't actually own. Try selling a collection of tracks you have downloaded – they are worthless, but there is always a demand for second-hand CDs.

If you listen to the record companies they would have us believe that soon, the only way you will be able to obtain recorded music is via downloading. On numerous occasions I have been in a record shop and have heard somebody say that they had downloaded a couple of tracks of a particular artist and now wanted to purchase their album. Very little has changed from those days when I would purchase albums after recording tracks from the Radio 1 *Chart Show*. The danger is that the industry is convincing itself that download is the only way to go and investing millions to encourage us to believe the same. Yet this is the same industry that only a couple of years ago was spending millions on trying to stop people downloading. The situation where mighty record companies were taking sixteen-year-old kids to court and suing them for downloading tracks from an illegal website was both disastrous PR and totally embarrassing, for everybody connected with the music industry. The record-buying public have been conned into thinking downloading is bigger than it is. Even though downloading is increasing, it only accounted for five per cent of album sales in 2007.

Downloading is causing more problems for the shops, as most CD single releases are available on download a month before the physical format is released. I watch with interest when I am in a shop and somebody asks for a new release. I look at the frustration in the dealer's face when, through gritted teeth, he informs them that it is only available on download and he won't have it in stock for a few weeks. This is most galling when the track is in the top 30 due to sales on download only. Downloading will continue to grow, but it is important for the record companies to recognise that the vast majority of the general public prefer to obtain their music on a physical format.

There is a huge difference between legal downloading, which affects independent record shops, and illegal uploading, which, in effect, is piracy and is a worldwide music industry problem. The internet provides the ideal means of transferring the digital files that music is stored on – the increasing portability of music, coupled with the penetration of broadband, enables swift file sharing and transfer. Alongside this, a sense of developed entitlement on behalf of those swapping the music. The attitude of illegal uploaders is that the record companies rip off the musicians anyway, so why pay them with their money? And if they did, haven't Bono or Phil Collins got enough anyway? All of a sudden, rock star excess became a rationalisation for what was (and is) theft.

A further problem was that the 80s boom years, where it was easy to make money, had produced a generation of music executives who, frankly, weren't very good at the business side of their job. The outcome was that there was no clear industry response to the challenge presented by download until the cat was well and truly out of the bag. Whereas the rest of the world viewed the 'home taping is killing music' campaign as risible; the music industry decided to embark on part two by insisting that 'all digital was bad'.

The outcome was similar to that which happened with the government cannabis laws. So many people have tried, used or know those that have taken cannabis that government scare tactics about the evils of the drug simply do not work. Sure, a number of those using cannabis move on to harder drugs, but the overwhelming majority do not. The outcome is that an illegal drug is readily available almost everywhere, with very little public disapproval.

And so it is with digital and other piracy. So many people enjoyed it, and then maybe bought CDs as a result. Also, the music industry's claims were so wild (the involvement of organised crime, for example) that it became socially acceptable to upload and download. When the Recording Industry Association of America (RIAA) prosecuted those who did so, the result was widespread condemnation of its behaviour, and not the uploader's.

One amusing tale concerning piracy involved Sony BMG. The company was prosecuted in 2005 for releasing CDs with built-in copy protection software so that, when played in PCs, the CD would send data from the computer back to the record company. Sony were sued in California under a law that bans collecting personal information by deceptive means. The group who launched the lawsuit were a non-profit-making consumer group called the Electric Frontier Foundation, who try to address the balance between civil liberties and new technology.[1] It was claimed that consumers who purchased Sony CDs received spyware which can damage a computer.[2] In an amusing postscript, it turned out there was a flaw in the technology. People could simply bypass the copy protection by drawing around the outer edge of the CD with a marker pen or covering it with tape. It was similar to when you bought pre-recorded cassettes. Simply by covering the holes on the top of the tape, you could re-use them. The copy protection worked by adding a bogus data track to the outer edge of the CD. As the computer read the data track from the CD first, it wouldn't then play the music tracks. By drawing on the CD, over the track, the computer is unable to locate the data track and so goes ahead with music playback. The millions spent on developing this technology were undone by something as simple as a felt-tip pen.

On 30 January 2007, the US Federal Trade Commission announced a settlement with Sony BMG on charges that its CD copy protection had violated federal law. The settlement required Sony BMG to reimburse all consumers up to $150 to repair damage resulting directly from their attempts to remove the software installed without their consent.[3] The company also agreed to remove all affected CDs from sale and offered to exchange any CD already purchased. My own feeling on piracy and downloading is that record shops should be given a licence to download for the general public. I have been in shops on so many occasions when a customer is after a track; the single is deleted or part of an expensive compilation and the customer has walked out without purchasing any music. The over-40s are the non-download generation and giving shops the opportunity to provide downloads to the public in return for an annual licence fee would be a money spinner for everybody. Artists would receive money from the licence, more customers would go into record stores, who in turn would

1 http://news.bbc.co.uk/1/hi/technology/4459620.stm
2 *Ibid.*
3 http://en.wikipedia.org/wiki/2005_Sony_BMG_CD_copy_protection_scandal

make more money, and customers would be able to obtain the music they want. Although Andy has lost a fair amount of student business to downloading, he has recognised this and, like many other shops, is aiming at a more mature clientele.

I asked him if he would be one of the 'Last Shops Standing'. Andy replied that, as long as record companies are still trading, he will be there, but in ten years will there be such a thing as a record company?

* * *

From Aberystwyth I drive north a long a beautiful road to visit the only record shop for miles, Cob Records, which has branches in Portmadog and Bangor The rise to international fame of Cob Records began inauspiciously in Porthmadog North Wales in 1967 when Brian Davies started selling ex-juke box singles at 1/6d. (7½p) each as a side-line designed to bring in extra income to what was then a thriving cafe. It soon became apparent that there was a demand for current LPs and Singles as there was no record shop in the area. Accounts were opened with all the record companies and the whole basement of the cafe was fitted out as a record shop. Although LPs were only 32/6d. (£1.62) in those days they were still not affordable to many, so they offered a service of "any 3 of your old LPs for any 1 new of ours" and before long they had a large selection of used LPs along with the new stock. They still operate a similar service, but in today's more complex market they now offer a part exchange price against the new items required.

It was then decided to advertise internationally offering new LPs at discount prices. This proved to be such a success that they closed down the cafe and concentrated solely on the record business, moving up from the basement to acquire more space, to where they still are now – over 40 years later. By 1971 business was booming – they were mailing on average about 7,500 LPs per week to some 25,000 customers (many of whom are still dealing with them today) in over 50 countries worldwide employing about 25 staff members. Shortage of space again became a problem, so they bought and custom fitted out a warehouse directly opposite and moved in the whole mail-order operation separating it from the shop sales. The bulk of mail-order sales was, and still is, to private individuals. Some exceptions they can remember, in particular, sending three orders of £1,000's worth each of cassettes to a store in Port Stanley for the troops during the Falklands War.

The fact that such a relatively small record shop in a small town like Porthmadog was exporting in such volume to countries world-wide attracted so much media attention that many documentaries featuring the business were made for local and national television and radio.

In the 70s and 80s the bulk of their trade was done by mail order. They were probably very fortunate in establishing the mail -order business – especially the export side – at the right time, when they could supply LPs to most countries weeks and sometimes months before they were released abroad. Nowadays there is a near enough worldwide release date. They also lost a great deal of business in the former Yugoslavia, where they had some 5,000 customers, with the events leading up to the conflict and the conflict itself. They were also adversely affected by new European customs regulations when the U.K. joined the E.C. Mail-order sales inland are also more difficult nowadays, with so many multiples and the advent of the Internet, which was not in existence when Cob was in its heyday. But through thick and thin the mail-order trade is still operational, albeit on a smaller scale. Gone are the days when they were placing orders for 500 copies of the latest LP by Led Zeppelin, Stones, Moody Blues, Santana and the likes Their main direct mail-order sales today are for items not necessarily "in the charts" which many stores do not stock and have no desire to order for customers.

In December 1979 Cob opened a second branch up the coast in Bangor. Taken on, as a young assistant on a 6-week trial Owen Hughes is still there 30 years later as the owner of that branch. Owen was originally an enthusiastic customer of the Porthmadog shop and it was his enthusiasm and knowledge that led to Brian offering him a job. Soon he worked his way up to manager and in 1995 when Brian decided to take life a little easier, he offered Owen the chance to buy the Bangor shop himself. This was an offer Owen couldn't refuse, as it had always been a dream to own his own record shop. Although the shops are now under separate ownership, they still work closely together and share a similar ethos. Owen distinctly remembers his first day in work at Cob Bangor as both Pink Floyd's The Wall and Abba's Greatest Hits Volume 2 came out that week and sold like hot cakes. Over the years Owen has played drums with many bands, one of the first being called Hot Water- a great band with a lukewarm name. They became John Peel favourites with the great DJ giving them a session and coming up to do a gig with the band in Bangor, an area he was familiar with, as he had done his National Service on Anglesey. In return Owen accommodated John at his house but was in such awe of his hero that he doesn't recall saying a word all evening giving the impression to John that he was mute.

After two singles and much touring, the band split and Owen went on to join the wonderfully named cult band Fay Ray. Named after the blonde actress who starred in the original King Kong movie, they must be the only band in history who achieved a record deal due to a couple of men chatting whilst taking a piss in a urinal (as you do). One of the men was the boyfriend of the bands manager and unbeknown to him the man next to him who he was enthusing about Fay Ray to was the head of Elektra Records in America.

He was given a cassette of the band, which he took back to New York with him, and upon hearing it, immediately signed the band to a major record deal. Nigel Gray produced their two singles and only album "Contact You" at his studio in Leatherhead. At the time Gray was Producer of the Year following his work on the first three Police albums and was also producing Siouxsie and the Banshees and The Professionals during the same period. After initial success, particularly in Europe, like many bands Fay Ray fell victim to record company politics and due largely to a lack of promotion album sales in the UK were disappointing. The label then got cold feet and shelved plans for a second album despite reasonable sales in Europe and the US. Disillusioned with the music biz in general, the band split in 1982, but despite the passing of over 25 years, it is still fondly remembered especially in its North Wales heartland.

These days Owen plays with a local band called Cajuns Denbo. They started off as a blues band called the Jukes backing various touring American bluesmen such as Lowell Fulson, Lazy Lester, Honeyboy Edwards and numerous others. In 1990 they were offered the chance to appear on a Welsh TV programme called Celtic Magic. There was one problem, the show was based around folk music and the band was asked if they could change their sound.

The band brought in a renowned local fiddle player while their keyboard player switched to accordion and did their performance in a Cajun/Zydeco style with Welsh lyrics. They went down a storm and were so inundated with offers of work that they never looked back.

Cajuns Denbo are the premier (and only!) purveyors of Welsh language Cajun and Zydeco music and are festival favourites all over Europe. They have released three CD's and as Mike Harding recently said of them on his BBC Radio 2 show "I didn't understand a word of it, but it sounded brilliant!"

These days Owen combines running the shop with playing in various bands and also promotes touring Roots and Blues artists at several local venues which he feels complements and enhances the shops activities.

One thing Owen has noticed over the last 5 years is the rise of the technology generation. The shop used to rely heavily on the students of Bangor University but nowadays the students download much of their music and the shop relies more on sales to the over 30's.

I asked Owen who was the daftest customer they had call in the shop. He found it difficult to choose but eventually narrowed it down to two contenders. The first was a punter who came in very late one Christmas Eve and asked how the CDs were filed, was it by forename or surname?

Tired but wishing to be helpful, Owen replied that it was by surname and enquired which artist he was after?

He replied "Janet Jackson"!!!!

The other contender was the elderly lady who asked for the Paper Serviettes.

Thinking it was the latest hot band the new Saturday girl Tina checked the P section to no avail.

She then checked the S section, no joy. Another staff member came to the rescue and asked the lady if she was after an LP or a single." Don't be stupid" she replied ,"they're for putting on the table"

I feel confident that both Cob stores will be amongst the Last Shops Standing The Porthmadog store still has a healthy mail order operation; whilst the Bangor shop relies more on an extensive back-catalogue, specialist knowledge and healthy sales of second hand vinyl and CD's. It is also proud of being a vital part of the local musical community, a place where people can not only find that that much sought after Meic Stevens LP, but also find out where he might be playing. A place where local bands can sell their own label CD's or find that new nose flute player on the shop's noticeboard. It is also a place where music matters and as with many of the independent record shops, it provides a soulful oasis in a High Street that is becoming increasingly dominated by corporate homogeny. Both shops are grateful to their long serving staff and even more so to their loyal customers.

*   *   *

I drive over to Welshpool to meet a real character – the owner of Rainbow Records, Mike Breeze.

Like a lot of shop owners, he started off in music as a DJ. Noticing an advert in *World Fair* from a company in Bedfordshire, who were offering packs of 100 7" singles for £6, he took the plunge and started buying regular batches. He found that in each batch he could use around twenty, leaving him with another 80 to dispose of. He then took a leaf out of the company's book and offered batches of 80 singles for £10 in his local paper.

As well as being a DJ, he worked during the day for an insurance company. After falling asleep at his desk the company gave him an ultimatum: it was either insurance or his evening employment. For a music fan it was no contest and he resigned from insurance. Knowing that he would not earn enough as a DJ he opened his first store in Shrewsbury in 1979, taking £38 on his first day. Over the years he gradually expanded and at one point had seven stores in Newtown, Oswestry, Welshpool, Colwyn Bay, Llandrindod Wells and Whitchurch. However, he is now sadly back to just the one shop, based in the market in Welshpool, because of the difficulties independent dealers have faced in recent years. However, I suspect that he is happier than ever now, with a lot more time to take things easy.

The way Mike ran Rainbow was unlike most record stores. He concentrated on bargains and collectable products as opposed to chart CDs and singles. If a store was closing down, Mike would be on the phone to see if they had any stock they wanted to sell; he would be on to receivers and would attend auctions anywhere he was likely to be able to purchase vast quantities of CDs for next to nothing. Often at Proper we would take back stock from stores who were unable to pay their bill (being the nice company we are, we would do anything we could to help stores who were struggling). Mike was always keen to purchase all of our mixed stock at a reasonable price (naturally).

He is also one of the hardest-working men I have ever come across. As well as the Rainbow stores, Mike is also a DJ on Radio Shropshire, as well as running record fairs. When I visited him it was often in the evening. I would usually spend three days visiting shops in Wales, so rather than sit in my B&B watching TV, I would utilise my time to gain extra sales. One day, as I was heading to Wales, I received a phone call from one of my customers who worked for Mike Lloyd, a small chain of three record stores based in Hanley in The Midlands. He informed me that they were about to go into receivership and it might be wise for me to come up as soon as possible to withdraw Proper's stock from the store. Whenever a store goes into receivership it is unlikely that we get the money back on that stock, so we always try to retrieve it before the receivers take control. Mike Lloyd owed us nearly £3,000. I realised I was never going to get this amount of stock into my car, so I called Mike Breeze, knowing he would appreciate a bargain. He met me at the store with his van and I gave him first choice on the stock I was collecting.

It soon became clear to me that, although Mike Lloyd owed us £3,000, he had nowhere near that value of our stock left, because he had run a closing down sale over the previous few days. After I collected all of our stock they still owed us £1,500. By this time the staff were completely disinterested, as they were all leaving the following day. I suggested to the manager that I pick out 500 CDs from the racks and value them at £3 per CD to clear the debt. "No problem," he replied.

Meanwhile, Mike Breeze had arrived and I had boxes full of 200 CDs and offered them to him at £3.50 per unit; he was in his element and I noticed that he was taking around 80 per cent of the stock. Mike informed me that he would take the lot if he could have them for £2.50 per CD. We eventually agreed on £3.10; he was happy, and I felt that at least I was making some kind of profit on the deal.

Mike Breeze had some great tales from his radio show. Back in February 1991 he allowed a new rock trio from London to play a session on the show. They turned out to be nice guys and they appreciated the chance to perform. Two members of the band had long hair and bushy beards, whilst the third was short with cropped hair. To repay Mike, they offered to take him for a meal. So Mike and the boys trooped off to the local Beefeater, where the staff knew Mike as the local radio DJ. Although greeted warmly, the manager explained that they were no longer serving, despite it only being 9.45pm. In desperation, Mike told the manager that the trio were in fact ZZ Top, who had just flown in from Texas and had been looking forward to some Welsh hospitality. The manager looked at the band and then disappeared into the kitchen. He shortly re-appeared with the head chef and they embraced and hugged the band as if they were long lost brothers; they really believed that this band was ZZ Top! The service was fantastic and they were all treated like royalty, getting the restaurant to themselves. When the time came to pay the bill, the manager said that it was on the house, as he was honoured to have such a famous band eating there. Just as they were finishing their coffees, the chef reappeared holding his own copy of ZZ Top's *Eliminator* and asked the band to sign it. Somehow managing to keep straight faces, each member of the band signed the album and then made a hasty retreat. Mike has, understandably perhaps, never been in a Beefeater since.

One person who will never forget meeting Mike was 60s star Billy J Kramer, who after being interviewed by Mike for his radio show, invited him to his gig later that evening. Mike attended with his wife, Sue, and Billy gave them seats on their own in the wings. Dressed in a pure white catsuit, Billy was going down a storm and halfway through the set launched into his most famous hit 'Little Children'. Billy thought it good fun to dance backwards to where Mike and Sue were sitting, where he would let rip a large fart in time to the music. Twice he did this, much to the amusement of the band's drummer. Unfortunately, the third time he attempted it he followed through and, to Mike and Sue's horror, a dark brown stain the size of a 50 pence piece appeared on the pure white trousers. As the song went on the stain got larger; in fact, it seemed to be getting bigger by the second. As soon as the song finished, Billy rushed off stage only to appear minutes later in a clean black suit. Only Mike, Sue and the drummer understood why there was an unexpected musical interlude.

In 1993 Mike was contacted by the management of Ben E King, ex-lead singer of The Drifters, and asked if he would like to interview him for his Radio Shropshire show. Mike was delighted and even more so when Ben E King agreed to do a signing in his store to promote his new album. The only problem was that King could not drive, so Mike had to arrange for his friend, Paul, to pick him up from a top Birmingham hotel.

On his arrival Paul asked the receptionist if she could contact Mr King and ask him to come down to the lobby. But to Paul's horror this caused a catastrophe, as the receptionist telephoned the wrong room and spoke to the wrong Mr King; by sheer coincidence two Mr Kings were staying in the hotel that night and strutting down the stairs, surrounded by a bunch of heavies, was boxing promoter Don King. Needless to say, Don King was not impressed to be dragged down to the lobby. However, on the plus side, Ben E King laughed all the way to the studio and Mike had a great interview before he and King popped down to the shop to the record signing.

A less successful signing was that of Peter Sarstedt, when he came to the shop to promote his greatest hits album. As well as the signing, Peter performed an acoustic set singing his number one classic 'Where Do You Go To My Lovely' and his other, sadly often overlooked hit 'Frozen Orange Juice'. After the performance, Mike closed the store and took Peter to do an interview on his radio show. When they had finished, they went for a meal (needless to say it wasn't at the Beefeater) and, at around midnight, they bade each other farewell as Peter set off on the long journey back from Wales to his home in Surrey. Back home and in bed, Mike heard the phone ring. He looked at the clock. It was 3am ... who could this be? It turned out to be Peter Sarstedt, who was outside his house without his keys – he had left them along with his wallet in his briefcase, which was still in Mike's shop. Peter travelled back to Wales where a bleary eyed Mike met him outside the store just as the sun was coming up.

Rainbow was graced with the presence of another celebrity when a six-foot American covered in gold jewellery smoking a huge cigar called in with his girlfriend on his arm. "Rock 'n' roll!" he barked at Mike, who pointed out his section and, to Mike's delight, started piling up a stack of CDs he wished to purchase. The American noticed another customer purchasing a Dolly Parton CD. He shouted so everybody could hear, "Dolly can't sing, she just has big tits". He then noticed a nervous looking student with a 12" single by the Pet Shop Boys. "A couple of poofs," he remarked, no doubt encouraging sales in the shop no end. Noticing that a crowd had gathered, he burst out singing and dancing, performing a superb version of 'Jailhouse Rock'. It turned out he was the trouser-splitting star from the 60s, PJ Proby, and his quiet girlfriend was Billie Davis, who had hits with 'Tell Him' and 'I Want You to Be My Baby'. They were on a Solid Gold 60s Tour and had played at Aberystwyth Arts Centre the previous evening. After purchasing his CDs, Mike got chatting with PJ and asked him if he would like to appear that evening on his radio show to promote the tour.

"Would love to, son," PJ replied. Mike pushed his luck further – he had a record fair in town later and he asked PJ if he would be his guest of honour and officially open it.

"Would love to, son." Mike was delighted until, as PJ left he asked him whether the charge for opening the fair should be $2000.

"You must be joking," Mike replied.

"I never joke about money, son," he retorted. Needless to say, the record fair had no guest of honour.

I asked Mike who his favourite celebrity was and he told me that it was the late great Edwin Starr who came on to Mike's radio show many times and also popped into Mike's shop to sign autographs. He also always had a good story to tell. Mike will never forget the first time they met. Edwin was to be a guest on the show, but whilst Mike was on air, he received a phone call from a very disillusioned Edwin Starr who was hopelessly lost. He said he wasn't going one step closer unless Mike arranged a police escort. Mike gained enough information from Edwin to work out roughly where he was. Not wishing to let his listeners down, he reassured Edwin that the police would arrive soon and accompany him to the studio. In desperation, Mike phoned the local police and fortunately the officer that took the call was a huge Motown fan and volunteered to do the job himself. Edwin was delighted when the police motorcyclist turned up and escorted him to the studio – even more so when the officer dismounted from his motorcycle and gave Edwin a salute.

Mike's most unusual store was on Colwyn Bay Pier. I don't normally associate piers with record stores, but Mike's reason for shutting the shop down was rather unique. The shop was run by a 35-year-old married man called Keith. A young girl named Jane assisted him. It was the middle of June, one of the hottest days of the year, so Mike was anxious to hear how well his store had done that day; with all those holidaymakers around he was expecting big takings. Unfortunately, he could get no reply from either Keith or Jane's phone. Rather perplexed, he phoned the owner of the pier and asked him to check out the store. The reply came soon after with a rather nervous pier-owner stammering that he had bad news – the store was closed with a 'Back Soon' sign on the door. The good news was that the staff were safe and sound; unfortunately, he had found them in the storeroom having a quick bonk. Needless to say, the lease expired soon after. Mike closed the store; he just couldn't get the staff.

Another sex-related tale occurred when a customer brought a huge collection of LPs into the store to sell, as he was going through a divorce and needed the cash. As there were over 1,000 albums, Mike asked him to leave them with him and to call back later. Mike started inspecting the LPs and was delighted with the quality. As he took the LP out of the sleeve of the classic Bryan Ferry album *Bride Stripped Bare*, a package dropped to the floor. On closer examination it turned out to be twenty photos of this man's wife using a vibrator. Was this the reason for the divorce? Mike was left with a dilemma – should he return the photos to the man? His wife, Sue, who had also seen the photos, took the decision out of his hands by cutting them up and putting them into the bin.

I often ask the shops I visit what their best-ever sale was and Mike proudly told me of how he had turned £100 into £1,400 in 24 hours. One cold, wet day a man walked in and informed Mike that he was moving flats that day and wished to dispose of his record collection. He lived in a nearby town and had around 300 LPs, all Elvis Presley! Mike turned up at the block of flats and, as would be the case, the gentleman lived on the top floor. The lift was out of order and the gentleman explained he had a bad back and Mike would have to carry all of the records down himself. Already cold and wet, he wasn't in the happiest mood when the gentleman asked him how much he would offer. Although he had looked through the boxes, he had not really studied the records and offered the man £100, expecting him to turn down the opening offer. He was pleasantly surprised when the gentleman reluctantly accepted this derisory offer.

The next day he unloaded his purchase into his Newtown shop and suddenly realised what a great deal he had made. Many of the LPs were first pressings. There were lots of picture discs and plenty were on coloured vinyl. There were even two mint condition 10" singles on the HMV label. Whilst still deciding how much to charge for them, a couple walked into the shop and started flicking through the Elvis collection.

"These are nice!" they commented, and then proceeded to talk at great length in Welsh, constantly nodding their heads in agreement.

After fifteen minutes the guy came over and said, "We collect Elvis records, and although we have many of these, yours are in better condition. Can you do me a good deal on the entire contents of the five boxes?"

Chancing his luck Mike said, "You can have them for £1,400."

The couple seemed very cool and discussed the offer in Welsh before asking Mike to give them half an hour to raise the cash. The half an hour seemed to last an eternity, but fifty minutes later they called back with £1,400 in crisp £20 notes; so, in 24 hours, Mike had turned £100 into £1,400.

I often ask my customers who their maddest customer has been. Mike provided me with a list as long as my arm, so I have narrowed it down to a top ten.

Number 10 – The customer who asked Andy, Mike's trusted assistant, if they had a CD by Daniel O'Donnell featuring 'Danny Boy'. Andy scoured the racks and eventually found what she was looking for. The lady was most impressed. "Can you write the name of the CD on a piece of paper please?"

"No trouble," Andy replied. When the lady turned to leave, Andy asked her whether she wanted the CD.

"Oh no," she replied. "I like to give my business to WHSmith."

Number 9 – The lady who returned her Bee Gees cassette demanding a refund. Mike stood his ground and refused and wouldn't even change it for her. The woman became more upset, ranting and raving and saying that she knew her rights and would get trading standards involved unless Mike relented, but Mike stood firm. Exasperated, the woman demanded to know on what grounds Mike was refusing to give her her money back. At this point, Mike felt it apt to point out to the woman the Woolworths sticker on the top right-hand corner of the cassette.

Number 8 – Mike had a clear-out of his albums, so he placed a huge sign in the window saying 'Vinyl Sale'. A couple of hours later an old lady popped in and asked for some 6×4 lino for her back kitchen.

Number 7 – The customer who kicked off in front of a packed shop demanding a refund on a Siouxsie and the Banshees album and called Mike everything under the sun as one side of the album played Jimi Hendrix. He was given a refund of £5.99, but being the shrewd salesman he is, Mike marketed it as a Jimi Hendrix rarity and re-sold it for £20.

Number 6 – The man who asked to see all of the Fleetwood Mac CDs that Mike had in stock. He then proceeded to take his mobile phone out and took a picture of the front and back of each CD. Then, to Mike's utter amazement, he phoned up his partner and said, "Darlin' these are the CDs I am after. Can you contact Play.com and order them for me?"

Number 5 – Mike had a sign instore saying '12" only 99p'. An old lady popped in, pointed at the sign and asked for a pair of size twelve's. Not really understanding what she meant, or wishing to hurt her feelings, he replied, "We only have size tens and fourteens left."

"Not to worry. I will pop back later in the week."

Number 4 – The regular customer who would purchase everything by Led Zeppelin, and would ask every time he came in, "Anything new?" Mike had just purchased a Japanese 7" single called 'Trampled Water', which he proceeded to show him. Mike said that it was deleted. Immediately the customer said that he must have it, as he had everything by Led Zeppelin, but he hadn't got one called 'Deleted'.

Number 3 – The man who picked out a collection of Bob Marley CDs and, when he got to the counter, told Mike that he had no money, but he would give Mike some powders in exchange. I think Mike realised that the powders were unlikely to be Ariel, Bold or Daz, and thus rejected this unusual offer.

Number 2 – There is a very fine line between doing your job properly by being a good salesman and giving the impression that you want to get into ladies' knickers. A couple of years ago a very large lady walked in and started purchasing all of Mike's line dancing CDs. She became a regular and moved on to purchasing all of his Bon Jovi CDs. As with all regular customers, Mike had a chat with her and week-by-week she started to reveal all of her personal problems. Her biggest problem, however, was her smell. One day she revealed that her partner had left her, which was probably something to do with the pong. Suddenly she started becoming over-friendly and complimenting Mike, who had been happily married for the last 26 years. Things took a turn for the worse when knickers would be posted through the letterbox of the shop on a daily basis; on the plus side, they were clean. The woman then resorted to following Mike around. Things came to a head one day when she was in the shop filling it with her pungent smell and turned to Mike and said, "Mike, if you take me out I promise I will have a bath."

Luckily Mike's wife, Sue, was in the back of the shop and came out and gave her a piece of her mind. The stalker has never returned. Sadly for Mike sales of Bon Jovi CDs are down, but he is saving a fortune on air fresheners.

Number 1 – The thief who Mike watched take two empty cassette cases off the wall, bring them to the counter and demand a refund as there were no cassettes inside. "I have just seen you take them off the wall," Mike said, but the man kept to his story and became very abusive, upsetting all of the customers in the shop. Mike only got rid of him by saying he was calling the police. Feeling the guy was trouble, Mike walked down to the other record shop in town, the now-defunct Our Price, to warn them about this character and, lo and behold, standing at the counter of Our Price was the same guy screaming abuse at the manager and demanding a refund for the two cassettes he had claimed he had purchased, neither of which had a cassette in.

I asked Mike about his plans for the future and whether he had any regrets. He informed me that he was happy to keep working in his last shop as long as it was still viable; he had worked for nearly forty years in something he enjoyed; the only other thing that had ever appealed to him was working in a circus. Although he never achieved that ambition, he met plenty of clowns in the music industry.

A nice postscript to the Rainbow tale is that Mike Lloyd is one of the great survivors. Despite his business crashing, at the time of the collapse he owned five record shops, a ticket agency and a theatre. He bounced back with a new venture, Music Mania, based in Hanley. The shop is run by one of his ex-managers, the affable Ian Gadsby. The long-term vision of the shop was to keep it simple. They sell tickets and second-hand product as well as a great range of rock, world, blues, folk and reggae. As with all record shops, Ian has had a good laugh at the antics of his customers. These are his three favourite tales.

1) 'The Bearded Abba Lady'
   Customer: "I love Abba."
   Ian: "Do you?"
   Customer: "They are the best band ever, do you like them?"
   Ian: "Not my cup of tea, don't get me wrong, after a few drinks I'll sing along to 'Dancing Queen'."
   Customer: "The women were very beautiful."
   Ian: "Yeah."
   Customer: "All three of them."

To this day Ian wondered who he preferred, the blonde, the brunette or the one with the beard!

2) 'Does Nana Mouskouri Live in Hanley?'
    Ian was approached by a man who sometimes just stared at the walls in
    the shop and asked "Do you know Nana Mouskouri?"
    "I don't think we've got anything in," he replied.
    "No, do you know Nana Mouskouri?"
    "I know of her," he replied.
    "No, no, no, do you know her?"
    "Do you mean personally?" he asked.
    "Yes," he said.
    The guy had written a letter but didn't have her address.
    "No, I don't know her," Ian said.
    "Do any of your friends know her?" he then asked.
    "I know, send it to Nana Mouskouri – Greece."
    "Will it get to her?"
    "Oh yeah, easy," said an exasperated Ian.

3) 'The self-styled Viscount of Trentham'
    Ian's favourite customer was an eccentric old gent he dealt with whilst
    working at the Mike Lloyd shop – the self-styled Viscount of Trentham, Sir
    Alan Maddocs. He would ask to listen to ballroom records and then dance
    around the shop.
    One busy Saturday he arrived carrying a balloon. He had a big bag of
    records saved and was paying by cheque, but he did not have a cheque guar-
    antee card. The floor manager at the time was a very uptight person, who
    informed him that they couldn't accept the cheque without the card.
    "Dear boy, present this cheque at the Newcastle-under-Lyme branch of
    Lloyds Bank and the funds will be there."
    The manager was now very red-faced and tried to explain modern
    banking to Sir Alan.
    "In that case I will write my credentials on the back."
    In the tiniest writing he wrote "I am Earl Mountbatten's cousin, I knew
    the Queen as a baby," and much more. Eventually the general manager was
    called. He took Sir Alan into his office and had a cup of tea and a nice chat.
    After about half an hour he raised the subject and said, "I'm sorry, we can't
    take this cheque."
    "Oh dear boy," replied Sir Alan, "you should have said." He then pulled
    a wad of twenties from his wallet and paid. The likes of Sir Alan are now
    long-gone and sorely missed.

Chapter 15

Resurrection of The Record Shop

lthough at times it sounds as though everything is doom and gloom, I truly believe independent record shops have a great future. There were many shops that had lazy and arrogant management who thought because they had a chart return machine the record companies would always look after them – many have bitten the dust.

The record shops that have survived are the crème de la crème.

Record shops have been forced to diversify. No longer can they rely on sales of chart albums or CD singles. The shops I have featured in this book are still standing for two main reasons:

1. They recognized the need to diversify early enough, by increasing their selection of folk, blues, country, jazz and world music: genres not widely offered in supermarkets. They embraced importing CDs only released in Japan, Australia and the USA. Nearly all shops now have bargain sections for CDs and music DVDs. The resurgence in vinyl sales is also having a huge impact. Your record shop is the place to buy vinyl as it is unlikely that the supermarkets will ever stock it. Most satisfying of all is that young people are discovering the joys of vinyl. Not only have they diversified in the genres but also in the product they stock. Many now sell music books, T-shirts, accessories, radio and CD players along with musical instruments.

2. The other reason these shops are still standing is customer service. The stores featured in this book all offer outstanding customer service and they will all make an extra effort to find that elusive CD for you. Record shops are part of the community and any area is enriched for

having one. I feel sad when I go to a town that does not have a record shop. It is as though something is missing.

In 2009 the future for the independent record shop suddenly took a turn for the better when 900 Woolworths stores closed along with 150 Zavvi shops. This was bad news for the staff, however, it was a turning point for many independents. People who shopped at Woolworths and Zavvi did so because they wanted to purchase physical product. Although a percentage of these people then started purchasing via the internet, many sought out their local independent record shop.

Suddenly, after the carnage of the last 10 years in which record shops were closing almost daily – new record shops were opening. Shops such as Backtrax in Totnes, who had closed down, now decided the time was right to start again. Shops such as the excellent Rise Records in Cheltenham, founded by the father and son combination of Gordon and Lawrence Montgomery, expanded by opening branches in Warwick and Bristol. Gordon had originally been the founder of Fopp Records who had been one of the great independent chains but these days is owned by HMV. Shops such as Raves From The Grave in Frome opened another branch in Warminster, whilst Powerplay expanded into Leicester. Even in my home-town of Chippenham a new record shop, Magpie, opened its doors. In my job at Proper Music I speak to many independent record shops every day; 90% of them have increased turnover in the last year despite us being in one of the worst ever economic recessions. These positive developments are not just confined to the UK, but are happening all over the world. People are rediscovering vinyl again. In Los Angeles, three vinyl record shops (On Vacation, Origami Records, and the strangely named Territory Barbeque and Records) have all opened in the past year. There is a really positive vibe emanating from the record shops.

Writing 'Last Shop Standing' has shown me is that the public love record shops and wish to support them. I would like to think my little book, originally written to highlight the plight faced by the UK record shops, has contributed to the feel good factor. The biggest factor in confirming that record shops have a future is an event started in the USA in 2008. Record Store Day has done more than anything to raise the profile of the great independent record shops of the world. I find it hard to believe that an event first held in 2008 could have such a great impact in such a short time. I asked founder Michael Kurtz about the event's background and how they managed to get the record shops of the world to take part. Michael has had a great history in the business, having been a member of cult band 'Three Hits', who were signed to Sony back in 1987 and since they split has been involved in many projects that have benefited the independent record shops of the USA.

Here, in Michael's own words, is the story of Record Store Day – how a little idea has developed into one of the most important dates in the music calendar:

'Record Store Day was originally pitched to me as an idea by Chris Brown (one of the guys who runs Bull Moose out of Portland, Maine. Bull Moose is the largest retailer of new and second hand music, movies and video games in Maine and Seacoast New Hampshire with 10 stores, employing over 100 people. Chris had observed how the comic book industry ran an event called Free Comic Day here in the USA and suggested that we organize a similar event for independently owned record stores. I run an organization called the Music Monitor Network. MMN is now the largest of the indie coalitions in the US and Canada. Part of my job is bringing together indie retail stores for an annual event called Noise In the Basement, held in Baltimore. At the 2008 event I posed the idea for Record Store Day to folks in my group, as well as to Newbury Comics, Criminal Records, and the Coalition of Independent Music Stores. At the time everyone was grousing about all the negative press on record stores and how, even though there had been a good deal of expansion in our world over the past few years, everything that was reported about record stores in the media was bad. Record Store Day would simply be an excuse to throw a party for ourselves and the artists we love, as well as get the real story on record stores out to the media. Chris originally pitched the idea of Record Store Day, which I took to some of the other great indie stores in the country as well as to the Coalition of Independent Music Stores and the Alliance of Music Stores (two noteworthy indie coalitions). After getting the stores on board, I felt that the best way to see if the idea had legs was to see if the artists themselves would support us. Paul McCartney had recently released "Memory Almost Full," and had celebrated its release with an intimate in-store event at Amoeba Records, in Los Angeles, (with Ringo in the audience!). Shooting for the stars I reached out to the Hear Music/Concord label (owned by TV producer, and huge music fan Norman Lear). I asked them if they would alert Paul to what we were doing with Record

Store Day and see if Paul would give us a word of support. I was stunned when an email from Paul appeared in my inbox saying "There's nothing as glamorous to me as a record store. When I recently played Amoeba in LA, I realized what fantastic memories such a collection of music brings back when you see it all in one place. This is why I'm more than happy to support Record Store Day and I hope that these kinds of stores will be there for us all for many years to come. Cheers!" Almost all of the folks who run record stores grew up with the Beatles so getting a note from Paul gave us the strength to say "Yes, we are pretty cool. We can do this!" From there the messages started cascading in from the likes of Chuck Berry, Mike Patton, Tom Waits, Nick Hornby and Cameron Crowe, amongst many others. I then took the message of Record Store Day to Mike Sherwood at Warner Bros and to Marc Reiter who was based at a management firm called Q Prime to see if Metallica would get involved in their hometown of San Francisco. One of the most exciting days of my life was getting the call from Mike saying that the band loved record stores and the idea of Record Store Day so they would help launch it at Rasputin in their hometown of San Francisco. Having Metallica participate was especially gratifying to me as I always thought Lars Ulrich got a raw deal from the media for having the audacity to speak up about not embracing peer-to-peer networks because he thought Metallica, along with other artists, should be paid for their work. What a concept! Anyway, Metallica ended up being incredibly nice to work with and they treated their fans like royalty insisting that they be given time to meet and talk with each and every one of them circling and fanning out from the store for what seemed like miles. It was, as Lou Reed, once sang, a "perfect day,"

Others joined in like Steve Earle who performed at Manifest Discs in Charlotte, NC and Panic at the Disco played at Waterloo Records in Austin, TX. Pretty much all the major labels and distribution companies embraced the idea and created wonderful promotional/collectible pieces like vinyl LPs and 7" singles to give out freely to music fans on the day. We even had various commercial products made for us by artists like REM, Stephen Malkmus, Built To Spill, Death Cab For Cutie, and Jason Mraz. A group of about 500 or so stores in the USA jumped into the fray and before we knew it the news media was reporting our positive story pretty much everywhere from the NY Times to the BBC to CNN. This was our beginning.

2009 was our second year for Record Store Day and I don't think anyone was prepared for what took place, or how exciting it would be. The labels and distributors showed record stores a massive amount of love and created close to 100 commercial pieces made specifically for Record Store Day and independent record stores. We had Radiohead, The Flaming Lips, Wilco, The Smiths, Iggy Pop and the Stooges, Iron and Wine, Tom Waits, Bruce Springsteen, Sonic Youth, Leonard Cohen, The Killers, Bob Dylan, Slayer, Dead Weather and The Black Kids involved in one way or another. Apple Records even gave the stores beautiful hand numbered Beatles' lithographs. Jeff Tweedy from Wilco issued a statement saying, "My introduction to a lot of great music and to the music business came from hanging around and eventually working at independent record stores... It's the life I know. Nothing beats browsing in your favourite store, listening to music, finding something new or old that you've been searching for, being ignored by the store clerks, all that. Without these stores, there's just no way Wilco would still be around. They've been there with us from the very beginning, through thick and thin. Even if I wasn't in a band, I'd still support Record Store Day." With artist statements like Jeff's coming out with regularity and a press release from NYC Mayor Michael Bloomberg declaring Record Store Day as an officially recognized day by the city of New York, media coverage on Record Store Day began to build. By the time the day hit, Record Store Day reached the number 5 Google news item of the day, ranking #34 as the most googled term of the day. 10% of all tweets for that day were about Record Store Day, and our story went worldwide. The result was the creation of a new event that hundreds of both established and developing artists embraced, including Ani DiFranco, Wilco, Disturbed, Erykah Badu, The Eagles of Death Metal, Talib Kweli, the Silversun Pickups, Chris Cornell, Ashford & Simpson and so on. Record Store Day now brings even more people through the doors than Christmas.

The dark side of Record Store Day was having a few embittered indie stores attack the organizers of Record Store Day. This was a bit of a shocker, but as I reached out to each of the stores to work with them so that they could fully understand what we were doing, everything came together. For the most part, the American indie record store community is fully now behind Record Store Day so all of the hard work was worth it and we accomplished what we set out to do.

The bad press, paranoia and the weirdness has gone, replaced by innovation fuelled by local community spirit. It's the essence of rock n' roll. You could see this in the indie record store that Record Store Day erected on site with Zia Records (out of Arizona) at the Coachella Music Festival in California. Over 80 bands stepped in to participate and meet fans and over 30% of everything sold was on vinyl. It was a huge success allowing us to take our story directly to the music fans at arguably the world's coolest three-day music festival. Progress in rolling out Record Store Day internationally has gone well with over 300 stores joining in from around the world. Our main task now is working to help international stores get commercial pieces made for Record Store Day in their respective countries so that Record Store Day can continue to grow and strengthen local record stores everywhere.'

Michael Kurtz

Everybody involved in Record Store Day can be proud of their efforts. It has focused so much positive media attention on an industry so many of us love. Record Store Day is now a brilliant global event. Why can't every day be like this for independent record shops? How can it be that only one day a year record shops are offered this exclusive product by record companies? They are missing a golden opportunity to encourage people into shops where new music and local bands are supported. Without independent record shops the music scene stagnates.

If only the record companies were prepared to help the record shops by releasing CDs throughout the year with exclusive bonus tracks not available online. This would encourage fans to visit the shops.

During my tour of the UK to write 'Last Shop Standing' I drove 2,750 miles visiting record shops. As I sit here with my bottle of red wine thinking about how to end this book, I raise my glass to all the great characters throughout the world who run record shops, providing a fantastic service bringing great music and a lot of pleasure to music fans everywhere.

Speak to your grandparents and they will tell you the High Street of their childhood contained stamp shops, coin shops and candlestick shops. Who remembers them now? Don't let record shops go the same way. Who knows, one MD of a major record company might even say 'I too love record shops and my company is going to support them every day of the year!' Well, we can all dream.

Check out your local record shop. Use it or lose it.

Artist Quotes about record shops and Record Store Day:

Paul McCartney
There's nothing as glamorous to me as a record store. When I recently played Amoeba in LA, I realised what fantastic memories such a collection of music brings back when you see it all in one place. This is why I'm more than happy to support Record Store Day and I hope that these stores will be there for us all for many years to come. Cheers!

Bruce Springsteen
"I buy CDs all the time. I'll go into a record store and just buy $500 worth of CDs. I will! I am single-handedly supporting what's left of the record business.

I hate to see record stores disappear and I'm old-school in that I think you should pay for your music. But what my kids do is download a lot of things, pay for them and then if they love something, they'll get the CD. That may be the future."

Tom Waits
"Folks who work here are professors. Don't replace all the knowers with guessers. Keep 'em open, they're the ears of the town"

Jack White
"I think it's high time the mentors, big brothers, big sisters, parents, guardians, and neighborhood ne'er do wells, start taking younger people who look up to them to a real record store and show them what an important part of life music really is. I trust no one who hasn't time for music. What a shame to leave a child, or worse, a generation orphaned from one of life's great beauties. To the record stores, artists, labels, dj's and journalists; we're all in this together. Show respect for the tangible music that you've dedicated your careers and lives to and stop it becoming nothing more than disposable digital data."

Robyn Hitchcock
Records used to mean vinyl, then cassettes, then CDs and now downloads. Like currency, they got smaller and are now almost invisible. The record stores were a great network where music fans could listen to what was out there without necessarily having to buy it. But if they did, they came away with a black disc embedded with grooves, mostly enshrined in a cardboard sleeve that contained vital additions to the music inside. These sacred objects (and their slightly less sacred descen-

dants, the tape and the compact disc) were the closest you could get to the act itself: like portable shrines with holy relics.

Scott McCaughey, Peter Buck and Bill Rieflin, who comprise the Venus 3, my American band, all heard my songs for the first time in the record stores where they worked. It's probable they also first heard each other's music like that, too. I have fond memories of hanging out in US record shops, particularly the Used Record Shoppe in the Sunset district of San Francisco. Shops like Let It Be in Minneapolis, Bill's in Dallas, Tower on 4th & Broadway, Easy Street in Seattle, Criminal in Atlanta, Amoeba in LA and many others gave us a platform to perform live on tour and unfailingly stocked our records (Robyn Hitchcock & the Egyptians, my solo work, The Soft Boys and now me & the Venus 3) where the larger chains found us unprofitable. Independent record stores gave my career a solid base.

John Mellencamp
"Immersing yourself in the environment of a real record store where music is celebrated and cherished adds real value to the experience of buying music. In some ways, that retail experience is as important as the music."

Joe Satriani
"Independent record stores are a vital source of the ever-changing cool. They respond to the street faster than the chains can. They help us tele-graph to each other what's "now" and what's not, what we should be telling our friends and neighbors about and what's about to take off, or, no longer hot. Musical trends are confirmed at the local independent record store by you and me. Hanging out, listening to something you've never heard before, being enlightened by the staff, getting into some-thing new, finding that old recording you've been searching for, having your local band's newest offering stocked right next to major label stuff, it all happens at the local indie shop. Why would we want to do away with all that?"

Tim Rice-Oxley (Keane)
"Growing up in the UK I've loved and lost a series of great independent record stores over the last twenty years. These days I go into David's Music in Letchworth whenever I can and always leave with a swag bag full of vinyl and CDs. I especially love flipping through endless boxes of musty second-hand vinyl, picking out things I'd never have gone looking for. I've discovered loads of incredible music that way. It's a way of

shopping for records that is discouraged by the layout of huge chain record stores and totally denied by the dreaded supermarkets. So here's to the indie stores – beacons of diversity, discovery and passion in an ever more homogenised world."

James Morrison
"Record stores have a magic about them that's totally unique. They are places where you can come across music and culture that you're not open to in any other way, often by accident. I love that hands-on experience of browsing and buying music, so I wish the Record Store Day every success."

Peter Gabriel
"I was introduced to lots of great music through my local record store. It was a place where people knew music and they knew me and could make great suggestions and discoveries. Whether it is in the physical world or on-line, the value of a great and knowledgeable record store has not gone away."

David and Don Was
"In the beginning was the record store, more like a modern-day temple with its attendant priesthood and initiates, a holy repository of the culture's most sacred beats and rhymes. By comparison, the internet is a clean room in a hospital – it lacks the funk and feeling of a place with floors and ceilings and racks full of soul-stirring goodness. May they persist till someone turns the lights out on this small planet! Here's to the true believers – keep the faith, brothers and sisters!"

Norah Jones
"It's important to keep indie record stores alive because their unique environments introduce music lovers to things in a very personal way."

Wayne Coyne (The Flaming Lips)
"The 'cool' record store. It is where you can talk to people who are like you. They look like you, think like you and, most tellingly like the same music as you – the only comparable experience these days would probably be an art museum – an actual place where you can stand and simply be surrounded by your heroes."

Henry Rollins
"I have watched independent record stores evaporate all over America and Europe. That's why I go into as many as I can and buy records whenever

possible. If we lose the independent record store, we lose big. Every time you buy your records at one of these places, it's a blow to the empire."

Chuck Berry
"Music is an important part of our culture and record stores play a vital part in keeping the power of music alive."

Damon Albarn
"My local independent record shop (Honest Jons) is a library, where you can go to listen to music, learn about it, exchange ideas about it and be inspired by it. I think independent record shops will outlive the music industry as we know it because long term their value to people is far greater, because even in our era of file-sharing and blogs, you can't replace the actual look on someone's face when they are playing something they really rate and think you should listen to it too. It's special."

Joan Jett
"The indie record stores are the backbone of the recorded music culture. It's where we go to network, browse around and find new songs to love. The stores whose owners and staff live for music have spread the word about exciting new things faster and with more essence than either radio or the press. Any artist that doesn't support the wonderful ma and pa record stores across America is contributing to our own extinction."

Ziggy Marley
"Record stores keep the human social contact alive and bring people together. Without the independent record stores the community breaks down with everyone sitting in front of their computers"

Regina Spektor
"I just really love anything that's not faceless, where people know each other and work together to build, like, a community. People that work there know their stuff; they're not coming in today to sell music and tomorrow to sell TVs and the next day to sell whatever. Somebody can come in and say, "I want somebody who plays piano music" or something and somebody will actually tell them to listen to my record and they'll play it in the store for them and they'll talk about it. You can connect in some way with somebody who's doing something that they love. It is important to have something that is done out of true love for new music and is being welcomed into the world. People should go to their indie record store and find out what is happening."

Sam Phillips (A&R / producer for Elvis Presley, Johnny Cash, Carl Perkins, and many others

"There would be no Elvis, no Johnny Cash, no B.B King, no Roscoe Gordon, no Carl Perkins, no Jerry Lee Lewis or Roy Orbison. I can just tell you. We owe all of that to the independents and the independent people that work so hard for us to have something that could be accepted through their efforts, hard work and desire to keep a personal feeling in every record."

Ian Gillan (Deep Purple)

"Buy real records in real shops, or I'll come round your house and scream at your mother."

KT Tunstall

"Independent record stores are like casinos where you put down your money and you always win. How amazing to discover gems you didn't know about, to meet someone more passionate than you are and to feel at home in a place you may never have been to before. I'm convinced they will never lose their place – Long may they rule."

Steve Wilson (Porcupine Trees)

"Independent retail has always been the backbone of Porcupine Tree's exposure in the USA and from the very beginning; the band was proactive in trying to associate with as many indie retail stores as possible. We've always respected the aesthetics of the "pure" record store and the importance of knowledgeable staff who can recommend great stuff to you because they truly love music, know what they're talking about, and are not selling vacuum cleaners or washer/dryers in the next section over. Porcupine Tree would never have reached its level of retail exposure without the indie stores; we'll always stand with them."

DJ Jazzy Jeff

"The Independent Record Store is the reason why I still do music. It seems like they're the only ones who really care about the real music lovers. We need them...they're our balance to all of the music we are forced to listen to...they're the only ones that may still suggest something new and fresh instead of just what's popular."

Nick Hornby

"Yes, yes, I know. It's easier to download music and probably cheaper. But what's playing on your favourite download store when you walk into it? Nothing, that's what. Who are you going to meet in there?

Nobody. Where are the notice boards offering flatshares and vacant slots in bands destined for superstardom? Who's going to tell you to stop listening to that and start listening to this? Go ahead and save yourself a couple of quid. The saving will cost you a career, a set of cool friends, musical taste and, eventually, your soul. Record stores can't save your life, but they can give you a better one."

Paul Quirk (Chairman of ERA Entertainment Retail Association UK)
It may be apocryphal, but the story goes that in the first 12 months after the launch of the talking pictures in the US, 50,000 piano players lost their jobs. Tinkling along while a scratchy, black and white Buster Keaton, Louise Brooks or Lillian Gish emoted wordlessly on the silver screen was a job rendered redundant by technology.

In some ways independent record shop owners — and I was one myself — are the Noughties equivalent of those piano players. In a world of on-demand streaming (Spotify) and digital downloads (iTunes), when supermarkets have decided to sell CDs at rock-bottom prices alongside the washing powder and baked beans and when you can freely — though often illegally — download the entire history of popular music at the click of the mouse, it is really no wonder that smaller shops have increasingly found it difficult to compete. In that sense Last Shop Standing is a book tinged with sadness, a love letter to a world fast-disappearing. On the other hand, by identifying some of those stores who even now are prospering, the book gives cause for optimism that while the indie stores of the future will be fewer in number, they will be truly great stores.

No amount of technology can ever replace the feel, the atmosphere, the community — and sometimes the smell! — of a committed, customer-focused store run by real music fans. Even now we are seeing some clear indications of a renewed sense of purpose in the indie sector. Initiatives like Record Store Day and indications of real revival of interest in limited editions and vinyl, a format unlikely ever to be re-adopted by supermarkets for instance, give real cause for optimism that those "last shops standing" have a real chance of making it through.

Graham Jones has cast a long-overdue spotlight on the culture and history of Britain's independent record stores. I whole heartedly commend this book and just wish that I was still one of those record stores out there on the front line.

Here is a listing of great record shops in the world. The vast majority will be taking part in Record Store Day. Get in touch with your nearest store.

AUSTRALIA

Ace Music	Sydney	www.acemusic.net.au
Arkitekt Records	Melbourne	www.arkitektrecords.com/
The Basement Discs	Melbourne	www.basementdiscs.com.au/
Beatdisc Records	Parramatta	www.beatdisc.com.au/
Collectors Corner	Melbourne	www.brella.org/collectors/
Egg Records	Sydney	www.eggrecords.com/
Egg Records	Brisbane	www.eggrecords.com/
Elevator Music	Adelaide	
Greville Records	Melbourne	www.grevillerecords.com.au/
HearNow	Melbourne	www.hearnow.net.au/
Hum on King	Newtown	www.hum.com.au/
Hum on Oxford	Daringhurst	www.hum.com.au/
Licorice Pie Records	Melbourne	
Mojo Music	Sydney	www.mojomusic.com.au/
Music Shop Wooden	Canberra	www.musicshop.com.au/
Music Shop	Bondi Junction	www.musicshop.com.au/
Northside Records	Fitzroy	www.northsiderecords.com.au/
Polyester Records	Melbourne	www.polyesterrecords.com/
Polyester Records	Fitzroy	www.polyesterrecords.com/
Pure Pop Records	St Kilda	www.purepop.com.au/
Radical Records	Dandenong	www.radicalrecords.com.au/
Rare Records	Melbourne	
Record Collector's Corner	Albury	www.brella.org/collectors/
Record Paradise	St Kilda	
Redback Music	Wollongong	www.redbackmusic.com.au/
Red Eye Records	Sydney	www.redeye.com.au/
Reload Records	Rosebud	www.reloadrecords.com.au/
Red Eye Records	Sydney, N.S.W.	www.redeye.com.au/
Repressed Records	Sydney	www.repressedrecords.com/
Reload Records	Sydney	www.reloadrecords.com.au/
Rockaway Records	Brisbane	www.rockaway.com.au/
Round & Round Records	Brunswick	
The Rock Factory	Wollongong	
Sunflower Music	Broadbeach	
S.W.O.T (Sense Working Over Time) Gallery	Apollo Bay	
Squirrell Gripp Records	Adelaide	www.vinylpusher.net/
The Music Shop – Fortitude Valley	Fortitude Valley	www.musicshop.com.au/
The Music Shop – Bondi Junction	Bondi Junction	www.musicshop.com.au/
The Music Shop – Belconnen	Canberra	www.musicshop.com.au/
The Music Shop Burleigh	Burleigh Head	www.musicshop.com.au/
The Music Shop Parramatta	Parramatta	www.musicshop.com.au/
Utopia Records	Sydney	www.utopia.com.au/
Wow Music	Sydney	

BELGIUM

JJ Records	Leuven	www.jjrecords.com/
Metalzone	Malle	www.metalzone.be/
Vynilla	Gent	www.vynilla.be/

CANADA

Atomix Records	St. Catharine's	www.atomixrecords.com/
Argy's Collectables	Winnipeg	www.argy.ca/
Audiopile	Vancouver	www.audiopile.com/
Aux 33 Tours	Montreal	www.aux33tours.com/
The Beatmerchant	Richmond	www.beatmerchant.com/
Beatnick Music	Montreal	www.beatnickmusic.com
Blackbyrd	Edmonton	www.blackbyrd.ca/
Aux 33 Tours	Montreal	www.aux33tours.com/
Bluestreak Records	Peterborough	
Compact Music	Ottawa	www.compactmusic.ca/
CD Warehouse	Nepean	www.cdwarehouse.ca/
Criminal Records	Toronto	www.crimedoesntpay.ca/
Ditch Records & CDs	Victoria	www.ditchrecords.com/
Dandelion Records	Vancouver	www.dandelionrecords.ca/
Dixie Records	Mississauga	
Dr. Disc	Hamilton	
Encore Records	Ottawa	www.endhits.ca/
End Hits	Hamilton	
Encore Records	Kitchener	
Freecloud Records	Edmonton	www.freecloud.ca/
FrÈquences Le Disquaire	Saint-Hyacinthe	www.frequencesledisquaire.com/
Grooves	London	
Into The Music	Winnipeg	www.intothemusic.ca/
Le Pick Up	Montreal	
Listen Records & CDs	Edmonton	www.listenrecords.net/
Melodiya Records	Calgary	www.melodiyarecords.ca/
Meow Records	Prince George	www.meowrecords.ca/
Neptoon Records	Vancouver	www.neptoon.com/
Penguin Music	Toronto	www.penguinmusic.com/
Planet of Sound	Winnipeg	www.planetofsound.ca/
Records on Wheels	Sudbury	
Records on Wheels	Dundas	
Ric's Recollections	Vancouver	www.redcat.ca/
Red Cat Records	Mississauga	www.ricrec.com/
Salt Spring Sound	Salt Spring	www.bookbill.com/sss.html
Scratch Records	Vancouver	www.scratchrecords.com/
Sonic Boom Records	Toronto	www.sonicboommusic.com/
Sound Connection	Edmonton	
Soundscapes	Toronto	www.soundscapesmusic.com/
Speed City Records	London	www.speedcityrecords.com/
Spinners Sound Centre	Kamloops	
Spin-It Records	Moncton	
Star Records	Oshawa	
Sunrise Records	Scarborough	www.sunriserecords.com/

Taz Records	Halifax	www.tazrecords.com/
The Danger Room	Regina	
The Inner Sleeve	Calgary	www.theinnersleeve.com/
The Record Works	Woodstock	www.therecordworks.com/
Vinyl Encore Records	Mill Bay	www.vinylencore.com/
Vertigo Records	Ottawa	www.vertigorecords.ca/
Vinyl Records	Vancouver	www.vinylrecords.ca/
Zulu Records	Vancouver	www.zulurecords.com/

DENMARK
Repo Man Records	Copenhagen	
Moby Disc Records	Odense S	www.mobydisc.dk/

FRANCE
Alain Solivaret	Saint Priest	
Sasprodiex	Paris	www.sasprodiex.com
Groove Store	Paris	www.groove-store.com/

GERMANY
Asphalt Tango	Berlin	
Fatplastics	Jena	www.fatplastics.com/
Groove Attack Recordstore	Cologne	www.grooveattackrecordstore.com/
Mr Dead & Mrs Free	Berlin	www.deadandfree.com/
HHV.DE Selected Store	Berlin	www.hhv.de/
Musikgarage Bensheim	Bensheim	www.musikgarage.de/
Optimal Records Store	Baveria	www.optimal-records.de/
Parallel Schallplatten	Cologne	www.parallel-schallplatten.de/
Resonanz Schallplatten	Munchen	www.resonanz-schallplatten.de/
Underdog Recordstore	Koeln	www.underdogrecordstore.de/
Woodstock Record Store	Erfurt	www.woodstock-ef.de/

GREECE
Mister CD	Chakidaa	
Vinyl Kiosk	Athens	www.vinylkiosk.com/

HONG KONG
White Noise Records	Causeway Bay	www.whitenoiserecords.org/

IRELAND
Beatfinder Records	Dublin	www.beatfinderrecords.com/
BPM Records	Waterford	www.bpmrecords.ie/
City Discs	Dublin	
Cooldiscs Music	Derry	www.cooldiscsmusic.com/
e2 Music	Mullingar	www.e2music.ie/
e2 Music	Navan	
Freebird Records	Dublin	
Musicmaster	Omagh	www.irishmusicmaster.co.uk/
Plugd Records	Cork City	
Road Records	Dublin	www.roadrecs.com/
Tower Records	Dublin	www.towerrecords.ie/

Rollercoaster Music	Kilkenny	
Zhivago	Galway	

ISRAEL

Third Ear Records	Tel Aviv	www.third-ear.com/

ITALY

1st Pop Vinyl & CDs	Verona	www.1stpop.net/
Always CD	Ferrara	www.leadingedgemusic.com.au/ warriewood
Carillon Dischi	Monza	
Caru' Dischi	Gallargate	www.caru.com/
Casa del Disco di Galletti	Faenza	
Casa del disco	Varese	www.musictownsa.com/
Casa Musicale Niccoli	Prato	www.dischiniccoli.it/
Cigna Dischi dal 1940	Biella	www.italianmusicstore.com/
Disclan	Salerno	
Disco Club	Genova	www.discoclub65.it/
Discoteca Laziale	Rome	www.discotecalaziale.com/
Discopiu	Roma	
Discovalante	Via Principi Di	
Diskotic	Genova	www.diskotic.com/
DJ Land	Mottola Ta	
Dodicilune Shop	Lecce	www.dodiciluneshop.com/
Doodah	Salerno	www.rarerecords.com.au/
Exit Music	Savigliano	www.hellnation.it/
Hellnation Record Store	Rome	
Jumpin Jack	Torri di Quartesolo	
Jungle Records	Conegliano	www.mixeduprecords.com/
Kandinski	Brescia	
Les Yper Sound	Via Rossini	www.lysrecords.com/
Mono Music Shop	Cagliari	www.monomusic.com/
Moses Vibes Reggae Store	Lecce	www.monomusic.com/
Melody Maker	Legnano	
Musicando	Vimercarte	www.musicando.eu/
Music Box Records	Perugia	
Musica Musica	Perugia	
Musicland Records	Vasto	www.musiclandrecords.com/
Musicland Records	San Salvo	
Musicomania	Valdarno	www.musicomania.eu/
Musis Store Genova	Genoa	www.topten.it/
New Record	Bari	
Nordovest	Frosinone	www.nordovestrock.splinder.com/
One Love Music Corner	Roma	www.onelovehp.com/
Pat Record	Castellamonte	www.patrec.gemm.com/
Psycho	Milano	
Record Runners	Varese	www.recordrunners.com/
Rock & Folk	Torino	www.rockandfolk.com/
Sanantonio42 Records Shop	Pisa	www.sanantonio42.it/
Sonicrocket – cd4sale	Bologna	

Transylvania Dischi	Jesi	
Vinyl Refresh	Rome	
Vieri Dischi	Arezzo	
Vi-R-Us Beatquarter	Pescara	
8 Ball Records	Reggio Emllia	www.8ballrecords.it/

JAPAN

45Tours	Fukuoka	www.45tours.org/
Beavers Books	Sapporo	www.bvsbooks.com/
Beginners Records	Kumamoto	www.begireco.sakura.ne.jp/
Big Beat Record	Kawasaki	
Bout Records	Nagoya	www.boutrecords.com/
Cocobeat Records	Fukushima	www.cocobeat-records.com/
Coconuts Disk	Tokyo	www.coconutsdisk.com/kichijoji
Cornershop	Shizuoka	www.cornershoprecords.com/
Disc Shop Zero	Tokyo	www.discshopzero.com/
Disk Note Morioka	Morioka	www.morioka-record.com/
Disk Union	Tokyo	www.diskunion.co.jp/
Flake Records	Osaka	www.flakerecords.com/
Ganban	Tokyo	www.ganban.net/
Greenhouse Records	Okayama	www.greenhouse-records.jp/
Jet Set	Kyoto	www.jetsetreocrds.net/
Kent Record	Hamamatsu	www.kentjapan.com/house/index. html
Konpaku Dou	Yokkaichi	www.conpakudou.jp/
Llamalabo Record	Kyoto	
Lot Record	Hatogaya	www.ameblo.jp/lotrecord
Mezurashiya	Tokyo	www.10.ocn.nc.jp/%7Emezurasi/
More Music	Matsuyama	www.moremusic.co.jp/
Music First	Nagoya	www.musicfirst.biz/index.html
Musique69	Osaka-city	www.musique69.com/
Oasis Records	Tokyo	www.oasisstore.jp/
Ondoko	Sapporo	www.ondoko.jp/top.shtml
Outside Records	Okazaki	
Panda Panda Records	Osaka	www.pandapandarecords.com/
Parks Records	Fukuoka	www.parks-records.com/
Penny Lane	Komaki	www.komaki-pennylane.net/
Pet Sounds	Tokyo	www.petsounds.co.jp/
Reco Fan	Tokyo	www.recofan.co.jp/
Record Shop Disco	Tokyo	www.koiwa-disco.com/
Record-Ya Kurashiki	Kurasahiki	www.ameblo.jp/recordya
Records-Records	Sapporo	www.records-records.co.jp/
Reggae Music Records	Sapporo	www.rmrrmr.blog39.fc2.com/
Snow Records Japan	Osaka	www.snowrecords.co.jp/
Sunny Boy	Nagasaki	
Takechas Record	Sapporo	
Thirty Three	Fukuoka	www.thirty-three.org/
Time Bomb Records	Osaka	www.timebomb.co.jp/
Used Shop Seconds	Sapporo	www.seconds.main.jp/

Weird Meddle Record	Sapporo	www.d.hatena.ne.jp/meddle/

NETHERLANDS

Concerto	Amsterdam	www.concertomania.nl/
Plato	Utretch	www.platomania.nl/
La La Land Music	Den Haag	www.lalalandmusic.nl/
Plato Apeldoorn	Apeldoorn	www.platomania.nl/
Plato Deventer	Deventer	www.platomania.nl/
Plato Enschede	Enschede	www.platomania.nl/
Plato Groningen	Groningen	www.platomania.nl/
Plato Leiden	Leiden	www.platomania.nl/
Plato Rotterdam	Rotterdam	www.platomania.nl/
Plato Zwolle	Zwolle	www.platomania.nl/
Rush Hour records	Amsterdam	www.rushhourmusic.com/
Sounds Recordshop BV	Venio	www.sounds-venlo.nl/
Velvet Music Breda	Breda	www.velvetmusic.nl/

NEW ZEALAND

Beat Merchants	Auckland	
Conch Records	Auckland	www.conch.co.nz/
Music Oasis	Waihi	www.musicoasis.co.nz/
Slow Boat Records	Wellington	www.slowboatrecords.co.nz/
Real Groovy	Auckland	www.realgroovy.co.nz/
Real Groovy	Christchurch	

SWEDEN

Bengans	Gothenburg	www.bengans.se/
Bengans	Stockholm	
Dotshop	Fristad	www.dotshop.se/
Folk Â Rock	Malmo	www.folkarock.se/
Pet Sounds Records	Stockholm	www.petsounds.se/
Record Hunter	Stockholm	www.recordhunter.se/
Sound Pollution	Stockholm	www.soundpollution.se/
Skivlagret	Linkoping	www.skivlagret.se/
The Beat Goes On	Stockholm	www.beatgoeson.se/
Repulsive Records	Stockholm	www.repulsive.se/
Vinylium	Gothenburg	www.vinylium.se/
We Love Music	Stockholm	www.welovemusic.se/

UNITED KINGDOM

101 Collectors Records	Farnham	www.101collectorsrecords.co.uk
2 Funky	Leicester	www.2-funky.co.uk
A&A	Congleton	www.aamusic.co.uk
Aardvark	Paignton	
Abergavenny Music	Abergavenny	www.abergavennymusic.com
Acorn Music	Yeovil	www.acornmusic.co.uk
Action	Preston	www.actionrecords.co.uk
Action Replay	Windermere	

Adrian's	Wickford	www.adrians.co.uk/
All Ages Music	London	www.allagesrecords.com/
Andy's Records	Aberystwyth	www.andys-records.co.uk
Ape	Brighton	
Apollo Music	Paisley	
Avalanche Records	Glasgow	www.avalancheglasgow.co.uk
AW Jazz	Haverfordwest	
Avalanche Records	Edinburgh	www.avalancherecords.co.uk
Backtrax	Totnes	
Badlands Records	Cheltenham	www.badlands.co.uk
Bakewell Bookshop	Bakewell	www.bakewellbookshop.co.uk
Banquet Records	Kingston	www.banquetrecords.com
Ben's Collectors	Guildford	www.bensrecords.com
Beatin Rhythm	Manchester	www.beatinrhythm.com
Better Leisure	Great Yarmouth	
Blackcat Records	Taunton	www.blackcat-records.co.uk
BM Soho	London	www.bm-soho.com
Borderline	Brighton	
Bridport Music	Bridport	www.bridportmusic.co.uk
Brill	London	www.musiccoffeebagels.com
Broad Street Jazz	Bath	
Bruce Miller	Aberdeen	www.brucemillers.co.uk
Cavern Records	London	
CD Shop	Eastcote	
Chalkys	Banbury	www.chalkys.com
Changing World	Glastonbury	www.fatplastics.com
Clampdown Records	Manchester	www.clampdownrecords.com
Clerkenwell Music	London	www.clerkenwellmusic.co.uk
Clives Records	Lerwick	
Cob Records	Bangor	www.cobrecordsbangor.com
Cob Records	Porthmadog	www.cobrecords.com
Coda Music On The Mound	Edinburgh	www.coda-music.com
Compact	Sudbury	
Compact	Sevenoaks	www.bluesandjazz.co.uk
Concorde	Perth	www.concordemusic.com
Crash Records	Leeds	www.crashrecords.co.uk
Counter Culture	High Wycombe	
Cruisin'	Welling	
Dada	Chiswick	
Dales Records	Tenby	
David's Music	Letchworth	www.davids-music.co.uk
Derricks	Swansea	www.derricksmusic.co.uk
Disc Discovery	Hull	
Diskery	Birmingham	
Diverse Music	Newport	www.diverserecords.com
Drift	Totnes	www.driftrecordshop.com
Duck Son & Pinker	Bath	
Dyskworld	Scarborough	
Eastern Block	Manchester	
Endless Music	Manchester	www.endlessmusic.co.uk

Fine	Hove	
Fives Records	Leigh On Sea	www.fives-records.co.uk
Flashback	London	www.flashback.co.uk
Focus Sounds	Waterlooville	
Folk Devils	Whitby	www.folkdevils.co.uk
Gatefield Sounds	Whitstable	
Gojo	Hexham	
Grainger CD	Newcastle	
Groove	Orkney	www.orkneymusic.co.uk
Hellraiser Records	Leeds	
Herrick Watson Ltd.	Skegness	www.herrickwatson.co.uk
Honest Jon's	London	www.honestjons.com
Hudson's	Chesterfield	
If Music	London	www.ifmusic.co.uk
Imperial Music	Inverness	
Intoxica	London	www.intoxica.co.uk
Jam	Falmouth	www.jamrecords.co.uk
JG Windows Ltd	Newcastle	www.jgwindows.com
Jumbo Records	Leeds	www.jumborecords.co.uk
Kaleidoscope	St Helens	
Kanes Records	Stroud	www.kanesrecords.com/
King Bee	Manchester	
Les Aldrich	London	www.lesaldrich.co.uk
Lewks	Downham Market	www.lewks.co.uk/
Malcolm's Musicland	Chorley	
Martian	Exeter	www.martianrecords.co.uk/
Mixed Up Records	Glasgow	
Monorail	Glasgow	
Morning After Music	Machlynlleth	
Movie Mix	Ilfracombe	
Muse Music	Hebdon Bridge	
Musical Box	Liverpool	
Music Cellar	Preston	
Music Mania	Stoke-on-Trent	www.musicmaniauk.com/
Music Memorabilia	Alfriston	www.music-memorabilia-shop.com
Music Master	Omagh	
Nevermind	Boston	
News From Nowhere	Liverpool	www.newsfromnowhere.org.uk/
Number 19	Guernsey	
Octave	Lewes	
Off The Beaten Tracks	Louth	
One Up	Aberdeen	www.oneupmusic.com/
Phoenix Sound	Newton Abbot	www.cdblam.co.uk/
Phonica Records	London	www.phonicarecords.com/
Piccadilly Records	Manchester	www.piccadillyrecords.com/
Polar Bear	Birmingham	
Powerplay	Hereford	www.powerplaydirect.com
Prelude	Norwich	www.preluderecords.co.uk
Presto	Leamington Spa	www.prestoclassical.co.uk
Probe	Liverpool	www.probe-records.com

Pure Groove	London	www.puregroove.co.uk/
Rainbow	Welshpool	
Rapture	Evesham	
Rapture Entertainment	Witney	www.rapture-online.co.uk
Rebel Music	London	www.rebel-music.com/
Record Collector	Sheffield	
Record Corner	Godalming	www.therecordcorner.co.uk
Record Revivals	Scarborough	
Record Shak	Edinburgh	
Record Shop	Amersham	
Reflex	Newcastle	www.reflexcd.co.uk
Resident	Brighton	www.resident-music.com
Resurrection Records	London	www.resurrectionmusic.com
Rhythmic	Greenock	
Rise	Bristol	www.rise-music.co.uk
Rise	Cheltenham	www.rise-music.co.uk
Rock A Boom	Leicester	
Rock Hen's Coop	Okehampton	
Rooster Records	Exeter	
Rooted Records	Bristol	www.rootedrecords.co.uk/
Roots Records	Newcastle	www.rootstomusic.com/
Rounder Records	Brighton	www.rounderbrighton.co.uk
Rough Trade East	London	www.roughtrade.com/
Rough Trade West	London	www.roughtrade.com/
RPM Music	Newcastle	
Sister Ray	London	www.sisterray.co.uk
Skeleton	Birkenhead	
Sleeves	Kircaldy	
Slipped Discs	Carmarthen	
Slipped Discs	Billericay	www.slipped-discs.co.uk
Solo music	Barnstaple	www.solomusic.co.uk
Soul Brother Records	London	www.soulbrother.com/
Sound & Image	Chatham	www.soundandimagemusic.co.uk
Soundclash	Norwich	www.soundclash-records.co.uk/
Sound House	Deal	
Sound It Out Records	Stockton	www.sounditoutrecords.co.uk/
Sound Knowledge	Marlborough	
Sounds	Durham	www.soundsmusic.co.uk
Sounds Good	Cheltenham	
Sounds Interesting	Trowbridge	
Spillers Records	Cardiff	www.spillersrecords.co.uk/
Square Records	Wimborne	
Stamford Audio	Stamford	www.stamfordaudio.co.uk/
ST Records	Dudley	
Summit	Birmingham	
Tangled Parrot	Carmarthen	www.tangledparrot.com/
Tempest	Birmingham	www.temrec.com
Terminal	Haverfordwest	
Terry's	Pontypridd	www.vintagemusic.co.uk
The Collectors Room	Salisbury	

Last Shop Standing

The Heavy Sounds	Nottingham	www.theheavysounds.co.uk/
The Outback	Hereford	
Threshold	Cobham	
Townsend Records	Great Harwood	www.townsend-records.co.uk
Tor Records	Glastonbury	
Upbeat	Bude	
Vinyl Countdown	Ulverston	
Vibes Records	Bury	www.vibesrecords.co.uk
Vinyl Know How	London	www.knowhowrecords.co.uk
Vinyl Revival	Manchester	www.vinylrevivalmcr.com
Wall Of Sound	Huddersfield	www.wallofsound-records.com
Watermill	Aberfeldy	
Wee W.	Stornoway	
Wowie Zowie	Manchester	www.wowiezowie-online.com
X Records	Bolton	www.xrecords.co.uk

Recommended UK Second Hand Specialists

33 RPM	Romford	
Alans Record and CD Shop	East Finchley	
Astonishing Sounds	Burnley	
Better Daze	Leyburn	www.betterdaze.co.uk
Boiler Room Records	Poole	
Boogaloo on Broadway	Fulham	
Casbah Records	Greenwich	
Criminal Records	Huddersfield	
Grammar School Records	Rye	www.grammarschoolrecords.com
Groucho's	Dundee	
Helter Skelter Records	Chichester	
Media Mania	Berwick upon Tweed	
Midnight	Coventry	
Mister Tees	Kidderminster	
Mold Record Shop	Mold	
Music Nostalgia	Truro	www.musicnostalgia.co.uk
Pear Music Shop	Knaresborough	
Radar Records	Huddersfield	www.radarrecords.co.uk
Recollect Records	Rochester	
Records and Relics	Blackpool	
Rollin' Records	West Wickham	www.rollinrecordsuk.com
Rooster Records	Exeter	www.vinylera.co.uk
Rubber Soul Records	Stoke-On-Trent	
Second Sounds	Tunbridge Wells	www.camdenroad.co.uk
Select Sounds	Lincoln	
Shaking Street Gallery	London	
Sounds Original	Ealing	www.soundsoriginal.co.uk
The Record Shop	Cheltenham Spa	
The Rock Box	Camberley	www.rockbox.co.uk
Vinyl Exchange	Manchester	www.vinylexchange.co.uk
Wah Wah	Stockport	

USA

ALABAMA

CD Cellar	Anniston, AL	www.myspace.com/cdcellar01
Pegasus Records	Florence, AL	www.pegrecords.com
Vertical House	Huntsville, AL	www.theverticalhouse.com

ALASKA

Mammoth Music	Anchorage	www.mammothmusic.com

ARIZONA

Hoodlums Music and Movies	Tempe, AZ	www.hoodlumsmusic.com
Revolver Records	Phoenix, AZ	www.revolveraz.com
Rock It Man CDs &DVDs	Flagstaff, AZ	www.rockitmancds.com
Rockzone Records	Tempe, AZ	www.rockzonerecords.com
Stinkweeds	Phoenix, AZ	www.stinkweeds.com
Zia Records – Chandler	Chandler, AZ	www.ziarecords.com
Zia Records – Indian School	Phoenix, AZ	www.ziarecords.com
Zia Records – Oracle	Tucson, AZ	www.ziarecords.com
Zia Records – Speedway	Tucson, AZ	www.ziarecords.com
Zia Records – Tempe	Tempe, AZ	www.ziarecords.com
Zia Records – Thunderbird	Phoenix, AZ	www.ziarecords.com

ARKANSAS

Arkansas Record-CD Exchange	Little Rock, AR	www.arcd.com
Sound Warehouse	Fayetteville, AR	www.soundwarehouse.com

CALIFORNIA

1-2-3-4 Go! Records	Oakland, CA	www.1234gorecords.com
Amoeba Music	Hollywood, CA	www.amoeba.com
Amoeba Music	San Francisco, CA	www.amoeba.com
Aquarius Records	San Francisco, CA	www.aquariusrecords.org
Atomic Records	Burbank, CA	www.atomicrecordsla.com
Back Door Disc	Cotati, CA	www.backdoordisc.com
Backside Records	Burbank, CA	
Bedrock Music & Video	San Rafael, CA	www.bedrockmusicandvideo.org
Bombass Muzik	Los Angeles, CA	www.bombassmuzik.com
Boo Boo Records	San Luis Obispo, CA	www.booboorecords.com
Buffalo Records	Ventura, CA	www.buffalorecords.org
Cheap Thrills Records	San Luis Obispo, CA	www.cheapthrills.biz
Coachella Festival	Indio, CA	www.coachella.com
Creative Music Emporium	San Francisco, CA	www.creativemusicsf.com
CSL-California Sound & Lighting	San Diego, CA	www.calsound.com
Darkstar Records & Books	Bakersfield, CA	www.darkstarrecordsandbooks.com
Dimple Records (6)	Sacramento, CA	www.dimple.com
Disconnected Records	San Diego, CA	www.disconnectedrecords.com
Down Home Music	El Cerrito, CA	www.downhomemusic.com
Down Home Music	Berkeley, CA	www.downhomemusic.com
Dr Strange Records	Alta Loma, CA	www.rarepunk.com
Fabrik	San Diego, CA	

Fat Beats	Los Angeles, CA	www.fatbeats.com
Fingerprints	Long Beach, CA	www.fingerprintsmusic.com
Freakbeat Records	Sherman Oaks, CA	www.freakbeatrecords.com
Gearhead Records	Woodland, CA	www.gearheadrecords.com
Going Underground Records	Bakersfield, CA	
Groovetime Music Brokers	San Bernardino, CA	www.groovetime.com/
Headline Records	Los Angeles, CA	www.headlinerecords.com/
Last Record Store	Santa Rosa, CA	www.the-last-record-store.com/
Lou's Records	Encinitas, CA	www.lousrecords.com/
M-Theory	San Diego, CA	www.mtheorymusic.com/
Mad Platter	Riverside, CA	www.rhinorecords.cc/
Magic Disc Music	Carson, CA	
Medium Rare Music	San Francisco, CA	
Metamusic Records	Santa Cruz, CA	www.metamusiconline.com/
Midnight Records	Los Angeles, CA	www.midnightrecordsonline.com/
Mod Lang	El Cerrito, CA	www.modlang.com/
Music Revolution	Whittier, CA	www.musicrev.com/
Old Town records	Temecula, CA	www.oldtownrecords.com/
Origami Vinyl	Los Angeles, CA	www.origamiorigami.com/
Pearl Records	Sacramento, CA	
Penny Lane Records	Pasadena, CA	www.pennylane.com/
Pepperland Music	Orange, CA	www.pepperlandmusic.com/
R5 Records	Sacramento, CA	www.r5records.com/
Rare Records	Sacramento, CA	www.rare-records.net/
Rasputin Music and DVD	Berkeley, CA	www.rasputinmusic.com/
Record Alley	Palm Desert, CA	
Record City	San Diego, CA	
Record City	San Diego, CA	
Recycled Records	Monterey, CA	www.recycledrecordsmonterey.com/
Recycled Records	Monterey, CA	www.recycledrecords.net/
Red Devil Records	San Rafael, CA	www.reddevilrecords.net/
Rhino Records	Claremont, CA	www.reddevilrecords.net/
Rockaway Records	Los Angeles, CA	www.rockaway.com/
Salzer's	Ventura, CA	www.salzers.com/
South Shore Mad About Music	South Lake Tahoe, CA	www.southshoremadaboutmusic.com/
SpaceCat	San Jose, CA	www.superspacecat.com/
Spin Records	Carlsbad, CA	
Strawberry Alarm Clock	Merced, CA	
Streetlight Records	San Jose, CA	www.streetlightrecords.com/
Streetlight Records	Santa Cruz, CA	www.streetlightrecords.com/
TKO Records	Fountain Valley, CA	www.tkorecords.com/
Tune Town Music	Tehachapi, CA	
VIP Records	Long Beach, CA	
Vacation	Los Angeles, CA	www.vacationvinyl.com/
Vinyl Planet	Petaluma, CA	www.vinylplanet.org/
Vinyl Solution	Huntington Beach, CA	

Vinyl Solution Records	San Mateo, CA	www.vinylsolutionrecords.com/
VIP Music	Los Angeles, CA	www.vipmusic24.com/
VIP Music	Compton, CA	www.vipmusic24.com/
Visjon Records	Los Angeles, Ca	www.visjonrecords.com/
Watts Music	Novato, CA	

COLORADO

Albums on the Hill	Boulder, CO	www.albumsonthehill.com/
Angelo's CDs	Aurora, CO	www.angeloscds.com/
Angelo's CDs	Littleton, CO	
Angelo's CDs	Thornton, CO	
Angelo's CDs	Wheat Ridge, CO	
Bart's CD Cellar	Boulder, CO	www.bartscdcellar.com/
Cheapo Discs	Denver, CO	www.cheapodiscsdenver.com/
Eagle Valley Music	Vail, CO	
Finest Record Store	Ft. Collins, CO	www.thefinest.com/
Independent Record & Video (Denver)	Denver, CO	www.beindependent.com/
Independent Records & Video	Colorado Springs, CO	
Independent Records & Video	Fountain, CO	
Independent Records & Video	Pueblo, CO	
Independent Records & Video	Colorado Springs, CO	
Mojo Music	Avon, CO	www.mojomusicstore.com/
Pueblo Records and Tapes	Pueblo, CO	www.pueblorecordsandtapes.com/
Rock 'n' Robin's	Fort Collins, CO	www.rocknrobins.com/
Sgt Peppers Music & Video	Estes Park, CO	www.sgtpeppersmoab.com/
The Leechpit	Colorado Springs, CO	www.leechpit.com/
Twist & Shout	Denver, CO	www.twistandshout.com/
Wax Trax Records	Denver, CO	www.waxtraxrecords.com/

CONNECTICUT

Exile on Main St.	Branford, CT	www.exileonmain.com/
Gerosa Records	Brookfield, CT	www.gerosarecords.com/
Johnny's Records	Darien, CT	www.johnnysrecords.com/
Mystic Disc	Mystic, CT	www.themysticdisc.com/
Oldies & Goodies	Wallingford, CT	
Phoenix Record Shop	Waterbury, CT	
Phoenix Records	Litchfield, CT	
Power House music & Entertainment	Bridgeport, CT	
Redscroll Records	Wallingford, CT	www.redscrollrecords.com/
Replay Records	Hamden, CT	www.replayrecordsct.com/
Tumbleweeds	Niantic, CT	www.tumbleweedsct.com/

DELAWARE

Rainbow Music & Books	Newark, DE	www.rainbow-online.com/
Record & Tape Traders	Rehoboth Beach, DE	www.recordandtapetraders.com/

DISTRICT OF COLUMBIA

CD Warehouse	Washington, DC	www.thinkinground.com/
Crooked Beat Records	Washington, DC	www.crookedbeat.com/
DJ Hut	Washington, DC	www.djhut.com/
Melody Record Shop	Washington, DC	www.melodyrecords.com/
Politics & Prose Bookstore	Washington, DC	www.politics-prose.com/
Smash!	Washington, DC	www.smashrecords.com/
Som Records	Washington, DC	www.somrecordsdc.com/

FLORIDA

Alliance Entertainment	Coral Springs, FL	
Atlantic Sounds Records	Daytona Beach, FL	
Backbone Music	Delray Beach, FL	
Bananas Music	St Petersburg, FL	www.musicfinder.com/
CD Connection	Jacksonsville Beach, FL	www.cdconnection.net/
Central Square Records	Seaside, FL	
Daddy Kool Records	St. Petersburg, FL	www.daddykool.com/
East-west music & more	Orlando, FL	
Hear Again	Gainesville, FL	
Hot Wax	Tampa, FL	
Hot Wax	Ybot City FL	
Mojo Books & Music	Tampa, Fl	
MusicMatters	St. Augustine, FL	
Park Avenue CDs	Orlando, FL	www.parkavecds.com/
Radio-Active Records	Fort Lauderdale, FL	
Retro Records	Orlando, FL	
Rock & Roll Heaven inc	Orlando, FL	www.rock-n-rollheaven.com/
Selected Records	Miami beach, FL	www.selectedrecords.com/
Sound Exchange	Tampa, FL	
Sound Idea	Brandon, FL	www.soundideadistribution.com/
Sweat Records	Miami, FL	
TJ's CDs & More	Port Charlotte, FL	
Tonevendor	Gainesville, FL	www.tonevendor.com/
Uncle Sam's	Miami Beach, FL	www.unclesamsmusic.com/
Vinyl Fever	Tampa, FL	www.vinylfevertampa.com/
Vinyl Fever	Tallahassee, FL	www.vinylfever.com/
Vinyl Frontier	Jacksonville, FL	
Wax on the Tracks	Pensacola, FL	
Yesterday and Today Records	Miami, FL	www.vintagerecords.com/

GEORGIA

Criminal Records	Atlanta, GA	www.criminal.com/
Da Spot	Carrollton,GA	www.daspotstore.com/
DBS Sounds	College Park, GA	www.dbssounds.com/
DBS Sounds II	Forest Park, GA	
Decatur CD	Decatur, GA	www.decaturcd.com/
Fantasyland Records	Atlanta, GA	
Low Yo Yo Stuff	Atlanta, GA	
Moods Music	Atlanta, GA	www.moodsmusic.net/

North Georgia Compact Disc	Norcross, GA	www.securmusic.com/
Pyramid Music and More	Augusta, GA	www.pyramidmusicandmore.com/
School Kids Athens	Athens, GA	www.schoolkidsrecords.com/ athens.php
Super Sound Music	Decatur, GA	
Super Sound Music	Atlanta, GA	
Sweet Melissa Records	Marietta, GA	www.sweetmelissarecords.com/
The Atlanta Bench	Atlanta, GA	
Wax'n'Facts	Atlanta, GA	
Wuxtry	Decatur, GA	www.wuxtryrecords.com/
Wuxtry	Athens, GA	

HAWAII

Hungry Ear Records	Kailua, HI	www.hungryyear.com

IDAHO

Big Hole Music	Driggs, ID	
Record Exchange	Boise, ID	www.therecordexchange.com/
The Long Ear	Coeur d Alene, ID	www.longear.com/

ILLINOIS

Algonquin Records	Des Plaines, IL	www.algonquinrecords.com/
Any Frequency	Monticello, IL	
Beverly Records	Chicago, IL	www.beverlyrecords.com/
Chicago Digital	Oak Park, IL	
Co-Op Records	Moline, IL	
Co-Op Records	East Peoria, IL	
Co-Op Records	Pekin, IL	
Cyklopx	Forest Park, IL	www.cyklopx.com/
Dave's Records	Chicago, IL	www.davesrecordschicago.com/
Deadwax	Chicago, IL	
Dr Wax	Chicago, IL	www.drwax.com/
Dusty Groove America	Chicago, IL	www.dustygroove.com/
Exile on Main St.	Champaign, IL	www.exilemain.com/
Gramaphone Records	Chicago, Il	www.gramaphonerecords.com/
Groovin High, Inc	Chicago, IL	
Hard Boiled Records	Chicago, IL	www.hardboiledrecords.blogspot.com/
Jazz Record Mart	Chicago, IL	www.jazzmart.com/
Kiss The Sky	Geneva, IL	www.kissthesky.net/
Laurie's Planet of Sound	Chicago, IL	www.lauriesplanetofsound.com/
Metal Hedz	Granite City, IL	www.metalhedz1.com/
P-Mac Music	Carbondale, IL	www.pmacmusic.net/
Permanent Records	Chicago, IL	www.permanentrecordschicago.com/
Platterpus Records	Addison, IL	www.platterpus.com/
Plaza Records	Carbondale, IL	
Raffe's Record Riot	Chicago, IL	
Rainbow Records	Barrington, IL	
Reckless Records	Chicago, IL	www.reckless.com/
Recycled Records, Inc.	Springfield, IL	www.recycledrecords.com/
Rolling Stone Records	Norridge, IL	www.rollingstonesmusic.com/
Second Hand Tunes	Evanston, IL	www.2ndhandtunes.com/

Shake, Rattle & Read	Chicago, IL	
Shandis Music and More	Canton, IL	
Shooting Stars Records	Carpentersville, IL	
Slackers CDs and Games	Alton, IL	www.slackers.com/
Slackers CDs and Games	Glen Carbon, IL	
Slackers CDs and Games	OFallon, IL	
Sunshine Daydream CDs & Gifts	Mt. Prospect, IL	www.sunshinedaydream.biz/
The Music Experience	Chicago, IL	www.amusicexperience.com/
The Old School Records	Forest Park, IL	www.theeoldschoolrecords.com/
Toad Hall Books and Records	Rockford, IL	
Val's Halla Records	Oak Park, IL	www.valshalla.com/
Vintage Vinyl	Evanston, IL	www.vvmo.com/
Waiting Room Records	Normal, IL	www.waitingroomrecords.com/

INDIANA

13th Floor Music	Seymour, IN	
House O' Hits	Madison, IN	www.houseohits.com/
Indy CD & Vinyl	Indianapolis, IN	www.indycdandvinyl.com/
JL Records	West Lafayette, IN	
Joe's Records	Evansville, IN	www.joesrecords.com/
Karma Plymouth	Plymouth, IN	
Karma Records	Indianapolis, IN	
Landlocked Music	Bloomington, IN	www.landlockedmusic.com/
Luna Music	Indianapolis, IN	www.lunamusic.net/
Missing Link Records	Indianapolis, IN	www.missinglinkrecords.com/
Park Co Music	Kingman, IN	
Record Cellar Audio Video	Vincennes, IN	
Side 1 Music	Richmond, IN	
TDs CDs and LPs	Bloomington, IN	
The Underground Record Shop	Indianapolis, IN	
Tracks Records	Bloomington, IN	www.tracksrocks.com/
Vibes Music 2	Indianapolis, IN	
Village Green Records	Muncie, IN	

IOWA

CDs-4-Change	Dubuque, IA	
CD Warehouse	Des Moines, IA	
Co-op Records	Clinton, IA	
Moondog Music	Dubuque, IA	
Real Compact Discs and Records	Iowa City, IA	
Weird Harold's Records	Burlington, IA	www.weirdharolds.com/
Zzz Records	Des Moines, IA	www.zzzrecords.com/

KANSAS

Acoustic Sounds, Inc.	Salina, KS	www.acousticsounds.com/
House Of Sight and Sound	Salina, KS	
Keep It Real Records	Kansas, KS	
Kief's Downtown Music	Lawrence, KS	www.downtown.kiefs.com/
Love Garden Sounds	Lawrence, KS	www.lovegardensounds.com/

Needmore Discs	Shawnee, KS	
Rewound Sounds	Wichita, KS	rewoundsounds.blogspot.com/
Sisters Of Sound Music	Manhattan, KS	www.sistersofsoundmusic.com/
Vinyl Renaissance	Shawnee, KS	www.vinyl-renaissance.com/

KENTUCKY

CD Central	Lexington, KY	www.cdcentralmusic.com/
Ear X-Tacy	Louisville, KY	www.earx-tacy.com/
Terrapin Station	Murray, KY	
The Great Escape Bowling Green	Bowling Green, KY	www.thegreatescapeonline.com/
The Great Escape Louisville	Louisville, KY	
Ticket To Ride	London, KY	
Underground Sounds	Louisville, KY	

LOUISIANA

Jim Russell Records	New Orleans, LA	www.jimrussellrecords.com/
LaRhythms Music Store	Baton Rouge, LA	www.larhythms.com/
Odyssey Records	New Orleans, LA	
Peaches Records	New Orleans, LA	www.peachesrecordsneworleans.com/
Record store	La Accra, LA	
Skully'z Recordz	New Orleans, LA	
The Mushroom	New Orleans, LA	www.mushroomnola.com/

MAINE

Bill O'Neil's House of Rock 'n Roll	Saco, ME	
Bull Moose (Bangor)	Bangor, ME	
Bull Moose (Brunswick)	Brunswick, ME	
Bull Moose (Sanford)	Sanford, ME	
Bull Moose (Waterville)	Waterville, ME	
Bull Moose (Windham)	Windham, ME	
Bull Moose Music	Portland, ME	www.bullmoose.com/
Bull Moose (Scarborough)	Scarborough, ME	
Everyday Music	Farmington, ME	www.everydaymusicme.com/
Music Plus	Biddeford, ME	

MARYLAND

El Suprimo Records	Baltimore, MD	www.elsuprimo.com/
Blinding Sun Records	Frederick, MD	www.blindingsunrecords.com/
Celebrated Summer Records	Towson, MD	
Dimensions In Music	Baltimore, MD	www.dimensionsinmusic.com/
Kemp Mill Music	Temple Hills, MD	www.kempmillonline.com/
Kemp Mill Music	Hillcrest Heights, MD	
Platters That Matter Records	Frederick, MD	
Record & Tape Traders	Towson, MD	www.recordandtapetraders.com/
Record & Tape Traders	Catonsville, MD	
Record & Tape Traders	Frederick, MD	
Record & Tape Traders	Glen Burnie, MD	
Record & Tape Traders	Westminster, MD	

Sound Garden – Baltimore	Baltimore, MD	www.cdjoint.com/
Trax on Wax	Catonsville, MD	

MASSACHUSETTS

Aboveground Records	Martha's Vineyard, MA	
Booksmith/Musicsmith	Orleans, MA	
Listen up music	Natick, MA	www.listenupmusicusa.com/
Music DNA	Methuen, MA	
Newbury Comics	Boston, MA	www.newburycomics.com/
Rebel Sound Records	Pittsfield, MA	
Record Connection	Waterville, MA	
Spinnaker records	Hyannis, MA	www.spinnakercd.com/
Sunset Records	Somerset, MA	
That's Entertainment	Worcester, MA	www.thatse.com/
Turn It Up!	Northampton, MA	www.turnitup.com/
Weirdo Records	Cambridge, MA	www.weirdorecords.com/

MICHIGAN

Capeside Records	Saginaw, MI	
Dance zone	Eastpointe, MI	
Dearborn Music	Dearborn, MI	
Discs & Tapes Unlimited	Howell, MI	
Encore Recordings	Ann Arbor, MI	
Flat Black and Circular	East Lansing, MI	www.flatblackandcircular.com/
Green Light Music/ CD Warehouse	Kalamazoo, MI	
M&M	Eastpointe, MI	
Melodies & Memories	Eastpointe, MI	
Musicando	Vimercate, MI	www.musicando.eu/
Pearl's Music	Detroit, MI	
Puffer Red's	Ypsilanti, MI	www.pufferreds.com/
Record Time	Roseville, MI	www.recordtime.com/
Records & Tapes Galore	Saginaw, MI	
Rock Of Ages	Garden City, MI	
Rock-a-billy's	Utica, MI	www.rockabillys.com/
Schuler Books & Music	Walker, MI	www.schulerbooks.com/
Schuler Books & Music	Lansing, MI	
Schuler Books and Music – Okemos	Okemos, MI	
Shantinique Music	Detroit, MI	
Sound it Out Records	Traverse City, MI	www.sounditoutrecords.com/
Stormy records	Dearborn, MI	www.stormyrecords.com/
Street Corner Music	Beverly hills, MI	www.streetcornermusic.com/
The Corner Record Shop	Kalamazoo, MI	
The Corner Record Shop	Gandville, MI	www.cornerrecordshop.com/
The Full Circle	Holland, MI	
The Record Lounge	East Lansing, MI	
Underground Sounds	Ann Arbor MI	
Vertigo Music	Grand Rapids, MI	www.vertigomusiconline.com/
Wazoo Records	Ann Arbor, MI	www.wazoorecs.com/

MINNESOTA

Discland	Bloomington, MN	www.disclandonline.com/
Down In The Valley	Golden Valley, MN	www.downinthevalley.com/
Down In The Valley	Maple Grove, MN	
Down In The Valley	Crystal, MN	
Eclipse Records	St. Paul, MN	
Electric Fetus	Saint Cloud, MN	
Electric Fetus	Minneapolis, MN	www.electricfetus.com/
Electric Fetus	Duluth, MN	
Extreme Noise Records	Minneapolis, MN	www.extremenoise.com/
Fifth Element	Minneapolis, MN	www.fifthelementonline.com/
Know Name Records	Minneapolis, MN	www.knowname.com/
Last Stop CD Shop	Marshall, MN	
Mother's	Moorhead, MN	
Treehouse Records	Minneapolis, MN	
Tune Town Music and Video	Makato, MN	www.tunetowncds.com/

MISSISSIPPI

Be-Bop Record Shop (4)	Jackson, MS	
Cat Head Delta Blues & Folk Art	Clarksdale, MS	www.cathead.biz/

MISSOURI

Apop Records	Saint Louis, MO	
CD Reunion	St. Charles, MO	
CD Warehouse – Lebanon	Lebanon, MO	
CD Warehouse Independent	Springfield, MO	www.cdwarehouse.com/
Earwaxx Records & More	Gladstone, MO	
Euclid Records	St. Louis, MO	www.euclidrecords.com/
PMac Music	Cape Girardaeu, MO	www.pmacmusic.net/
Slackers CD's and Games	Columbia, MO	
Slackers CD's and Games	OFallon, MO	www.slackers.com/
Slackers CD's and Games	St. Peters, MO	
Slackers CD's and Games	Chesterfield, MO	www.slackers.com/
Slackers CD's and Games	St. Louis, MO	
Slackers CD's and Games	Jefferson City, MO	
Slackers Music Movies and Games	St. Charles, MO	
Surf Brothers	Raymore, MO	www.surfbrothers.com/
Vintage Vinyl	St Louis, MO	www.vintagevinyl.com/
Zebedee's RPM	Kansas City, MO	

MONTANA

Cactus Records	Bozeman, MT	
Conley's Books and Music	Livingston, MT	www.jimmysbooks.com/
Creative Leisure	Havre, MT	
Ear Candy Music	Missoula, MT	
Rockin Rudy's	Missoula, MT	www.rockinrudys.com/
Rockin Rudys	Missoula, MT	

NEBRASKA

Antiquarium Records	Omaha, NE	

Drastic Plastic	Omaha, NE	
Homer's	Omaha, NE	www.homersmusic.com/
Homer's	Lincoln, NE	
Homer's Old Market	Omaha, NE	
Homer's Orchard Plaza	Omaha, NE	
Homer's Saddle Creek	Omaha, NE	
Recycled Sounds	Lincoln, NE	
Spindle Records	Lincoln, NE	

NEVADA

Michael's Used Books and CDs	Las Vegas, NV	
Sundance Bookstore and Music	Reno, NV	www.sundancebookstore.com/
Wax Trax Records	Las Vegas, NV	www.pearlsent.com/waxtrax
Zia Records – Eastern	Las Vegas, NV	www.ziarecords.com/
Zia Records – Sahara	Las Vegas, NV	

NEW HAMPSHIRE

Bull Moose	Salem, NH	
Bull Moose	Portsmouth, NH	www.bullmoose.com/
Harlan Wolfe's Record Shop	Conway, NH	www.harlanwolfe.com/
Odyssey And Oracle	Portsmouth, NH	
Turn It Up!	Keene, NH	www.turnitup.com/

NEW JERSEY

Bus Stop Music Cafe	Pitman, NJ	
CD Exchange	Northfield, NJ	
Curmudgeon Records	Somerville, NJ	
Eyeconik Records & Apparel	Franklin, NJ	
EZ2collect	Fair Lawn, NJ	
Grooveground	Collingswood, NJ	www.grooveground.com/
Jack's Music Shoppe	Red Bank, NJ	www.jacksmusicshoppe.com/
Princeton Record Exchange	Princeton, NJ	www.prex.com/
Record City	Paterson NJ	www.recordcitydirect.com/
Record King	Hackensack NJ	www.therecordking.com/
Scotti's Record Shop	Morristown, NJ	www.scotticd.com/
Scotti's Record Shop	Summit, NJ	www.scotticd.com/
Sound City	Bayonne, NJ	
Sound of Trenton	Trenton NJ	
Sound Station	Westfield, NJ	
The Record Collector	Bordentown, NJ	www.the-record-collector.com/
The Record Store	Howell, NJ	www.therecordstorenj.com/
Tunes	Marlton, NJ	www.tunesonline.net/
Tunes	Hoboken, NJ	
Tunes	Voorhees, NJ	
Tunes	Turnersville, NJ	
Vintage Vinyl	Fords, NJ	www.vvinyl.com/
Yesterday's Treasures	Union, NJ	

NEW MEXICO

Taosound Tape and CD	Taos, NM	www.taosound.com/

NEW YORK

Academy Record Annex	Brooklyn, NY	www.academyannex.com/
Angry Mom Records	Ithaca, NY	
Armand Schaubroeck House of Guitars	Rochester, NY	www.houseofguitars.com/
Atomic Hi-Fi	Sugar Loaf, NY	
Basement Mix Records	Brooklyn, NY	www.basementmixx.com/
Black Star Music & Video	New York, NY	www.blackstarvideo.com/
Bleecker Street Records	New York, NY	www.bleeckerstreetrecords.com/
Bleeckerbobs	New York, NY	
Bop Shop Records	Rochester, NY	www.bopshop.com/
Breakdown Records	Queens, NY	
CD Exchange	Rochester, NY	
CD Island	Rockville Centre, NY	www.cdislandny.com/
Downtown Music Gallery	New York, NY	www.downtownmusicgallery.com/
Earwax records	Brooklyn, NY	
Etherea	New York, NY	www.etherea.net/
Fat Beats	New York, NY	www.fatbeats.com/
Generation Records	New York, NY	
Gimme Gimme Records	New York, NY	
Halcyon the shop	Brooklyn, NY	www.halcyonline.com/
Hall of Fame	Jamaica, NY	www.hfmstores.com/
Harmony records	Bronx, NY	
Hot Waxx Record Store	St. Albans, NY	
House of Guitars	Rochester, NY	
Infinity Records Ltd	Massapequa Park, NY	www.infinityrecords.net/
J&R Music World	New York, NY	www.jr.com/
Jack Wolak's Rare Necessities	N. Syracuse, NY	www.jackwolak.com/
Jack's Rhythms	New Paltz, NY	
Kim's Video & Music	New York, NY	
Lakeshore	Rochester, NY	www.alternativemusic.com/
Last Vestige Music Shop	Albany NY	
Last Vestige Music Shop	Saratoga, NY	www.lastvestige.com/
Last Vestige Music Shop	Albany, NY	
Looney Tunes	West Babylon, NY	www.looneytunescds.com/
Majors records & video	Staten island, NY	
Music Alley	Wellsville, NY	
No Radio Records	Ithaca, NY	www.noradiorecords.com/
Oblong Books & Music	Millerton, NY	www.oblongbooks.com/
Off-Center Records	Utica, NY	
Other Music	New York, NY	www.othermusic.com/
Platinum Hits	Riverhead, NY	
Rebel Rebel	New York, NY	
Record Archive	Rochester, NY	
Record Archive	Rochester, NY	
Record Express	Brooklyn, NY	

Record Stop	Lake Ronkonkoma, NY	www.amberrosemarie.com/
Record Theatre	Buffalo, NY	www.recordtheatre.com/
Record Theatre	Hamburg, NY	
Record Theatre	Buffalo, NY	
Records n Stuff	Bonx, NY	
Rhino Records New Paltz	New Paltz, NY	www.rhinonewpaltz.com/
Rock and Soul	New Nork, NY	
Sit and Spin	Buffalo, NY	www.sitandspin.com/
Sound Fix	Brooklyn, NY	www.soundfixrecords.com/
Sound Garden – Syracuse	Syracuse, NY	www.cdjoint.com/
Soundtraks	Huntington, NY	
Soundtraks	Huntington, NY	
Spiral Scratch Records	Buffalo, NY	
Townhouse Records and Film	Jamestown, NY	
Utopia	Centereach, NY	www.shoputopia.com/
Utopia	Hicksville, NY	
Volume Records	Ithaca, NY	
Whirlin Disc Records	Farmingdale, NY	www.whirlindisc.com/
Ye Olde Hippie Shoppe of Woodstock	Woodstock, NY	

NORTH CAROLINA

641rpm	Boone, NC	www.641rpm.com/
AzioMedia: Used Books & Vinyl Records	Shallotte, NC	www.aziomedia.com/
BB's Compact Discs	Greensboro, NC	
Bull City Records	Durham, NC	www.bullcityrecords.com/
CD Alley	Chapel Hill, NC	www.cdalley.net/
CD Alley	Wilmington, NC	
East coast music and video	Greenville, NC	
Edward McKay Used Books & More	Raleigh, NC	www.wefeedyourhead.com/
Edward McKay Used Books & More	Winston-Salem, NC	
Edward McKay Used Books & More	Greensboro, NC	
Edward McKay Used Books & More	Fayetteville, NC	
Edward McKay Used Books & More	Raleigh, NC	
Gravity Records LLC	Wilmington, NC	
Green Eggs and Jam	Boone, NC	
Harvest Records	Asheville, NC	www.harvest-records.com/
In Your Ear Music Emporium	Sylva, NC	
Lunchbox Records	Charlotte, NC	www.lunchboxrecords.com/
Manifest Records	Charlotte, NC	www.manifestdisc.com/
Nits Nats Music	Henderson, NC	
Offbeat Music	Durham, NC	www.offbeatmusic.blogspot.com/
Play It Again Records,	Valdese, NC	

Schoolkids Records	Raleigh, NC	www.schoolkidsrecords.com/
Static Age Records	Asheville, NC	www.staticagerecords.com/
The Music Box	New Bern, NC	

NORTH DAKOTA

Budget Music	Grand Forks, ND	www.budgetmusic.net/
Budget Music & Video	Minot, ND	
Orange Records	Fargo, ND	

OHIO

Ace in the Hole Music	Columbus, OH	www.aceintheholemusic.com/
Allied Record Exchange	Toledo, OH	
CD/Game Exchange	Cleveland, OH	www.cdgamexchange.com/
Crazy Dee's Muzic Palace	Warrensville Heights, OH	www.lordlandonline.com/
Culture Clash Records	Toledo, OH	www.thecultureclash.com/
Everybody's Records	Cincinnati, OH	www.everybodysrecords.com/
Evil Empire Records at Kafe Kerouac	Columbus, OH	www.evilempirerecords.com/
Evil Empire Records at What The Rock!?	Columbus, OH	
Finders Records	Bowling Green, OH	www.findersrecords.com/
Galaxy CDs	Hamilton, OH	www.galaxycds.com/
Gem City Records	Dayton, OH	www.gemcityrecords.com/
Haffa's Records	Athens, OH	
Indie Wax	Youngstown, OH	www.indiewax.com/
Lost Weekend Records	Columbus, OH	www.lostweekendrecords.com/
Magnolia Thunderpussy	Columbus, OH	www.thunderpussy.com/
Moles Records and CDs	Cincinnati, OH	
Music Saves	Cleveland, OH	www.musicsaves.com/
My Mind's Eye	Lakewood, OH	www.mymindseyerecords.com/
Nikki's Music	Cleveland, OH	www.nikkismusic.com/
Phonographic Arts	Cleveland, OH	
Rama Lama Records	Toledo, OH	
Record Den	Mentor, OH	
Shake It	Cincinnati, OH	www.shakeitrecords.com/
Shakin' Street Records	Toledo, OH	
Shattered	Cleveland, OH	
Singing Dog Records	Columbus, OH	www.singingdogrecords.com/
Singing Dog Records	Columbus, OH	
Spin-More Records	Kent, OH	
Square Records	Akron, OH	www.squarerecordsakron.com/
The Joy of Music	Cleveland, OH	
The Music Box	Olmsted Falls, OH	www.themusicboxohio.com/
Time Traveller CDs	Cuyahoga Falls, OH	
Toxic Beauty Records	Yellow Springs, OH	

Turnup Records	Kent, OH	
Ultrasound Music	Willoughby, OH	

OKLAHOMA

CD Warehouse	Shawnee, OK	
Guestroom Records	Norman, OK	www.guestroom-records.com/
Guestroom Records	Oklahoma City, OK	
Randy's M&M'S	Edmond, OK	
Size records	Oklahoma City, OK	
Starship Records	Tulsa, OK	
Under The Mooch	Tulsa, OK	

OREGON

360 Vinyl	Portland, OR	www.360vinyl.com/
CD or not CD	Ashland, OR	www.cdornotcd.com/
CD World	Eugene, OR	www.gotocdworld.com/
CD/Game Exchange	Eugene, OR	
Everyday Music	Portland, OR	www.everydaymusic.com/
Everyday Music	Beaverton, OR	www.everydaymusic.com/
Exiled Records	Portland, OR	www.exiledrecords.com/
Green Noise Records	Portland, OR	www.greennoiserecords.com/
Happy Trails Records	Corvallis, OR	
House of Records	Eugene, OR	
Jackpot Records	Portland, OR	www.jackpotrecords.com/
Music Coop	Ashland, OR	
Music Millennium	Portland, OR	www.musicmillennium.com/
Musichead	Medford, OR	
Off the Record	North Bend, OR	
One Stop music	Portland, OR	www.onestoprecordshop.com/
Platinum Records	Portland, OR	www.platinum-records.com/
Ranch Records	Bend, OR	
Timbuktunes World Music	Portland, OR	www.timbuktunes.com/

PENNSYLVANIA

720 Records	Pittsburgh, PA	www.720records.com/
A.K.A. Music	Philadelphia, PA	
Angry Young & Poor	Lancaster, PA	www.angryyoungandpoor.com/
Backstreet Records	Indiana, PA	
CI Records and Skates	Lancaster, PA	
City Lights Records	State College, PA	
Creep Industries	Phoenixville, PA	www.creepindustries.com/
Dave's Music Mine	Pittsburgh, PA	www.davesmusicmine.com/
Desolation Row	Pittsburgh, PA	
Digital Ferret	Philadelphia, PA	
Eide's Entertainment	Pittsburgh, PA	www.eides.com/
Embassy Vinyl	Scranton, PA	www.embassyvinyl.com/
Gallery of Sound	Willkes-Barre, PA	www.galleryofsound.com/
George's Song Shop	Johnstown, PA	www.georgessongshop.com/
Gold Million Records	Bryn Mawr, PA	www.goldmillionrecords.com/

Graham's Records	Erie, PA	
Hideaway Music	Philadelphia, PA	
Jazzsound	Philadelphia, PA	www.jazsound.com/
Jerry's Records	Pittsburgh, PA	www.jerrysrecords.com/
Mad Platter CDs	West Chester, PA	
Main Street Music	Philadelphia, PA	
Mr. Suit Records	Lancaster, PA	
Music Box	Philadelphia, PA	
Musical Energi	Wilkes-Barre, PA	
Newtown Book & Record	Newtown, PA	www.jerrysrecords.com/
Paul's CDs	Pittsburgh, PA	
Positively records	Levittown, PA	
Record Connection	Ephrata, PA	www.recordconnectionpa.com/
Repo Records	Philadelphia, PA	www.reporecords.com/
Shady Dog Records	Berwyn, PA	www.shadydog.com/
Siren Records	Doylestown, PA	
Sound of Norristown	Norristown, PA	
Soundcheck Records	Lehighton, PA	www.soundcheckrecords.com/
Tequila sunrise records	Philadelphia, PA	www.tequilasunriserecords.com/
The Attic Record Store	Millvale, PA	www.theatticrecordsstore.com/
The Main St. Jukebox	Stroudsburg, PA	
The One Storte Record Shop	Philadelphia, PA	
Vertigo Music	West Reading, PA	
Wayne's World Music	Dallas, PA	
Wayne's World of Used Cd's & More	Pittston, PA	www.waynesworldx.com/
Wicked Discs	Pittsburgh, PA	
Young Ones	Kutzo, PA	

RHODE ISLAND

Armageddon Shop	Providence, RI	www.armageddonshop.com/
In Your Ear/Zingg Music	Warren, RI	
Luke's Record Exchange	Pawtucket, RI	www.lukesmusic.com/
Music Box	Newport, RI	www.musicboxnewport.com/
What Cheer!	Providence, RI	
Zingg Music	Warren, RI	www.zinggmusic.com/

SOUTH CAROLINA

52.5	Charleston, SC	www.corporaterocksucks.com/
BJ Music	Greenville, SC	
Carousel Music	Gaffney, SC	
Cat's Music	Summerville, SC	www.catsmusic.com/
Earshot	Greenville, SC	www.earshot.com/
Horizon Records	Greenville, SC	www.horizonrecords.net/
Loco Record Shop	N Charledton, SC	www.locorecordshop.net/
Manifest Records	Columbia, SC	www.manifestdisc.com/
Monster Music	Charleston, SC	www.monstermusicandmovies.com/
Music Gator	Sumter, SC	www.musicgator.com/
Poco Music & More	Easley, SC	
Scratch n Spin Records	West Columbia, SC	

Soundwave Records	Summerville, SC	

SOUTH DAKOTA

Ernie November	Rapid City, SD	
Ernie November	Sioux Falls, SD	
Last Stop CD Shop	Sioux Falls, SD	
Mind Machine Records	Watertown, SD	www.mindmachinemusic.net/

TENNESSEE

Cat's Music	Nashville, TN	www.catsmusic.com/
Disc Exchange	Knoxville, TN	
Goner Records	Memphis, TN	www.goner-records.com/
Grimey's	Nashville, TN	www.grimeys.com/
Lost and Found Records	Knoxville, TN	
Pop Tunes	Memphis, TN	www.poptunesmemphis.com/
Shangri-La Records	Memphis, TN	www.shangri.com/
Spinstreet	Memphis, TN	www.spinstreet.com/
The Great Escape Charlotte	Nashville, TN	www.thegreatescapeonline.com/
The Great Escape Madison	Madison, TN	
The Great Escape Nashville	Nashville, TN	
The Groove	Nashville, TN	www.thegroovenashville.com/

TEXAS

180 Grams	San Antonio, TX	
All That Music & Video	El Paso, TX	www.allthatmusic.com/
All Records	Houston, TX	
Antone's Record Shop	Austin, TX	www.antonesrecordshop.com/
Backspin Records	Austin, TX	www.backspinrecords.net/
Cactus	Houston, TX	www.cactusmusictx.com./
CD Source	Dallas, TX	
CD Universe	Dallas, TX	
CD Warehouse	Arlington, TX	
Cheap Thrills Records and CDs	San Antonio, TX	www.cheapthrillstx.com/
Cheapo	Austin, TX	www.cheapotexas.com/
Disc Go Round	Corpus Christi, TX	www.welovecds.com/
Docs Records and Vintage	Fort Worth, TX	
Eargazum	Arlington, TX	
End of an Ear	Austin, TX	www.endofanear.com/
Evolution:Records	Baytown, TX	
Evolution:Records	Deer Park, TX	
Forever Young Records	Grand Prairie, TX	www.foreveryoungrecords.com/
Good Records	Dallas, TX	www.goodrecords.com/
Groove Net	Mesquite, TX	www.groove-entertainment.net/
Hastings Entertainment	Amarillo, TX	www.gohastings.com/
Hogwild Records	San Antonio, TX	
Immortal Performances	Austin, TX	
M&M Music Store	Tyler, TX	
Movie Trading Company	Dallas, TX	www.movietradingcompany.com/
Music Depot	Houston, TX	
Music Town	San Antonio, TX	

Music Town	Klein, TX	www.musictownsa.com/
Musicmania	Austin, TX	
Out of the Past Collectibles	Austin, TX	
Piranha Records	Round Rock, TX	
Ralph's Records	Lubbock, TX	
Remix Dallas	Dallas, TX	
Rewind Music & More	Dallas, TX	
RingTail Records	Alpine, TX	www.ringtailrecords.com/
Serious Sounds, Etc.	Houston, TX	
Sig's Lagoon	Houston, TX	www.sigslagoon.com/
Snake Eyes Vinyl	Austin, TX	www.snakeeyesvinyl.com/
Sound Exchange	Houston, TX	www.soundexchangehouston.com/
Sound Revolution CDs	Houston, TX	
Soundwaves	Houston, TX	www.soundwaves.com/
Surf Club Records	Corpus Christi, TX	
The Prestige	San Antonio, TX	
The Rock Box	San Antonio, TX	
Vinal Edge Records	Houston, TX	www.vinaledge.com/
Waterloo Records	Austin, TX	www.waterloorecords.com/

UTAH

Graywhale	Salt Lake City, UT	www.fatfin.com/
Groovacious	Cedar City, UT	www.groovacious.com/
Positively 4th St Music	Salt Lake City, UT	www.brothertimm.com/
Randy's Record Shop	Salt Lake City, UT	
Sgt Peppers Music & Video	Moab, UT	www.sgtpeppersmoav.com/
Slowtrain	Salt Lake City, UT	www.slowtrainmusic.com/

VERMONT

Buch Spieler Music	Montpelier, VT	www.bsmusic.com/
Burlington Records	Burlington, VT	www.burlingtonrecords.com/
Exile On Main Street	Barre, VT	www.exileonmainstreet.com/
In the Moment	Brattleboro, VT	www.inthemomentrecords.com/
Pure Pop Records	Burlington, VT	www.purepoponline.com/
Turn It Up	Brattleboro, VT	www.turnitup.com/
Vermont Music Library & Shop	Burlington, VT	www.vmls.org/

VIRGINIA

CD Cellar	Falls Church, VA	
Collectors Corner	Melbourne, VA	www.brella.org/collectors/
Fantasy	Newport News, VA	www.fantasyva.com/
Mountain Aire Music Sales	Bristol, VA	
Plan 9 Music	Richmond, VA	www.plan9music.com/
Plan 9 Music – Charlottesville	Charlottesville, VA	
Record & Tape Exchange	Fairfax, VA	www.recordandtapeexchange.com/
Sidetracks Music	Charlottesville, VA	

Skinnies Records	Norfolk, VA	www.skinniesrecords.com/
Sonic Music & DVDs	Bristol, VA	www.catsmusic.com/
Speakertree Records	Lynchburg, VA	www.speakertreerecords.com/
Turnstyle	Richmond, VA	www.turnstyleonline.com/
Vienna Music Exchange	Vienna, VA	

WASHINGTON

4000 Holes	Spokane, WA	www.4000holes.com/
Another Record Store	Seattle, WA	
Avalon Music	Bellingham, WA	
CD Exchange of Walla Walla	Walla Walla, WA	
Coog's Budget CDs and Tapes	Port Angeles, WA	
Disc Connection	Tacoma, WA	
Disc Connection Records	Tacoma, WA	
Easy Street	Seattle, WA	www.buymusichere.net/stores/ easystreet/
Everyday Music	Seattle, WA	www.everydaymusic.com/
Everyday Music	Bellingham, WA	www.everydaymusic.com/
Exploding Planet Records	Bremerton, WA	
Georgetown Records	Seattle, WA	www.georgetownrecords.net/
Gruv	Seattle, WA	
Holy Cow Records	Seattle, WA	
Hot Poop	Walla Walla, WA	www.hotpoop.com/
Nature and Reubon Kirkpatrick	Anacortes, WA	
Off the Record	Yakima, WA	www.offtherecord.com/
Phantom City Records	Olympia, WA	www.phantomcityrecords.net/
Platinum Records	Seattle, WA	www.platinum-records.com/
Quimper Sound	Port Townsend, WA	www.quimpersound.com/
Rainy Day Record Company	Olympia, WA	www.rainydayolympia.net/
Rubato Records	Seattle, WA	
Silver Platters	Bellevue, WA	www.silverplatters.com/
Sonic Boom	Seattle, WA	www.sonicboomrecords.com/
Sounds Great	Gig Harbor, WA	
The Business	Anacortes, WA	www.thebusinessanacortes.com/
Unified Groove Merchants	Spokane, WA	
Wall of Sound	Seattle, WA	www.wosound.com/
Zion's Gate Records	Seattle, WA	www.zionsgate.com/

WEST VIRGINIA

Cheap Thrills Records	Princeton, WV	www.cheapthrillsrecords.com/
Cheap Thrills Records	Beckley, WV	
Grafton WV Disk Exchange	Grafton, WV	

WISCONSIN

B-Side Records	Madison, WI	www.b-sidemadison.com/
Bullseye Records	Milwaukee, WI	
Doctor Freuds	Manitowoc, WI	
Dr. Freud's Institute of Fine Recordings	Manitowoc, WI	
Exclusive Company	Oshkosh, WI	

Exclusive Company	Milwaukee, WI	
Exclusive Company	Janesville, WI	
Exclusive Company	Greenfield, WI	
Exclusive Company	Green Bay, WI	
Exclusive Company	Appleton, WI	
Exclusive Company	Oshkosh, WI	
Exclusive Company	Madison, WI	
Fox Music Company	Watertown, WI	www.foxmusiccompany.com/
Mad Hatteur Music	Fond Du Lac, WI	www.madhatteur.com/
Mad City Music Exchange	Madison, WI	www.madcitymusic.net/
Off The Beaten Path	Wauwatosa, WI	www.offthepath.vpweb.com/
Rush More Records	Milwaukee, WI	www.rushmor.com/
Strictly Discs	Madison, WI	www.strictlydiscs.com/
Strictly Discs	Madison, WI	www.strictlydiscs.com/
Sugar Shack Records	Madison, WI	
The Exclusive Company Madison	Madison, WI	
The Exclusive Company West Bend	West Bend, WI	
The Exclusive Company	Appleton, WI	
The Vinyl Cave	Superior, WI	

WYOMING

2nd Chance CDs	Sheridan, WY
Mammoth Music Inc	Riverton, WY

Acknowledgements

This book would not have happened without the support of the following people:

My son Ben Jones for all the editing he did for me inbetween studying for his GCSEs. I owe a great debt to the music journalist David Sinclair for his constant encouragement, and for making me believe that I could write a book. I would also like to thank the following for their contributions and words of wisdom: Tony Maher, Sally King, Colin Burns my marathon-running next-door neighbour, Chris Lowe at Acorn and Mark Merriman. To all the team at Proper Music, particularly Malcolm Mills, thank you for all your support over the years, and to Steve Kersley for some great anec-dotes and for always offering me an alternative view. Thank you to Chris Charlesworth at Music Sales for giving his time to provide me with advice and guide a novice through the art of producing a book, and for agreeing to distribute it for me. For my friend, and the best penalty taker I have ever known, James Weston for doing a great job of designing the cover (and like a true mate doing it for a few pints). To my enthusiastic back-up team: Lucy Beevor for the proofreading, Charlie Harris and Lucy Dickinson at Midas PR and Paul Quirk at ERA. Michael Kurtz, Spencer Hickman and all the team involved in Record Store Day. Steve Redmond for all your help. Thanks to Anna and Ben Wood for the hours spent correcting my grammar. Howie Minns and Jimmy Hughes for all the fun I had with The Cherry Boys and Exhibit B, and for still making fantastic music. To John Peel, Johnnie Walker and Bob Harris for introducing me to some fantastic records. A special thank you also to Starkey for failing in his suicide bid. If successful, I may never have started work in the music industry. For the love and support of my Mum and Dad whom without their night of passion, I wouldn't exist. Finally, to all the record shop owners who contributed to this book: I thank you, and wish you all good luck for the future.

Special thanks must go to Richard and Judy for making *Last Shop Standing* their book of the week and to all the people responsible for nominating it for the Booker Prize, and not forgetting Steven Spielberg for buying the rights to turn this book into a film and hence lifting me out of poverty. (Well, we can all dream can't we?)

Thanks for reading.

Graham Jones
www.lastshopstanding.co.uk
graham@lastshopstanding.co.uk

WILCO

"My introduction to a lot of great music and to the 'music business' came from hanging around and eventually working at independent record stores in Belleville, IL and St. Louis many years back," said Wilco's Jeff Tweedy. "It's the life I know. Nothing beats browsing in your favorite store, listening to music, finding something new or old that you've been searching for, being ignored by the store clerks, all that. And without these stores, there's just no way Wilco would still be around. They've been with us from the very beginning, through thick and thin. Even if I wasn't in a band, I'd still support Record Store Day. It's a great thing and I'm glad we could do something special with them."

RECORD STORE DAY

Graham Jones was born in Anfield, Liverpool. After leaving school he worked in numerous dead-end jobs before getting his first break in the music industry thanks to a colleague's failed comical suicide attempt. Ever the optimist, Graham managed The Cherry Boys, a band that made *Spinal Tap* look mundane, and ran his own market stall, selling vinyl fruit bowls made from Beatles LPs melted into shape under a grill. He eventually found his vocation travelling the country selling records, tapes and CDs to independent record stores, and never looked back – until now. One of the founders of Proper Music Distribution, the largest independently owned music distributor in the UK, he lives in Chippenham, Wiltshire, with his son Ben.

ENTERTAINMENT RETAILERS ASSOCIATION

supporting independent retail | **since 1988**

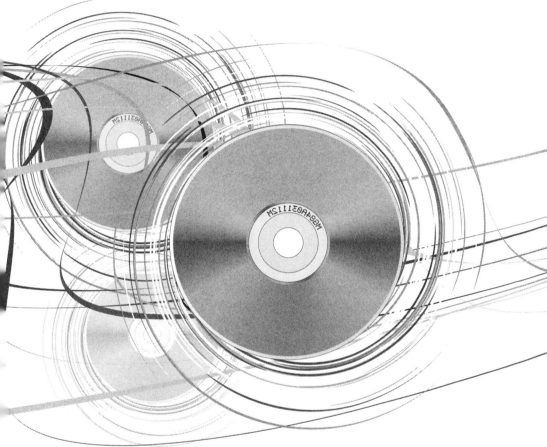

Save over £100 on your PRS and PPL licences.
Free legal advice and **reduced Streamline
rates**. Just some of the benefits enjoyed by over
150 independent music retailers who have joined
Era. With membership fees from just £90 pa, Era
represents the UK's music retailers at both industry
and Government level.

Contact sarah@eraltd.org
01202 292063 for more information

www.eraltd.org

in unity is strength | **era the voice of entertainment retail**